ADVANCE PRAISE FOR Our Fragile Freedoms

"A remarkable survey of American history and history writing, and a powerful set of reflections on the importance of historical study and thinking, *Our Fragile Freedoms* couldn't be more timely and essential. As much as any book it helps us recognize the centrality of history in our efforts to understand the present. And it demonstrates why Eric Foner is one of this country's greatest historians."

—Steven Hahn, author of *Illiberal America*

"Eric Foner is the foremost chronicler of our nation's past. In this timely book, he reminds us that democracy and freedom have always been contested. An urgent call to continue our freedom struggles, this book is required reading for our times."

—Lisa McGirr, author of *The War on Alcohol*

"Eric Foner is that rare historian who makes history speak to important contemporary issues while maintaining the highest standards of historical scholarship. These essays—as readable as they are insightful—are a fitting capstone to Foner's illustrious career."

—James Oakes, author of *The Crooked Path to Abolition*

"Whether this book is your introduction to Eric Foner or a reminder of the depth and breadth of his contributions to the study of U.S. history, you can find no better guide to American democracy."

—Kathleen DuVal, author of *Native Nations*

OUR FRAGILE
FREEDOMS

ALSO BY ERIC FONER

Free Soil, Free Labor, Free Men:
The Ideology of the Republican Party Before the Civil War (1970)

America's Black Past:
A Reader in Afro-American History (editor, 1971)

Nat Turner (editor, 1971)

Tom Paine and Revolutionary America (1976)

Politics and Ideology in the Age of the Civil War (1980)

Nothing but Freedom: Emancipation and Its Legacy (1983)

Reconstruction: America's Unfinished Revolution, 1863–1877 (1988)

A Short History of Reconstruction (1990)

A House Divided:
America in the Age of Lincoln (with Olivia Mahoney, 1990)

The New American History (editor, 1990; rev. ed. 1997)

The Reader's Companion to American History
(editor, with John A. Garraty, 1991)

Freedom's Lawmakers:
A Directory of Black Officeholders During Reconstruction (1993; rev. ed. 1996)

Thomas Paine (editor, 1995)

America's Reconstruction:
People and Politics after the Civil War (with Olivia Mahoney, 1995)

The Story of American Freedom (1998)

Who Owns History?: Rethinking the Past in a Changing World (2002)

Give Me Liberty!: An American History (2004)

Voices of Freedom: A Documentary History (editor, 2004)

Forever Free: The Story of Emancipation and Reconstruction (2005)

Herbert Aptheker on Race and Democracy:
A Reader (editor, with Manning Marable, 2006)

Our Lincoln: New Perspectives on Lincoln and His World (editor, 2008)

The Fiery Trial:
Abraham Lincoln and American Slavery (2010)

American History Now (editor, with Lisa McGirr, 2011)

Gateway to Freedom:
The Hidden History of the Underground Railroad (2015)

Battles for Freedom:
The Use and Abuse of American History (2017)

The Second Founding:
How the Civil War and Reconstruction Remade the Constitution (2019)

W. E. B. Du Bois, Black Reconstruction
(editor, with Henry Louis Gates Jr., 2021)

ERIC FONER

OUR FRAGILE FREEDOMS

Essays

W. W. NORTON & COMPANY

Independent Publishers Since 1923

For information about permission to reproduce selections from this
book, write to Permissions, W. W. Norton & Company, Inc.,
500 Fifth Avenue, New York, NY 10110

For information about special discounts for bulk purchases, please
contact W. W. Norton Special Sales at specialsales@wwnorton.com or
800-233-4830

Manufacturing by Lakeside Book Company
Book design by Brooke Koven
Production manager: Julia Druskin

Library of Congress Cataloging-in-Publication Data is available.

ISBN 978-1-324-11061-3

W. W. Norton & Company, Inc., 500 Fifth Avenue, New York, NY 10110
www.wwnorton.com

W. W. Norton & Company Ltd., 15 Carlisle Street, London W1D 3BS

10 9 8 7 6 5 4 3 2 1

To the memory of Ira Berlin, Alan Brinkley, Judith Stein, and Fred Siegel: colleagues, teachers, friends

The past is the key of the present and the mirror of the future.

—from the diary of Robert G. Fitzgerald (1840–1919), a free African American born in Delaware, a volunteer in both the Union cavalry and navy during the Civil War, and a founder of Freedmen's Bureau schools in North Carolina

CONTENTS

INTRODUCTION

O UR FRAGILE FREEDOMS gathers together nearly sixty book reviews and opinion pieces I have written over the past quarter-century. Originally published in venues such as the *New York Review of Books, London Review of Books, The Nation,* and *The New York Times,* they reflect a period of remarkable creativity among American historians but also intense controversy over the teaching, writing, and public presentation of history. The book examines history as refracted through the prism of some of the most influential recent works of scholarship, while at the same time shedding light on my own evolution as a historian.

The essays in this volume make clear that there is no single "correct" way to study history. The books discussed, which include biographies, accounts of broad time periods, local studies based on deep archival research, and syntheses of existing scholarship, underscore the fact that the study of history is a democratic enterprise, open to anyone who seeks to contribute to our understanding of the past. Few non-scientists feel qualified to express their opinions about, say, biology or nuclear physics. But everyone, it seems, from filmmakers to ordinary citizens, can and do make judgments about history. The authors whose books I discuss here are mostly faculty members at institutions of higher learning. But they also include journalists, a high school teacher, a museum curator, and a researcher at George Washington's estate, Mount Vernon. All are welcome members of the historical enterprise. All have helped to shape the current understanding of American history within and outside the academy.

Why should those interested in history read a collection of previously published book reviews and opinion pieces? Many such essays, I believe, continue to be of value well after their initial appearance. Book reviews alert readers to recent trends, current debates, and new insights in the study of history and direct attention to a constantly expanding cast of historical characters, many of them members of groups whose historical experience has traditionally been ignored. They illustrate the impact on scholarship of the profound changes the United States has experienced during the last fifty years and illuminate the complex relationship between history and the historian, and between past and present. Similarly, opinion essays that intervene in current political, legal, and historical controversies can remain valuable sources of civic education well after their original publication.

The pieces reproduced here also remind us of the current crisis of American democracy, reflected in intense political polarization, the weaponizing of base prejudice, and refusal to accept the outcomes of elections. This situation is not unprecedented. American democracy has always been a terrain of conflict. Our politics have always included those who believe that too many people, or people of the "wrong" kind, are voting and taking part in public debate. Various forms of violence—war, assassination, mob actions, political repression, the brutality intrinsic to slavery—have played more of a role in our history than is often recognized. I vividly recall watching televised images of the Capitol riot as it unfolded on January 6, 2021, and hearing a commentator declare that "nothing like this" had happened before in the United States. "That's wrong," I remarked to no one in particular. "What about the Battle of Liberty Place or the Colfax Massacre—violent uprisings a century and a half ago that sought to oust democratically elected state and local governments in Reconstruction Louisiana—or the 1898 coup d'etat in Wilmington, North Carolina, that marked the end of biracial government in that state?"

History was visible at the riot. It was shocking, although not really surprising, to see the Confederate battle flag unfurled inside the Capitol. Since the Civil War, Americans who reject inclusive definitions of democracy and freedom have often turned to the Confederacy for inspiration. A widely reproduced photograph taken that day links our conflict-ridden past with the violent present, depicting a rioter carrying a Confederate flag while on the walls behind him hang portraits of John C. Calhoun, a key architect of proslavery ideology, and Charles Sumner, a staunch defender of the rights of Black Americans. Also visible is a bust of Richard Nixon, the Republican president whose "southern strategy" employed thinly veiled racism to attract the votes of white Democrats alarmed by the social and political changes brought about by the civil rights revolution.

Many of the essays included here deal with books on the history of social and political change, and particularly the long struggle over slavery, abolition, and the place of formerly enslaved men, women, and children, and their descendants, in American life, subjects that have shaped my own scholarship. It is probably safe to say that the finest body of American historical writing to appear in the last fifty years has been produced by scholars of slavery and emancipation. This literature has not only established beyond question the centrality of slavery to the history of the United States, but it has also refashioned our understanding of how profound political and social changes frequently emerge from a symbiotic relationship between enlightened political leaders and engaged social movements. But as Thomas Wentworth Higginson, who commanded a celebrated unit of African American soldiers during the Civil War, noted in his diary, "revolutions may go backward." The destruction of slavery was followed, during the period known as Reconstruction, by a struggle to rid the country of slavery's legacy, including a remarkable expansion of democratic rights. In the South, however, Reconstruction soon gave way to a violent backlash and the imposition of a new system of racial subordination known by the shorthand "Jim Crow," leaving to the twentieth century and our own time the vexed problem of racial justice. The freedoms acquired by the emancipated slaves proved to be tragically transitory and incomplete. Jim Crow survived for many decades, finally succumbing to a mass movement of courageous citizens who braved police dogs, economic retaliation, and prison to breathe new life into our democracy and secure the rights of all Americans.

This long history has been among my major preoccupations during a career as a historian that began in the 1960s when the civil rights movement was at its peak and other social changes were sweeping the country. The subjects, indeed the titles, of many of my books reflect the centrality of ideas, practices, and debates relating to freedom in my account of American history. My doctoral dissertation and first book, *Free Soil, Free Labor, Free Men*, examined the ideas of the early Republican Party, which brought the antislavery impulse into American politics, leading directly to the election of Abraham Lincoln, the coming of the Civil War, and the destruction of slavery. My second book, *Tom Paine and Revolutionary America*, although dealing with a different time period, also traced the relationship between political leadership and social movements, in this case the connections between the leading pamphleteer of the struggle for independence and ordinary Americans who saw the revolution as an opportunity to democratize the social and political order. Later, in *The Fiery Trial*, I examined the evolution of Lincoln's ideas and policies regarding slavery, freedom, and the rights of Black Americans, tracing how changes in his outlook and policies were influenced by the unprecedented crisis of the Civil War and by Lincoln's complex relationship with abolitionists, Black and white. That book was followed by *Gateway to Freedom*, which chronicled the experience of fugitive slaves who risked their lives to seek freedom in the northern United States and Canada, and of the abolitionists who defied national law to assist them.

Most recently, in *The Second Founding*, I examined the constitutional amendments ratified during Reconstruction, which reframed the definition of American citizenship and expanded the rights it entailed. The Constitution was rewritten to incorporate the principle of birthright citizenship—the idea that anyone born in the United States is automatically a citizen and entitled to equal protection of the law—and, for Black men, the right to vote. The Thirteenth, Fourteenth, and Fifteenth Amendments gave new meaning to American freedom, linking it with equality regardless of race, and identifying the national government, in the words of Charles Sumner, as the "custodian of freedom."

Despite the passage of a century and a half since the end of the Civil War, questions central to that era still remain essential to our politics today. Who is entitled to citizenship? Who should enjoy the right to vote? What is the connection between political and economic freedom? How should authorities respond to terrorist violence? Our moment is one that Frederick Douglass in his later years would have recognized. "Principles which we all thought to have been firmly and permanently settled by the late war," Douglass declared in 1894 as the Jim Crow system was being fastened upon the South, "have been boldly assaulted and overthrown." In the late nineteenth century a conservative Supreme Court gave judicial sanction to the evisceration of the Reconstruction amendments, making it more and more difficult for the federal government to protect African Americans from violence, and allowing states to require racial segregation in public facilities and to disenfranchise Black voters. Today, as the Roberts Court embraces a retreat from the idea of equality and conservative politicians call for an end to birthright citizenship, key elements of the Second Founding remain controversial. The essays in this volume caution us to avoid reading history as a linear narrative of progress. Our freedoms can never be taken for granted.

My education as a historian began at home. My father, Jack D. Foner, was a historian, as was his twin brother, my uncle Philip. W. E. B. Du Bois and Paul Robeson were family acquaintances, and history was a frequent point of discussion around our dinner table in the suburbs of New York City. But the history my brother Tom and I absorbed was quite different from what we were taught at school. There, slavery and modern-day racism were rarely, if ever, mentioned. My parents, however, instilled in us the conviction that the Jim Crow system was a scandalous injustice and that radical dissenters such as Douglass, whose powerful speeches and writings my uncle collected and published in five influential volumes, were among the most heroic Americans. The only time I recall hearing my father use a common four-letter epithet was in

1955 when a radio news broadcast announced that an all-white Mississippi jury had acquitted the killers of the Black teenager Emmett Till.

Scattered throughout this book are recollections of how these convictions were reflected in my family history. In 1942, during a purge of "subversive" instructors in the City University of New York, my father and uncle lost their teaching positions. Later, my mother was dismissed from her job as a high school art teacher. Their experience taught another important historical lesson reflected in the essays included here—the fragility of civil liberties. Freedom of speech and the right to dissent were not ingrained in the American system from the outset. They grew in importance over time thanks in considerable measure to the actions of those outside the political mainstream, among them antislavery speakers who confronted proslavery mobs, members of the Industrial Workers of the World who demanded the right to deliver public speeches without prior approval from local authorities, and women's rights advocates who violated the law by disseminating information about birth control. It was through efforts like these that the words of the Bill of Rights were transformed from what James Madison called ineffective "parchment barriers" to violations of liberty to become living principles in a reinvigorated American democracy.

Black history is American history. This insight, a central theme of the National Museum of African American History and Culture, which opened to the public in the nation's capital in 2016, does not mean that other histories are of no importance, but rather that the Black experience has been central to the historic evolution of our politics and society and to our evolving understanding of freedom for all Americans. By inspiring other social movements that transformed our ideas about the meaning of freedom, African American struggles for justice played a major role in the emergence of the modern idea of universal human rights.

The essays included in this volume also illustrate how the work of historians is shaped by the social, intellectual, and political environment in which they live. We see how the reputations of historical figures change over time as new standards of judgment emerge. Woodrow Wilson, for example, was once lionized for attempting to lay the foundation for a post–World War I international order based on the self-determination of peoples. But in retrospect he has become the target of harsh criticism for presiding over the wartime suppression of civil liberties (one of the low points in the history of freedom in the United States) as well as his unwillingness to include African Americans and the colonial subjects of European empires in his pledge to make the world "safe for democracy." Our current political alignments have directed new attention to the once obscure George Wallace, father, so to speak, of Nixon's southern strategy and the racial politics of the modern Republican Party.

Although historians are often warned to avoid presentism—that is, reading present-day values and concerns back into the past—many draw on a knowledge of history to illuminate their own times. A number of the pieces collected here, for example, emphasize the continuing relevance of the Reconstruction era to the world in which we live. In the past two generations, no era of American history has undergone a more complete revision of historical interpretation. I contributed to this transformation through my books *Nothing but Freedom*, *Freedom's Lawmakers*, and *Reconstruction: America's Unfinished Revolution*, as well as by lecturing on Reconstruction to numerous non-academic audiences, co-curating a major museum exhibition on the era, serving as advisor to a prizewinning public television documentary series, and initiating the process that led to the establishment of a National Historical Park in Beaufort, South Carolina, devoted to Reconstruction.

The study of Reconstruction has left a deep imprint on my scholarship more generally. Research on those years led me to appreciate that freedom has never been a single, fixed idea. My work on Reconstruction made clear that in the aftermath of the Civil War, former owners, formerly enslaved African Americans, and millions of northerners held radically different ideas about what freedom meant and how it might be achieved in the aftermath of emancipation. This insight helped to inspire my book *The Story of American Freedom*, which traces debates over the meaning of freedom, who is entitled to enjoy it, and what kinds of social and political organization are necessary to make it a reality. That work, in turn, became the foundation for my American history textbook, *Give Me Liberty!*, in which the changing understandings of freedom form a unifying theme for understanding the American past. The titles of a good number of my books include the words freedom, free, and liberty.

Of course, freedom has been an American preoccupation ever since the Revolution gave birth to a nation that identified itself as a unique embodiment of freedom in a world overrun by oppression. The Declaration of Independence includes liberty among mankind's unalienable rights; the Constitution announces at the outset the aim of securing the "blessings of liberty." As the educator and statesman Ralph Bunche wrote in 1940, "every man in the street, white, red, black, or yellow, knows that this is "The land of the free . . . [and] the cradle of liberty."

Yet freedom is neither a fixed idea nor a story of progress toward a predetermined goal. The history of American freedom is a tale of debates and struggles. Often, battles for control of the idea illustrate the contrast between "negative" and "positive" meanings of freedom, a dichotomy elaborated by Sir Isaiah Berlin in an influential essay in 1958. Negative liberty defines freedom as the absence of outside restraints on individual action. Positive liberty is a form of empowerment—the ability to establish and achieve one's goals. The first sees government as a threat to individual freedom, the second often requires governmental action to remove barriers to its enjoyment.

Freedom played an unexpectedly large role in the presidential election of 2024. The Democratic national convention opened with a video of the popular entertainer Beyoncé performing her song "Freedom." Nearly a century earlier, in the wake of the Great Depression, Franklin D. Roosevelt had linked freedom to economic security for ordinary Americans. This definition of freedom, a product of the New Deal, assumed an active role for the federal government. But since the 1980s, when Ronald Reagan effectively redefined freedom as limited government, low taxes, and unregulated economic enterprise, Democrats had pretty much ceded the word to their opponents. Now they wanted it back. Harris crisscrossed the country talking about freedom. The most frequently articulated demand of Democrats, a response to the Supreme Court decision of 2022 overturning the constitutional right to terminate a pregnancy, was for "reproductive freedom"—the ability to make intimate decisions free of government interference.

There is another crucial element in the ongoing debate about freedom, reflected in many of the essays in this book: who is entitled to enjoy it? When the Constitution was ratified, and for decades afterwards, many understandings of freedom had a racial dimension. The first laws defining how immigrants could become naturalized citizens, enacted in the 1790s, limited the process to "white" persons. It took over half a century for slavery to be eradicated and for Black persons, briefly, to be incorporated into the body politic. This history, discussed in several of the books reviewed below, exemplifies what the historian Tyler Stovall has called "White Freedom." Freedom is often defined by exclusion. From the leaders of the Confederacy to modern-day Realtors determined to keep non-whites from purchasing a home in a segregated neighborhood, the "right to discriminate" has often been seen as a form of freedom. The vaunted independence of men, for example, long depended on limiting the freedom of women.

The 2024 campaign was not the first time a presidential election became, in part, a contest to define the meaning of freedom. In 1936, *The New York Times* observed that the fight for possession of "the ideal of freedom" was the central issue of that year's presidential election. In 1964, the journalist Theodore White observed that freedom was the "dominant word" of both civil rights activists and supporters of the conservative Republican candidate for president, Barry Goldwater, although they meant entirely different things by it. The United States, White concluded, sorely needed "a commonly agreed-on concept of freedom."

No recent president employed the word freedom more often, and more egregiously, than George W. Bush, who made it an all-purpose justification for the 2003 invasion of Iraq and the conflict that followed, dubbed by the president "Operation Iraqi Freedom." In his first inaugural address, Bush used the words freedom, free, or liberty on seven occasions. In his second, a ten-minute speech delivered after the invasion, they appeared no fewer than forty-nine times. Bush's invocation of the ideal of freedom to justify an unprovoked war seemed to make his immediate successors wary of using the word at all. Barack Obama did not speak often about freedom, preferring the language of community, equality, and personal responsibility. Nor has freedom been a major theme of Donald Trump, who prefers to speak of raw military and economic power (although one can purchase on the Internet T-shirts displaying the slogan "Trump Fighting for Freedom").

The only obligation we have to history, Oscar Wilde once remarked, is to rewrite it. New questions, new information, and the changing status of various groups of Americans will inevitably produce new historical insights. So will the changing composition of the historical profession. During my college and graduate student years, I was never once taught by a female or non-white historian, something all but impossible today. I look back with pride on the fact that the seventy-five or so historians whose dissertations I supervised during my teaching career included numerous members of previously underrepresented groups, notably women of diverse ancestries and non-white men. Inevitably, changes in the historical profession have altered the ways we think about the American past.

Historical interpretation both reflects and helps to shape the politics of the moment in which the historian is writing. For decades, the Dunning School, named for Columbia University professor William A. Dunning and his students, dominated historical writing on Reconstruction. In their account the post–Civil War era was a time of misgovernment caused by the supposedly misguided decision to grant political rights to Black men. The incapacity of Blacks was a foundational assumption of historical scholarship at a time when the study of the past was becoming professionalized. I have discussed the Dunning School in previous writings as well as in some of the essays in this book.

Suffice it to say here that like any complex social system, the South's Jim Crow order required a historical foundation to support its claim to legitimacy, and that for much of the twentieth century, historians played a major role in providing it.

Today, the writing and teaching of history has been drawn into the vortex of the culture wars. Why is history so controversial? The French historian Ernest Renan had an answer. Historical analysis, he famously wrote in the late nineteenth century, has always been linked to broader ideas about the nation state. National consciousness, or at least the sense of unity and patriotic pride that accompanies nation-building, he argued, rests in part on historical mythology. Indeed, Renan wrote, because "historical error" plays a significant role in the creation of a national consciousness, advances in the field of history, including the replacement of myth by accurate accounts of the past, are often seen as "a threat to the nation."

Over a century ago the historian Carl Becker made a similar point when he wrote that history is what the present chooses to remember about the past. We see this in recently enacted state laws barring the teaching of controversial or "disturbing" ideas and mandating a celebration of American history that gives short shrift to less than praiseworthy realities of our past. These laws reflect our current cultural and political polarization, with each side embracing its own concept of what the United States has been, is, and should be. As the historian Richard Slotkin remarks in his most recent book, because both sides in the culture wars claim historical justification for their political beliefs, dramatically different American histories are being taught in different parts of the United States.

The 250th anniversary of American independence is fast approaching. But rather than playing a unifying role, the study of history reinforces our society's divisions. So does the clash between two definitions of freedom, one exclusionary and linked to ethno-cultural identity, the other inclusive and egalitarian, both rooted in the American experience.

Heated controversy over what history books students and interested adults should encounter itself has a long history. In 1923, the historian James Truslow Adams warned that the "forces of reaction and obscurantism" were on the march, seeking to determine how history was taught. At around the same time, the Daughters of the Confederacy were successfully demanding the removal of history textbooks from southern classrooms (and, not infrequently, those in the North as well), if they failed to present slavery as a benign institution and the war for southern independence as a gallant struggle for liberty. A different memory survived in Black communities, a remembrance of the 200,000 Black men who served in the Union army and navy during the Civil War and of the tragedy of enslaved children separated from their families. Remembering history at a time when others distort or seek to forget it can itself be a form of resistance.

During the McCarthy era, works by supposedly disloyal historians, including a seemingly uncontroversial history of Jews in the United States by my uncle Philip, were removed from the Department of State's overseas libraries. In the 1990s, national history standards designed by teachers at the behest of the National Endowment for the Humanities became the subject of controversy for, in the eyes of detractors, devoting excessive attention to the role of women, African Americans, and other groups whose experiences had previously been slighted by historians. Too much Harriet Tubman, critics complained, not enough George Washington.

Whatever the outcome of current controversies, the teaching and public presentation of history have changed considerably since I became a historian. A number of the books discussed here complain of pervasive "amnesia" or, even worse, downright misrepresentation, in school textbooks, public monuments, and historical markers. But the situation today is complicated. Textbooks now offer a far more nuanced and bittersweet portrait of the American past than when I was in school. The previously mentioned National Museum of African American History and Culture has attracted millions of visitors, a powerful rebuke to the belief that the historical narratives students and the general public encounter should reinforce traditional lessons, assumptions, and prejudices rather than challenging them. Today, one can also visit the International African American Museum in Charleston, located on the site where many thousands of Africans disembarked from ships carrying them into American bondage. Another new historical venue is the National Memorial for Peace and Justice in Montgomery, Alabama, which opened in 2018 and whose unsparing exhibits commemorate the over 4,000 victims of lynching during the Jim Crow era. In Jackson, the exhibits at the Museum of Mississippi History and the adjacent Mississippi Civil Rights Museum offer a surprisingly candid account of that state's unsettling history. But the very dissemination of new historical perspectives has produced a countervailing reaction, laws that seek to limit what students are allowed to read and learn. Some of the essays included here deal directly with ongoing battles over the fate of monuments glorifying the Confederacy and, more broadly, the political and cultural functions of historical commemoration.

"The past is the key of the present and the mirror of the future." Robert G. Fitzgerald, an African American who fought in both the Union army and navy during the Civil War, wrote these words in his diary in the early days of Reconstruction. As our country confronts a troubled present, perhaps a candid account of our history, the mirror of a future we cannot yet know, will help lay the foundation for a more equal, more just nation and a reinvigorated American democracy.

————

The essays in this book republish book reviews and opinion pieces I have written over the years. With minor exceptions, mostly to avoid repetition, the essays are republished as they originally appeared. The identification of each piece appears at the bottom of its opening page. These note the place and date of original publication, and, for reviews, the title and author of the book under review. At the back of this book I have included a list of the original publications and the essays that appeared in each.

PART I

Slavery and Antislavery

THE RISE AND FALL OF
AMERICAN SLAVERY

I N THE SPRING of 2011, television viewers in Great Britain were treated to a six-part series on the rise (and possible fall, if China has its way) of the West, hosted by the Harvard historian Niall Ferguson. The show offered a highly reductive version of history, identifying "the West" with qualities such as competition, scientific inquiry, and the rule of law and denigrating societies from Asia to the Middle East and Latin America for lacking these virtues. In effect, it provided a usable past to those who see today's world as riven by a clash of civilizations.

One episode explored why after independence the United States forged ahead while nations of Latin America stagnated. In an unusual twist, Ferguson chose South Carolina, a state governed by a tightly knit planter oligarchy, as an exemplar of Jeffersonian democracy resting on small property ownership, in contrast to the autocratic societies south of the border organized around large latifundia. Only 45 minutes into the one-hour show did he mention the presence of slaves—the actual majority of South Carolina's population. When it finally made an appearance, slavery was presented not as a crucial structural feature of

———

Review of *The American Crucible: Slavery, Emancipation and Human Rights*, by Robin Blackburn, *The Nation*, August 29, 2011.

early American society but as a moral dilemma, an "original sin" now expiated by Barack Obama's election.

Among the many virtues of Robin Blackburn's *The American Crucible* is that it moves slavery from the periphery to the center of any account of western ascendancy. Without the colonization of the New World, he notes at the outset, the West as we know it would not exist, and without slavery there could have been no colonization. Between 1500 and 1820, African slaves constituted about 80 percent of those who crossed the Atlantic from east to west. More than any other institution, the slave plantation underpinned the extraordinary expansion of western power and the region's prosperity in relation to the rest of the world.

In two earlier books, published in 1988 and 1997, Blackburn traced the creation of New World slavery and its abolition in the British, French, and Spanish empires, covering the years down to 1848. These works established him as one of the foremost scholars of slavery as an international institution. Now he has written an incisive one-volume survey of the institution's rise and fall. In part, the book summarizes his earlier volumes, but it goes well beyond them, drawing on recent scholarship to amplify his previous arguments and taking the story to around 1900, soon after the end of slavery in Brazil in 1888. He now explores emancipation in the nineteenth century's three greatest slave systems—the United States, Cuba, and Brazil. The book is an outstanding example of a major trend in recent historical writing—the transcending of national boundaries in favor of Atlantic or transnational history. Yet Blackburn cautions that while both the growth and abolition of slavery were international processes, they took place "in national histories" and followed no single pattern or path. With its theoretical sophistication and combination of a broad international approach and careful attention to local circumstances, *American Crucible* takes its place alongside David Brion Davis's *Inhuman Bondage* as the finest one-volume histories of the rise and fall of modern slavery.

Blackburn emphasizes that far from being static, New World slavery was a constantly evolving institution, and he identifies three broad eras in its history. In the first, which he dates from around 1500 to 1650, slavery centered in the Spanish colonies. It was small-scale and mostly urban. By 1600, half the population of the great colonial cities Lima, Havana, and Mexico City consisted of African slaves and their descendants. But in the countryside, in the silver and gold mines that enriched the Spanish crown and on the haciendas ruled by powerful colonial settlers, the indigenous population performed most of the labor.

The Spanish empire at this point lacked an extensive plantation system. That developed first in Brazil and then quickly spread to the British and French colonies of the Caribbean and mainland North America, launching the second era of modern slavery's history (1650–1800). Sugar and tobacco produced by slave labor, along with African slaves themselves, six million of whom were transported across the Atlantic in the eighteenth century, now became key commodities of international commerce. Sugar was the first mass-marketed product in human history. By 1770, colonial exports and reexports, mostly of slave-produced goods, represented between a third and a half of Atlantic trade. The profits swelled merchants' coffers and the treasuries of European nation-states. By this time, too, the slave plantation had become a highly versatile economic unit, well adapted to the demands of the capitalist marketplace and quite modern in its methods of production, marketing, and credit arrangements. Far from a retrograde drag on economic development, slavery was "a sinew of national strength" and of economic prosperity.

During this second period slavery began to play a central role in key features of western economic development—the spread of market relations, industrialization, and the rise of a consumer economy. Carefully examining the old debate about the relationship between slavery and the industrial revolution, Blackburn concludes that the vast accumulation of capital derived from slave labor was a necessary but not sufficient cause of industrialization. Such profits did not boost manufacturing development in Spain and Portugal. For this to happen, not only money but also a large home market and a supportive state were needed, both of which only late-eighteenth-century Britain possessed. Once it got underway, early industrialization spurred the further growth of slavery, creating a giant market for cotton from the American South and fueling the spread of a "commodity-based notion of freedom," in which ordinary consumers demanded more and more goods like the sugar, tobacco, rum, and coffee produced on slave plantations.

In the nineteenth century, slavery entered its third era, one rife with contradictions. In the century's first four decades Haiti, born of a slave revolution, emerged as the hemisphere's second independent republic, and the northern United States, the independent nations of Latin America, and the British empire implemented steps toward abolition. Yet, Blackburn cautions against the idea of a preordained, "irresistible advance" toward emancipation. Even as slavery died elsewhere, it thrived in the American South, Brazil, and Cuba. Indeed in 1860, on the eve of the American Civil War, far more slaves (around six million) resided in the Western Hemisphere than ever before. And slave-grown products—Cuban sugar, Brazilian coffee, and American cotton—played a greater role than ever in the new economy of mass consumption. By this time, to be sure, industry had outstripped plantation slavery in supplying goods for the consumer marketplace. But, Blackburn insists, there was no purely economic reason why slave plantations could not continue to coexist with industrializing economies, supplying their demand for raw materials and consumer goods from the tropics.

Blackburn also rejects the idea that emancipation arose from what he calls "latent virtue"—a comforting notion sometimes invoked by American historians to excuse the founding fathers for lack of action against slavery on the grounds that even if not immediately, their ideals set in motion the abolition process. And while not neglecting slave agency, Blackburn argues that the concessions and customary rights wrested by slaves from their owners over a long period of day-to-day struggle did not pose a fundamental challenge to the system. Rather, he insists, emancipation emerged from specific historical circumstances—a nexus of slave resistance, ideological conflict, and political crisis.

Blackburn examines in detail the myriad sources of antislavery thought—religious, nationalist, humanitarian, economic—and the abolitionists' pioneering use of mass-produced pamphlets, lithographs, petitions, and the like to spread their message. By the early decades of the nineteenth century, a genteel antislavery sentiment had become a hallmark of enlightened opinion on both sides of the Atlantic. But Blackburn is quick to note the limited accomplishments of respectable antislavery. Often, these early emancipations consisted of "free womb" laws that ended slavery over a prolonged period by freeing future offspring when they reached adulthood, not living slaves. Moreover, in most times and places, abolitionists represented only a small minority of the free population. Only in times of crisis did abolitionists acquire the power to influence national policy.

It was not the slow accumulation of rights by slaves or the persuasiveness of antislavery arguments that produced emancipation but "revolutionary ruptures" and political crises. In revolutionary France, a Spanish empire wracked by wars of colonial independence, a Britain beset by the crisis over parliamentary reform in the early 1830s, and Civil War America, slave resistance suddenly acquired new salience and abolitionist arguments found a receptive audience among the general populace and political elites. As in his previous books, Blackburn also insists that emancipation was closely connected to the state-building process. The act of abolition itself presupposed the existence of a new kind of state, one intolerant of the special local sovereignty of slaveowners and capable of carrying out radical measures. It gave the state moral legitimacy, allowing it plausibly to claim to be the embodiment of liberty.

Blackburn offers an excellent narrative of the path toward emancipation in the United States and of Lincoln's own evolving attitudes and policies. The American Civil War clearly exemplified the linkage of nineteenth-century nationalism with abolition. And with the destruction of the hemisphere's largest and most powerful slave system, Cuba and Brazil saw the handwriting on the wall. Spain enacted a free womb law for its colony, Cuba, in 1870, but abolition there, as elsewhere, also involved violence. About half the rebel army in the war of independence of the 1870s consisted of present or former slaves, and patriots demanded equal citizenship for all, regardless of race, in an independent Cuba. Slavery in Brazil finally ended in 1888, seemingly peacefully, although numerous slave revolts and the enlistment of thousands of slave soldiers in the war against Paraguay between 1865 and 1870 preceded emancipation.

When it comes to the consequences of abolition, Blackburn presents a rather somber assessment. Antislavery ideas were always linked to notions of liberty and progress, but less often to racial equality. Indeed, as they extended their empires across the globe in the late nineteenth century, European powers "claimed to be inspired by abolitionist principles" even when acting in blatantly racist ways. Everywhere in the Western Hemisphere, new systems of racial and labor subordination succeeded plantation slavery. Emancipation's economic impact turned out to be less drastic than many had hoped or feared. The export value of the main crops—American cotton, Brazilian coffee, and Cuban sugar, quickly recovered.

Blackburn is particularly pessimistic about the post-slavery United States, warning against a scholarly tendency to "exaggerate the gains made by former slaves and their descendants." While acknowledging the remarkable effort during post–Civil War Reconstruction to create an interracial democracy in the South, he sees that era as a minor detour on the road to a new system of racial domination based on segregation, disenfranchisement, and economic subordination. Indeed, he goes so far as to say that in the entire hemisphere, "the Blacks of the US South gained least from the ending of slavery."

It is unclear what standard of comparison Blackburn is applying here, since, as he notes, post-emancipation societies in general remained highly unequal. Despite its failure, Reconstruction closed off even more oppressive possibilities in the United States. Moreover, the rewriting of the laws and Constitution during Reconstruction to enshrine the idea of equal citizenship rights for Blacks established the legal framework for subsequent challenges to the post-emancipation racial regime. And the creation of autonomous Black churches and schools put in place institutions that would serve as the springboards for future struggles. Without falling back on the idea of "latent virtue," it is worth noting that unlike in other countries, the South's Jim Crow system remained a regional, not a national system, and that Black Americans had options not matched elsewhere, especially the possibility of migration to the North and West, where a different (though hardly egalitarian) racial system prevailed.

Slavery and Emancipation form two of the three parts of Blackburn's subtitle. The third, Human Rights, receives less attention, but represents a new concern compared to his previous work. In part, Blackburn's discussion is a response to recent scholarship by Lynn Hunt, who locates the origins of human rights consciousness in the Enlightenment and French Revolution, and Samuel Moyn, who situates the idea's emergence much more recently, in the 1970s. Earlier definitions of human rights, Moyn points out, were tied to the nation-state, as the full title of one key such document, the Declaration of the Rights of Man and of the Citizen (France, 1789) makes clear. People enjoyed human rights by virtue of membership in a particular polity, not their common humanity. Only lately, Moyn claims, did the idea arise of human rights that transcend and challenge national sovereignty and are thus truly universal.

Blackburn acknowledges the force of Moyn's argument and has no desire to create a selective and ahistorical genealogy of human rights. He insists, however, rightly in my view, that the abolitionist movement played a major role in developing the concept of human rights unbounded by race and nationality. "In the heat of these momentous clashes over slavery," he writes, "a new notion of human freedom and human unity was proclaimed." Indeed, the attack on slavery also involved a critique of the pretensions and power of the nation-states that protected and profited from the institution.

Unlike previous scholars, Blackburn places the slave uprising in St. Domingue, the richest of all the sugar islands, which became the nation of Haiti, at the center of the early history of human rights. The Haitian revolution, he notes, is rarely given its due by historians. Half a century ago, R. R. Palmer wrote an acclaimed two-volume work, *The Age of the Democratic Revolution*, that barely mentioned Haiti at all. Lately, thanks in part to the bicentennial of Haitian independence in 2004, a spate of works have appeared. Drawing on this literature, Blackburn insists that the rebellious slaves profoundly affected Atlantic political culture and human rights consciousness. Not only did events in St. Domingue directly inspire the 1794 French decree abolishing slavery (later reversed by Napoleon), but the revolutionary Convention's decision to seat Black and brown delegates from the island marked a stunning affirmation that the entitlements of the Declaration of the Rights of Man were available to all French citizens, regardless of color.

Ironically, if "the West" is to celebrate the idea of universal human rights as one of its distinctive contributions to modern civilization, part of the credit must go to the mostly African-born slave rebels of Haiti.

THE SLAVE SHIP

THE BICENTENNIAL IN 1807 of Great Britain's outlawing of the Atlantic slave trade inspired a host of scholarly and popular commemorations, including conferences, exhibitions, and even a big-budget film, *Amazing Grace*, that made an unlikely matinee idol of William Wilberforce, a key leader in the movement to abolish the trade. All these events took place in an atmosphere suffused with self-congratulation. The crusade against the slave trade and the government's eventual response offers a usable past for a society increasingly aware of its multiracial character—a chapter of history of which all Britons can be proud.

As an excellent recent book on the abolition movement by Christopher Brown suggests, Britain, the world's leading slave trader in the eighteenth century, later presented abolition as irrefutable proof of virtuous motives as it embarked on a new era of imperialism. Previously, rhetoric celebrating "British liberty" had rung a bit hollow given the country's role in shipping Africans to the New World. Abolition, Brown suggests, accumulated a stash of "moral capital" that helped to

———

Review of *The Slave Ship: A Human History*, by Marcus Rediker, *London Review of Books*, July 31, 2008.

underpin the idea of liberal empire. Even today, it has not been entirely expended. Lost in all this self-satisfaction is the reality that slavery itself survived in the British empire into the 1830s and in the United States until the end of the Civil War in 1865.

Also lost of late, according to Marcus Rediker, has been the human experience of slavery. Historical debate has focused on the trade's economic impact, the causes of abolition, and the precise numbers transported from Africa. The most widely accepted figure today is that over the course of four hundred years, beginning in the late fifteenth century, eleven million Africans were transported involuntarily to the New World. About three million more perished onboard the ships or in the process of capture and enslavement in Africa. This was "history's greatest forced migration," Rediker writes.

Rediker has established himself as the leading historian of maritime labor in the eighteenth century, the "golden age" of the slave trade. He has previously written about the era's pirates and its rebellious sailors and dockworkers. Now, he directs his attention to the captains and crews who worked the slave ships and to the slaves themselves. The book is not conceived as a full history of the trade. There is no mention of the part played by other European powers, nor does Rediker enter into the long-standing debate, originally inspired by Eric Williams's *Capitalism and Slavery* (1944), on the economic causes of abolition. Rediker sees the slave ship as a microcosm of economic exchange and political and military power, the "linchpin" of the world's first era of "globalization."

Slave ships carried the labor that built the first British empire. They enriched planters, merchants, investors, insurance companies, ship-builders, and the government. On their return voyages to Europe they flooded the market with sugar, coffee, and tobacco, the first mass-marketed consumer goods. The trade involved high costs, high risks, and high profits. Rediker does not mince words in describing the "terror"—unleashed against sailors as well as slaves—that enabled it to function. *The Slave Ship* is dramatic, moving, and kaleidoscopic. It draws on a remarkable array of sources: memoirs, eyewitness accounts, government documents, merchants' record books, and the database of slaving voyages compiled in the 1990s by a group of historians headed by David Eltis and Herbert Klein. It ranges from the counting houses of Liverpool and Bristol to the "factories" (slave-trading outposts) of West Africa and the slave markets of the Caribbean. The book is also episodic and sometimes confusing. It lacks a clear principle of organization, and there is much repetition concerning the purchase of slaves, the recruitment of crews, and discipline and resistance at sea. But its virtues considerably outweigh these flaws. This is truly an Atlantic history—something frequently called for but much less frequently achieved.

Rediker certainly knows his ships: how and where they were built, how a normal trading vessel was transformed into a slave ship by the addition of cannon and the building of a "barricado," a barrier across the main deck behind which armed crewmen could retreat in the event of an uprising. He takes us on a tour from stem to stern, from captain's quarters to the levels below decks where slaves were incarcerated. He knows the crew and their tasks—the mates, carpenters, gunners, and common sailors. And he knows how slaves were captured, transported, and terrorized.

The Slave Ship makes it clear that while Europeans financed, directed, and profited from the trade, it could not have functioned without the active participation of rulers and traders in Africa. Domestic slavery and the trading of slaves across the Sahara to Arab merchants existed centuries before Europeans arrived in West Africa. But the rise of the transatlantic trade transformed African societies. By the eighteenth century, militarized states like Asante and Dahomey had come into existence. They thrived by warring on and enslaving their neighbors. The trade exacerbated class tensions within African societies, as merchants and rulers profited from selling commoners to the slavers.

But Rediker's interest lies primarily with the victims. He draws heavily on the memoir of Olaudah Equiano—the son of a West African village chief who was kidnapped at the age of 11 by traders but eventually went on to a notable career as an abolitionist—to describe how Africans were brought from the interior to the coast and first encountered the slave ship, a vessel far larger and more menacing than anything they had ever seen. Even if, as some historians have recently suggested, Equiano was actually born in South Carolina, not Africa, his vivid account, Rediker argues, derived from conversations with those who lived through the experience of capture and transportation.

Once onboard ship, the slaves entered what Rediker calls "a world unto itself," a combination of warship, prison, and workplace. The vessels were of every size, from small pleasure craft dispatched to pick up a handful of slaves in Africa and sell them in the West Indies, to behemoths like the *Parr*, a 566-ton ship fitted out to carry seven hundred slaves and a hundred crewmen. (An explosion, its cause unknown, destroyed the *Parr* during its first voyage.) Then there was the *Brooks*, the most famous of all slave ships. Abolitionists circulated a diagram of the vessel crammed with slaves on both sides of the Atlantic; this was the era's most effective piece of visual propaganda. The trade's defenders claimed the ship was an invention: human beings could not possibly be packed together for a long voyage with so little space. Rediker shows that, not only was the *Brooks* real, but she made ten slaving voyages, sometimes carrying even more slaves than the number shown in the famous engraving.

Whatever the size, every slave ship was a rigidly hierarchal environment headed by a captain wielding a power, one wrote, "as absolute...as any potentate in Europe." Beneath him were the sailors, drawn from impoverished residents of port cities, ex-felons, debtors, and others who could be lured into service by advance payment of two months' wages, often spent before departure in taverns and brothels. As soon as the ship left port, captains established their authority over the crew, sometimes sadistically, with whippings and other punishments for minor or non-existent infractions. James Stanfield, a sailor whose epic poem about his experiences Rediker quotes at length, wrote of the "demon cruelty" of his captain. Stanfield felt that in some ways the slaves were better off than the crew, since the captain had an economic incentive to deliver them alive and well for sale.

Once the ship arrived on the African coast and began to load slaves, however, captain and crew found common cause in fear of insurrection. Now, from captain to cabin boy, all were white men. This hardly guaranteed them equality, but it did ensure that they would not be sold. (Even African traders could find themselves ensnared if they weren't careful.) Captain and crew now terrorized the human cargo: there were whippings and brandings with hot irons and the widespread rape of slave women. Sharks gathered around the ships—some followed them all the way across the ocean—waiting to feed on the corpses of those who perished. To discourage escape attempts, some captains threw food overboard to keep the predators nearby.

On the ship, Africans from different societies, speaking different languages, practicing different religions, began to create a new identity. If, Rediker argues, sailors became white men, the slaves, previously Igbo or Yoruba, became "Blacks" or "Africans." The trade threw together individuals who would never otherwise have encountered one another and who had never considered their color or residence on the same continent a source of unity. Their new bond was forged not from kinship, language, or even "race," but from slavery itself. Although the process of creating a cohesive African American culture would take place over many years, it began, Rediker shows, onboard the slave ships.

Rediker's account of this "shipboard community" is unavoidably speculative, but it helps to explain the resistance that broke out at every stage of the commerce. As Benjamin Franklin pointed out at the Constitutional Convention of 1787, the difference between the trade in slaves and all other commerce was that other cargoes do not rebel. The book begins with a failed attempt at resistance—a woman leaping from a canoe while being ferried from the African shore to a waiting slave ship and quickly being recaptured—and subsequently moves on to detail many instances of refusal to eat, jumps overboard, attempted suicide, and actual insurrection. A few uprisings succeeded; most were suppressed by the heavily armed crew. Barbaric punishments followed these attempts. Leaders were whipped to death, placed in cages and left to die by slow starvation, or had their body parts cut off one by one and thrown to the sharks.

Resistance raised costs, making it necessary to increase the size of crews and the number of weapons on board and causing insurance companies to increase their rates. It did not end the slave trade, but it did help to inspire the abolitionist movement. In 1792, Parliament seemed on the verge of voting for gradual abolition of the trade. The following year, with the outbreak of war with France, the plan was shelved. The movement was revived in 1806, and in 1807 Parliament decreed abolition. But the Spanish and Portuguese trade continued, and three million more Africans would be carried to the New World before the commerce ended.

Rediker, however, does not end with a celebration of British abolition. Rather, he directs our attention to the slave ports of the Caribbean and its population of "wharfingers": impoverished, diseased sailors who had been left behind when their vessels departed to prevent shipboard epidemics. Some of them, an official of the Royal Navy reported, had been taken in by "Negro women, out of compassion, and are healed in time." That some of the slave trade's victims cared for men responsible, in part, for their enslavement, echoes Equiano's eventual realization, with which his memoir opens, that mankind is "of one blood."

AMERICAN SLAVERY: THE FIRST TWO CENTURIES

MORE THAN A century and a half since the Emancipation Proclamation, Americans have yet to arrive at a generally agreed-upon understanding of either the history or legacy of slavery. Probably the most popular film among white Americans remains *Gone with the Wind*, in which slavery, for both races, seems little more than an occasion for a prolonged party. Back in 1997, when director Steven Spielberg tried to update the celluloid portrayal of slavery, he chose to do so via the *Amistad* case, which involved not American slaves but Africans who seized control of a Spanish slave ship in 1839. The rebels did end up in Connecticut, but their celebrated legal battle for freedom had nothing to do with slavery in the United States. It did, however, provide the occasion for one of Hollywood's patented happy endings, in which former president John Quincy Adams moves the Supreme Court to a recognition of human rights by eloquently invoking the Declaration of Independence. The justices did, indeed, in 1841, send the Africans home, but their deci-

Review of *Many Thousands Gone: The First Two Centuries of Slavery in North America*, by Ira Berlin, *London Review of Books*, February 2, 1999.

sion turned on maritime law and international treaty obligations, not mankind's inalienable right to liberty. In 1857, the same Court, in the Dred Scott decision, declared that Black persons had no rights that "a white man is bound to respect"—a more typical expression of judicial opinion regarding slavery.

Actually, America's historical memory of slavery tends more to amnesia than romanticization, although of late this has begun to change. The national desire to forget slavery stands in stark contrast to historians' preoccupation with the subject—an example of the well-known disconnect between the academy and general public. Since Kenneth Stampp launched the golden age of slavery studies with the publication in 1956 of *The Peculiar Institution*, no part of the American past has been the subject of so large and outstanding a body of historical scholarship. For many years, research tended to focus on the antebellum years, the age of the Cotton Kingdom and irrepressible conflict. More recently, a growing number of historians have turned their attention to slavery in colonial America, seeking to explain the system's origins. Ira Berlin's book is an outstanding contribution to this literature. It propels the study of slavery in new directions.

Berlin, who taught at the University of Maryland and was the author of a well-regarded study of free Blacks in the nineteenth-century American South, for many years directed the Freedmen and Southern Society editorial project. Documentary editing rarely receives much public attention, but this undertaking, in which a team of scholars combed through literally millions of documents in the National Archives to illuminate the drama of emancipation during the Civil War, has profoundly affected how scholars interpret that era. The first volume published by the project, which dealt with the experience of Black soldiers, made it impossible to write about the war without taking into account how their service changed the nature of the conflict. Succeeding volumes have examined the complex causes that brought down slavery, and how the transition from slave to free labor occurred in different parts of the South.

Some of the themes of *Many Thousands Gone* were evident in Berlin's earlier work, especially the vital importance of regional and temporal variations within slavery. He showed how conditions of free Blacks evolved over time and distinguished sharply between their status in the Upper and Lower South. In his new book, too, Berlin emphasizes that slavery, too often treated by historians as a static institution, was in fact constantly changing. The range of subjects he covers is indeed impressive—from work patterns to family life, naming practices, religion, race relations, and modes of resistance. By organizing his account of the first two centuries of North American slavery—from the settlement of Jamestown, Virginia, in 1607 to the abolition of the Atlantic slave trade by Britain and the United States in 1808—along the axes of space and time, Berlin provides coherence to what would otherwise have been an account encyclopedic in its detail and complexity.

Berlin divides the history of slavery into four regions and three broad time periods. The regions are the northern colonies; the Chesapeake (Virginia and Maryland); the coastal lowcountry of South Carolina, Georgia, and Florida; and the lower Mississippi Valley. By including Louisiana, at various times under the control of France and Spain, and the Spanish colony of Florida, Berlin drives home the point that the modern United States is far more than the descendant of British settlement. He also subtly undermines a familiar historical legend. In 1693, he points out, Spain offered freedom to fugitive slaves who converted to Catholicism, inspiring a significant number of slaves to flee to Florida from adjacent South Carolina. The spectacle of inhabitants of an English colony seeking liberty under Spanish rule offers a jarring counterpoint to the familiar narrative that poses Anglo-Saxon love of liberty as the mirror opposite of Spanish tyranny.

In tracing how slavery and African American culture evolved within his four regions, Berlin distinguishes three broad chronological experiences: the "charter generation" (the first arrivals and their children); the plantation generation, which experienced the full brunt of slavery's consolidation; and the revolutionary generation, which sought to turn the rhetoric of American patriots into an instrument of their own liberation. Perhaps Berlin's most original section deals with the earliest

Africans brought to the New World—those he calls "Atlantic Creoles." The descendants of encounters between Europeans and Africans on the west coast of Africa beginning in the fifteenth century, these were literally and figuratively "people in the middle." Familiar with white society's laws, economy, and religious practices, they often brokered the movement of goods and people on the African coast and were among the first Africans transported to the New World.

In the earliest days of North American settlement, Berlin empha-sizes, slavery was far more open and indeterminate than it would later become. Slaves and white indentured servants worked together, drank together, engaged in sexual relations, and frequently ran away in inter-racial groups. Creole slaves adopted Christianity, took their masters to court, and sometimes were able to gain their freedom—they were, in brief, a recognizable part of colonial society. In many ways they were not equal to whites, but in a society of brutal labor exploitation that affected white indentured servants as well as Black slaves, slavery was one form of inequality among many, and color did not have the salience it would later achieve as a line of social division.

"The fluidity of colonial society, the ill-defined meaning of slavery, and the ambiguous notions of race," writes Berlin, referring to the seventeenth century, "allowed Atlantic Creoles to carve a place for themselves" and occasionally obtain freedom and "achieve a modest prosperity." Borrowing a distinction developed by Moses Finley in his studies of ancient slavery, he calls these early settlements "societies with slaves" (that is, ones in which slavery was of marginal economic impor-tance), as opposed to "slave societies" where the institution stood at the center of economic and political life.

In some, but not all, of Berlin's regions, the consolidation of plan-tation agriculture and the achievement of political dominance by the planter class inaugurated a new and far harsher era of slavery, in which avenues to freedom were effectively curtailed. History, however, does not move along a linear or predetermined path, and the pace and direc-tion of change differed markedly from place to place. In Louisiana, the French introduced the plantation at once, only to see their slave society devolve "backward" into a society with slaves after an uprising of Indians and Africans in 1729 thoroughly destabilized the system and wrecked the dream of creating a plantation-based colony such as existed in the Caribbean.

In the North, the plantation never entrenched itself and the indeterminacy of the charter generation lasted into the eighteenth century. In the Chesapeake, initially settled in 1607, it was not until the 1680s that the society with slaves turned into a slave society. In South Carolina, the initial "charter" period was little more than a fleeting moment, for as soon as planters discovered the viability and profitability of growing rice, the consolidation of the plantation and the transition to a slave society took place.

With the establishment of plantation economies came a fundamental change not only in the nature of work, access to freedom, and the power and profits of the planter class, but in Black culture as well. Race took on far greater social significance, as planters filled the statute books with laws distinguishing between white and Black, and subjected free Blacks to more and more onerous regulations. Indeed, even in the northern colonies, the situation of free Blacks deteriorated in the eighteenth century. Throughout the colonies, "free" increasingly became a term associated only with whites. It is now almost a cliché that race is "invented" or "socially constructed." Berlin is one of a handful of scholars who, through careful empirical research, shows how the invention of race actually took place.

The new demand for plantation labor led to a massive influx of slaves imported directly from Africa. In place of Creoles at home in two worlds, Black society was increasingly composed of men and women born in Africa and culturally quite alien. Because of this "re-Africanization" of Black culture, the process of assimilation had to begin over again. It occurred more swiftly in the Chesapeake, where a high birth rate among slaves soon produced a new generation of American-born Blacks who spoke English, were familiar with white ways, and, like whites, were swept up in the mid-eighteenth-century religious revivals known as the Great Awakening. It proceeded fitfully in the lowcountry, where large groups of African-born slaves lived in virtual isolation on rice and indigo plantations, while their owners spent much of their time in Charleston town houses. Here, a sharp split developed between the African-oriented rural slaves and urban slave artisans and domestic workers, far more assimilated into the larger society.

The American Revolution transformed slavery once again, but as always the pattern varied from place to place. Thousands of slaves obtained their freedom by running away during the turmoil of war, enlisting in the Continental Army, or accompanying the British when they evacuated cities like New York, Charleston, and Savannah. Black men and women seized on the revolutionary ideology to point up the hypocrisy of slaveholders who trumpeted their commitment to the rights of man, and brought eloquent "freedom petitions" before courts and legislatures. The northern states took steps for the gradual abolition of slavery. Nonetheless, Black freedom did not mean the same as freedom for whites. Northern Blacks were barred from skilled trades and, as time went on, from the right to vote, a central emblem of citizenship in a democratic society.

In the Chesapeake, a considerable number of slaveholders, inspired by revolutionary ideology (and moved as well by the declining need for year-round labor as the region shifted from tobacco to grain production) voluntarily manumitted their slaves. Thus, a large free Black community came into existence. In South Carolina and Georgia, however, the disruptions of the War for Independence produced not a weakening of commitment to slavery, but the demand that the Atlantic slave trade be reopened. At the insistence of these states, the Constitutional Convention of 1787 forbade Congress from abolishing the importation of slaves until 1808. Given this window of opportunity, South Carolina brought in tens of thousands of new slaves, further reinforcing the African presence in lowcountry Black society.

Thus, the Revolution both weakened and strengthened slavery. But the melancholy fact is that in 1810, when Berlin's account ends, there were far more slaves in the United States than when the Declaration of Independence was written. Not only had slavery failed to wither and die as some of the founders had hoped, but the institution stood poised on the eve of an era of tremendous territorial and economic expansion based on rapidly growing world demand for cotton.

With its continental perspective and nuanced account of the evolution of slavery as an institution and the shaping of African American culture, *Many Thousands Gone* is likely to remain for years the standard account of the first two centuries of slavery in the area that became the United States. Berlin argues that while slavery produced and reinforced racism, the fundamental reasons for its establishment were economic. Slavery was the byproduct of the voracious appetite of European consumers for products of slave labor such as sugar, rice, and tobacco. By virtue of being different, Blacks were deemed enslavable in ways that English or French laborers never were, but it was desire for profits, not racial prejudice, that actually inspired slave trading. Race for Berlin is an evolving set of social relationships, not a fixed attitude or deus ex machina, as so many other historians treat it.

Berlin is sensitive to subtle differences between slave systems in different parts of the hemisphere. His account, however, raises questions about the utility of the distinction between slave societies and societies with slaves. To be sure, this seems a common-sensical way of differentiating between colonies like Massachusetts and Pennsylvania, where slaves accounted for less than 10 percent of the population, and Virginia and South Carolina, where they came to dominate the labor force. Yet Berlin demonstrates the deep reliance on slavery of both the non-plantation colonies and the metropolitan powers. Massachusetts ships transported slaves and slave-grown sugar to northern colonies and Europe. The slave plantations of the West Indies were the major export market for grain grown by the free farmers of Pennsylvania. Merchants, small farmers, consumers, and political rulers all profited from its existence. The point is that in a slave-based empire, everyone, in a sense, was part of a slave society. Berlin reminds us of the complexity of the institution of slavery. He makes clear the centrality of slavery to American history from the earliest days of colonial settlement. Understanding this basic fact is the first step toward exorcising the divisions and inequalities that are among slavery's most enduring legacies.

THE LINE

NOT MANY GEOPOLITICAL boundaries occupy a place in Americans' historical imagination. The Mason-Dixon line is one that does. Surveyed in the 1760s by the English astronomers Charles Mason and Jeremiah Dixon to settle a long-running boundary dispute between Pennsylvania and Maryland, it has inspired responses as diverse as an early twentieth-century popular song, "Cross the Mason-Dixon Line," and Thomas Pynchon's late twentieth-century novel, *Mason and Dixon*. To be sure, not many Americans know the full names of Mssrs. Mason and Dixon. But quite a few know that before the American Civil War "the Line," as Edward G. Gray refers to it throughout his deeply researched and very readable new book, *Mason-Dixon*, marked the boundary between political economies based on slave and free labor.

Actually, as Gray points out, this definition of the Line is somewhat misleading, since at the time of American independence there was no boundary between slavery and freedom. Slavery was legal in all thirteen states. And when Pennsylvania, in 1780, enacted the new nation's

---

Review of *Mason-Dixon: Crucible of the Nation*, by Edward G. Gray, *Times Literary Supplement*, January 26, 2024.

first law for abolition (Vermont preceded it, but was not recognized as part of the Union until 1791), the measure did not free any living slaves. Instead, it provided for the future emancipation of children henceforth born into slavery.

This was typical of laws for "gradual" abolition in northern states, some so gradual that slavery lingered in parts of the North well into the nineteenth century. But the 1780 law did focus attention on an increasingly rancorous national divide about the future of slavery that over time greatly enhanced the Line's significance.

At a time when a crisis at the nation's southern border has inflamed American politics, it is perhaps not surprising that scholars have turned their attention to the history of "borderlands"—meeting grounds of diverse peoples characterized by the interpenetration of cultures and competing claims to political authority. The Line, however, was not a border in a modern sense. With the significant exception of African Americans, who were required to demonstrate their right to cross, it did not impede the movement of people. Maryland, however, did require members of the state's large free Black population to carry official documents attesting to their legal status or, in the case of slaves, an owner's permission for them to travel.

Of course, drawing boundary lines on a map often means very little on the ground. This, Gray writes, was the fate of the Proclamation line of 1763, meant to end violent disputes over access to land between speculators, European settlers, and Native Americans by reserving a large area west of the Appalachians for the exclusive occupation of indigenous peoples. In reality, settlers continued to flood into Indian Territory, exacerbating, Gray writes, the "internecine racial violence of the borderlands." These events encouraged the emergence of what Gray calls a politics of "aggrievement and alienation" still on display today in parts of the United States, a political outlook that demands physical protection and economic assistance from public authorities but simultaneously is quick to oppose governmental regulation of people's behavior. To dispossess the Native population required a vigorous exercise of military power (and taxation to help pay for it), but as soon as this had been accomplished settlers insisted on being left alone.

Founded, respectively, in 1681 and 1732, Maryland and Pennsylvania were proprietary colonies, meaning that they originated in large land grants (the borders not clearly defined, hence the need for a definitive survey) accompanied by sweeping political powers, to Cecil Calvert and William Penn, wealthy Britons influential at court. Both proprietors had mixed motives. They hoped to profit from control of their colonies' commerce, but also aspired to establish sanctuaries for persecuted co-religionists in Britain—Roman Catholics in the case of Calvert, Quakers for Penn. To attract settlers and avoid war, which could be very expensive, Penn made real estate available on generous terms and cultivated friendly relations with local Indians. But things did not work out as planned. Rather than a model of religious toleration, Maryland was beset by "incessant sectarian conflict" between Protestants and Catholics, while Penn's dream of harmonious relations among a diverse population foundered on the shoals of settlers' land hunger, which opened the door to what Gray calls "ethnocidal slaughter" directed at Native Americans. As thousands of European farmers, artisans, and merchants arrived to take advantage of Penn's largesse, the Pennsylvania-Maryland borderland emerged as one of the most violent regions in all of North America. Despite this, its great port cities, Philadelphia and Baltimore, thrived as the population grew, becoming key entrepots for the export of crops produced by a vast agricultural hinterland.

After the United States achieved independence, the main cause of conflict in the Mason-Dixon borderlands arose from the physical proximity of freedom and slavery. Unlike Pennsylvania, Maryland was a colony dominated by tobacco plantations. Slaves knew that freedom lay on the other side of the Line, especially since the border counties were home to Quaker farm families willing to defy state and national law by assisting runaway slaves. Meanwhile, despite efforts to restrain them, kidnappers from Maryland operated what historians have called a "reverse underground railroad," seizing free Black persons, including children, on the streets of Philadelphia for sale into southern slavery. Cross-border legal disputes sparked by the escape of slaves and the kidnapping of African Americans embroiled the courts and led to the enactment of two national Fugitive Slave Acts. The first, in 1793, essentially authorized owners to enter northern states and apprehend runaways by themselves. The second, in 1850, made the federal government responsible for the capture and return of fugitive slaves while mandating draconian penalties for assisting or even refusing to help capture them. These conflicting imperatives led to further violence along the Line. In 1851, in Christiana, Pennsylvania, armed African Americans, free and fugitive, engaged in an altercation with a posse led by federal marshals and an owner seeking to retrieve runaway slaves, leading to the enslaver's death.

Events in the Mason-Dixon borderland reflected in microcosm the conflict that was tearing the nation apart. Some of the most famous fugitive slaves, including Frederick Douglass and Harriet Tubman, escaped from Maryland to the other side of the Line. Key figures in national politics were products of this region, among them Roger B. Taney, Chief Justice of the United States, whose infamous Dred Scott decision denied that any Black person could be an American citizen; President James Buchanan, during whose administration the Union shattered; and Thaddeus Stevens, leader of the antislavery forces in Congress during the Civil War. John Brown chose a farm in Hagerstown, Maryland, not far from the Line, as the headquarters for his band of abolitionists who in 1859 tried to incite a slave revolution.

During the Civil War two slave states in the Mason-Dixon borderland, Delaware and Maryland, remained in the Union, becoming known, along with Kentucky and Missouri, as the border states. Because geography placed them in the military crosshairs, they experienced severe devastation. The war's greatest battle took place in Gettysburg, Pennsylvania, a few miles north of the Line. More Americans died at Antietam, in Maryland, just south of the Line, than on any other day in the nation's history. The war quickly inspired demands for emancipation, but also, in the borderland, strong resistance to change. Not long after fighting began, Lincoln offered Delaware (located at the eastern end of the Line) financial incentives to adopt a plan of gradual emancipation. Delaware had only 1,800 slaves, but its political leaders clung to the institution's decaying body for the entire war. Slavery did not end in Delaware until 1865, with the ratification of the Thirteenth Amendment to the U.S. Constitution. In a futile but revealing gesture, the state refused to ratify the amendment until 1901. Unlike Delaware, Maryland abolished slavery during the Civil War; this required a social and political revolution that ousted planters from power. Gray's sub-title, *Crucible of the Nation*, suggests that some of the patterns he has identified still roil the country, including hostility to racial "others," intense political and cultural polarization, and recurring violence. Also familiar today is the conviction that people can enjoy a better life by crossing borders, legally or illegally.

In a book published four years after the end of the Civil War, Harriet Tubman described a vision she had experienced. There was "a line," and on the other side "green fields, and lovely flowers, and beautiful white ladies who stretched out their arms to me." At first, Tubman "always fell" before reaching the line. But eventually she succeeded: "I had crossed the line. I was free."

WASHINGTON AND SLAVERY

O NE OF THE few facts of American history of which Donald Trump appears to be aware is that George Washington owned slaves. Trump mentioned this in 2019 as one reason for his opposition to the removal of the monuments to Confederate generals that dot the southern landscape. In Trump's view owning slaves probably enhances Washington's reputation: like him, the first president knew how to make a buck. Not everyone agrees. In June this year, the San Francisco school board voted to cover over a series of New Deal–era murals at George Washington High School that depicted the great man's career: some students found their depictions of a dead Native American and of slaves working in Washington's fields upsetting. Lost in the debate was the fact that the artist, Victor Arnautoff, a communist, had used the murals to challenge the prevailing narrative of Washington's life and, indeed, American history more broadly. His murals were intended to show that the country's economic growth and territorial expansion—Washington took

Review of *The Only Unavoidable Subject of Regret: George Washington, Slavery, and the Enslaved Community at Mount Vernon*, by Mary Thompson, *London Review of Books*, December 19, 2019.

part in both—rested on the exploitation of slave labor and the violent seizure of Native American land.

Among historians, Washington's connection to slavery has inspired far less examination, and agonizing, than Thomas Jefferson's. Partly this is because of the patent contradiction between Jefferson's affirmation in the Declaration of Independence that "all men are created equal" and his ownership of more than a hundred slaves. Prurient interest also plays a part. Thanks to DNA evidence, it's now clear that Jefferson, a widower, fathered several children with his slave Sally Hemings. There is no equivalent in Washington's life, though some of his male relatives, including his wife's father-in-law in her first marriage, did have such offspring. An official at Mount Vernon, Washington's plantation on the Potomac River, once told me that he wished similar information would come to light about Washington, since Jefferson's plantation, Monticello, had experienced a substantial increase in visitor numbers after the historian Annette Gordon-Reed established beyond doubt the Hemings connection. In the apparent belief that visitors' imaginations need to be stirred even further, a room at Monticello next to Jefferson's bedroom is now identified as Hemings's living quarters, although the evidence that she actually slept there is slight.

Actually, Mount Vernon doesn't need any more visitors. Today, it attracts around a million a year, outstripping Monticello and even Graceland, the home of Elvis Presley. What tourists find there has changed dramatically in recent years. Slavery used to be pretty much ignored (if guides mentioned slaves at all, they referred to them as "servants"), but today the historical presentations deal candidly with the institution and Washington's relation to it. Visitors have the option to join an Enslaved People of Mount Vernon tour.

Washington grew up in a world centered on slavery. He inherited slaves from his father and his older half-brother. His wife, Martha, possessed dozens of "dower slaves" who had been owned by her first husband and legally remained under her control until her death, when they returned to his estate. During much of his life Washington bought and sold slaves. They were property, and he frequently referred to them as such, listing them in letters in the same sentence as horses, or saying he needed to sell cattle, sheep, furniture, tools, and slaves to pay his creditors. At the time of his death in 1799 the slave population of Mount Vernon exceeded three hundred.

Washington's sprawling estate consisted of eight thousand acres. There were five separate farms where tobacco and grain were the main crops, each worked by slaves directed by a white manager. There were also woodlands teeming with game, experimental gardens, stables, shops for carpenters, blacksmiths, and other craftsmen, and a mansion where Washington and his wife lived, attended by slaves dressed in red and white livery. Mary Thompson's book is the most detailed examination yet published of slavery at Mount Vernon. Thompson has worked for many years as a research historian at the estate and has a perhaps excessive admiration for Washington, whom she calls "one of the greatest—but still not perfect—men who ever lived." But she knows the sources better than anyone. When Washington died, his wife burned their forty-year correspondence. But documentation of other kinds is abundant. Washington kept a diary and detailed accounts of income and expenditure. A stickler for detail, he insisted on receiving weekly reports from his farm managers, which include revealing descriptions of slave labor. Periodically compiled lists of slaves by age, skill, and marital status offer insights into the structure of the slave community. Innumerable visitors, including relatives, friends, and perfect strangers, turned up at Mount Vernon expecting and receiving the Washingtons' hospitality, and in letters and memoirs many described the plantation's management and the condition of its slaves.

To be sure, virtually all the information Thompson draws on comes from whites; as she ruefully notes, "only occasionally can the voice of one of the slaves be heard." Nonetheless, her command of the sources makes possible an almost encyclopedic description of the conditions of slave life. What did slaves eat? At Mount Vernon, cornmeal, buttermilk, fish, and, at harvest time, meat, supplemented by food grown in their own gardens or stolen from the big house. What clothing did Washington provide? Aside from the livery for domestic slaves, male slaves each year received a wool jacket and two pairs of trousers, two coarse linen shirts, and a pair of shoes; females got a jacket, a skirt, a pair of stockings, and two linen shifts.

What about their living quarters? Apart from a brick House for Families near the mansion, most slave dwellings were poorly constructed log cabins that leaked in the rain, and because of their small windows were dark most of the day. The slaves grew crops in their gardens either to eat or to sell at a weekly market in the nearby town of Alexandria. With the proceeds, many managed to acquire household goods. Archaeological research has uncovered evidence of ceramics, glassware, silverware, furniture, and cooking implements in some of the slave quarters. On the much-debated question of whether African elements survived in slave culture, Thompson acknowledges that the evidence is scanty but cautiously suggests that some naming practices, religious beliefs, and methods of food preparation reflect an African inheritance.

Labor, of course, was the raison d'être of slavery, and Thompson devotes much attention to Washington's efforts to create a disciplined workforce and to the ways slaves resisted his demands. He was "by no means an easy man to work for." He insisted that slaves and hired workers adhere to his own highly demanding work ethic. "I expect my people," he wrote to one overseer, "will work from daybreaking until it is dusk," a regimen which in summer, as Thompson points out, meant a very long work day indeed. Every morning Washington went into the fields. He noticed when slaves were not at work and reprimanded them and the farm managers. Extremely concerned with his public reputation, he took pride in his own self-control. Those who knew him, however, were aware that he had a fierce temper. He was "tremendous in his wrath," Jefferson recalled after Washington's death, and slaves learned to steer clear when he was provoked.

Like other owners, Washington relied on a combination of incentives and punishments. When slaves worked on a holiday (such as the period around Christmas or Easter), he compensated them with small cash payments. Those who, he believed, were shirking their duties would be whipped, though unlike most planters, Washington set up a kind of appeals process to review physical punishments. Most of the whipping was done by overseers, but Washington himself sometimes applied the lash. Some historians have claimed that Martha Washington treated slaves more severely than her husband did, at least in terms of verbal abuse.

Thompson makes clear that Washington never succeeded in creating the work environment he desired. The most common forms of what historians call "day-to-day resistance" were doing poor work and feigning illness to avoid labor. Both Washingtons frequently criticized slaves' work habits and complained of their "tricks" to avoid labor and their lack of gratitude for all that had supposedly been done for them. As on most plantations, theft was commonplace at Mount Vernon, and there were constant complaints that wine, meat, and other items had disappeared, either consumed by slaves or sold at the Alexandria market. Oddly, Thompson suggests that these forms of resistance "may have backfired" by leading whites to consider Black men and women "lazy and clumsy workers . . . a stereotype that continues to this day." Washington certainly believed that Blacks were indolent by nature. But this was an integral part of the ideological justification for slavery, echoed throughout the world by colonizers and employers dissatisfied with workers of every race and nationality. As Alexander Hamilton noted, "the contempt we have been taught to entertain for the blacks makes us fancy many things that are founded neither in reason nor experience."

A more daring and dangerous form of resistance was escape. Between 1760 and 1799 at least forty-seven of Washington's slaves ran away. A group of seventeen, including three women, escaped during the War of Independence to seek refuge with the British army, which promised freedom to slaves. When Washington met the British commander Sir Guy Carleton in 1783 to implement the British withdrawal from New York, he asked Carleton to keep a lookout for "some of my own slaves" who had run off. He expressed surprise when Carleton replied that to deprive slaves of the freedom they had been promised would be a "dishonorable violation of the public faith."

Thompson believes that Washington showed some consideration for his slaves' feelings—for example by refusing to break up families when slaves were sold. She points out, however, that while most adult slaves at Mount Vernon were married, a majority lived on different farms from their spouses. Marital closeness took second place to work. She also claims that "affectionate ties" developed between the Washingtons and some of their slaves. Yet the story of Ona (or Oney) Judge, the subject of a prize-winning book by Erica Armstrong Dunbar, illustrates the limits of paternalism at Mount Vernon. From the age of ten, Judge worked as a personal maid and seamstress for Martha Washington. When she ran away in 1796, while living with the Washingtons in Philadelphia, the new nation's temporary capital, Martha was "extremely upset." Judge managed to reach New Hampshire, and George Washington made several attempts to recover her. Judge sent word that she would return if promised freedom on their deaths. Washington rejected her offer—"It would be neither politic or just to reward unfaithfulness," he replied. Why had Judge, certainly a privileged slave, run away? She learned that Martha Washington had promised her to her granddaughter as a wedding present. The Washingtons frequently referred to slaves as part of their family. But one does not typically give away a family member as a gift.

Visitors to Mount Vernon often ask whether Washington was a "good slaveowner." This language ought to be retired. Slaves themselves recognized that treatment varied considerably from owner to owner, but that was really irrelevant. During a visit to Richmond soon after the end of the Civil War, the Scottish minister David Macrae met a slave who complained of past mistreatment while acknowledging that he had never been whipped. "How were you cruelly treated then?" Macrae asked. "I was cruelly treated," the freedman answered, "because I was held in slavery."

Thompson ends with an account of the evolution of Washington's attitudes on slavery. Before the American Revolution, he seems to have had no qualms about the institution. Thompson believes that the revolutionary experience changed him. He came to recognize what the historian Edmund S. Morgan called "the American paradox"—the contradiction between the language of liberty invoked by the patriots and the reality of slaveholding. While Washington at first did not allow Black men to enroll in the revolutionary army, by the end of the conflict several thousand had served. (The army he commanded was more racially integrated than any American fighting force until the Korean War.) He emerged from the war with his views on slavery "radically altered." "There is not a man living," he wrote in 1786, who wished to see a plan for abolition adopted "more than I do." In the interim he decided to stop buying and selling slaves.

Yet he did nothing to promote the end of slavery and rejected any suggestion that he publicly call for Virginia or the country generally to adopt a plan for abolition. In Philadelphia, as president, he practiced what Thompson calls outright "duplicity," moving slaves back and forth between Mount Vernon and the city, "under pretext," he wrote, "that may deceive both them and the public." His purpose was to circumvent Pennsylvania's gradual abolition law of 1780, which provided that any slave brought into the state who remained there for six months could claim freedom. Washington signed the first national law for the rendition of fugitive slaves and his administration pressed Britain to abide by the Treaty of Paris, which ended the War of Independence and required the return of property, including slaves, seized from Americans.

Thompson offers various explanations for Washington's refusal to speak or act publicly against slavery. She points out that freeing his slaves would have meant financial disaster for his family. Like other Virginia planters, Washington was chronically in debt, largely because of a taste for luxury goods imported from Britain. Indeed, in 1789 he had to borrow money to pay for his journey to New York where his inauguration as the first president was to take place. She speculates that, having presided over the Constitutional Convention and witnessed bitter debates inspired by slavery, he feared that airing the question of abolition would destroy the new country. However, Benjamin Franklin also took part in the convention, and that didn't prevent him from adding his name to an abolition petition presented to Congress in 1790.

Washington seems to have had a number of private conversations in the last twenty years of his life about ending slavery. Nothing came of them, but when he died in 1799, leaving his estate to his wife, he directed his executors to free all the slaves (156 men, women, and children) who belonged to him on her death. Slave children were to be bound out to white employers until they were in their twenties, receiving an education and training in a craft. The will did not deal with Martha Washington's 153 dower slaves, in whom her husband had no property interest. Living among men and women anxiously awaiting the freedom that would come with her death, and fearing one of them might feel motivated to help that day arrive sooner, Martha freed her husband's slaves in 1801. When she died the following year, the dower slaves, many of whom were married to the former slaves owned by her late husband, reverted to the control of the Custis family and were divided among her four grandchildren. Thus the slave community that had existed for decades at Mount Vernon was destroyed.

Addressing current controversies about the historical reputation of men like Washington, Thompson warns against "judging a person from another time and culture" by today's moral standards. Yet antislavery ideas were hardly unknown during Washington's lifetime, and he himself expressed them privately. What about expecting an individual to live up to his own professed convictions? Washington deserves full credit for emancipating his slaves. Some Virginia planters, inspired by revolutionary ideals and religious convictions, did the same; many more did not. Yet manumission (freeing individual slaves) is not the same thing as abolishing the institution. Alongside the humane provisions of his will should be placed Washington's public silence when it came to slavery. Jefferson's will freed only five slaves, all relatives of Hemings's, but he did write the proposed Land Ordinance of 1784, which would have barred slavery from the country's western territories, and which narrowly failed to receive congressional approval. Washington was willing to place his life and property on the line to fight for American independence. He was by far the most esteemed statesman in the early republic. Imagine if he had used his reputation to promote a plan for abolition. When it came to taking action to end slavery, he, like most of the revolutionary generation, must be found wanting.

INSIDE THE LARGEST
SLAVE AUCTION

I N PRE–CIVIL WAR fugitive slave narratives—memoirs written
by men and, occasionally, women who had escaped to freedom and
hoped to convert readers to the cause of abolition—the most heart-
rending passages described slave auctions and the separation of families
that usually ensued. When the abolitionist journalist and underground
railroad activist Sydney Howard Gay interviewed fugitives who passed
through his office in New York City in the 1850s, he found that the
threat of sale was a major reason for the decision to run away.

Although most Americans today acknowledge the centrality of slavery to antebellum southern life, the ubiquity of the buying and selling
of slaves is less widely recognized. In 2016, many were shocked to learn
that Georgetown, a Jesuit university, sold nearly three hundred slaves in
the 1830s to remain afloat financially. A myth survives that slave trading was of marginal economic importance and that slave traders were
outcasts who operated on the fringes of southern society. In fact, after
the importation of slaves from Africa was outlawed by Congress in

Review of *The Weeping Time: Memory and the Largest Slave Auction in
American History*, by Anne C. Bailey, *London Review of Books*, March
22, 2018.

1808 a massive commerce in slaves developed within the United States. This "internal middle passage," as the historian Ira Berlin has called it, involved the sale of more than two million slaves in the decades before the Civil War, a large number of whom were sent from older states such as Virginia to the burgeoning Cotton Kingdom of the Lower South. Every southern newspaper carried advertisements for the sale of slaves and every major town had slave dealers who drew attention to their business with signs proclaiming "Negro Sales" or "Negroes Bought Here." In Charleston and New Orleans, there were large public slave markets. Slave trading was essential to the survival and profitability of the system, as well as to the financial success of individual owners.

The largest slave auction in American history, the sale of more than four hundred men, women, and children owned by Pierce M. Butler, took place in Savannah, Georgia, in 1859. Butler was the grandson and namesake of the signer of the U.S. constitution who proposed its notorious fugitive slave clause, which ensured that slaves who fled to another state were returned to their owners. He spent nearly all his time in a luxurious townhouse in Philadelphia and rarely visited his Georgia estates—a rice plantation near Darien and a plantation growing Sea Island cotton (the most sought-after and profitable strain of the crop) on St. Simon's Island, just off the coast—leaving them to be run by overseers.

Butler is best known to historians for his tempestuous marriage to the British actress Fanny Kemble, whom he courted after seeing her perform in Philadelphia. They married in 1834; two years later, he inherited half of his grandfather's estate. In 1838, Butler and Kemble embarked on a five-month visit to his plantations, and she later published an account of their stay in *Journal of a Residence on a Georgia Plantation*, an eye-opening account of how slavery operated. Kemble held antislavery views, which grew stronger after witnessing the institution at first hand. Arguments, separations, and reunions followed the couple's return to Philadelphia. In 1849 they divorced, an event much chronicled in the society pages. In keeping with the laws of the time, Butler was given custody of their two young children. To Kemble's dismay, their daughter inherited her father's outlook on slavery and strongly supported the Confederate cause during the Civil War.

Before then, however, Butler's gambling losses and financial reverses triggered by the Panic of 1857, the first worldwide economic crisis, led him to agree to a massive sale of slaves to satisfy his creditors. Some remarkable documents survive from the sale, held over two days in March 1859, beginning with the auction catalogue, which lists slaves by name, age, and skill. The first entries read: "George, age 27, prime cotton planter; Sue, age 26, prime rice planter; George Jr, age 4, boy child; Harry, age 2, boy child." Listings for 432 other slaves follow. Another indispensable source is a 28-page pamphlet published soon after the auction took place. Its author was Mortimer Thomson, a reporter for the *New York Tribune*, the country's leading antislavery newspaper, who posed as a potential buyer and wrote a detailed account of the proceedings, down to some of the conversations among the buyers. Thomson overheard one of them say that he could "manage ordinary niggers" with the whip, but when he encountered a really recalcitrant slave, "I just get my pistol and shoot him right down." Others eagerly looked forward to the reopening of the Atlantic slave trade, which some southern political leaders were advocating. Thomson mostly let the events speak for themselves, but occasionally he offered a sardonic comment. Some of Butler's slaves, he reported, had been known to "inquire into the definition of the word liberty, and the meaning of the starry flag which waves, as you may have heard, o'er the land of the free."

Half the slaves on the Butler plantations were included in the sale. Most were field hands, but there were also domestic servants and skilled craftsmen, among them coopers, carpenters, and blacksmiths. The catalogue did not list prices, but Thomson recorded what many of the slaves sold for. The auctioneer announced the terms: buyers would pay one-third down in cash, with the remainder in interest-bearing installments. The highest sum paid was $1750 for William, a carpenter—an immense amount at a time when the average working-class white person earned around $300 per year. George, Sue, and their two young sons together went for $2480.

The sale was managed by Joseph Bryan, a prominent slave dealer whose occupation does not seem to have impeded his acceptance by Savannah's white residents—he was also the city's chief of police. For several days, local hotels were filled with potential buyers, who made the three-mile trip to the Savannah racetrack, where the auction took place. There they closely examined the slaves, who were housed in stalls that usually accommodated horses.

The sale destroyed long-established slave communities. Most of the slaves, and their parents before them, had lived their entire lives on Butler's plantations. They were part of what is now known as the Gullah Geechee culture of coastal South Carolina and Georgia, where African traditions survived more fully than in other parts of the South, partly because most of the owners, like Butler, were absentees and the slaves had little contact with whites. Slaves in this region spoke a dialect that mixed African and English words, which Black persons further inland, slave and free, often could not understand.

They told stories about slaves who learned to fly and made their way back to Africa. Butler's slaves were required to attend religious services conducted by white ministers, who instructed them to serve their masters faithfully, but they also had their own religious leaders. One day one of them, Sinda, prophesied that the end of the world was nigh, and with it emancipation. Butler's slaves, the overseer reported, stopped working and refused to resume until the appointed day had come and gone.

Unusually, the auctioneer was instructed not to separate families, although as Thomson noted, this admonition was limited to not separating husbands from wives and parents from young children. Siblings, cousins, grandparents, and grandchildren were wrenched apart, as were couples who had not been formally married. The night before the auction began, the slaves Dembo and Frances somehow located a minister who agreed to marry them so that they could be sold together; they were bought for $1320 each by a cotton planter from Alabama. Jeffrey, age 23, begged his buyer also to purchase Dorcas, proclaiming: "I loves her well and true." But they weren't married so his plea was to no avail. With his business agent, Butler made the trip from Philadelphia to watch the auction, which netted more than $300,000, enough to wipe out his debts. He stayed until the final lot was spoken for and then, Thomson reported, handed out "one whole dollar, in specie," to each of the slaves who had been sold.

The Savannah auction is the starting point of *The Weeping Time* by Anne C. Bailey, who teaches African American and African history. Her opening chapter recounting the sale of the Butler slaves is riveting but somewhat brief: one wishes that she had devoted more space to this harrowing story. But she seems anxious to move on to larger questions, to use the auction as a window into slavery itself. She discusses issues ranging from Black culture in the Georgia lowcountry to the way agricultural skills brought from Africa—especially complex methods of cultivating rice—enriched the slaves' owners. She probes the way subsequent generations remembered (or forgot) the institution's brutality and its centrality to American development. These are all weighty subjects, perhaps too weighty for a book of fewer than two hundred pages. Some of those pages cover subjects of dubious relevance, such as Britain's involvement in the Atlantic slave trade, and the presence of Islam in West Africa, where the ancestors of these slaves originated (although evidence for its presence on the Butler plantations is meager).

Bailey also spends too much time establishing points already widely accepted among historians. "This book affirms the view that the Black family is a resilient institution," she writes, a finding demonstrated more than forty years ago by Herbert Gutman in *The Black Family in Slavery and Freedom*. Other aspects of the story cry out for further analysis. The book devotes considerable attention to establishing "links to the slaves' African pasts" in their work routines, religious practices, and folkways such as ring dances. There is less on how Africans became African Americans, or the extent to which they were influenced by the values of the society around them. When emancipation finally arrived, Bailey notes, the former slaves saw the right to vote "as the heart and soul of their freedom." This outlook is more likely to have originated in nineteenth-century America than ancestral Africa.

During the Civil War, the slaves who had not been put on sale were moved inland, as Butler, like other local planters, acted to prevent them from running off to join the Union army, which occupied the Sea Islands early in the war. Once peace and emancipation arrived, former slaves throughout the South, including some from the Butler sale, set out to locate those from whom they had been separated. Only a few succeeded. Many of Butler's former slaves returned to his estates, the only place they knew as home. They hoped to claim some of the land for themselves, an aspiration that seemed plausible in January 1865, when General William T. Sherman set aside a large swathe of land on the Sea Islands and along the Georgia and South Carolina coasts for the settlement of Black families, and barred whites entirely from the islands. Later that year, however, President Andrew Johnson, who took office after Lincoln's assassination, ordered that the confiscated territory be returned to its owners. Butler and his daughter traveled to Georgia, hoping to put the former slaves back to work, but soon complained about their "laziness"—in other words, they were unwilling to work as if they were slaves. The frustrated Butlers eventually hired immigrants from China and Ireland to get their plantations running again.

Bailey's book is as much about memory as history. In Black communities the memory of lost children, husbands, wives, and other family members was seared into the culture of post-emancipation generations. How did the Butler slaves and their descendants, and African Americans more generally, confront and try to overcome the trauma of slavery, and to reconstitute families that had been torn apart? Bailey pays tribute to "the noble efforts of modern-day descendants . . . to restore the pieces of their fragmented past," despite not only a paucity of documentation but also the silence of former slaves and their immediate descendants about their experiences. Remarkably, however, ten families have managed to map out their ancestry, representing 15 percent of those sold at the Savannah auction. Over the course of generations, some of these families thrived. They learned to read and write, and became property owners. Several served in the armed forces, following in the footsteps of two Butler slaves who enrolled in the Union military during the Civil War. Some families suffered the kinds of loss all too familiar in the Jim Crow South. One eighteen-year-old was killed with an ice pick in Texas in 1940 by a white man who had been overheard earlier in the day saying he was "going to get him a nigger."

As Bailey notes, the heroic attempts of these families to reconstruct their lineages form part of a much broader effort among African Americans, many of whom have turned to companies that analyze DNA samples to identify their ethnic and geographic ancestry. Bailey tells us that she has had samples of her own DNA examined in order to locate her forebears' origins in West Africa. Although no direct evidence exists, she believes she "may have an ancestral link to the people of this study." She rightly insists that such genealogical explorations can lead to increased historical knowledge. She does not, however, take into account some of the problems raised by genetic testing, which has become big business, even spawning genome-themed tours of ancestral African homelands. The sociologist Alondra Nelson's recent book *The Social Life of DNA* explores these themes in depth, and raises questions about whether science can really be the vehicle for healing old wounds and answering questions about personal identity and heritage. Nelson points out that relatively few of the many hundreds of ethnic groups in West Africa have had their DNA studied, yet companies offer definitive-sounding findings about an individual's ethnic ancestry. She wonders whether the reliance on DNA is reviving the long-discredited biological understanding of race as something inborn and immutable that determines a person's capabilities. For her part, Bailey seems to believe that the impact of traumatic experiences, such as the Holocaust and slavery, can be transmitted genetically, that descendants can "unconsciously" inherit "environmental stresses akin to historical trauma." Studies of rats, she reports, reveal the reality of "transgenerational stress."

If Bailey's account of the transmission of memory borders on the metaphysical, she occupies solid ground in pointing to the inadequacy of public understandings of slavery. Of course, the way the Civil War is commemorated in public statues and monuments has become a highly controversial matter in the United States. There is nothing uniquely

American about these debates. Since the collapse of the Soviet Union and the fall of communism in Eastern Europe such artifacts have been removed with increasing frequency. Many Americans who oppose taking down statues of Confederate leaders applauded when Muscovites upended the statue of Felix Dzerzhinsky, a founder of the Soviet secret police, when Hungary shifted its communist-era monuments to a museum outside Budapest, and when U.S. troops toppled the statue of Saddam Hussein in Baghdad. Generally, as regimes change so does the public presentation of history. But this has aroused considerable opposition in the United States. The problem isn't simply the nostalgia for the Confederacy (and its underlying raison d'être of white supremacy) inscribed in many hundreds of monuments scattered across the South, but that the public commemoration of the history of the region, and the U.S. generally, is entirely one-dimensional. As Bailey notes, the experience of slavery is conspicuously absent from public representations of history. What is needed, she writes, is a "democratization of memory."

Some progress is being made. Bailey chides the National Park Service for having "obscured" the significance of slavery at its Civil War sites. This seems somewhat unfair since at the direction of Congress the service has in fact included discussions of slavery at many of its locations. And in 2016 the Obama administration designated Beaufort, South Carolina, just up the coast from the Butler plantations, as the site of a national monument devoted to the history of Reconstruction. But Bailey's larger point has merit.

A few years ago, President Sarkozy of France dedicated a monument in the Luxembourg Gardens intended to commemorate both the long travail of French slavery and the slaves' own contributions, through their struggles for freedom, to "the universality of human rights" and to French traditions of liberty. A historical marker now stands in Savannah showing the site of the "Largest Slave Sale in Georgia History." But to this day there is no monument anywhere in the United States to the millions of victims of American slavery or to the ways their labor helped to produce the world in which we live.

ISRAEL HILL

THE WORK OF historians of the last forty years has made clear the centrality of slavery to American history. Far less attention has been paid to the nearly half-million free Blacks who lived in the United States on the eve of the Civil War, a majority in the slave states. In a society that equated "Black" and "slave," free Black persons were seen as an anomaly. They had the right to enter into legally recognized marriages and own property (including, on occasion, slaves). But in nearly all the states, North and South, they could not vote, serve on juries, testify in court against white people, or attend public schools. "Free Negroes," a South Carolina judge declared in 1848, "belong to a degraded caste of society" and must conduct themselves "as inferiors."

Previous historians have described the limits of free Blacks' freedom. But none has examined the quality of their lives in the detail or with the sophistication of Melvin Patrick Ely in *Israel on the Appomattox*. Ely takes as his subject free Black life in Prince Edward County, in the

Review of *Israel on the Appomattox: A Southern Experiment in Black Freedom from the 1790s Through the Civil War*, by Melvin Patrick Ely, *Los Angeles Times Book Review*, September 12, 2004.

Virginia Piedmont southwest of Richmond. Best known today for having closed its public schools in the early 1960s for five years rather than accept integration, Prince Edward County before the Civil War was the site of a remarkable experiment in race relations initiated by Richard Randolph, a member of one of the state's most prominent families.

Like many aristocratic Virginians of the Revolutionary era, Randolph became convinced that slavery contradicted the ideals that inspired American independence. In 1796, shortly before his death at 26, Randolph drafted a will that condemned slavery as an "infamous practice," provided for the freeing of his slaves, and set aside part of his land for them. Because Randolph died in debt, it took fourteen years for his plan to be implemented. But in 1810 his widow gave some ninety men, women, and children their freedom, and divided 350 acres of land among their families. Steeped in the biblical story of Exodus, they called their settlement Israel Hill.

By 1860, the county's free Black population had risen to nearly 500, a number small enough to enable Ely to trace out their experiences family by family. He does this with remarkable energy and ingenuity. Ely has immersed himself in local documents—tax lists, road repair orders, census figures, and especially court records. From them he develops a striking portrait of free Black life as a day-to-day social reality, rather than simply a legal category.

Ely insists that despite the legal disabilities under which they suffered, and their complete exclusion from political participation, free African Americans effectively used local institutions to assert their rights and defend their interests. Local courts and public officials treated them pretty much the same as they did white Virginians. Free blacks accused of crimes were acquitted at the same rate as white defendants, and frequently won judgments against whites who owed them money. A landless free Black man sued a white employer for unpaid wages and won in court. An all-white jury awarded damages to a free African American plaintiff whose hogs were shot by a white farmer after they trampled his crops, since the law required landowners to maintain adequate fences. Meanwhile, state laws such as the requirement that free Black tax delinquents be hired out for involuntary labor remained unenforced in Prince Edward.

As the defense of slavery solidified after 1830, articles appeared in the southern press claiming that the residents of Israel Hill had degenerated since becoming free. Ely shows that this picture grossly distorted reality. Free Blacks were hard-working, ambitious, and economically successful. Many worked as skilled craftsmen—carpenters, blacksmiths, bricklayers, and boatmen who transported goods to market for both Black and white neighbors. Some employed whites to work for them, and a few seem to have owned or hired slaves.

Ely's portrait is of a society of "live and let live" rather than onerous repression. Free Blacks shared with their white neighbors, including slaveowners, common values—evangelical religion, devotion to their families, the quest for economic independence. The county even witnessed interracial marriages, which did not seem to stir up much resentment. Ely offers persuasive evidence that in Prince Edward County at least, free Blacks were a successful and widely accepted part of the social fabric.

Ely has done a remarkable job of examining how a complex system of race relations operated on the local level. Unfortunately, he sometimes caricatures the views of others to exaggerate the originality of his own findings. Ely chides Ira Berlin, the leading scholar of free Blacks in the Old South, for assuming that repressive laws accurately reflected day-to-day social reality. Yet the broad compass of Berlin's account, which covers free Blacks in the entire South from 1790 to 1860, allows far more scope for generalizations, regional comparisons, and examination of change over time than Ely's investigation of a single county, especially one where their connections with the prominent Randolph family may well have affected the overall treatment of Israel Hill's residents.

Local histories, so valuable in bringing into sharp relief the details of daily life, seem to have an inherent bias toward continuity as opposed to historical change. The rhythms of life in agricultural societies change slowly, and national events seem remote. Indeed, Ely insists that the momentous events of that era—Nat Turner's rebellion, the growing slavery controversy, even the Civil War itself—had "astoundingly little effect" on day-to-day race relations. His treatment of the impact of the Civil War and emancipation on free Blacks is cursory, to say the least. He notes, for example, that in Prince Edward, unlike other parts of the South, formerly free Blacks did not step forward during Reconstruction to take positions of political leadership. But he fails to offer an explanation, or to consider whether this reticence may have reflected a dependence on white good will fostered by the very racial closeness that his book depicts.

Israel on the Appomattox presents a valuable account of free Black life. But Ely has a larger ambition—to recast our understanding of slavery itself as a living institution. In this, his reach far exceeds his grasp. He insists that master–slave relations were marked by the same "human empathy" he finds operated with regard to free Blacks. This conclusion cannot be sustained by the evidence he offers.

The court records and other public documents on which Ely relies do not reveal the texture of slavery as a lived experience. Nearly all discipline and punishment took place on the plantation, at the whim of individual owners. Ely's local focus, moreover, makes it impossible for him to place slave life in its full context. He never tells us how many of the county's slaves were sold. As slave trading became a more central element in Virginia's economy, the number surely reached into the thousands.

The constant threat and frequent reality of sale undercuts Ely's conclusion that "at its core" slavery "revolved around personal bonds between individual Blacks and whites." Moreover, since so many free Blacks married slaves or in other ways enjoyed close ties to the slave community, the buying and selling of slaves affected them as well. This is why Willis A. Hodges, a free Black Virginian whose brother was jailed for assisting fugitive bondsmen, later described slaves and free Blacks as "one man of sorrow."

Scholars who study laboring people often find themselves torn between emphasizing the repressiveness of the social system and making their subjects active historical agents. Too much stress on oppression makes the lower classes appear simply as victims rather than actors on the stage of history. Too much attention to resiliency and accomplishment may obscure the system's inhumanity. Ely hopes to shift the emphasis in the study of free Blacks from disempowerment to accomplishment, and he goes a long way toward reaching this goal. Where he falters is precisely where Edward P. Jones succeeded in his fine recent novel about free Black life, *The Known World*. For Jones makes clear the system's capriciousness with regard to free Blacks' privileges, and delineates the overall structure of power—the "known world" within which people lived their lives and which determined the limits of the possible for white and Black alike.

STATES RIGHTS AND
FUGITIVE SLAVES

W HENEVER I LECTURE to non-academic audiences about the Civil War era, someone is bound to insist that the South fought for states' rights rather than the long-term survival of slavery. In an extreme version of this view, Abraham Lincoln was not the Great Emancipator but a tyrant, the creator of the leviathan national state that essentially enslaved white Americans. This reading of the conflict is why a remarkable number of libertarians—self-proclaimed defenders of individual freedom—sympathize with the Confederacy, and why some even make excuses for slavery. But this account omits one important part of antebellum history: When it came to enforcing and maintaining the peculiar institution against an increasingly antislavery North, the Old South was all too happy to forget its fear of federal power—a little-remembered fact in our modern retellings of the conflict.

The slavery exception to the South's otherwise robust support for states' rights was a recurring feature of antebellum politics. Southerners wrote into the Constitution a clause requiring the return of slaves who escaped from one state to another, and in 1793, only four years after

Politico, January 23, 2015.

George Washington assumed the presidency, they persuaded Congress to enact a law putting that clause into effect. Ironically, when it came to runaway slaves, the white South, usually vocal in defense of local rights, favored robust national action, while some northern states engaged in the nullification of federal law, enacting "personal liberty" laws that barred local officials from cooperating in the capture and return of fugitives.

The Old South also invoked federal power in other ways to strengthen slavery—for example, when it came to employing federal troops in the 1830s to remove Native Americans from southern lands ripe for cotton cultivation. But the most striking example of the South's embrace of national power was the Fugitive Slave Act of 1850. This law was the most robust expansion of federal authority over the states, and over individual Americans, of the antebellum era.

In the 1840s, as increasing numbers of slaves pursued freedom by running away to the North, and a network of local groups, collectively known as the underground railroad, came into existence to assist them, southerners demanded national action. As part of the Compromise of 1850, which abolished the slave trade in the nation's capital and allowed territories recently acquired from Mexico to decide whether or not to allow slavery, Congress enacted the new, draconian fugitive slave law. The measure created a new category of federal officeholder, U.S. commissioners, authorized to hear cases of accused fugitives and issue certificates of removal, documents that could not be challenged in any court. The fugitive could neither claim a writ of habeas corpus nor testify at the hearing, whose sole purpose was to establish his or her identity. Federal marshals could deputize individuals to execute a commissioner's orders and, if necessary, call on the assistance of local officials and even bystanders.

The act included severe civil and criminal penalties for anyone who harbored fugitive slaves or interfered with their capture, as well as for local officials who failed to carry out a commissioner's order or from whom a fugitive escaped. No local law could interfere with the process; northern personal liberty laws were specifically mentioned in the act as examples of illegitimate "molestation" of the slaveowner. To forestall resistance, the federal government at its own expense could deliver the fugitive to his or her owner.

This law could hardly have been designed to arouse greater opposition in the North. It overrode numerous state and local laws and legal procedures and "commanded" individual citizens to assist, when called upon, in capturing runaways. It certainly did not reveal any sensitivity to states' rights on the part of slaveholders. Southern political leaders insisted that northern compliance with the new law constituted the key test of the Compromise of 1850.

Antislavery activists predicted that this measure would, in fact, strengthen their movement. The American and Foreign Anti-Slavery Society predicted that it would awaken northerners to the plight of fugitive slaves and change how the underground railroad operated. "Heretofore," it declared, "the fugitive has been aided in secret." Now, "men will strive who can most openly do him service." The infringement on northerners' liberties would inspire greater defiance. This is, indeed, what happened.

The first arrest under the Fugitive Slave Act of 1850 took place in New York—a city whose economic fortunes were closely tied to the cotton trade, and whose political establishment was decidedly pro-southern. On September 26, 1850, eight days after President Millard Fillmore signed the measure, two deputy U.S. marshals arrested James Hamlet at his job as a porter in a local store. Hamlet had escaped from Baltimore two years earlier and settled in Williamsburg, a Brooklyn village with a small Black population, along with his wife and three children, all born in Maryland.

The hearing before a U.S. commissioner took place the day after Hamlet's arrest. (The Hamlet case, the *New York Tribune* noted sardonically, exhibited "very little of the 'law's delay.'") One might add that it also exhibited little respect for individual rights. The representatives of Hamlet's owner identified him as a slave. Hamlet, who insisted that he and his parents had been previously set free, was not, in accordance with the provisions of the new law, allowed to testify. The commissioner directed marshals to deliver Hamlet to Baltimore at the federal government's expense. Hamlet was handcuffed and hurried to a waiting steamboat. The day after his arrest he was back in Maryland, lodged in prison. His wife knew nothing of these events until after his departure.

Hamlet's story, however, did not end there. His newly reinstated owner announced that Hamlet's freedom could be purchased for $800. Two thousand members of New York's Black organizations, "with a slight and visible sprinkling of white abolitionists," according to a local antislavery newspaper, gathered at the African Methodist Episcopal Zion Church to collect contributions and secure Hamlet's freedom. A week after his arrest, Hamlet was back in Brooklyn, a free man. Few apprehended fugitives were as fortunate. Fugitive slave renditions continued to take place in New York City and in many other parts of the North until the eve of the Civil War. Before 1850, many runaways had settled in the free states; after the passage of the new law most continued on to Canada, which refused to extradite them. They were joined there by free Blacks who were in danger of being caught up in the new law's procedures. The spectacle of individuals fleeing to another country to enjoy freedom mocked the prevailing self-image of the United States as an asylum for those denied liberty in foreign lands.

At antislavery public meetings, speakers, Black and white, invoked the heritage of the American Revolution to justify violent resistance to an unjust law. An abolitionist in New Bedford, Massachusetts, called on fugitives to "practice the art of using firearms" so that they could shoot slave catchers. Such rhetoric often amounted to little more than bravado, but in some parts of the North, efforts to assist fugitives did take a decidedly violent turn. Dramatic attempts to rescue runaway slaves punctuated the 1850s—one study counts over eighty such confrontations. In October 1850, hundreds of armed Blacks gathered at a jail in Detroit where a fugitive was being held. The frightened owner quickly agreed to allow his freedom to be purchased.

In September 1851, a predominantly Black crowd in Christiana, Pennsylvania, routed a group of slave catchers that included a federal marshal and a Maryland owner, who were attempting to apprehend four fugitives. The crowd was led by William Parker, a runaway slave at whose home two of the fugitives were hiding. The slaveowner died in the affray, Parker and the fugitives fled to Canada, and the administration of Millard Fillmore obtained indictments for treason—a capital crime—against forty-one men, the largest such mass indictment in American history. Pursuing the case proved almost impossible in an area with strong antislavery sentiment. Only one person, a white miller who claimed to have been an innocent bystander, was brought to trial. After deliberating for only 15 minutes, the jury returned a verdict of not guilty.

Boston, a center of abolitionism, witnessed several confrontations over the rendition of fugitives. In February 1851, a slaveowner arrived in the city seeking to retrieve Shadrach Minkins, who had escaped from Virginia in 1850 and found a job in a Boston coffee house. Two deputy U.S. marshals arrested Minkins, the first fugitive seized in New England under the new law. But as the hearing before a U.S. commissioner progressed, a crowd of men led by the Black abolitionist Lewis Hayden entered the courtroom "like a Black squall" and carried Minkins off. Eight, including Hayden, were put on trial for taking part in the rescue, but none was convicted. Minkins ended up in Montreal.

Sometimes, Boston's activists failed, most dramatically in 1854, when Anthony Burns, a 21-year-old fugitive slave from Richmond, was brought before Edward G. Loring, a prominent jurist acting as U.S. commissioner. Hundreds of persons gathered at the courthouse, but guards repulsed a rescue attempt. Following the letter of the law, Loring ordered Burns returned to slavery. It took some 1,600 men—police, militia units, and three companies of federal infantry and marines—to march Burns to a waiting ship. The case was a striking illustration of the use of federal power in the interests of slaveholders, but it also reinforced antislavery sentiment. A new Massachusetts personal liberty law, enacted in 1855 over the governor's veto, barred state and local officials from assisting in renditions, granted accused fugitives a jury trial, and required any state judge who accepted appointment as a federal commissioner to resign from the bench. Loring himself was dismissed from a position at Harvard Law School and four years later removed from his judgeship. President James Buchanan then appointed him to the federal judiciary, where he served until his death in 1877. Anthony Burns proved to be the last person remanded to slavery from anywhere in New England. But in other parts of the country, the Fugitive Slave Law continued to be enforced until the outbreak of the Civil War.

Southerners had little sympathy for northern resistance to the federal law. Even though few fugitive slaves reached the North from South Carolina (the state most vocal in asserting its right to nullify federal law), the longest paragraph in the state's "Declaration of the Immediate Causes" of secession of December 1860 related to northern obstruction of the capture of fugitives. "An increasing hostility on the part of the non-slaveholding states to the institution of slavery," the document maintained, had led the free states to render "useless" the Constitution's fugitive slave clause, without which the document would never have been ratified. With the North having "broken" the constitutional compact, South Carolina, in turn, was "released from her obligation" to it.

Even though it became a dead letter as the Civil War progressed, the Fugitive Slave Act was not repealed until 1864, over a year after Lincoln issued the Emancipation Proclamation. During Reconstruction, it enjoyed an ironic afterlife when Lyman Trumbull, chair of the Senate Judiciary Committee, used the infamous 1850 statute as a model for the Civil Rights Act of 1866, which extended to Black Americans many of the rights previously enjoyed exclusively by whites. To do so, Trumbull drew on the 1850 law's enforcement mechanisms and the way it superimposed federal power on state law in order to establish a national responsibility for securing a constitutionally protected right (in 1850 the right to retrieve fugitive slaves; in 1866 the right of Blacks to liberty, recently secured in the Thirteenth Amendment). "The act that was passed that time for the purpose of punishing persons who should aid Negroes to freedom," Trumbull declared, "is now to be applied . . . to the punishment of those who shall undertake to keep them in slavery." Thus, as Rep. James Wilson of Iowa put it, in the aftermath of the Civil

War Congress turned "the arsenal of slavery upon itself," wielding "the weapons which slavery has placed in our hands . . . in the holy cause of liberty."

That the Fugitive Slave law served as a blueprint for the Civil Rights Act suggests in a nutshell the lesson of this chapter of history. Neither federal power nor states' rights exist in a vacuum. Both can be threats to the liberties of citizens and both can be modes of protecting them. It all depends on the uses to which federal and state power are put. And interpretations of the Constitution can be strategic tools as much as unwavering sets of principle. The point is not that constitutional doctrines have no meaning, but that constitutional consistency is no match for political and social self-interest.

The same might be said for views of history. It would be more accurate to acknowledge that slavery was the fundamental cause of the Civil War—a point made straightforwardly by Abraham Lincoln in his great Second Inaugural Address. But for those conservatives and libertarians of today who trace their intellectual lineage to the Old South's supposed commitment to states' rights, it's inconvenient to remember the region's motivation as the preservation of slavery. So I expect to continue to see that raised hand in the back of the lecture hall, ready to protest that the war was all about states' rights—despite what the historical record shows.

LINCOLN AND BROWN

ABRAHAM LINCOLN, MEMORIALIZED as a child of the frontier, self-made man, and liberator of the slaves, has been the subject of more than 16,000 books, according to David S. Reynolds's new biography, *Abe*. That's around two a week, on average, since the end of the American Civil War. Almost every possible Lincoln can be found in the historical literature, including the moralist who hated slavery, the pragmatic politician driven solely by ambition, the tyrant who ran roughshod over the Constitution, and the indecisive leader buffeted by events he could not control. Conservatives, communists, civil rights activists, and segregationists have claimed him as their own. *Esquire* magazine once ran a list of "rules every man should know." Rule 115: "There is nothing that can be marketed that cannot be marketed better using the likeness of Honest Abe Lincoln."

It seems safe to assume that even the most diligent researcher will not be able to discover significant new material about Lincoln—a diary,

Review of *Abe: Abraham Lincoln in His Times*, by David S. Reynolds, and *The Zealot and the Emancipator: Abraham Lincoln, John Brown, and the Struggle for American Freedom*, by H. W. Brands, *London Review of Books*, December 17, 2020.

say, or previously unknown speeches and letters. Instead, the biographer must devise an original interpretative approach. And, against all odds, Reynolds manages to say new and important things about Lincoln in his elegantly written book. Rather than a conventional account of Lincoln's life, *Abe* is a "cultural biography." The familiar trajectory of Lincoln's career is here, from his youth in Kentucky and Indiana to his emergence as a national figure forced to preside over a cataclysmic war and its "astounding" (Lincoln's word) result: the emancipation of four million slaves. But Reynolds is more interested in the way Lincoln's character and political outlook reflected "the roiling cultural currents" of the nation in which he lived.

Lincoln's America, Reynolds says, was suffused with sensationalism, violence, raw humor, and spectacles high and low. On the streets of New York, theatergoers attending performances of Shakespeare rubbed shoulders with the audiences for blackface minstrel shows. Nearby, P. T. Barnum's American Museum featured General Tom Thumb (an adult less than three feet tall) alongside such frauds as the "Feejee Mermaid." Lincoln felt at home with both elite and popular culture. Reynolds believes that his success as a politician stemmed from his engagement with the diverse cultural phenomena around him. For Reynolds, Lincoln really was "Abe," the everyman depicted in his campaign literature.

To situate Lincoln in his cultural context, Reynolds takes the reader down numerous narrative byways. A discussion of Lincoln's taste in music, including the erotic ballad "I won't be a nun" and, improbably, "Dixie," a paean to the Old South, leads to a long examination of nineteenth-century popular song. When, after the death of their 11-year-old son Willie, Lincoln and his wife Mary arrange for seances in the White House, we learn about the popularity of spiritualism. Mention of *Uncle Tom's Cabin* leads to a discussion of the emotional intensity of mid-century writing and what Reynolds calls the "opportunistic sensationalism" of reformers who dwelled on the degradation of drinkers and the physical abuse of slaves, an approach Lincoln rejected as counterproductive.

The relevance of these excursions is sometimes open to question. Some political cartoonists depicted Lincoln in the guise of Charles Blondin, a tightrope walker famous for crossing Niagara Falls on a high wire, navigating a dangerous course without leaning too far to the left or right. Reynolds describes Lincoln as a "political Blondin," who chose an ideologically balanced "Blondin-like" Cabinet and sought a "Blondin-like balance in the military" by appointing both Democrats and Republicans to command troops. The repeated invocation of Blondin is certainly original, and Lincoln did mention him in an 1862 meeting with an abolitionist delegation, but Reynolds's claim that Lincoln "identified strongly" with the celebrated daredevil is a bit of a stretch.

Reynolds's Lincoln is not simply a sponge who absorbs what's going on around him in the culture. *Abe* devotes far more attention than most biographies to Lincoln's formative years on the frontier, where he learned to trust his own judgment. Unlike most frontiersmen, he did not hunt, gamble, drink, or use tobacco. At a time of intense religious revivalism, Lincoln never joined a church. He even expressed admiration for Tom Paine's Deist tract *The Age of Reason*. Lincoln didn't share the prevailing hatred of Native Americans, and despite his physical presence (he was 6'4") tried to avoid the brutal altercations that marked the region's rough-and-tumble male culture. At an early point in his career Lincoln even suggested that property-owning women should enjoy the right to vote. Despite Reynolds's subtitle, *Abraham Lincoln in His Times*, the Lincoln of *Abe* sometimes seems like a woke inhabitant of our own era: "environmentally conscious," forward-looking with regard to gender, kind to animals, and sympathetic towards "ethnic others."

Reynolds sees nineteenth-century America as a country that lacked coherence, the site of rampant individualism and weak established institutions. The resulting "formlessness," he argues, gave Lincoln a desire for structure in both his own life and the larger world. As a counterweight to the centrifugal forces around him, he revered the national Union, represented by the Declaration of Independence and the Constitution, documents that his speeches brilliantly enlisted in the cause of antislavery. As a party leader in Illinois, Lincoln understood the need to maintain peace among the various Republican factions—radicals and conservatives, nativists and immigrants, former Democrats and former Whigs. Union was as essential to the party as to the nation. In his personal life, Lincoln sought to enlist reason against his tendency towards bouts of intense emotion and occasional depression.

Politically, Reynolds writes, Lincoln "stuck close to the center," seeking a middle ground between abolitionists, whose intemperate attacks on individual slaveowners seemed to him to endanger the Union, and northerners indifferent to the evil of the South's "peculiar institution." Because of his reverence for the Union, Lincoln called for northern acquiescence in measures he privately abhorred, notably the draconian Fugitive Slave Act of 1850, since the Constitution established the right of owners to have runaways captured and returned. His idol was Senator Henry Clay of Kentucky, known as the Great Compromiser. Clay died in 1852, and Lincoln must have realized that his fifty-year effort to rid Kentucky of slavery had accomplished nothing. But well into the Civil War, Lincoln clung to Clay's plan for abolition: gradual emancipation, monetary compensation to the owners, and "colonization"— that is, encouraging freed slaves to leave the United States for Africa or the Caribbean.

What does all this tell us about what Reynolds calls the "hotly contested" subject of Lincoln's racial attitudes? In the year 2000, Lerone Bennett Jr., an African American historian, published *Forced into Glory*, which drew on Lincoln's pre-war statements opposing civil and political rights for African Americans (his comment on female suffrage was limited to whites), and his advocacy of colonizing freed slaves, to depict him as an inveterate racist. The book had the drawbacks of any prosecutor's brief, but it forced historians and the general public to confront aspects of Lincoln's career that had mostly been swept under the rug. Outraged members of what one scholar has called the "Lincoln-Industrial Complex" rushed to defend the Great Emancipator.

Insisting on "the complete falsity of the charges of innate racism," Reynolds joins the defense. He insists that in interactions with individual African Americans, Lincoln did not display signs of prejudice. To mitigate the fact that Lincoln, like many of his white contemporaries, enjoyed blackface minstrel shows, Reynolds advances the not entirely convincing argument that these racist performances communicated a "cloaked progressiveness," because their white performers made up as Blacks sometimes assumed, for comic effect, positions of power. Reynolds makes clear that no one with political ambitions could ignore the deeply ingrained racism of Illinois. The state's notorious Black Laws denied Blacks basic rights, and racist language suffused politics. In the 1858 debates during the campaign for one of Illinois's seats in the Senate, Lincoln's antagonist, Senator Stephen A. Douglas, freely used the word "nigger" and accused Lincoln and the "Black Republicans" of wanting freed slaves to move to Illinois, take the jobs of whites, and marry white women. Warned that Douglas's assault was weakening his party's electoral chances, Lincoln denied that he believed in "Negro equality." But unlike Douglas, Reynolds points out, he did not waver from the conviction that the inalienable rights identified in the Declaration of Independence—life, liberty, and the pursuit of happiness—applied to all persons, regardless of race. These are valid points. Nonetheless, it is fair to say that unlike the abolitionists, who demanded not only an immediate end to slavery but full citizenship rights for Blacks, Lincoln found it impossible to imagine the United States as a biracial society of equals.

A writer who chooses his words with care, Reynolds struggles to find the right ones for Lincoln's racial views. At one point he refers to his subject's "hidebound" outlook. He writes that Lincoln "associated himself" with colonization, a weak way of describing his service on the Board of Managers of the Illinois Colonization Society and his numerous speeches and presidential messages promoting the policy. At a notorious 1862 meeting with a group of free African Americans, Lincoln urged his listeners to encourage emigration among their people. Reynolds sees this encounter, which outraged most Black leaders and seems to have inspired racial violence in the North, as a calculated performance to prepare conservative whites for the coming announcement of emancipation.

Once he issued the Emancipation Proclamation on January 1, 1863, Lincoln's racial views underwent rapid evolution. Unfortunately, while devoting a chapter to a careful analysis of Lincoln's two greatest speeches, the Gettysburg Address and the Second Inaugural, Reynolds says relatively little about the Proclamation, although that pivotal document offers compelling evidence of the changes in Lincoln's thinking. In it, Lincoln abandoned his long-held plan for gradual emancipation in favor of immediate freedom for more than three million slaves (about 750,000 were not covered, mostly because they lived in states that had not seceded) and dropped the idea of colonization, urging Blacks to "go to work for reasonable wages" in the United States. For the first time, he authorized the enrollment of African Americans in the Union army. Lincoln doubtless understood that military service would lead to demands for equal citizenship after the war. He never became egalitarian in a modern sense, but in the last two years of his life, spurred by the crucial role of Black soldiers in the ongoing conflict, his thinking changed dramatically. In his final speech, in 1865, he publicly advocated the right to vote for educated Blacks and those who had served in the army. By then he had moved well beyond his culture: at the time only a tiny number of Black men enjoyed the right to vote.

In *The Zealot and the Emancipator*, H. W. Brands has written a dual biography of Lincoln and the abolitionist John Brown, who in 1859 led a band of twenty-two men to seize the federal arsenal at Harper's Ferry, Virginia, in the hope of sparking a slave insurrection. The divergent paths chosen by Brown and Lincoln illuminate a problem as old as civilization itself—what is a person's moral responsibility in the face of glaring injustice?

Lincoln and Brown never met. Both came from humble origins, but in many ways they could not have been more different. Lincoln thrived in the world of nineteenth-century American capitalism, rising through ambition, hard work, and continual self-improvement to solid middle-class status, while Brown, who failed at numerous ventures and more than once experienced bankruptcy, seemed to sink

beneath the economy's turbulent waters. Where Lincoln the rational-
ist declared that man could not know the will of God, Brown "knew"
that he had been chosen for a divine mission to overthrow slavery. Lincoln condemned mob violence and insisted that respect for the rule of
law must become the nation's "political religion." Brown, like many
abolitionists, believed in a "higher law" that legitimized resistance to
unjust man-made statutes.

As with Lincoln, the historical literature contains many John
Browns—freedom fighter, terrorist, civil rights pioneer, madman. For
an earlier generation of historians, who saw the Civil War as needless carnage brought on by irresponsible fanatics, Brown was Exhibit
A. But African American radicals have long hailed Brown as a rare
white person willing to sacrifice himself for the cause of racial justice.
Stokely Carmichael, who popularized the idea of "Black Power" in the
1960s, identified Brown and the Radical Republican leader Thaddeus
Stevens as the only white figures in American history worthy of admiration. Lately, with the destruction of slavery occupying a central place
in accounts of the era's history, Brown has come to be widely admired.
In 2005, Reynolds published an adulatory biography, whose hyper-
bolic subtitle describes Brown as the man who "killed slavery, sparked
the Civil War and seeded Civil Rights." Fifteen years later, Brown was
a major character in a TV series, *The Good Lord Bird*, starring Ethan
Hawke. Brands writes that his students in Austin, Texas, "can't get
enough of John Brown."

Lincoln and Brown both hated slavery but that conviction by itself
did not tell a person how to take action against it. When the Fugitive
Slave Act became law, Brown formed the League of Gileadites, a mostly
Black group pledged to armed resistance. Later, he spirited a group of
Missouri slaves to freedom in Canada. Lincoln, by contrast, insisted
that no matter how reprehensible, the law must be obeyed. When
the Kansas-Nebraska Act of 1854 opened territories in the Trans-
Mississippi West to the expansion of slavery, Brown armed himself and
headed there with several of his sons to take part in the local civil war

over slavery known as "Bleeding Kansas." During this preview of the national conflict, they murdered five proslavery settlers. Lincoln joined the new Republican party and committed himself to seeking legislation that barred slavery's expansion.

A skilled narrative writer, Brands offers a vivid account of the raid on Harper's Ferry and its aftermath. In military terms, the event was a disaster. No slaves rose up to join Brown (in fact there weren't very many in the mountains of what is now West Virginia, where the arsenal was located, far from the plantation belt). After commandeering weapons, Brown abandoned his plan to retreat into the Alleghenies and fight a guerrilla war against the slave system. Instead, he and his men remained in place and were quickly overwhelmed by local militia and a contingent of Marines led by Robert E. Lee. But Brown's demeanor at his trial for treason, where he cited the Bible as his inspiration, and his subsequent execution, made him a martyr in the eyes of many northerners. He had made the gallows "as glorious as the cross," Ralph Waldo Emerson exclaimed. Lincoln, the lawyer and constitutionalist, saw the raid as a setback for the antislavery cause and strove to dissociate the Republican Party from Brown's action. Among those who witnessed Brown's hanging was the actor John Wilkes Booth, later Lincoln's assassin. He called Brown "a man inspired, the greatest character of the century," and resolved to outdo him.

Lincoln and Brown differed not only on strategy but on underlying principles. Unlike Lincoln, Brown saw the struggles against slavery and racism as interconnected. He was determined to live an antiracist life. Richard Henry Dana Jr. (the author of *Two Years Before the Mast*) was astonished when visiting Brown's farm in upstate New York to find Black guests seated at the dinner table. Brown introduced them not by their first names but as "Mr." and "Mrs." It was obvious to Dana that they had not been spoken to that way very often in their lives. Brown was inspired by the example of Black abolitionists, many of whom he knew well, and by slave rebels such as Nat Turner. His armed band was interracial, although Brands tells us little about the motives and goals of the five black men who fought at Harper's Ferry. Brands observes that one of the reasons Lincoln promoted colonization, despite recognizing the near impossibility of transporting millions of men, women, and children out of the country, was that history offered no example of "a successful biracial republic." Brown, however, thought the United States could become just that.

Both Brands and Reynolds conclude their books by noting that the paths chosen by Lincoln and Brown eventually seemed to converge. In 1864, convinced he would not win re-election because of northern war weariness, Lincoln proposed that the Black abolitionist Frederick Douglass raise a force of soldiers who would move into the South, spread word of the Emancipation Proclamation and encourage slaves to seek freedom behind Union lines. The idea bore a striking resemblance to Brown's original plan at Harper's Ferry.

Today, Lincoln is widely revered, while many Americans, including some historians, consider Brown insane. Yet it was Brown's strategy that brought slavery to an end. In a note written shortly before his execution in 1859, Brown wrote: "The crimes of this guilty land will not be purged away but with blood." And Lincoln, the centrist politician, ended up presiding over slaughter on a scale neither he nor Brown could possibly have imagined. At his Second Inaugural, in March 1865, Lincoln embraced Brown's insight that slavery was already a system of violence and could not be eradicated peacefully. Echoing Brown, Lincoln explained the Civil War's staggering death toll as divine retribution for two and a half centuries of "blood drawn by the lash." He was reminding his listeners that violence in America did not begin when John Brown unsheathed his sword; it was embedded in slave society from the outset. And in the end, as Brands concludes, "Union arms, not Union arguments, overthrew slavery."

LINCOLN AND DOUGLASS

THE ABOLITION OF slavery in the United States appears in retrospect so inevitable that it is difficult to recall how unlikely it seemed as late as 1860, the year of Abraham Lincoln's election as president. Slaveowners had pretty much controlled the national government since its inception. The four million slaves formed by far the country's largest concentration of property (their economic worth as property exceeded the value of all the factories, railroads, and banks in the country combined). Racism was deeply entrenched, North as well as South. Black Americans, free as well as slave, had few rights anywhere, and abolitionists were a despised minority. Lincoln's election and the Civil War it triggered made emancipation possible. But Lincoln campaigned for president pledging to prevent slavery's expansion into western territories, while insisting he had no intention of interfering with the institution where it already existed. It was by no means certain when the war began that it would become a crusade to destroy slavery.

—

Review of *The Radical and the Republican: Frederick Douglass, Abraham Lincoln, and the Triumph of Antislavery*, by James Oakes, *The Nation*, February 5, 2007.

Who was responsible for the end of slavery? Over the past two decades, historians have avidly debated this question. Did the Union's initial lack of military success, the actions of slaves who, in increasing numbers, fled the plantations for Union lines, and the pressure exerted by abolitionists and Radical Republicans compel a reluctant president to embrace emancipation? Or did Lincoln sagely wait until public opinion was ready and then act upon a lifelong desire to see slavery abolished?

A spate of recent books has sought to restore Lincoln's standing as the Great Emancipator, a reputation somewhat tarnished by studies of his far-from-egalitarian racial views. These books rightly emphasize Lincoln's genuine hatred of slavery. But too often, they insist that the road he took to emancipation was the only possible one. Lincoln is hailed as a "responsible realist," a practitioner of the "politics of prudence." His opposites in this interpretation are the abolitionists, portrayed as self-righteous moralists who lacked a sense of practical politics.

The argument is entirely circular: we know Lincoln's course was the only possible one because the pragmatic Lincoln chose it; anyone who demanded more was, by definition, asking for the impossible. These writers fail to understand that the abolitionists' efforts to arouse public sentiment regarding slavery was itself a political strategy. They helped to make the impossible possible. Without the abolitionists, there could have been no Lincoln.

One of the ways in which James Oakes's *The Radical and the Republican* advances the study of Lincoln and emancipation is by making Frederick Douglass a co-equal protagonist. The addition of Douglass significantly deepens the analysis and the range of political views represented, and allows Oakes to reach beyond the tunnel vision that afflicts so many recent studies of Lincoln.

Oakes does not entirely avoid some of the pitfalls that bedevil Lincoln scholarship. Like many other writers, he reproduces verbatim a number of Lincoln "quotations" of doubtful credibility. Did Lincoln really say in 1850, "the slavery question can't be compromised," as his former law partner John T. Stuart later claimed? Or speak in 1860 of the day "when there will not be a single slave within the borders of this country," as Julian Kune, a Hungarian immigrant, asserted half a century later? After Lincoln's death, memory, even among his close friends, was filtered through the knowledge of his role in ending slavery.

Oakes himself cannot fully escape the gravitational pull of Lincoln's image as Emancipator, but he refuses to reduce Douglass to a foil for Lincoln's greatness. Both played a role in the end of slavery. Emancipation, Oakes writes, shows "what can happen in American democracy when progressive reformers and savvy politicians make common cause." This formulation enables us to understand emancipation as the product of a broad social and political movement, not a single individual.

The Radical and the Republican does not claim to chronicle a personal relationship between the two men, because none existed. They met only three times. On the first occasion, in August 1863, Douglass urged Lincoln to order that Black soldiers receive the same pay as white. Lincoln responded that the enlistment of Blacks had offended many whites and that Black soldiers would have to wait for their pay to be equalized. A year later, at a low point of his presidency when he anticipated defeat in the upcoming presidential election, Lincoln asked Douglass to devise a plan to encourage as many slaves as possible to flee to Union lines, so that his successor could not undo emancipation. Then, in March 1865, Douglass spoke briefly with Lincoln to congratulate him on his Second Inaugural Address. This is the extent of their personal encounters.

More significant are the two men's paths of personal and political development, and these Oakes traces expertly. A lively writer, Oakes offers striking portraits of their very different personalities. Douglass, the escaped slave who became a towering figure of the abolitionist movement, "had the blustery, oversize persona of the nineteenth-century Romantic." He held his views with fierce commitment, even when he sometimes impulsively changed them. He spoke from personal experience of the bloody horrors of slavery.

Lincoln, a grandchild of the Enlightenment, was a man of iron self-control. Unlike Douglass, he never denounced slaveholders as sinners and sadists, and was more apt to condemn slavery for denying Black men and women the fruits of their labor than to dwell on whippings and the breakup of slave families. Only in his majestic Second Inaugural Address would he speak of the "blood drawn by the lash." He appealed to his listeners' logic and idealism, not their passions.

Oakes's main theme is how, from very different beginnings, the views of Douglass and Lincoln converged. He is especially good at outlining Douglass's shift from a follower of William Lloyd Garrison, who insisted that the Constitution was inherently pro-slavery and that therefore abolitionists should stand aloof from the electoral arena, to a supporter of antislavery politics. By the 1850s, instead of seeing the United States as fatally compromised by slavery and racism (a position that led some of his Black contemporaries, like Martin R. Delany, to support emigration to a country where former slaves could rule themselves), Douglass insisted that African Americans were as entitled to the rights of citizens as their white fellow-countrymen. But, as Oakes shows, he could not decide how to pursue this goal politically, vacillating between support for fringe groups like the Radical Abolitionist party, and for the Republicans who, despite their limitations, were at least battling the Slave Power. Douglass's first mention of Lincoln came in 1858, when he praised him for upholding antislavery principles. But in 1860, he announced that while he hoped for a Republican victory, he could not vote for Lincoln because he was not an abolitionist.

On this point, of course, Douglass was correct—Lincoln was not an advocate of immediate abolition or the rights of Black Americans. At one point in the Lincoln-Douglas debates of 1858 (which pitted him against Stephen A. Douglas, not Frederick), Lincoln said the end of slavery in the United States might not come for a hundred years. But like Frederick Douglass, his political outlook went through a metamorphosis. From an Illinois Whig concerned mostly with internal improvements and the tariff Lincoln evolved into a Republican committed to placing slavery in the course of what he called "ultimate extinction." By 1860, Oakes claims, Douglass and Lincoln were frequently "saying the same thing"—that slavery was a moral abomination, that the founders were antislavery but the country had tragically diverged from their views, that the United States faced a momentous choice over whether freedom or slavery would shape the nation's future.

If indeed, Lincoln and Douglass converged during the 1850s, they moved sharply apart once the Civil War began. Almost immediately, Douglass demanded that Lincoln free the slaves and enroll Black men into the Union army. Like other writers, Oakes explains Lincoln's slower path to emancipation by saying that he "had to wait until public opinion caught up with him." This formulation cannot explain why equally pragmatic politicians in Congress—not only Radicals but many moderate Republicans as well—moved much more quickly toward emancipation than Lincoln, enacting laws for abolition in Washington, D.C., and the Confiscation Acts of 1861 and 1862, which granted freedom to hundreds of thousands of slaves well before the Emancipation Proclamation.

Douglass, meanwhile, tried in his own way to change public sentiment, speaking throughout the North and publishing a monthly magazine. In 1862, with Lincoln resisting demands for emancipation, Douglass wrote, "the friends of freedom, the Union, and the Constitution, have been most basely betrayed." He was ecstatic when Lincoln issued the Emancipation Proclamation, recognizing how it changed the character of the Civil War, but by 1864, upset by Lincoln's failure to remedy the unequal treatment of Black soldiers or to support Black suffrage in a reconstructed South, he lent his support to the Radical Republican effort to replace Lincoln with John C. Frémont as the party's presidential candidate. On the other hand, in their personal encounters, Douglass was impressed by how Lincoln treated him with respect, never making him feel their difference in station or race. Lincoln, Oakes writes, was "radicalized by the war," and by the end of his life had adopted Douglass's positions on emancipation and Black troops, and was even contemplating the right to vote for some Black southerners.

On one key point, as Oakes notes, this convergence was far from complete. Douglass saw the struggles against slavery and racism as a single crusade. He insisted that Republicans betrayed their own supposed moral beliefs when they opposed Black suffrage, as Lincoln himself did for most of his life (one reason Douglass refused to support him in 1860). Lincoln saw slavery and racism as two separate and in some ways unrelated questions. He claimed for African Americans the natural rights enumerated in the Declaration of Independence, which he understood to include the right to the fruits of their labor, but that was all. He had little contact with Black people and said almost nothing about race relations before the Civil War except when accused by Democrats of favoring "Negro equality," which he emphatically denied.

Oakes says that it is impossible to know how much of this Lincoln actually believed, and how much was a concession to political expediency. But he leans toward the explanation that Lincoln practiced "strategic racism," hoping to deflect Democratic charges so that the "real issue"—slavery—could occupy political center stage. Otherwise, he could never have been elected. But is this self-evidently true? Salmon P. Chase, who devoted much of his career to promoting the rights of free Black persons, was elected governor of Ohio in 1855. Lyman Trumbull, who won a reputation as "attorney for fugitive slaves" in Illinois was elected and reelected to the U.S. Senate. Lincoln's actions should not be taken as the sole barometer of the politically "possible."

Oakes does not acknowledge that even "strategic racism" compromised Lincoln's antislavery logic. As Richard Hofstadter pointed out sixty years ago in his brilliant essay on Lincoln in *The American Political Tradition*, Lincoln never confronted the question of how Black persons were supposed to defend the natural rights to which he thought them entitled, if deprived of the right to vote, testify in court, and move freely from one state to another—rights taken for granted by white Americans. Lincoln's answer, to the extent that he had one: they should emigrate to some other country, where they could enjoy all these rights.

Like many other writers on Lincoln, Oakes finds it impossible to take seriously Lincoln's long embrace of colonization—that is, encouraging African Americans to leave the United States. "I cannot make it better known than it already is, that I strongly favor colonization," Lincoln said in a message to Congress less than a month before he issued the Emancipation Proclamation. Oakes calls Lincoln's August 1862 meeting with Black leaders (not including Douglass), where he urged them to support colonization, "bizarre," and explains it as an effort to "make emancipation more palatable to white racists." As he notes, Douglass reacted with one of his most bitter criticisms of the president. "Mr Lincoln," he wrote, "assumes the language and arguments of an itinerant colonization lecturer, shows all his inconsistencies, his pride of race and blood, his contempt for Negroes and his canting hypocrisy. How an honest man could creep into such a character as that implied by this address we are not required to show." The real task of a statesman, he concluded, was not to patronize African Americans by deciding what was best for them, but to allow them to be free. Douglass realized what Lincoln did not—that advocacy of colonization exacerbated racism. But after issuing the Emancipation Proclamation, Lincoln abandoned the idea of colonization and began to think seriously about the aftermath of slavery in a biracial society.

After his death, Lincoln was succeeded in the White House by Andrew Johnson, a southern Unionist who was everything Lincoln was not—stubborn, narrow-minded, and incorrigibly racist. In 1866, Johnson met with Douglass and a group of Black leaders, and hectored them about his opposition to Black suffrage. When they left, Johnson remarked to an aide that Douglass was "just like any nigger, and he would sooner cut a white man's throat than not." Johnson's sheer incompetence and resistance to equal rights for the former slaves eventually propelled Congress to embark on Radical Reconstruction, the failed attempt to build an interracial democracy on the ruins of slavery.

Douglass fervently embraced Reconstruction and became more and more alarmed in the 1870s as the Republican Party retreated from its commitment to equality. In 1876, with Reconstruction in its final months, he delivered a remarkable speech in Washington at the dedication of an emancipation monument built with funds donated by freedmen and women. Douglass seems to have been taken aback when the monument was unveiled—it showed a standing Lincoln holding his hand over a kneeling slave, not the image of Black self-reliance Douglass favored. In the speech, he called Lincoln "preeminently the white man's President, entirely devoted to the welfare of white men." Fourteen years after the event, Lincoln's colonization meeting of 1862 still rankled—Douglass could not forbear mentioning that Lincoln had "strangely told us that we were to leave the land in which we were born."

But, he went on, Lincoln was also the author of great achievements, especially emancipation and the enlistment of Black soldiers, and his name would always be cherished by Black Americans. Douglass chided abolitionists, presumably including himself, for excessive criticism of Lincoln during his presidency. Overall, as Oakes notes, the speech was both an insightful assessment of Lincoln and a remarkable example of self-criticism on Douglass's part.

Like so many other Americans of his and succeeding generations, Douglass invoked Lincoln for a political purpose—to demand that the nation remember that slavery had been the central issue of the Civil War and to recommit itself to equal rights for Black countrymen. In memory, Lincoln and Douglass reached a convergence they never quite achieved in life.

PART II

The Civil War and Reconstruction

DEATH AND MEANING IN THE CIVIL WAR

O NE OF THE most arresting lectures I have ever heard at a historians' convention was delivered in 2004 by Drew Gilpin Faust at the annual meeting of the American Historical Association. Taking as her starting point Robert E. Lee's possibly apocryphal remark, "it is well that war is so terrible for otherwise we should grow too fond of it," Faust chastised historians for succumbing to war's seductive power. By ascribing moral purposes and profound causes to what is really pointless slaughter, she insisted, historians obscure war's horror. Exhibit number one was the American Civil War. More than 60,000 books, she observed, have been published dealing in one way or another with that conflict—an average of more than one per day since it ended. If historians need war to add drama to their grand narratives, Faust suggested, war, to achieve legitimacy, very much needs historians.

Faust, of course, is best known today as the first woman president of Harvard in the university's 370-year history. But before reaching this milestone, she established a reputation as a leading scholar of

Review of *This Republic of Suffering: Death and the American Civil War*, by Drew Gilpin Faust, *The Nation*, January 28, 2008.

nineteenth-century southern history. Indeed, one of her earlier books, *Mothers of Invention*, accomplished something almost impossible— coming up with a genuinely new explanation for Confederate defeat. Faust attributed it to the withdrawal of support by women on the southern home front, who abandoned the fight because of the damage the war was inflicting on their families and on traditional gender relations. Now, with *This Republic of Suffering*, a work by turns fascinating, innovative, and obsessively morbid, Faust returns to the task of stripping from war any lingering romanticism, nobility, or social purpose.

Faust begins by reminding us of the Civil War's appalling harvest of death. In a nation of thirty-one million, over 700,000 died as members of the Union and Confederate armed forces, a total nearly equal to the deaths in all other American wars combined, and the equivalent of six million in terms of today's population. These figures do not include thousands of civilians who became collateral victims or who perished in disease-ridden camps for runaway slaves or in internecine conflict between Unionist and Confederate families that raged in parts of the South. This slaughter of the young could not be assimilated into the cultural ideal that Faust calls the Good Death—the passing at home of a man or woman of advanced age, surrounded by family members and imparting last words of religious and social wisdom.

Of course, untimely death was hardly unknown in mid-nineteenth-century America, given the primitive state of medicine. During the course of his life, for example, Abraham Lincoln lost a baby brother and two sons to disease, and saw his sister die in childbirth. But the scale of loss in the Civil War dwarfed anything in the American experience. And unlike today, when the government carefully shields images of the war dead from public view, the new art of photography, in the words of one newspaper, "brought the bodies and laid them in our dooryards." The war's extensive and very public carnage, Faust writes, "required that death be given meaning." Drawing on a wide range of sources, including sermons, memoirs, newspapers, poetry, and soldiers' letters, Faust probes how Americans tried to cope with mass death and how the experience affected everything from business practices to religious attitudes, literary culture, and the organization of the state.

In some ways, Faust points out, death was good for business. Transportation companies, North and South, made tidy profits bringing the bodies of dead soldiers home for burial. Embalmers operated near the battlefields, preserving bodies and then demanding payment from grieving families. Entrepreneurs promised, for a fee, to locate information about missing loved ones. A burgeoning market developed in mourning attire, not only dresses and veils but items with names unrecognizable today: bareges, challies, balzerines. There were elaborate rules, for the upper classes at least, about how to remain part of fashionable society while still in mourning. Faust even takes note of the extensive sales of the "planchette," a kind of Ouija board that supposedly enabled the living to communicate with the dead.

War, Randolph Bourne would write during World War I, "is the health of the state." One of the most profound changes wrought by the Civil War was the creation of a powerful national government, evidenced by the mobilization of economic resources, conscription, the issuance of the first national currency, and the emancipation, by presidential decree, congressional action, and constitutional amendment, of four million slaves. Coping with death, Faust shows, also required unprecedented state action, from notifying next of kin to accounting for the dead and missing. Both Union and Confederacy established elaborate systems for gathering statistics and maintaining records of dead and wounded soldiers, an effort supplemented by private philanthropic organizations.

After the war ended, Washington embarked on what Faust calls "the most elaborate federal program undertaken in nearly a century of American nationhood," the location and reburial of hundreds of thousands of Union soldiers in national military cemeteries. The scale of death in engagements like Shiloh, Antietam, Gettysburg, and many others was so vast that many bodies lay untended for days, eventually buried in unidentified shallow graves near the battlefield. Between 1865 and 1871, the federal government reinterred over 300,000 Union (but not Confederate) soldiers, including Black ones, buried, as they had fought, in segregated sections of military cemeteries. Faust points out that officials seeking to locate the remains of deceased Union soldiers often found that they had been buried, and their graves cared for, by local African Americans in the South.

If Civil War death "required an explanation," Americans increasingly found one in religion. The pre-Socratic philosopher Xenophanes first pointed out that man creates God in his own image. The same is true of heaven. Of course, equating death with eternal life was a central tenet of Christianity. But mass death, Faust argues, led to a "transformation of heaven," as Americans imagined future celestial family reunions that seemed more and more like decorous gatherings in Victorian living rooms. "I don't like Paradise," the poet Emily Dickinson jested, in response to this domestication of heaven, "because it's Sunday—all the time." Some Americans could not wait until their own deaths to see the departed. Spiritualism—belief in the ability to communicate with the dead—proliferated. Mary Todd Lincoln held seances in the White House to experience again the presence of her young son Willie, who succumbed to disease in 1862.

But religion also gave a larger meaning to wartime sacrifice. What Faust calls "a new sense of national destiny" emerged from the war, a belief that God had willed the conflict to purge the nation of the sin of slavery, and that America's manifest destiny to serve as a worldwide embodiment of freedom had been hallowed by all the blood that had been shed. Lincoln, in his magnificent Second Inaugural Address, invoked Biblical language to explain the war, but warned that ultimately, God's will cannot be known by man. The North's Protestant clergy expressed no such humility. To them, God's purposes were clear and the soldiers' deaths merged with the Union's triumph in what Faust calls a "consoling narrative of divine purpose and sacrifice." The dead had not died in vain.

Faust sees this providential view of the war as essentially a device to make sense of pointless slaughter. In a chapter on the way American writers responded to the bloodshed, she gives pride of place to Ambrose

Bierce, Emily Dickinson, and Herman Melville, each of whom tried, through ironic detachment, to "undeceive" readers by stripping the war of comfortable, exalted meaning. To Faust, war remains, as in her 2004 lecture, meaningless violence.

Except, that is, for the 200,000 Black men who served in the Union army and navy. Faust notes the special dangers Black soldiers confronted. The Confederacy viewed them not as legitimate soldiers but as rebellious slaves (unlawful combatants, to use a current phrase). "We cannot treat negroes . . . as prisoners of war without a destruction of the social system for which we contend," one southern newspaper declared. Many atrocities took place in which Black soldiers were massacred after surrendering, most infamously at Fort Pillow, Tennessee, where nearly 200 perished at the hands of southern soldiers under the command of General Nathan B. Forrest. Nor were white officers of Black troops spared, and unlike other officers, Confederates did not return their bodies to the Union army for proper burial.

"Black soldiers," Faust writes, "approached war's violence differently from white Americans." They saw the war as a righteous struggle against slavery, offering not only spiritual redemption but an equal place in American society. The struggle for freedom gave the war a "special meaning" for Black troops. But her treatment of Black soldiers stands in sharp contrast to Faust's account of the white combatants, northern and southern. When they wrote home of service to nation, to God, to their comrades, Faust seems to see little more than a rationalizing of violence by giving it a nationalist and Christian overlay. Indeed, her chapter on white soldiers' response to death mixes letters by Union and Confederate soldiers to show the essential sameness of their responses. Here she diverges from Chandra Manning's *When This Cruel War Was Over*, a recent examination of soldiers' letters that demonstrates that as time went on, more and more Union soldiers saw the war as a struggle over the future of slavery in a nation dedicated to freedom. For Faust, pointless violence and mass death compelled Americans to seek meaning in the war; for Manning, what led northerners and southerners to be willing to lay down their lives was a difference in essential values.

All history, the saying goes, is contemporary history. Current concerns affect the questions we ask of the past and, frequently, the answers we find. The Civil War offers a striking example. During the 1930s and 1940s, in part because of a revulsion against what they saw as the needless slaughter of World War I, historians presented the Civil War not as an irrepressible conflict between two societies with fundamentally different systems of labor and social outlooks, but as an unnecessary struggle brought on by a "blundering generation" of politicians. In the aftermath of World War II, historians reinterpreted the Civil War in light of the struggle against fascism and a growing civil rights consciousness. Refracted through the lens of those experiences, the moral was clear: if it was worth a war to destroy the Third Reich, it was worth one to rid the nation of slavery.

Today, war has taken on a different aspect and historians have followed suit. Like Faust's book, *On the Altar of the Nation*, a recent work by the Yale scholar of religious history Harry Stout, condemns the Civil War clergy for justifying slaughter. It is hard not to see the shadow of the Iraq War—a prime example of senseless carnage cynically overlain with exalted rhetoric—hovering over these books. And at a time of the increasing militarization of our society and politics, any reminder of the true costs of war is certainly welcome.

Yet, on the question of whether the Civil War did have any larger meaning, *This Republic of Suffering* is oddly agnostic. At one point, Faust does refer to "a war about slavery." But overall, the war's meaning for her lies in death, not life, in destruction and suffering, not any other outcome. The Civil War was, indeed, a terrible tragedy. But because of her unrelenting preoccupation with death, Faust strips the war of political meaning. She never steps back to ask what the price of avoiding war might have been.

A look at the unsuccessful "compromise" proposals advanced during the secession winter of 1860–61 suggests that war could have been averted only at a very high cost, if not in lives then in the nature of American society itself. To try to bring the South back into the Union, these plans included, among other things, a ban on northern criticism of southern institutions, a southern veto on national policies, and the recognition of slavery as a permanent feature of American life. In other words, the price of peace would have been the destruction of freedom of speech, political democracy, and any hope for an end to slavery.

What about letting the "erring sisters" depart in peace, as Horace Greeley, editor of the *New York Tribune*, advocated? Confederate leaders were bent on expanding their slave-based empire into Mexico and the Caribbean. Either way—a compromise settlement or peaceable disunion—the United States and, indeed, the entire Western Hemisphere, would look very different today if the Civil War had not taken place.

THE CIVIL WAR IN "POST-RACIAL" AMERICA

IN 1877, SOON after retiring as president, Ulysses S. Grant embarked on a two-year tour of the world. At almost every location he was greeted with adulation. In London, the Duke of Wellington, whose father had vanquished Napoleon, praised Grant as a military genius, the architect of victory in one of the greatest wars known to human history. In Newcastle, tens of thousands of parading English workers, arrayed with the banners of their various crafts, hailed him as the man who had saved the world's leading experiment in democratic self-government, and as a Hero of Freedom for his role in the abolition of American slavery. In Berlin, Otto von Bismarck, the chancellor of Germany, welcomed Grant as a nation-builder who had accomplished something on the battlefield—national unity—that Bismarck was attempting to create for his own people. "You had to save the Union," Bismarck commented, "just as we had to save Germany."

Grant's contemporaries recognized the Civil War as an event of international significance. One hundred and fifty years after the conflict began, the meanings they ascribed to it offer a useful way of outlining why it was so pivotal in our own history. The Civil War changed the

The Nation, October 10, 2011.

nature of warfare, gave rise to an empowered nation-state, vindicated the idea of free labor, and destroyed the modern world's greatest slave society. Each of these outcomes laid the foundation for the country we live in today. But as with all great historical events, each outcome carried with it ambiguous, even contradictory, consequences.

Because of the war, the nation survived. Yet in its physical destruction and massive loss of life (the equivalent of over seven million in today's population), and encouragement of a patriotism that equated criticism of the government with treason, the Civil War can be seen as an ominous harbinger of twentieth-century total war, with its erasure of the distinction between civilian and military targets and serious infringements on civil liberties.

The nation-state created by the war, Abraham Lincoln insisted, embodied the principle of self-government. But it could also be used for undemocratic purposes. Shortly after the guns fell silent, Treasurer Frances Spinner (whose signature adorned every "greenback" issued by the federal government—the first national currency, itself a symbol of expanded national power) observed: "The thing to be feared now is that we will be running around the world with a chip on our shoulder. If we can avoid this, a glorious future is ours." Just as Spinner feared, the reunited nation soon embarked on a career of imperial expansion, beginning with the acquisition of Alaska two years after the war ended and culminating at the turn of the century in the conquest and annexation of Hawaii, the Philippines, and Puerto Rico. Indeed, the abolition of slavery, an indisputably moral exercise of national power, gave new meaning to Jefferson's description of the United States as an "empire of liberty." No matter how violent or oppressive, American expansion now meant, by definition, the expansion of freedom—a rhetoric alive and well today.

The principle of free labor may have triumphed with the Union's victory, but the national banking system, high tariffs, and other economic policies instituted by the Lincoln administration in an effort to mobilize the North's resources for the war underpinned a long-lasting alliance between the Republican Party, the national state, and an emerging class of industrial capitalists and financiers. Partly because of the war, Lincoln's America—the world of small shops and farms—gave way to an industrial leviathan. It was left to the Gilded Age labor movement to warn that a new industrial aristocracy had taken the place of the Slave Power as the enemy of ordinary working people.

Even abolition had mixed results. Long after the war ended, Lincoln and the emancipated slave would remain global symbols of universal liberty. But the new system of racial inequality that followed the overthrow of postwar Reconstruction seriously tarnished the idea that the Civil War had produced a new birth of freedom, as Lincoln claimed at Gettysburg. What people choose to remember about the Civil War has always been tinged by politics. The abandonment of the nation's commitment to equal rights for the former slaves was one basis on which former white antagonists could reunite. The displacement of slavery from a central role in the memory of the war accorded with the new racial realities under Jim Crow.

Forgetting some aspects of the past is as much a part of historical understanding as remembering others. For decades it remained a cliché that the Confederacy lost the war but won the battle over historical memory. In the highly influential writings of Charles and Mary Beard early in the last century, the war was brought on by a conflict between industrial and agricultural elites, and slavery hardly deserved a footnote in the narrative. In Black communities, the legacy of the 200,000 Black men who fought in the Union army and navy remained alive. But the memory of their participation receded in the broader society. The conflict was remembered as a "brothers' war" pitting northern against southern whites. Well beyond the borders of the South, the Lost Cause of the Confederacy remained a potent cultural force in American life.

Among historians, all this began to change after World War II. If World War I, with its massive slaughter and disappointing aftermath, had fueled Civil War revisionism by instilling skepticism about war in general, the Good War proved that in certain circumstances military action is necessary and desirable. In an influential article in 1949, historian Arthur Schlesinger Jr. challenged the underlying premise of prevailing Civil War scholarship. The South, he pointed out, had shown no evidence of a willingness to end slavery; indeed, over time it had become ever more hysterical in its defense. With one eye firmly on the recent past, Schlesinger insisted that a society closed in support of evil could not be appeased. But not until the 1960s, under the impact of the civil rights revolution, did historians en masse repudiate a half-century of Civil War scholarship, concluding that the war resulted from an irreconcilable conflict between two fundamentally different societies, one resting on slavery, the other on free labor. Historians pushed emancipation to the center of their account of the Civil War, and it has remained there ever since.

If historians have reached a considerable degree of consensus, the same cannot be said of the general public. Americans do not share either a single understanding of the war's meaning or a unified conception of its relevance to our own times. As the war's sesquicentennial proceeded in the early years of the twentieth century, Americans did not appear to be in a celebratory mood. In the wake of combat in Iraq, a truly needless war cynically justified in the language of freedom, many Americans seemed reluctant to commemorate an earlier conflict. Several recent books have insisted that the Civil War—and indeed all war—has no meaning other than death and destruction, and that by ascribing lofty motives to the combatants, historians fall into the trap of legitimizing past and present carnage.

Both left and right have grown more suspicious of exercises of power by the national state. Civil libertarians are appalled by the persistent violations of individual freedoms since September 11. The party of Lincoln, its center of gravity now located in the states of the Confederacy, has little desire to recall a time when its ancestors believed in a federal government that actively promoted racial equality and paid for war with tariffs and taxes (including the dreaded income tax, inaugurated in 1862). Moreover, the whole business of historical commemoration has been somewhat tarnished of late. Ever since 1992, when Native Americans and their allies disrupted efforts to celebrate the 500th

anniversary of Columbus's first voyage by drawing attention to the deleterious consequences that flowed from the European conquest of the
Western Hemisphere, historical anniversaries have exposed fault lines
in today's society.

As always, a gap remains between historical scholarship and popular understandings of history. In April 1961, when Charleston, South
Carolina, marked the anniversary of the firing on Fort Sumter, the city
was bedecked with Confederate flags and the commemorations made
no mention of slavery. Fifty years later, in April 2011, the city fathers
and National Park Service sponsored a gathering that included reflections on slavery's role in the war and on post-slavery race relations. As in
1961, a band played "Dixie," but now it was accompanied by "The Battle
Hymn of the Republic," recognition that a majority of South Carolina's
population (the slaves) sided with the Union, not the Confederacy. But
the event attracted far smaller crowds than the first time around.

Of course, the centennial celebrations of the 1960s took place at the
high tide of the civil rights revolution, which underscored the Civil
War's continuing relevance. At one of these anniversary gatherings the
headquarters hotel in Charleston denied accommodations to a Black
delegate from New Jersey. In response, President Kennedy moved the
event to a nearby naval base, whereupon southern delegates seceded to
hold their own Confederate States Centennial Conference.

A half-century later, the election of the nation's first Black president
produced the ironic result of removing issues related to the legacy of
emancipation from the national agenda. In the absence of a vibrant
movement for racial justice and in an era that has been misleadingly
labeled "post-racial," the Civil War's relevance appears far less clear
than fifty years ago. In 1963 it seemed entirely appropriate for Martin
Luther King Jr. to begin his "Dream" speech at the Lincoln Memorial
with a reference to the unfulfilled promise of the Emancipation Proclamation. Such rhetoric is rarely heard today, when the Black freedom
struggle has been transformed into a narrative of national unity, a fulfillment of bedrock American principles. Even neo-Confederates portray the Old South as a multicultural paradise of racial harmony, and

invent imaginary legions of Black Confederate soldiers to demonstrate that both sides can claim credit for the end of slavery.

Polls show that a majority of Americans identify issues other than slavery—states' rights, the tariff, etc.—as the war's fundamental cause. Yet contemporaries had little doubt that slavery "somehow" lay at the root of the conflict, as Lincoln put it in his Second Inaugural Address, and that emancipation was its most profound outcome. The Confederacy's founders forthrightly announced that they had created a republic whose "cornerstone," as Confederate vice president Alexander Stephens declared, was the principle that "slavery, subordination to the superior race," was the "natural and moral condition" of Black Americans. When Bismarck identified preservation of the Union as the war's purpose, Grant corrected him: "Not only to save the Union, but destroy slavery...a stain to the Union." Despite America's post-Reconstruction retreat from the ideal of equality, the destruction of slavery remains an epochal victory for human rights, worthy of celebration. Moreover, as Lincoln recognized, the service of Black soldiers, most of them emancipated slaves, proved essential to Union victory. No narrative of the Civil War can ignore the centrality of slavery to its origins, conduct, and legacy.

In May 2011, at a ceremony in Paris, French president Nicolas Sarkozy unveiled a monument to the victims of slavery (something we have yet to erect in the United States). Its inscription reads: "By their struggles and their strong desire for dignity and liberty, the slaves of the French colonies contributed to the universality of human rights and to the ideal of liberty, equality, and fraternity that is the foundation of our republic." In other words, the monument posits not simply that the nation conferred freedom on the slaves but that it learned about freedom, in part, from them. Here is a model of sober celebration, of triumph laced with humility, that we might seek to emulate.

THE EMANCIPATION OF ABRAHAM LINCOLN

O N JANUARY 1, 1863, Abraham Lincoln presided over the annual New Year's reception at the White House. Late that afternoon, he retired to his study to sign the Emancipation Proclamation. When he took up his pen, his hand was shaking from exhaustion. Briefly, he paused—"I do not want it to appear as if I hesitated," he remarked. Then Lincoln affixed a firm signature to the document.

Like all great historical transformations, emancipation was a process, not a single event. It arose from many causes and was the work of many individuals. It began at the outset of the Civil War when slaves sought refuge behind Union lines. It did not end until December 1865, with the ratification of the Thirteenth Amendment, which irrevocably abolished slavery throughout the nation. But the Emancipation Proclamation was the crucial turning point in this story. In a sense, it embodied a double emancipation: for the slaves, since it ensured that if the Union emerged victorious, slavery would perish, and for Lincoln himself, for whom it marked the abandonment of his previous assumptions

—

New York Times, December 31, 2012.

about how to abolish slavery and the role Blacks would play in post-emancipation American life.

There is no reason to doubt the sincerity of Lincoln's statement in 1864 that he had always believed slavery to be wrong. During the first two years of the Civil War, despite insisting that the conflict's aim was preservation of the Union, he devoted considerable energy to a plan for ending slavery inherited from pre-war years. Emancipation would be undertaken by state governments, with national financing. It would be gradual, owners would receive monetary compensation, and emancipated slaves would be encouraged to find a homeland outside the United States—this last idea known as "colonization."

Lincoln's plan sought to win the cooperation of slaveholders in ending slavery. As early as November 1861, he proposed it to political leaders in Delaware, one of the four border states (along with Kentucky, Maryland, and Missouri) that remained in the Union. Delaware had only 1,800 slaves; the institution was peripheral to the state's economy. But Lincoln found that even there, slaveholders did not wish to surrender their human property. Nonetheless, for most of 1862, he avidly promoted his plan to the border states and any Confederates who might be interested.

Lincoln also took his proposal to Black Americans. In August 1862, he met with a group of Black leaders from Washington. He seemed to blame the presence of African Americans for the conflict: "but for your race among us there could not be war." He issued a powerful indictment of slavery—"the greatest wrong inflicted on any people"—but added that, because of racism, Blacks would never achieve equality in America. "It is better for us both, therefore, to be separated," he said. But most Blacks refused to contemplate emigration from the land of their birth.

In the summer of 1862, a combination of events propelled Lincoln in a new direction. Slavery was disintegrating in parts of the South as thousands of slaves ran away to Union lines. With the war a stalemate, more northerners found themselves agreeing with the abolitionists, who had insisted from the outset that slavery must become a target.

Enthusiasm for enlistment was waning in the North. The Army had long refused to accept Black volunteers, but the reservoir of Black manpower could no longer be ignored. In response, Congress moved ahead of Lincoln, abolishing slavery in the District of Columbia, authorizing the president to enroll African Americans in the army, and freeing the slaves of pro-Confederate owners in areas under military control. Lincoln signed all these measures that summer.

The hallmark of Lincoln's greatness was his combination of bedrock principle with open-mindedness and capacity for growth. That summer, with his preferred approach going nowhere, he moved in the direction of immediate emancipation. He first proposed this to his cabinet on July 22, but Secretary of State William H. Seward persuaded him to wait for a military victory, lest it seem an act of desperation.

Soon after the Union victory at Antietam in September 1862, Lincoln issued the Preliminary Emancipation Proclamation, a warning to the Confederacy that if it did not lay down its arms by January 1, he would declare the slaves "forever free." Lincoln did not immediately abandon his earlier plan. His annual message to Congress, released on December 1, 1862, devoted a long passage to gradual, compensated abolition and colonization. But in the same document, without mentioning the impending proclamation, he indicated that a new approach was imperative: "The dogmas of the quiet past are inadequate to the stormy present," he wrote. "We must disenthrall our selves, and then we shall save our country." Lincoln included himself in that "we." On January 1, he proclaimed the freedom of the vast majority of the nation's slaves.

The Emancipation Proclamation is perhaps the most misunderstood of the documents that have shaped American history. Contrary to legend, Lincoln did not free all of the nearly four million slaves with a stroke of his pen. The proclamation had no bearing on slaves in the four border states since they were not in rebellion. It also exempted certain parts of the Confederacy occupied by the Union army. All told, it left perhaps 750,000 slaves in bondage. But the remaining 3.1 million, it declared, "are, and henceforward shall be free."

The proclamation did not end slavery in the United States on the day it was issued. Indeed, it could not even be enforced in most of the areas where it applied, which were under Confederate control. But it ensured the eventual death of slavery—assuming that the Union won the war. Were the Confederacy to emerge victorious, slavery, in one form or another, would undoubtedly have lasted a long time.

A military order, whose constitutional legitimacy rested on the president's power as commander in chief of the armed forces, the proclamation often disappoints those who read it. It is dull and legalistic; it contains no soaring language enunciating the rights of man. Only at the last minute, at the urging of Treasury Secretary Salmon P. Chase, an abolitionist, did Lincoln add a conclusion declaring the proclamation an "act of justice."

Nonetheless, the proclamation marked a dramatic transformation in the nature of the Civil War and in Lincoln's own approach to the problem of slavery. No longer did he seek the consent of slaveholders. The proclamation was immediate, not gradual, contained no mention of compensation for owners, and made no reference to colonization. In it, Lincoln addressed Blacks directly, not as property subject to the will of others but as men and women whose loyalty the Union must earn. For the first time, he welcomed Black soldiers into the Union army; over the next two years some 200,000 Black men would serve in the army and navy, playing a critical role in achieving Union victory. And rather than urging freed slaves to leave the country, Lincoln urged them to go to work for "reasonable wages"—in the United States. He never again mentioned colonization in public.

Having made the decision, Lincoln did not look back. In 1864, with casualties mounting, there was talk of a compromise peace. Some urged Lincoln to rescind the proclamation, in which case, they believed, the South could be persuaded to return to the Union. Lincoln refused. Were he to revoke the promise of freedom, he told one visitor, "I should be damned in time and eternity."

Wartime emancipation may have settled the fate of slavery, but it opened another vexing question: the role of former slaves in

American life. Colonization had allowed its proponents to talk about abolition without having to confront this issue; after all, the Black population would be gone. After January 1, 1863, Lincoln for the first time began to think seriously of the United States as a biracial society.

While not burdened with the visceral racism of many of his white contemporaries, Lincoln shared some of their prejudices. He had long seen Blacks as an alien people who had been unjustly uprooted from their homeland, and, though entitled to freedom, were not an intrinsic part of American society. During his Senate campaign in Illinois, in 1858, he had insisted that Blacks should enjoy the same natural rights as whites (life, liberty, and the pursuit of happiness), but opposed granting them legal equality or the right to vote.

By the end of his life, Lincoln's outlook had changed dramatically. In his last public address, delivered in April 1865, he said that in reconstructing Louisiana, and by implication other southern states, he would "prefer" that limited Black suffrage be implemented. He singled out the "very intelligent" (educated free blacks) and "those who serve our cause as soldiers" as most worthy. Though hardly an unambiguous embrace of equality, this was the first time an American president had endorsed any political rights for Black persons.

And then there was his magnificent Second Inaugural Address of March 4, 1865, in which Lincoln ruminated on the deep meaning of the war. He now identified the institution of slavery—not the presence of the Black population, as in 1862—as its fundamental cause. The war, he said, might well be a divine punishment for the evil of slavery. And God might will it to continue until all the wealth the slaves had created had been destroyed, and "until every drop of blood drawn with the lash, shall be paid by another drawn with the sword." Lincoln was reminding Americans that violence did not begin with the firing on Fort Sumter. What he called "this terrible war" had been preceded by 250 years of the terrible violence of slavery.

In essence, Lincoln asked the nation to confront unblinkingly the legacy of slavery. What were the requirements of justice in the face of this reality? What would be necessary to enable former slaves and their descendants to enjoy fully the pursuit of happiness? Lincoln did not live to provide an answer. A century and a half later, we have yet to do so.

ON JEFFERSON DAVIS

O F THE MYRIAD explanations for Union victory in the Civil War, perhaps the most arresting was proposed by the historian David Potter. If the Union and Confederacy had exchanged presidents, he wrote, the South might well have won the war. Potter's aim was to direct attention from the battlefield to the political arena, where wars are often won and lost. If one considers success inevitable for the side with the greater population and material resources (a position hardly tenable since Vietnam, Iraq, and Afghanistan), then presidential leadership makes little difference. If, as many scholars believe, the South had a reasonable chance of winning, one must find other explanations for its failure. Blame often falls on the Confederate president, Jefferson Davis.

Davis has been the subject of more than a dozen biographies, few of them laudatory. His historical reputation can never escape the burden of Confederate defeat or the shadow of his great antagonist, Abraham Lincoln. During the war, many southerners denounced him as a tyrant or a weakling. Afterward, he never achieved the saintly stature

---

Review of *Jefferson Davis, American*, by William J. Cooper Jr., *Los Angeles Times Book Review*, November 19, 2000.

accorded to Robert E. Lee. His most recent biographer, William C. Davis, described the Confederate president as "cold, aloof, obstinate, petty, enigmatic, vindictive, and bitter"—and this in a book whose author said he hoped to upgrade Jefferson Davis's reputation! As the adage goes, to be a real southerner, one has to have a granddaddy who fought with Stonewall Jackson and to hate Jefferson Davis.

William J. Cooper Jr., the author of several well-regarded works on nineteenth-century southern history, has combined assiduous archival research with a command of the vast secondary literature on the Old South and Civil War to produce *Jefferson Davis, American*, a generous although not uncritical study of the man. This book is biography on a grand scale, the most comprehensive treatment of Davis and his times yet to appear. Although scholars will find little that is strikingly new, readers interested in the Civil War era will surely enjoy Cooper's well-written and up-to-date treatment of the South's enigmatic president.

Born in 1808, within eight months and 100 miles of Abraham Lincoln, Davis grew up in a Kentucky farm family that owned a few slaves but never achieved more than modest wealth. After his father's death, Jefferson's brother Joseph, twenty-four years his senior and a cotton planter in Mississippi, became a surrogate paternal figure, arranging for him to attend West Point. Once Jefferson had served a stint in the army, Joseph settled him on Brierfield plantation at Davis Bend, a peninsula formed by the tortuous course of the Mississippi River.

Although Cooper says relatively little about Davis as a slaveholder, the information he does offer is fascinating: By the 1850s, Davis owned more than 100 slaves, and their labor in the rich cotton fields of the Mississippi Valley made him an exceptionally wealthy man. At a time when the annual per capita income of white Mississippians was $124, Davis took in about $35,000 per year. Davis seems to have been a humane owner who tried to keep Black families intact. While holding office in Washington, he left his slave James Pemberton, who had accompanied him during his military career as a body servant, in charge of the labor force. But life for Davis's slaves was harsh—very few of them lived past age 40. Cooper insists there is no contemporary evidence to support Davis's wife's later claim that slaves at Davis Bend administered justice themselves through a slave jury, which is often cited as an example of Davis's leniency toward his slaves. Contrary to legend, Cooper concludes, Brierfield was not a "plantation paradise."

Davis entered public life as a Democrat in the 1840s. His heroic conduct in the Mexican War, when his regiment helped turn the tide of battle at Buena Vista, made him a national figure. He soon came to dominate the public life of Mississippi, then served in Franklin Pierce's cabinet and the U.S. Senate. Davis quickly emerged as a proslavery extremist, favoring the institution's unrestricted westward expansion, adamantly opposing the Compromise of 1850, and in general echoing the positions of his ideological mentor, John C. Calhoun.

Davis's speeches were devoted to states' rights, the legitimacy of slavery, and the racial inferiority of Blacks. He portrayed slavery as a benevolent system in which laborers fared better than in the capitalist economy of the North. Slavery, for him, was the foundation of southern life and of true freedom (for whites). He criticized only one aspect of the institution, slave trading, even though he made purchases from slave dealers.

Those who today maintain that the Confederate flag stands for something other than slavery—states' rights, for example, or local heritage—will find little support in this book or in Davis's own words at the time. "The Confederacy," Cooper writes, "had come into existence over slavery, and with slavery as its fundamental institution." Years later, to be sure, in his book *The Rise and Fall of the Confederate Government* (1881), Davis tried to rewrite history, portraying the war as a battle over local autonomy, with slavery "in no wise the cause of the conflict."

Unlike most previous biographers, Cooper devotes more space to Davis's antebellum career than to the Civil War. The surprising result is that readers may find the treatment of Davis's life before 1860 fuller and more satisfying than Cooper's account of his presidency. The problem, however, is not really one of space. In his chapters on the war years, Cooper offers a clear narrative but not clear judgments. He relates how

Davis strove to forge a nation out of a fractious group of states that often seemed unwilling to surrender their traditional powers for the common war effort. He presents some familiar criticisms of Davis's presidency. Cooper notes, for example, that Davis was unable to delegate authority, immersing himself in the minutiae of military administration while failing to develop a strategic overview of the war. He had little understanding of public finance. And although known before the war as the "Cicero of the Senate," he lacked Lincoln's ability to communicate the war's meaning effectively to ordinary men and women. But these scattered observations are never brought together in an overall assessment of Davis as president.

Nor does Cooper engage the broad issues that concern current historians of the Civil War. Did slavery doom the Confederacy? Was internal division among whites responsible for southern defeat? Was the Confederacy, which forged a powerful central state in a region devoted to local autonomy, a "revolutionary experience," as historian Emory Thomas has claimed? The war chapters end with a dramatic account of Davis's flight from Richmond in 1865 and capture by federal soldiers. But nowhere does Cooper offer his own explanation for the war's outcome.

Confederate defeat, Cooper makes clear, did not change Davis's views of slavery, secession, race, or the justness of the southern cause. Although not involved in Reconstruction politics, he strongly opposed extending civil and political rights to the freedmen. Struggling to make ends meet, he fought to regain possession of Davis Bend. Before his death, Joseph Davis had sold the estate to his former slave, Benjamin Montgomery. Knowing Montgomery would have difficulty meeting the mortgage payments, Joseph in his will directed his heirs to offer him every leniency. But Jefferson Davis, even though he had never in fact acquired legal title to Brierfield from his brother, sued to evict Montgomery. After white supremacist Democrats regained control of the Mississippi government in 1875, Davis won his lawsuit. Joseph's grandchildren fought him every step of the way: evidently, they had a greater sense of honor, that quintessential southern attribute, than Jefferson Davis.

Cooper warns against judging Davis by the standards of our time rather than his own. Davis's belief that slavery was the foundation of white freedom, and that Blacks were innately inferior, he points out, were hardly "unique" in nineteenth-century America. The book's title drives home Cooper's point. Davis, he insists, was a "patriotic American" who shared his society's basic values and aspirations. He participated fully in the key developments of his era: westward expansion, economic growth, democratic politics. He revered the legacy of the American Revolution and insisted that Confederates were its inheritors because they attempted to implement the principle that government rests on the consent of the governed.

Cooper's point is that there was no contradiction between American traditions and a defense of slavery. For white Americans, liberty included the right to dominate and even own Blacks. This is a powerful corrective to patriotic grandiloquence about our past. But Cooper's zeal to avoid retrospective finger-pointing ends up producing a curiously agnostic narrative. It is misleading to describe Davis as an "American" and leave it at that. Racism was indeed widespread, but even in the nineteenth century it was not universal. Not every American believed that slavery was ordained by God or that Blacks must forever be slaves. Jefferson Davis represented one America, but there were others, more worthy of our respect. Davis made his choice, and the country has been living with the consequences ever since.

THE MAKING AND THE
BREAKING OF THE
LEGEND OF ROBERT E. LEE

I N THE BAND'S popular ballad "The Night They Drove Old Dixie Down," an ex-Confederate soldier refers to Robert E. Lee as "the very best." It is difficult to think of another song that mentions a general by name. But Lee has always occupied a unique place in the national imagination. The ups and downs of his reputation reflect changes in key elements of Americans' historical consciousness—how we understand race relations, the causes and consequences of the Civil War, and the nature of the good society.

Born in 1807, Lee was a product of the Virginia gentry—his father a hero of the War of Independence and governor of the state, his wife the daughter of George Washington's adopted son. Lee always prided himself on following the strict moral code of a gentleman. He managed to graduate from West Point with no disciplinary demerits, an almost impossible feat considering the complex maze of rules that governed the conduct of cadets.

While opposed to disunion, when the Civil War broke out and Virginia seceded, Lee went with his state. He won military renown for defeating a succession of larger Union forces, until Gettysburg. Eventu-

New York Times, August 28, 2017.

ally, he met his match in Ulysses S. Grant and was forced to surrender his army in April 1865. At Appomattox he urged his soldiers to accept the war's outcome and return to their homes, rejecting talk of carrying on the struggle in guerrilla fashion. He died in 1870, at the height of Reconstruction, when biracial governments had come to power throughout the South.

But, of course, what interests people who debate Lee today are his connection with slavery and his views about race. During his lifetime, Lee owned a small number of slaves. He considered himself a paternalistic master but could also impose severe punishments, especially on those who attempted to run away. Lee said almost nothing in public about the institution. His most extended comment, quoted by all biographers, came in a letter to his wife in 1856. Here he described slavery as an evil, but one that had more deleterious effects on whites than Blacks. He felt that the "painful discipline" to which they were subjected benefitted Blacks by elevating them from barbarism to civilization and introducing them to Christianity. The end of slavery would come in God's good time, but this might take quite a while, since to God a thousand years was just a moment. Meanwhile, the greatest danger to the "liberty" of white southerners was the "evil course" pursued by the abolitionists, who stirred up sectional hatred. In 1860, Lee voted for John C. Breckinridge, the extreme proslavery candidate for president. (A more moderate southerner, John Bell, carried Virginia that year.)

Lee's code of gentlemanly conduct did not seem to apply to African Americans. During the Gettysburg campaign, he did nothing to stop soldiers in his army from kidnapping free Black farmers for sale into slavery. In Reconstruction, Lee made it clear that he opposed political rights for the former slaves. Referring to Blacks (30 percent of Virginia's population), he told a congressional committee that he hoped the state could be "rid of them." Urged to condemn the Ku Klux Klan's terrorist violence, Lee remained silent.

By the time the Civil War ended, with the Confederate president, Jefferson Davis, deeply unpopular, Lee had become the embodiment of the southern cause. A generation later, he was a national hero. The

1890s and early twentieth century witnessed the consolidation of white supremacy in the post-Reconstruction South and widespread acceptance in the North of southern racial attitudes. A revised view of history accompanied these developments, including the triumph of what the historian David Blight calls a "reconciliationist" memory of the Civil War. The war came to be seen as a conflict in which both sides consisted of brave men fighting for noble principles—union in the case of the North, self-determination on the part of the South. This vision was reinforced by the "cult of Lincoln and Lee," each representing the noblest features of his society, each a figure Americans of all regions could look back on with pride. The memory of Lee, *The New York Times* wrote in 1890, was "the possession of the American people."

Reconciliation excised slavery from a central role in the story, and the struggle for emancipation was now seen as a minor feature of the war. The Lost Cause, a romanticized vision of the Old South and Confederacy, gained adherents throughout the country. And who symbolized the Lost Cause more fully than Lee? This outlook was also taken up by the southern Agrarians, a group of writers who idealized the slave South as a bastion of manly virtue in contrast to the commercialism and individualism of the industrial North. At a time when traditional values appeared to be in retreat, character trumped political outlook, and character Lee had in spades. Frank Owsley, the most prominent historian among the Agrarians, called Lee "the soldier who walked with God." Indeed, many early biographies directly compared Lee and Christ. Moreover, with the influx of millions of Catholics and Jews from southern and eastern Europe alarming many Americans, Lee seemed to stand for a society where people of Anglo-Saxon stock controlled affairs.

Historians in the first decades of the twentieth century offered scholarly legitimacy to this interpretation of the past, which justified the abrogation of the constitutional rights of southern Black citizens. In the 1920s and 1930s, a group of mostly southern historians known as the revisionists went further, insisting that slavery was a benign institution that would have died out peacefully. Instead, a "blundering generation" of politicians had stumbled into a needless war. But the true villains, as in Lee's 1856 letter, were the abolitionists, whose reckless agitation poisoned sectional relations. This interpretation dominated the teaching of history throughout the country.

As far as Lee was concerned, the culmination of these trends came in the publication in the 1930s of a four-volume biography by Douglas Southall Freeman, a Virginia-born journalist and historian. For decades, Freeman's hagiography would be considered the definitive account of Lee's life. Freeman warned readers that they should not search for ambiguity, complexity, or inconsistency in Lee, for there was none—he was simply a paragon of virtue. Freeman displayed little interest in Lee's relationship to slavery. The index to his four volumes contained 22 entries for "devotion to duty," 19 for "kindness," 53 for Lee's celebrated horse, Traveller. But "slavery," "slave emancipation," and "slave insurrection" together received five. Freeman observed, without offering details, that slavery in Virginia represented the system "at its best." He ignored the postwar testimony of Lee's former slave Wesley Norris about the brutal treatment to which he had been subjected. In 1935 Freeman was awarded the Pulitzer Prize in biography.

That same year, however, W. E. B. Du Bois published *Black Reconstruction in America*, a powerful challenge to the mythologies about slavery, the Civil War, and Reconstruction that historians had been disseminating. Du Bois identified slavery as the fundamental cause of the war and emancipation as its most profound outcome. He portrayed the abolitionists as idealistic precursors of the twentieth-century struggle for racial justice, and Reconstruction as a remarkable experiment in democracy. Most of all, Du Bois made clear that Blacks were active participants in the era's history, not simply a problem confronting white society. Ignored at the time by mainstream scholars, *Black Reconstruction* pointed the way to an enormous change in historical interpretation, rooted in the egalitarianism of the civil rights movement of the 1960s and underpinned by the documentary record of the Black experience ignored by earlier scholars. Today, Du Bois's insights are taken for granted by most historians, although they have not fully penetrated the national culture.

Inevitably, this revised view of the Civil War era led to a reassessment of Lee, who, Du Bois wrote elsewhere, possessed physical courage but not "the moral courage to stand up for justice to the Negro." Even Lee's military career, previously viewed as nearly flawless, underwent critical scrutiny. In *The Marble Man* (1977), Thomas Connelly charged that "a cult of Virginia authors" had disparaged other Confederate commanders in an effort to hide Lee's errors on the battlefield. James M. McPherson's *Battle Cry of Freedom*, since its publication in 1988 the standard history of the Civil War, compared Lee's single-minded focus on the war in Virginia unfavorably with Grant's strategic grasp of the interconnections between the eastern and western theaters.

Lee's most recent biographer, Michael Korda, does not deny his subject's admirable qualities. But he makes clear that when it came to Black Americans, Lee never changed. Lee chose to take up arms in defense of a slaveholders' republic. After the war, he could not envision an alternative to white supremacy. What Korda calls Lee's "legend" needs to be retired. And whatever the fate of his statues and memorials, so long as the legacy of slavery continues to bedevil American society, it seems unlikely that historians will return Lee, metaphorically speaking, to his pedestal.

LONGSTREET

DURING THE SUMMER of 1997, my wife and I picked up our
9-year-old daughter from a ballet camp in Carlisle, Pennsylvania, and drove to the nearby Gettysburg National Military
Park, which they had never seen and I barely remembered from a boy-
hood visit. The park's presentation of history left much to be desired.
The visitor center's small museum and the numerous monuments scattered across the battlefield conveyed a great deal about how the battle had been fought in July 1863, while offering almost no explanation
of why the combatants were fighting. The park commemorated the
Union's greatest military victory, but its emotional centerpiece was the
disastrous southern assault known as Pickett's Charge, identified, in
the romantic glow of nostalgia, as the "high-water mark" of the Confederacy. In labels accompanying the display of historic artifacts and
images, the words valor and glory were almost always applied to soldiers
who fought for the South, not for the Union.

That the place where the Civil War reached its turning point had
become a shrine to the courage of those who fought to destroy the

———

Review of *Longstreet: The Confederate General Who Defied the South*,
by Elizabeth R. Varon, *The Atlantic*, December 2023.

nation and preserve slavery should not have been a surprise. It has long been a commonplace that the South lost the Civil War but won the battle over historical memory. For decades, almost from the moment of surrender, the ideology of the Lost Cause shaped both popular and scholarly understanding of the conflict.

As Elizabeth R. Varon observes in *Longstreet: The Confederate General Who Defied the South*, her compelling new biography of James Longstreet, Robert E. Lee's second in command, the Lost Cause was far more than a military narrative. It provided a comprehensive account of the war's origins, conduct, and consequences. The conflict, in this telling, had little to do with slavery, but instead was caused, depending on which book you read, by the protective tariff, arguments over states' rights, or white southerners' desire for individual liberty. Confederate soldiers were defeated not by superior generalship or greater fighting spirit but by the Union's advantages in manpower, resources, and industrial technology. And the nation's victory was marred by what followed: the era of Reconstruction, when the southern white population was subjected to the humiliation of "Negro domination." This account of history was easily understandable and, like all ideologies, most convincing to those who benefitted from it—proponents of white supremacy.

Just how widely and publicly memorialized the Lost Cause narrative remained more than 150 years later became glaringly clear in the fallout from tragic events such as the Charleston, South Carolina, church massacre in 2015; the deadly altercation in Charlottesville, Virginia, in 2017; and the murder of George Floyd by Minneapolis police officers in 2020. The legacy of slavery was propelled to center stage in today's culture wars. With unexpected rapidity, the Confederate battle flag came down from many public buildings. And dozens of monuments to southern military leaders—most of them erected in the late nineteenth and early twentieth centuries to help provide historical legitimacy for the Jim Crow system of racial inequality, then being codified into law—were removed from their pedestals.

Of course, omission, not simply falsehood, can be a form of lying (as Alessandra Lorini, an Italian historian, noted earlier this year in an excellent survey of debates about historical monuments, titled *Le Statue Bugiarde*, or, roughly, "Statues That Lie"). For many years, the Civil War was remembered as a family quarrel among white Americans in which their Black countrymen played no significant role—a fiction reflected in the paucity of memorials indicating that enslaved men and women had been active agents in shaping the course of events. Lately, some historical erasures have begun to be remedied. For example, a memorial honoring Robert Smalls, the enslaved Civil War hero who famously sailed a Confederate vessel out of Charleston Harbor and turned it over to the Union navy, and later served five terms in the U.S. House of Representatives, is now on display in Charleston's Waterfront Park.

Back when we visited, the Gettysburg battlefield was beginning to be swept up in changing views of history. The site is strewn with monuments, memorials, markers, and plaques—1,328 of them, according to the National Park Service, approximately a quarter of which memorialize Confederate officers and regiments. (Visitors sometimes ask guides whether all these monuments "got in the way of the battle.") The Park Service and the Gettysburg Foundation, which jointly administer the site, were raising funds to build a new museum and visitor center. And in 1998, an equestrian statue was installed of James Longstreet, one of the Confederacy's most successful generals, present at the battle but never before memorialized at Gettysburg. Longstreet had warned Lee in vain that Pickett's Charge courted disaster. (To his credit, after the attack, which left about half of the 12,500 Confederate troops dead or wounded, Lee declared, "All this has been my fault.")

But the defeat at Gettysburg was not what explained Longstreet's exclusion from the pantheon of southern heroes. Rather, his conduct during Reconstruction was the problem—an assessment that was endorsed by the branch of the Sons of Confederate Veterans that commissioned his statue. (Some observers view the statue as intentionally insulting. Longstreet, a large man, sits awkwardly astride a small horse or pony, and looks behind him, as if to locate a route for retreat.) The general, the group explained, was being honored for his "war service," not his "postwar activities." What were those activities? After the war, Longstreet had emerged as a singular figure: the most prominent white southerner to join the Republican Party and proclaim his support for Black male suffrage and office holding. Leading the biracial Louisiana militia and the New Orleans Metropolitan Police, he also battled violent believers in white supremacy.

Among the challenges of writing the history of the Reconstruction period is avoiding the language devised by the era's contemporary opponents as terms of vilification. One such word is scalawag, applied to a white southerner who supported Reconstruction. White-supremacist Democrats viewed scalawags, who could be found in many parts of the South, as traitors to their race and region. The largest number were small farmers in up-country counties such as the mountainous areas of western North Carolina and northern Alabama and Georgia. There, slavery had not been a major presence before the Civil War, many white residents had opposed secession, and more than a few had enlisted in the Union army. Even though supporting Reconstruction required them to overcome long-standing prejudices and forge a political alliance with Black voters, up-country scalawags saw Black male suffrage as the only way to prevent pro-Confederate plantation owners from regaining political power in the South. All scalawags were excoriated in the white southern press, but none as viciously as James Longstreet.

Longstreet's life (1821–1904) spanned the era of sectional conflict, Civil War, and Reconstruction. Although unique in many ways, his postwar career illuminates both the hopes inspired by the end of slavery and the powerful obstacles to change. To write his biography requires a command of numerous strands of the era's complex history. Varon, a history professor at the University of Virginia, is the author of a general account of the conflict. She has also written books about the coming of the war and Lee's surrender at Appomattox, and is as adept at guiding the reader through the intricacies of Civil War military campaigns as she is at explaining the byzantine factional politics of

Reconstruction Louisiana. Her knowledge of the historical context is matched by her balanced appraisal of Longstreet's attitudes, personal and political.

Longstreet's unusual postwar political career, Varon insists, did not arise from lack of enthusiasm for slavery or doubts about southern independence. The owner of several slaves, he was a true believer in the Confederate cause. His grandfather was a plantation owner in Edgefield District, South Carolina, widely known as a center of cotton production, proslavery ideology, and secessionism. He was brought up by his uncle Augustus Longstreet, a prominent jurist who made very clear his belief in Black inferiority. Educated at West Point, Longstreet resigned from the U.S. Army in 1861 to join the Confederate war effort. Varon points out that unlike Lee, who on occasion recklessly risked casualties that his army could not afford by attacking Union forces, Longstreet preferred to fight on the defensive. This is why he advised Lee not to send Major General George E. Pickett's troops to assault the well-fortified Union lines at Gettysburg. But defenders of the Lost Cause—especially those who could never forgive Longstreet's strong embrace of political rights for former slaves—would blame him retroactively for the defeat at Gettysburg, accusing him of sabotaging Pickett's Charge by deliberately arriving late on the battlefield with his troops.

Longstreet was at Lee's side in the tiny village of Appomattox Court House in April 1865 when a note arrived from Ulysses S. Grant demanding the surrender of Lee's army to avert further bloodshed. Longstreet, who had known Grant since their West Point days, was impressed by the leniency of his old friend's terms of surrender, which allowed Confederate soldiers to return home on "parole." They would remain unpunished, and even keep their personal weapons, so long as they did not take up arms against the nation or violate local laws.

In her earlier work on the Appomattox surrender, Varon offered a provocative interpretation of the long-term consequences of Grant's generosity, making a case that Lee's officers and many ordinary soldiers saw it as a kind of homage to Confederate bravery. Indeed, a substantial number, she now writes, expected to receive another call to go to war for southern independence. They later argued that the radical expansion of Black rights forced on them during Reconstruction violated the terms of surrender. Those terms, they claimed, did not empower the Union to impose its will on the white South. Thus, resistance to Reconstruction did not violate the promise that paroled soldiers would obey the law.

Longstreet rejected any such interpretation of Lee's surrender, seeing in it "the flaw of hubris." He understood that Grant's terms were an effort to facilitate reconciliation (among white Americans) in the reunited nation and in no way justified political violence. In urging the white South to accept the reality of defeat, Longstreet made the obvious point that the losing party should not expect to impose its perspective on the victor. The white South, Longstreet declared in 1867, had "appealed to the arbitrament of the sword," and had a moral obligation to accept the outcome: "The decision," he wrote, "was in favor of the North, so her construction becomes the law." He believed Confederates should accept that the Union's victory demonstrated the superiority of a society based on free labor over one based on slavery, and seize the opportunity presented by Reconstruction to modernize the South. Longstreet's understanding of the lessons and consequences of Confederate defeat, Varon writes, helps explain the mystery of how a man who went to war to destroy the nation and protect slavery decided to join the Republican Party and work closely with Black political leaders during Reconstruction.

Soon after the surrender, Longstreet moved his family to New Orleans, where he established a cotton brokerage and became the president of an insurance company. Then, as now, New Orleans was a city with a distinctive history and an unusually diverse population. Occupied by Union forces early in the war, it harbored a large anti-secession white population. Its well-educated, economically successful free Black community was positioned to take a leading role in the Reconstruction project of revamping southern society, eliminating the vestiges of slavery, and establishing the principle of equal citizenship across racial lines. Many Black men—both those recently liberated and those already free before the war—were elected to public office after Congress, in 1867, ordered the creation of new governments in most of the former Confederate states. New Orleans, and by extension Louisiana, seemed to be a place where Reconstruction could succeed. But the newly created Republican Party was beset by factionalism as various groups jockeyed for political influence. The city was also home to a belligerent population of former Confederates willing to resort to violence to restore their dominion over Black residents.

Very quickly, Longstreet plunged into Louisiana politics, having applied for a pardon from President Andrew Johnson, Abraham Lincoln's successor. This would enable him to hold public office and retain his property, except for slaves. Johnson refused, but in 1868, as provided in the Fourteenth Amendment, Longstreet received amnesty from the Republican Congress. Lee, who had appealed to Grant personally for immunity from charges of treason but declined to condemn the violence of the Ku Klux Klan, chastised Longstreet for recognizing the legitimacy of Congress's Reconstruction policy.

But Longstreet, as Varon relates, was adamant that he was anything but a traitor to the white South. The first requirement of reconciliation, he wrote, was to accept frankly that "the political questions of the war" had been settled and should be "buried upon the fields that marked their end." There was no avoiding Black suffrage and the participation of Black men in southern government. In 1868, Governor Henry Clay Warmoth, a former Union army officer, created the biracial Metropolitan Police Force, where Longstreet went on to play a leading role. The sight of armed Black men patrolling the streets of New Orleans outraged much of the local white population. Longstreet was also appointed adjutant general of the state militia, which was racially segregated but had Black and white officers.

Over the course of eight years, Longstreet was active on a remarkable number of fronts in Reconstruction New Orleans. Grant appointed him to the lucrative position of customs surveyor. He sat on the New Orleans school board, which began operating the city's public education system on a racially integrated basis. Meanwhile, the legislature enacted a pioneering civil rights law, barring racial discrimination by transport companies and in some public accommodations. Louisiana Republicans split over this measure, with many white leaders—including Governor Warmoth, who vetoed it—opposing it as too radical, while Black officials embraced it. Realizing that Black voters constituted, to use a modern term, the Republican Party's "base," Longstreet aligned himself with the state's activist Black leaders, including P. B. S. Pinchback, who served briefly as the country's first Black governor after Warmoth was impeached. Uniquely among prominent ex-Confederates, Longstreet frequently spoke out in favor of Black voting rights, further eroding his reputation among white Democrats. Being condemned as a Judas only bolstered his support for Reconstruction.

Violence was endemic in Reconstruction Louisiana, and Longstreet played a major role in trying to suppress it. Terrorist groups such as the White League and the Knights of the White Camellia flourished. In 1874, after a series of disputed elections in Louisiana, the White League launched an armed assault on the state's Reconstruction government. In charge of defending New Orleans, Longstreet took part in the fighting. But the militia and police were overwhelmed, and only the intervention of federal soldiers restored order. The event exposed a reality that recent scholars such as Gregory Downs have strongly emphasized: The presence of Union troops was essential to Reconstruction's survival. In 1891, anti-Reconstruction Democrats erected a stone obelisk paying tribute to what they called the Battle of Liberty Place. The accompanying text, added in 1932, celebrated the insurrection as an attempt to restore "white supremacy." The memorial was removed in 2017, two years after then-Mayor Mitch Landrieu had approved a city council resolution to do so.

By 1875, the persistent violence had convinced Longstreet that Reconstruction should proceed more slowly and try not to "exasperate the Southern people"—by whom he meant white people. Meanwhile, in response to what Varon calls a giant "misinformation campaign" by southern newspapers and Democratic politicians that depicted the South as mired in government corruption, northern support was on the wane, an ominous sign for the future of Reconstruction. Longstreet essentially abandoned participation in Louisiana politics and moved his family to Georgia, where he soon became a leader of that state's Republican Party.

With Reconstruction ending, southern Republicans searched for ways to stabilize their party and maintain a presence in local government. In Georgia, Longstreet pursued a strategy different from the course he had embraced in New Orleans. Instead of cultivating alliances with Black leaders, he now worked more closely with white Republicans, many of them scalawags, who urged northern Republicans to help "southernize" the party by boosting the power of its white members and limiting that of Black politicians. The "colored man," Longstreet wrote to Thomas P. Ochiltree, a politician from Texas, had been "put in the hands of strangers who have not understood him or his characteristics." By "strangers," he was alluding to carpetbaggers (another of those tainted terms), northerners who took part in Reconstruction in the South and were derided by Democrats as merely seeking the spoils of office. Varon calls this letter "a blatantly racist piece of paternalist pandering." Despite Longstreet's efforts to reduce the political power of Black Republicans, white Democrats accused him of trying to "Africanize the South." He remained popular, however, with Black Americans after Reconstruction ended, even winning praise from Frederick Douglass for his continued endorsement of Black suffrage and his condemnation of lynching. Longstreet also spent much of his time setting the record straight, as he saw it, regarding his wartime accomplishments. In 1896, he published a 690-page memoir, roundly denounced by adherents of the Lost Cause.

Varon offers a mixed verdict on Longstreet's career. He could be arrogant and opportunistic, eager to bolster his own reputation. He benefitted personally from the numerous positions to which he was appointed (in particular the patronage posts he enjoyed after the end of Reconstruction, including ambassador to the Ottoman empire and federal marshal for northern Georgia). But he also demonstrated remarkable courage, refusing to abandon the Republican Party, as many scalawags eventually did, or to change his mind about Black citizens' political and civil rights.

Longstreet seems to have thought of himself, Varon writes, as "a herald of reunion." And yet, she notes, his life exemplified the "elusiveness" of various kinds of postwar reconciliation—between white northerners and white southerners, between white and Black Americans, between upholders of the Lost Cause and advocates of a "New South." His willingness to work closely with Black Americans, speak out in favor of their rights, and even lead them into battle in the streets of New Orleans overshadowed his military contributions to the Confederacy in the eyes of most white southerners. As a letter to a Georgia newspaper declared, when "it became a question of [the] Negro or white man," Longstreet chose the former and could never be forgiven. No statues of Longstreet graced the southern landscape.

Varon closes with a brief look at memorialization, focusing on the efforts of Longstreet's second wife in the 1930s and '40s to raise money to erect a statue at Gettysburg. A formidable woman forty-two years his junior, Helen Longstreet at age 80 worked as a riveter in a factory building bombers during World War II. The service of Black soldiers in the fight against Nazism inspired her to defend Black voting rights, a stance much praised by the African American press. She died in 1962 at the age of 99. One wonders what she would have thought of the statue itself and the descendants of Confederate veterans who finally installed her husband on horseback at Gettysburg yet felt obliged as late as 1998 to dissociate themselves from his efforts to secure the equal rights of all Americans.

Longstreet believed that peaceful and just reunion would only be possible when the white South moved beyond the myth of the Lost Cause. The end of his erasure from historical memory highlights what a long and complicated evolution that has proved to be. Perhaps his restoration is also a sign that the time has come to shift attention from taking down old monuments to putting up new ones, including some to the Black and white leaders of Reconstruction, who braved white-supremacist violence in an effort to bring into being the "new birth of freedom" that Abraham Lincoln envisioned at Gettysburg.

THE WAR WITHIN THE
CONFEDERACY

T HE BICENTENNIAL OF Abraham Lincoln's birth has come
and gone, and with it a flood of books about the sixteenth president. But the sesquicentennial of the Civil War now looms
on the horizon, promising its own deluge of books of every size, shape,
and description. We will be fortunate indeed if in sheer originality
and insight they measure up to *Confederate Reckoning* and *The Long
Shadow of the Civil War*, new works by Stephanie McCurry and Victoria Bynum, respectively, on the Confederate experience.

Most scholarly history on the Confederacy has been shaped, implicitly or explicitly, by a desire to explain southern defeat. Devotees of the
Lost Cause insist that gallant southern soldiers inevitably succumbed
to the Union's overwhelming advantages in manpower and economic
resources. The stronger side, however, does not always win a war, as the
United States learned in Vietnam. This fact has led historians to try to
locate internal causes for the failure of the quest for southern indepen-

———

Reviews of *The Long Shadow of the Civil War: Southern Dissent and Its
Legacies*, by Victoria E. Bynum, and *Confederate Reckoning: Power and
Politics in the Civil War South*, by Stephanie McCurry, *The Nation*,
August 4, 2010.

dence. They have identified such culprits as poor political leadership, excessive individualism, desertion from the army by non-slaveholding soldiers, waning enthusiasm for the war among upper-class white women, and disaffection among the slaves.

McCurry and Bynum are less interested in why the South lost—although their books shed light on this question—than in the social and political consequences of how it conducted the war. Taken together, they show how the effort to create a slaveholders' republic sundered southern society and changed the contours of southern politics. The subtitle of McCurry's book—"Power and Politics in the Civil War South"—is surely meant to be ironic. Most readers will no doubt expect another study of Jefferson Davis's administration or the battle between advocates of states' rights and central control. But McCurry challenges us to expand our definition of politics to encompass not simply government but the entire public sphere. The struggle for southern independence, she shows, opened the door for the mobilization of two groups previously outside the political nation—white women of the non-slaveholding class and slaves.

McCurry begins by stating what should be obvious but is frequently denied, that the Confederacy was something decidedly odd in the nineteenth century: "an independent proslavery nation." The Confederate and state constitutions made clear that protecting slavery was their raison d'être. Abandoning euphemisms like "other persons" by which the U.S. Constitution referred to slaves without directly acknowledging their existence, Confederates forthrightly named the institution, erected protections around it, and explicitly limited citizenship to white persons. McCurry implicitly pokes holes in other explanations for southern secession, such as opposition to Republican economic policies like the tariff or fear for the future of personal freedom under a Lincoln administration. Georgia, she notes, passed a law in 1861 that made continuing loyalty to the Union a capital offense, hardly the action of a government concerned about individual liberty or the rights of minorities.

The Confederacy, McCurry writes, was conceived as a "republic of white men." But since more than three million of its nine million people were slaves and half of the remainder disenfranchised white women, the new nation faced from the outset a "crisis of legitimacy." However much the law defined white women as appendages of their husbands, entitled to protection but not a public voice, and slaves simply as property, southern leaders realized early that they would have to compete with the Union for the loyalty of these groups, treating them, in effect, as independent actors. The need to generate consent allowed "the Confederate unenfranchised" to step onto the stage of politics, with their own demands, grievances, and actions.

McCurry's chapters delineating the political emergence of poor white women constitute the most dramatic and original parts of *Confederate Reckoning*. She makes clear that introducing gender as a category of analysis changes the definition of politics and power, but simultaneously warns against considering "woman" a unitary identity independent of class. All Confederate women struggled to cope as their loved ones were drawn off into the army, many never to return. Women of all classes called upon the state for assistance during the war. But when wealthy women made demands on the Confederate government, they did so as members of a national elite.

Poorer women forged a different political identity. They spoke the language not of southern nationalism or upper-class identity but of family and community. They described themselves as soldiers' wives and invoked what McCurry calls a "politics of subsistence." Lacking the aid of slave labor, they found that the absence of their husbands from their previously self-sufficient farms made it impossible to feed themselves and their children. As the war progressed and the economic situation deteriorated, they flooded Confederate authorities with petitions seeking assistance, not as charity but as a right. In demanding aid from local, state, and national governments, these women articulated a new vision of themselves as citizens with legitimate claims upon the state. Eventually, poor women took to the streets in food riots in major Confederate cities, the most dramatic example of their emergence as a political force.

The policies of the Confederate government and the actions of slave-owning planters exacerbated these women's sense of grievance. The

Confederate Congress enacted the "twenty-Negro" exemption, allowing one adult man to remain at home for every twenty slaves on a plantation in order to forestall slave resistance. Policies like impressment
and the tax-in-kind, which allowed the army to appropriate farm goods,
were applied much more rigorously against poorer southerners than
wealthy ones. Planters showed little interest in assisting their suffering
neighbors and resisted calls by Confederate authorities to grow edible
crops instead of cotton. "The rich people about here there hearts are of
steel," one Virginia woman wrote to Jefferson Davis. Indeed, planters'
unwillingness to sacrifice self-interest for the common good is a recurring theme of *Confederate Reckoning*. Having created a nation based on
slavery, they proved reluctant to provide Blacks for military labor, fearing this would interfere with their hold on their slave property. "You
cheerfully yield your children to your country," one anti-planter broad-
side asked, "how you refuse your servants?"

Later generations would create the myth of the ardently patriotic southern woman. Contemporaries knew better. The agitation of poor women,
McCurry shows, alarmed southern officials and directly affected Confederate policy. Politicians could not ignore the pleas of soldiers' wives.
Congress moved to exempt poor families from taxation. Governors like
Zebulon Vance of North Carolina and Joseph Brown of Georgia distributed supplies to needy families. By the end of the war, McCurry writes,
the Confederacy had created a significant "welfare system." Georgia
spent more money on relief in one year than Massachusetts (a state with
a significant poor population) did during the entire war.

In the second half of *Confederate Reckoning*, McCurry turns to the
actions of slaves during the war. Here she covers more familiar ground
but still manages to offer striking new insights. It is now widely recognized that the actions of slaves who ran away to Union lines helped to
put the slavery issue on the agenda of the Lincoln administration, and
that by serving in the Union army Black soldiers staked a claim to citizenship in the post-bellum world. Most slaves, however, lived out the
war behind Confederate lines. The government they had to deal with,
McCurry points out, was Davis's, not Lincoln's.

From the outset, McCurry shows, slaves carefully followed national politics and the course of the war. Even before Lincoln's election, the planter Charles Manigault noted, his slaves had "very generally got the idea of being emancipated when 'Lincon' comes in." Once the war began, slaves took every opportunity to aid Union forces and resist the demands of their owners. McCurry describes Manigault's plantations as being "in a state of barely suppressed insurrection." How to characterize slaves' actions has long posed a challenge for historians. W. E. B. Du Bois wrote of a "general strike" in the Confederacy. McCurry goes even further, using the phrase "a massive slave rebellion." This seems an exaggeration. But she is on firm ground when she insists that a battle ensued between North and South for slaves' "political allegiance."

Like the actions of white women, those of slaves strongly affected public policy, in ways that weakened southern unity and wartime mobilization. Unrest on the plantations led to the "twenty-Negro" exemption, which, in turn, heightened discontent among non-slaveholding farm families. Slaves' propensity to escape when near Union lines explains why planters resisted their use as military laborers, weakening the war effort. Planter resistance to the army's impressment of slave labor drew support from state governments that tried to undermine the policies of the Davis administration. The well-known battles over states' rights in the Confederacy, McCurry convincingly argues, were really arguments over whether the needs of the national government should take precedence over the property rights of slaveholders.

The struggle over slave impressment offered a prelude to the well-known debate of 1864–65 over the enrollment of slaves in the Confederate army. In the Emancipation Proclamation Lincoln had authorized Black enlistment, and by war's end some 200,000 Black men had served in the Union army and navy. As the Confederacy's situation worsened, military leaders including Robert E. Lee called for enrolling Blacks. Lee went so far as to propose coupling enlistment with a plan for "gradual and general emancipation." This was far more than the Confederate Congress could stomach. In March 1865, it finally authorized slave enlistment, in a law that made no mention of freedom. In his implementation order, however, Jefferson Davis promised freedom to those who agreed to serve. In other words, Davis acknowledged that slaves were able to make independent decisions and that their loyalty had to be won, not simply commanded.

McCurry correctly points out that enlisting Blacks in the Confederate army and offering them freedom did not necessarily mean the end of slavery. Both the British and the Americans had used slave soldiers in the War of Independence, yet slavery survived. It did so as well in the West Indies, where the British raised and freed slave regiments. Had the Confederacy emerged victorious, slavery would certainly have continued. In any event, a few days before the war ended, two companies of Confederate Black soldiers from Richmond were sent to the front. Most of these men had already been impressed to work in a Confederate hospital; whether they were truly volunteers may be doubted. Certainly, as McCurry makes clear, the idea that legions of slaves fought for the slaveholders' republic—a notion propagated by neo-Confederate organizations and widely disseminated on the Internet—is a myth.

Confederate Reckoning offers a powerful new paradigm for understanding events on the Confederate home front. Unfortunately, the book's structure to some extent stands at cross-purposes with its argument. Its two parts are not really integrated. White women pretty much disappear from the second half of the narrative, and there is little attention to how the political mobilization of slaves and white women of the non-slaveholding class, so expertly delineated, intersected. Moreover, a full account of how the war politicized previously marginalized groups and heightened tensions within southern society would require attention to a group neglected in this study—disaffected white men from the non-slaveholding class.

McCurry explains her decision not to write about these white men by pointing out that, thanks to studies of desertion from the Confederate army, we already "know a great deal" about them. But as Victoria Bynum notes in *The Long Shadow of the Civil War*, the "communities of dissent" that emerged in the Civil War South involved both men and women. Bynum studies three areas of disaffection within the Confederacy: the "Quaker belt" of central North Carolina; Jones County in southern Mississippi's Piney Woods; and the Big Thicket of East Texas. These localities lay outside the main plantation region and were populated mostly by non-slaveholding families. The three regions shared more than a similar demography. Many of the Mississippi Unionists had relatives in North Carolina, and some of the Texas guerrillas had emigrated from Jones County.

Bynum's subjects "hated the Confederacy" and in some cases took up arms against it. In these areas, bands of deserters plagued the Confederate war effort, and an internal civil war took place that pitted neighbor against neighbor. Unionist activity rested on extended family networks. The wives of deserters and draft dodgers acted not as Confederate soldiers' wives but as anti-Confederate cadres. They threatened public officials; stole from wealthier neighbors; and provided shelter, food, and information to male relatives hiding out in the woods.

Bynum, whose well-regarded book on Jones County, *The Free State of Jones: Mississippi's Longest Civil War*, dispelled the idea that it actually "seceded" from the Confederacy, clearly sympathizes with her subjects. Some of her ancestors, she writes, were among these lower-class Unionists. But she avoids over-romanticization. Bill Owens, the leading Unionist guerrilla in North Carolina, she notes, was a cold-blooded killer. But heinous acts were not limited to one side. Confederate soldiers tortured Owens's wife to gain information about his whereabouts. Local militia units mistreated Unionist women and children. Owens himself, after his capture toward the end of the war, was taken from his jail cell by unknown parties and murdered.

Bynum's book is not so much a narrative history as a series of discrete, overlapping, and somewhat disjointed case studies. But it adds a dimension to McCurry's far broader study by taking the story beyond the end of the Civil War to trace the long-term legacy of pro-Union activism. One chapter shows how family traditions of dissent survived in new forms as veterans of the "inner Civil War" and their descendants joined the biracial Republican Party during Reconstruction, and emerged as leaders of Populism in the 1890s and the Socialist Party of

Eugene Debs. The legacy of violent white supremacy also survived. The wartime Confederate militia was succeeded by the Ku Klux Klan after the war and "whitecappers" around the turn of the century.

Bynum invokes court cases to track the shifting political fortunes of the postwar South. In one North Carolina county, the members of an extended family challenged the right of a female relative to inherit land on the grounds that she had African ancestry. In 1892 a court ruled against the woman, and she lost the farm she and her late husband had tilled for two decades. Honor, supposedly a central characteristic of white southern culture, seems to have been in short supply after the Civil War.

One of the more fascinating figures Bynum discusses is Newt Knight, the leader of an armed band of Unionists in Jones County, who lived with a Black woman and became "the patriarch of an extensive mixed-race community." Bynum relates his long, unsuccessful campaign for monetary compensation from the federal government for his wartime activities. She also explores the fate of his mixed-race children and grandchildren. Some identified as people of color; some disappeared into white society. One descendant, David Knight, served in the army during World War II, married a white woman in 1946, and two years later was convicted in Mississippi of the crime of miscegenation. The Confederacy certainly cast a long shadow.

WHY RECONSTRUCTION
MATTERS

T
HE SURRENDER OF Confederate Gen. Robert E. Lee at
Appomattox Court House in April 1865 effectively ended
the Civil War. Preoccupied with the challenges of our own
time, Americans have devoted little attention to the sesquicentennial
of Reconstruction, the turbulent era that followed the conflict. This is
unfortunate, for if any historical period deserves the label "relevant," it
is Reconstruction. Issues that agitate American politics today—access
to citizenship and voting rights, the relative powers of the national and
state governments, the relationship between political and economic
democracy, the proper response to terrorism—all these are Reconstruction questions. But that era has long been misunderstood.

Reconstruction refers to the period, generally dated from 1865 to
1877, during which the nation's laws and Constitution were rewritten to guarantee the basic rights of the former slaves, and biracial governments came to power throughout the defeated Confederacy. For
decades, these years were widely seen as the nadir in the saga of American democracy. According to this view, Radical Republicans in Congress, bent on punishing defeated Confederates, established corrupt

---

New York Times, March 28, 2015.

southern governments presided over by carpetbaggers (unscrupulous northerners who ventured south to reap the spoils of office), scalawags (southern whites who supported the new regimes) and freed African Americans, unfit to exercise democratic rights. The heroes of the story were the self-styled Redeemers, who restored white supremacy to the South.

This portrait, which received scholarly expression in the early twentieth-century works of William A. Dunning and his students at Columbia University, was popularized by the 1915 film *The Birth of a Nation* and by Claude Bowers's 1929 best-selling history, *The Tragic Era*. It provided an intellectual foundation for the system of segregation and Black disenfranchisement that followed Reconstruction. Any effort to restore the rights of southern Blacks, it implied, would lead to a repeat of the alleged horrors of Reconstruction.

Historians have long since rejected this lurid account, although it retains a stubborn hold on the popular imagination. Today, scholars believe that if the era was "tragic," it was not because Reconstruction was attempted but because it failed.

Reconstruction actually began in December 1863, when Abraham Lincoln announced a plan to establish governments in the South loyal to the Union. Lincoln granted amnesty to most Confederates so long as they accepted the abolition of slavery, but said nothing about rights for freed Blacks. Rather than a blueprint for the postwar South, this was a war measure, an effort to detach whites from the Confederacy. On Reconstruction, as on other questions, Lincoln's ideas evolved. At the end of his life, he called for limited Black suffrage in the postwar South, singling out the "very intelligent" (pre-war free Blacks) and "those who serve our cause as soldiers" as most worthy.

Lincoln did not live to preside over Reconstruction. That task fell to his successor, Andrew Johnson. Once lionized as a heroic defender of the Constitution against Radical Republicans, Johnson today is viewed by historians as one of the worst presidents to occupy the White House. He was incorrigibly racist, unwilling to listen to criticism, and unable to work with Congress. Johnson set up new southern governments controlled by ex-Confederates. They quickly enacted the Black Codes, laws that severely limited the freed people's rights and sought, through vagrancy regulations, to force them back to work on the plantations. But these measures aroused bitter protests among Blacks and convinced northerners that the white South was trying to restore slavery in all but name.

There followed a momentous political clash, the struggle between Johnson and the Republican majority (not just the Radicals) in Congress. Over Johnson's veto, Congress enacted one of the most important laws in American history, the Civil Rights Act of 1866, still on the books today. It affirmed the citizenship of everyone born in the United States, regardless of race (except Native Americans, still considered members of tribal sovereignties). This principle, birthright citizenship, is increasingly rare in today's world and deeply contested in our own contemporary politics, because it applies to the American-born children of undocumented immigrants.

The act went on to mandate that all citizens enjoy basic civil rights in the same manner as "enjoyed by white persons." Johnson's veto message denounced the law for what today is called reverse discrimination: "The distinction of race and color is by the bill made to operate in favor of the colored and against the white race." Indeed, in the idea that expanding the rights of non-whites somehow punishes the white majority, we still hear the voice of Andrew Johnson in our discussions of race.

Soon afterwards, Congress incorporated birthright citizenship and legal equality into the Constitution via the Fourteenth Amendment. In recent decades, the courts have used this amendment to expand the legal rights of numerous groups—most recently, gay men and lesbians who wish to marry. As the Republican editor George William Curtis wrote, the Fourteenth Amendment changed a constitution "for white men" to one "for mankind." It also marked a significant change in the federal balance of power, empowering the national government to protect the rights of citizens against violations by the states.

In 1867 Congress passed the Reconstruction Acts, again over Johnson's veto. These set in motion the establishment of new governments in the South, empowered southern Black men to vote, and temporarily disenfranchised several thousand leading Confederates. In 1870, the Fifteenth Amendment extended Black male suffrage to the entire nation.

The Reconstruction Acts inaugurated the period of Radical Reconstruction, when a politically mobilized Black community, with its white allies, brought the Republican Party to power throughout the South. For the first time anywhere in the United States, African Americans voted in large numbers and held public office at every level of government. It was a remarkable, unprecedented effort to build an interracial democracy on the ashes of slavery.

Most offices remained in the hands of white Republicans. But the advent of African Americans in positions of political power aroused bitter hostility from Reconstruction's opponents. They spread another myth—that the new officials were propertyless, illiterate, and incompetent. As late as 1947, the southern historian E. Merton Coulter wrote that of the various aspects of Reconstruction, Black office holding was "longest to be remembered, shuddered at, and execrated."

There was corruption in the postwar South, although given the scandals of New York's Tweed Ring and President Ulysses S. Grant's administration, Black suffrage could hardly be singled out for blame. In fact, the new governments had a solid record of accomplishment. They established the South's first state-funded public school systems, sought to strengthen the bargaining power of plantation laborers, made taxation more equitable, and outlawed racial discrimination in transportation and public accommodations. They offered financial aid to railroads and other enterprises in the hope of creating a New South whose economic expansion would benefit Black and white alike.

Reconstruction also made possible the consolidation of Black families, so often divided by sale during slavery, and the establishment of the independent Black church as the core institution of the emerging Black community. But the failure to respond to the former slaves' desire for land left most with no choice but to work for their former owners.

It was not economic dependency, however, but widespread violence, coupled with a northern retreat from the ideal of equality, that doomed

Reconstruction. The Ku Klux Klan and kindred groups began a campaign of murder, assault, and arson that can only be described as American terrorism. Meanwhile, as the northern Republican Party became more conservative, Reconstruction came to be seen as a misguided attempt to uplift the lower classes of society. One by one, the Reconstruction governments fell. As a result of a bargain after the disputed election of 1876, Republican Rutherford B. Hayes assumed the presidency and disavowed further national efforts to enforce the rights of Black citizens, while white Democrats controlled the South.

By the turn of the century, with the acquiescence of the Supreme Court, a comprehensive system of racial, political, and economic inequality, known by the label Jim Crow, had come into being across the South. At the same time, the supposed horrors of Reconstruction were invoked as far away as South Africa and Australia to demonstrate the necessity of excluding non-white peoples from political rights. This is why W. E. B. Du Bois, in his classic 1935 work *Black Reconstruction in America*, saw the end of Reconstruction as a tragedy for democracy, not just in the United States but around the globe.

While violated with impunity, however, the Fourteenth and Fifteenth Amendments remained on the books. Decades later they would provide the legal basis for the civil rights revolution, sometimes called the Second Reconstruction.

Citizenship, rights, democracy—as long as these remain contested there will be need for an accurate understanding of Reconstruction. More than most historical subjects, how we think about this era truly matters, for it forces us to think about what kind of society we wish America to be.

DONALD TRUMP'S UNCONSTITUTIONAL DREAMS

I N AN INTERVIEW with the news program *Axios* on HBO, Donald Trump announced that he plans to issue an executive order ending birthright citizenship, the principle that everyone born in the United States, with a handful of exceptions, is automatically a citizen. "It was always told to me," the president declared, "that you needed a constitutional amendment. Guess what? You don't." In fact, such an order would undoubtedly be unconstitutional. It would also violate an essential American ideal—that anybody, regardless of race, religion, national origin, or the legal status of one's parents, can be a loyal citizen of this country.

Birthright citizenship is established by the Civil Rights Act of 1866, still on the books today, and by the Fourteenth Amendment to the Constitution, ratified two years later. The only exceptions, in the words of the amendment, are persons not "subject to the jurisdiction" of the United States. Members of Congress at the time made clear that this wording applied only to Native Americans living on reservations—then considered members of their own tribal sovereignties, not the United States—and American-born children of foreign diplomats. (Congress

---

New York Times, October 31, 2018.

made all Native Americans citizens in 1924.) Embedding birthright citizenship in the Constitution was one of the transformative results of the Civil War and Reconstruction.

Before the war, no uniform definition of citizenship existed. Soon after the conflict ended, members of Congress asked Horace Binney, a prominent lawyer and a former congressman, to explore the meaning of citizenship. "The word citizen," he responded, "is found ten times at least in the Constitution of the United States, and no definition of it is given anywhere." States determined who was a citizen and the rules varied considerably. Massachusetts recognized free African Americans as citizens; most other states did not. For persons immigrating from abroad, moreover, racial distinctions were built into federal law. The first Naturalization Act, in 1790, limited the process of naturalization to "white persons." In 1857, on the eve of the Civil War, the Supreme Court, in the Dred Scott decision, declared that no Black person, slave or free, could be a citizen of the United States or part of the national "political community." Echoes of this outlook persist to this day, including in Trump's long campaign to deny the birthright citizenship status of Barack Obama.

Long before the Civil War, abolitionists Black and white had proposed an alternative understanding of national citizenship severed from the concept of race, with citizens' rights enforced by the federal government. Gatherings where northern free Blacks agitated for equal rights called themselves conventions of "colored citizens" to drive home this idea. And by the conclusion of the war, the end of slavery and the service of nearly 200,000 African Americans in the Union army and navy propelled the question of Black citizenship to center stage of American politics.

The Fourteenth Amendment was meant to provide, for the first time, a uniform national definition of citizenship, so that states would no longer be able to deny that status to Blacks. It went on to require the states to accord all "persons," including aliens, the equal protection of the laws, as part of an effort to create a new, post-abolition egalitarian republic. The birthright citizenship provision, explained Senator Jacob

Howard of Michigan, one of the founders of the Republican Party and the floor manager of the amendment's passage in the Senate, was intended to "settle the great question of citizenship once and for all." The amendment formed part of a constitutional revolution. In 1870, Congress amended the naturalization laws to allow Black immigrants to become citizens. The bar to Asians, however, persisted; they could not be naturalized until well into the twentieth century.

Trump's prospective order would deny citizenship to children born in the United States to non-citizen parents. It is especially aimed at undocumented immigrants who supposedly pour into the country to have "anchor babies"—one of the president's numerous exaggerations when it comes to the dangers posed by immigration. When the Fourteenth Amendment was ratified, the category of illegal or undocumented immigrants did not exist. The closest analogy to children born today to such immigrants were the American-born offspring of newcomers from China. Their parents could not become citizens, but in 1898, following the plain language of the Fourteenth Amendment, the Supreme Court affirmed that a person of Chinese origin born in the United States was a citizen by birthright.

In the interview in which he discussed his plan to issue the executive order, Trump claimed that the United States is "the only country in the world where a person comes in and has a baby, and the baby is essentially a citizen of the United States." This, too, is an exaggeration, as many countries in the Western Hemisphere do recognize birthright citizenship. But it is true that in the past decade or two the nations of Europe have retreated from this principle. All limit automatic access to citizenship in some way, making it depend not simply on place of birth but also on ethnicity, culture, religion, or extra requirements for the children of parents who are not citizens. That has not been our way. Adopted as part of the effort to purge the United States of the legacy of slavery, the principle of birthright citizenship remains an eloquent statement about the nature of American society, a powerful force for assimilation of the children of immigrants, and a repudiation of our long history of racism.

President Trump's order, if issued, will not only violate the Constitution and repudiate ideals deeply rooted since Reconstruction, but will also set a dangerous precedent. If the president can unilaterally abrogate a provision of the Constitution by executive order, which one will be next?

WE SHOULD EMBRACE THE AMBIGUITY OF THE FOURTEENTH AMENDMENT

O N JULY 9, 1868, Louisiana and South Carolina approved the Fourteenth Amendment, bringing the number of ratifications to three-quarters of the states and making it part of the Constitution. Today, when the future of the Supreme Court and the fate of many American freedoms hang in the balance, it is worth recalling the amendment's complex, contradictory history.

On the one hand, the amendment fundamentally changed the Constitution. It declared nearly everyone born in the country an American citizen, and went on to bar the states from denying them the "privileges or immunities" of citizenship, or depriving any person (including aliens) of life, liberty, or property without due process of law, or of the equal protection of the laws. While its immediate focus was guaranteeing the essential rights of the four million emancipated slaves, its language is universal. As a result, it made it possible for all sorts of movements for equality to be articulated in constitutional terms. The Fourteenth Amendment led numerous Americans to view the federal government as the protector of their rights and to expand the definition of those rights far beyond anything known before the Civil War. In our own

The Nation, July 9, 2018.

time, the amendment's guarantees of liberty and equality have under-pinned Supreme Court decisions establishing the "one man, one vote" rule, overturning state laws denying the right to utilize contraception, and discriminating in marriage on the basis of sexual orientation.

But there is a profound irony at the heart of the Fourteenth Amend-ment's history. When it comes to the status of Black Americans, its promise has never been fulfilled. Beginning during Reconstruction itself, only a few years after ratification, the Supreme Court severely restricted the amendment's scope as a weapon for racial equality. It defined almost out of existence the "privileges or immunities" aris-ing from American citizenship. It made a fetish of the idea of "state action," insisting that the amendment barred racially discriminatory measures by state governments and officials, but not by private individ-uals, as a result making it all but impossible for the federal government to prosecute racially motivated violence or racial discrimination in transportation and public accommodations. In 1896, the Court ruled that state laws requiring racial segregation did not violate the equal protection of the laws. The Court also refused to enforce the Fifteenth Amendment, which sought to guarantee the right of Black men to vote throughout the nation. The Justices did nothing when southern states disenfranchised them.

Of course, the Warren Court of the 1950s and 1960s gave consti-tutional sanction to the civil rights revolution. But with the excep-tion of overturning *Plessy v. Ferguson* (the decision upholding racial segregation), it did not directly confront the long train of decisions that restricted the Fourteenth Amendment's reach regarding African Americans. Instead, the Court opted to work around existing juris-prudence. For example, in affirming the constitutionality of the Civil Rights Act of 1964, which barred discrimination by private busi-nesses, the Justices relied not on the Fourteenth Amendment's guar-antee of equal rights but on the Constitution's clause empowering Congress to regulate interstate commerce. The elevation of the com-merce clause into a pillar of human rights in this and other decisions made the judiciary look ridiculous. Everyone knows that guaranteeing the free flow of goods was not the motivation of those who took to the streets in the 1960s to demand passage of the Civil Rights Act, or of the members of Congress who voted for it. The Justices could not bring themselves to say that for eighty years the Court had simply been wrong. Lately, the Court has proved more sympathetic to white and Asian American plaintiffs complaining of "reverse discrimination" because of affirmative action policies than to Blacks seeking assistance in overcoming the legacies of slavery and Jim Crow. The majority seems to feel that "racial classifications," not racism, pose the greatest danger to equality.

But there is another way of reading the Fourteenth Amendment, one pioneered by the former slaves and their allies during and after Reconstruction and articulated in legal terms by the country's first generation of Black lawyers, who challenged the emerging jurisprudence of the late nineteenth century. It is too often forgotten that in 1867 and 1868, the all-white southern governments created by President Andrew Johnson, with the exception of Tennessee, rejected the Fourteenth Amendment, making ratification impossible. Congress responded by requiring the creation of new state governments, chosen through elections in which Black men voted in large numbers, leading to many hundreds holding public office. These new biracial governments ratified the amendment. In other words, no Black suffrage in the South, no Fourteenth Amendment. Yet when the Court has sought to construe the amendment's purposes and meaning, the Black voice is almost never heard.

The counter-interpretation developed by Black lawyers and their allies remains available today. Certainly it is as plausible, if not more so, than existing jurisprudence. There is no reason, for example, why the "privileges or immunities" of citizens must remain a dead letter, why they cannot be understood to encompass rights not only denied by slavery but essential to full membership in American society, such as access to an adequate education and protection against economic discrimination. There is no reason why what the Court dismissively refers to as "societal racism" cannot be taken into account in assessing affirmative action and school integration programs, or why the "state action" doctrine must hamstring national efforts to protect the rights of Americans against violation by private parties.

The language of the Fourteenth Amendment—equal protection, due process, privileges or immunities—is imprecise. It cries out for future interpretation. This "indefiniteness of meaning" was a "charm" to John A. Bingham, the Ohio congressman most responsible for the amendment's wording. To be sure, this ambiguity also opened the door to the cramped reading that still hangs over the jurisprudence of race. But rather than lamenting ambiguity, we should, in the spirit of Bingham, embrace it. Ambiguity creates possibilities. Ambiguity paves the way for future struggles.

By themselves, constitutional amendments cannot address all the legacies of slavery. Charles Sumner, the abolitionist senator from Massachusetts, remarked that rewriting the Constitution was not an end in itself but "an incident in the larger struggle for freedom and equality." With conservatives having fastened their grip on the Court, it would be foolhardy to expect the latent power of the Fourteenth Amendment to be invoked any time soon. But one day, in a different political climate, this "sleeping giant" (to borrow a phrase from Sumner) may yet be awakened, and its power employed to implement in new ways the Reconstruction vision of equal citizenship for all.

BOSTON'S BLACK
ACTIVISTS

THE 150TH ANNIVERSARY of the Emancipation Proclamation, issued on January 1, 1863, is fast approaching. Yet amid what will undoubtedly be an atmosphere of celebration, those professional killjoys known as historians are striking a more somber note. Where once the abolition of slavery was seen as the great watershed of African American life—a point of view epitomized in the title of John Hope Franklin's highly influential Black history textbook, *From Slavery to Freedom*—historians of late have taken to emphasizing the failure, or at least inadequacy, of the freedom brought about by the Civil War. Current scholars tend to stress continuity as much as change over the course of the nineteenth century. Racism and Black subordination persisted despite emancipation. Reconstruction, when an alternative outcome seemed possible, failed. A few months ago, Yale's Gilder-Lehrman Center for the Study of Slavery entitled a conference on new directions in the study of emancipation "Beyond Freedom."

Historians of the years following slavery have always spoken directly

——

Review of *More Than Freedom: Fighting for Black Citizenship in a White Republic, 1829–1889*, by Stephen Kantrowitz, *The Nation*, July 30, 2012.

to modern-day concerns. The Dunning school, with its emphasis on the alleged horrors of postwar Reconstruction (corruption, misgovernment, and "Black supremacy") provided scholarly legitimacy for Jim Crow and the disenfranchisement of southern Black voters. The revisionist school, which saw Reconstruction as a noble experiment in interracial democracy, arose in tandem with the civil rights movement. Today's more gloomy view of emancipation and its aftermath reflects, in part, a sense that the modern civil rights revolution failed to address adequately the economic plight of most Black Americans. The Freedom Movement may have succeeded on the legal front, but as the title of a recent work by Nancy MacLean about modern-day economic inequality puts it, *Freedom Is Not Enough*.

Stephen Kantrowitz's new book places him firmly in the camp of historians who conclude that freedom, when it came, was not enough to undo the centuries-long legacy of slavery. Kantrowitz is the author of a prize-winning study of "Pitchfork" Ben Tillman, who took part in the violent overthrow of Reconstruction in South Carolina and later rose to the governorship on the strength of lurid warnings that Black demands for equality posed a threat to the purity of white womanhood. In *More Than Freedom*, Kantrowitz turns his attention to the North, chronicling the struggles of Boston's Black activists over the course of the nineteenth century. The key figures in his book are hardly household names, even among historians—men like the former slave turned underground railroad activist Lewis Hayden; William C. Nell, whose book, *The Colored Patriots of the American Revolution*, laid claim for Blacks to the revolutionary heritage; and John S. Rock, who became the first Black attorney admitted to the bar of the Supreme Court and wrote articles ridiculing contemporary theories of racial hierarchy and inborn racial difference. Kantrowitz has done a remarkable job of bringing them to life and situating them in social context. Boston's Black community represented only 2 percent of the city's population. Most of its members lacked education and were confined to menial, low-wage employment. In this world the activists constituted an elite. But, as Kantrowitz makes clear, they themselves often lived on the edge of poverty. Nell remained in debt throughout the 1850s and resided in a boarding house. Hayden's clothing store failed, and he was only able to make ends meet when hired as a messenger by the secretary of state of Massachusetts. Thus, Kantrowitz insists, these leaders understood the experiences of ordinary Black Bostonians and can plausibly be taken as spokesmen for them.

Kantrowitz argues convincingly that the familiar story of sectional crisis, Civil War, and emancipation takes on a different cast when viewed from the perspective of these Black activists. The slavery controversy unleashed a complex, far-reaching debate about the role that racial difference should play in defining such core American values as freedom, equality, and citizenship. Boston's Black leaders inserted themselves into this debate, using every means at their disposal—petitions, speeches, pamphlets, lawsuits, and direct action—in pursuit of their goals. In so doing they directly challenged the prevailing assumption that "public life was for whites only." Kantrowitz insists, moreover, that the familiar label "Black abolitionists" is a misnomer, since their goals extended well beyond ending slavery.

Unlike most books on the era, *More Than Freedom* does not begin or end with the Civil War. Tracing these activists' careers over six decades allows Kantrowitz to drive home the point that their struggle did not end with emancipation. As the book's subtitle indicates, their aim was not simply freedom but full and equal citizenship for Black Americans. To be sure, citizenship itself was a contested concept in these years. One of only a handful of states to allow Black men to vote before the Civil War, Massachusetts long recognized its free Black population as citizens, although numerous racial inequalities existed in everyday life. Nationally, in the Dred Scott decision of 1857, the Supreme Court ruled that no African American could be a citizen of the United States. After the war, the Fourteenth Amendment granted citizenship to all persons born in the country regardless of race, in effect abrogating Dred Scott. Beginning in the 1870s, however, the Court severely limited the actual rights that went along with that citizenship. But Black activists, Kantrowitz argues, embraced an expansive definition of citizenship, understanding it as the enjoyment of equal rights in all areas of life, including political participation, access to public facilities, and much more.

In his most striking departure from previous scholarship, Kantrowitz argues that Black activists' "vision of belonging" encompassed not simply a set of specific rights but recognition by white Americans as "brothers and equals," including the establishment of "bonds of trust and even love across the color line." Only when white Americans embraced what Black activists called "the fraternal unity of man" would the country fully leave behind the legacy of slavery. In pursuit of this goal, Black Bostonians, excluded from white schools, churches, and organizations, created their own institutions, "a world apart" as Kantrowitz calls it. But their ultimate aim was not separation but inclusion. Kantrowitz's account differs dramatically from the most influential book on nineteenth-century Black politics published in the last decade, Steven Hahn's *A Nation Under Our Feet*, which emphasized Blacks' desire for group power rather than integration or white good will. Neither historian is necessarily right or wrong. Both strands—integration and self-determination—have always existed in Black life, not infrequently in the outlook of the same individual. The difference may arise from Hahn's focus on Black communities of the rural South, where Blacks had to rely on their own efforts for advancement, while Boston, as Kantrowitz shows, although rife with racism, was also home to a cadre of whites willing to work closely with Blacks in pursuit of abolition and racial equality.

Kantrowitz faults white abolitionists for paternalism toward Blacks, but he acknowledges that Boston's Black activists experienced a degree of interracial cooperation virtually unknown elsewhere in the United States. Frederick Douglass long remembered how Wendell Phillips "shared my hardships with me," insisting, for example, on remaining with Douglass on the frigid deck of a Boston–New York steamer because the captain would not allow Douglass to sit inside with the white passengers. It was this kind of experience that enabled Boston's Black radicals to imagine a future world of genuine equality, freed from the tyranny of race.

Boston may have been atypical. But, Kantrowitz argues, its Black radicals spearheaded the city's antislavery activism and helped to shape broader national events. The most striking example before the Civil War was the militant, sometimes violent opposition of Boston's abolitionists to the Fugitive Slave Act of 1850. Although the Boston Vigilance Committee, which worked to assist fugitives, had mostly white managers, the day-to-day work was done by Blacks. During the 1850s, the Committee assisted over 400 fugitives who passed through the city. And while many (although by no means all) white abolitionists adhered to the Garrisonian principle of non-resistance and eschewed violence as a way to oppose the law, Blacks quite literally put their lives on the line when legal procedures failed. In perhaps the most dramatic instance, hundreds of Black Bostonians in February 1851 descended on a court house where Shadrach Minkins, a fugitive slave from Virginia, was being held by local authorities. One armed group broke in and spirited him to safety; eventually Minkins made his way to freedom in Canada.

Not all such efforts ended in success. In 1854, while the Committee of Vigilance stood by helplessly, a force of police and federal soldiers escorted another fugitive, Anthony Burns, down State Street to Boston's docks, from where he was returned to slavery. But violent rescue attempts, both successful and unsuccessful, not only dramatized the fugitive slave issue but moved the abolitionist movement away from its commitment to non-violence. These events widened the breach between North and South and helped to bring on the Civil War.

Nine years after the rendition of Anthony Burns, a different procession marched down State Street to the cheers of onlookers. This was the 54th Massachusetts, a Black Union regiment (whose exploits would be celebrated in the film *Glory*). The contrast between these two events illustrated the transformation wrought by the Civil War. But as Kantrowitz shows, Boston's Black radicals divided on the question of Black military service. Some saw enlistment as a step toward equality. But given that the army maintained racially segregated regiments and paid Black soldiers less than their white counterparts, many Black Bostonians insisted that no one should fight unless accorded equal treatment. Their argument seems to have struck home—the 54th was unable to fill its ranks with Massachusetts men and had to seek recruits from throughout the North. Those who did enlist in the regiment refused to accept their pay until Congress agreed to retroactive equality. The soldiers' campaign eventually succeeded, producing the first national law explicitly based on the principle of racial equality.

By the war's end, slavery had been destroyed, 200,000 Black men had served in the Union army and navy, and the question of Black citizenship occupied a central place on the national political agenda. From one point of view, the gains made by Black Bostonians after the war were remarkable. Harvard enrolled its first Black undergraduate in 1865, the law school a year later. Some Black Bostonians headed south to take part in the democratic experiment of Reconstruction. Despite enjoying the right to vote, Black men had never held public office in Massachusetts, except for a justice of the peace or two. Now, some won election to the state legislature (including Edward Garrison Walker, who carried the names of two great abolitionists, one of whom was his father, David Walker, whose pamphlet, "An Appeal . . . to the Colored Citizens of the World," launched the militant abolitionist movement in 1829). Ironically, Edward Walker and Charles Mitchell, the first Black legislators, were among a handful to vote against ratification of the Fourteenth Amendment on the grounds that it failed to grant Blacks the suffrage. That would soon come, however, in the Fifteenth Amendment. By 1870, in the Constitution and on the statute books, Blacks nationwide were fully equal to white Americans. The abolitionist dream of a national citizenship without racial difference had been achieved.

Freedom had arrived. Or had it? Kantrowitz entitles his postwar section "The Disappointments of Citizenship." Most Blacks in Boston remained desperately poor; their only avenue for economic advancement was taking the place of striking white workers, as occurred during a railroad walkout in 1868. Exclusion and de facto segregation continued in many realms of life. Lewis Hayden's long battle to integrate the

Freemasons came to nothing. More broadly, Kantrowitz writes, "Black hopes for a broader sense of belonging," a "fraternal embrace across the color line," failed to materialize. Instead, foes of Reconstruction in the South and of Black equality in the North seized on the very ideal of "social equality" to discredit the entire egalitarian project. Blacks, they claimed, were trying to force themselves into places where they were not wanted—railroad cars, hotels, restaurants, homes, even bedrooms. As befits the author of a book on Ben Tillman, Kantrowitz emphasizes how opponents of Black rights took Black Bostonians' utopian goal of fraternity and love between the races and turned it into a synonym for interracial "amalgamation."

Kantrowitz concludes with a thirteen-page epilogue that takes the story rather breathlessly down to the present. We have not yet, he claims, achieved the "more than freedom" of the book's title—the "emotional, spiritual, and intuitive sense of kinship" envisioned by Boston's Black radicals. The discussion is far too brief to explain why. But length is less of a problem than a misplaced emphasis. In the end, the goal of all Americans sitting at a common "table of brotherhood," as Kantrowitz puts it, seems more a spiritual than a political aspiration. The idea is indeed a noble one. But what is less clear is whether it constitutes a viable basis for political action. Political coalitions generally revolve around shared goals and interests, rather than fraternal feelings. Indeed, Kantrowitz's own evidence suggests that to ordinary Black Bostonians access to jobs, political influence, and equal treatment in public spaces was of greater concern than whether white people loved them. Certainly, if the advent of universal brotherhood is the standard against which it is to be judged, freedom as it actually exists is bound to appear inadequate.

There is a compelling irony here. Today, we all embrace the brotherhood of man, at least rhetorically. Polls show that most white Americans believe that we have achieved the "raceless" (or as it is now called, color-blind) society envisioned by the Boston radicals. After all, Blacks have achieved all the legal rights demanded by the abolitionists. We even have a Black president, something utterly inconceivable then. Intimate interracial relationships, including marriages across the color line, so dreaded in the nineteenth century, are not only widely accepted but commonplace in television shows and in popular culture. Where the racial gap remains glaring is in more mundane areas—incarceration rates, family wealth, unemployment, health, victimization by banks and mortgage lenders.

Of course, the insistent claim that we have achieved a color-blind utopia too often serves as an excuse for ignoring the inequalities in American life that, in part, are the legacy of centuries of slavery and racism. And despite its weakness for a psychopolitics that elevates fraternal feelings above practical realities, *More Than Freedom* succeeds admirably in bringing vividly to life a group of all but forgotten Black political activists, and with them, a neglected chapter in the long struggle for racial justice.

COLFAX

U NBEKNOWNST TO MOST Americans, our nation's history includes home-grown terrorism as well as attacks from abroad. Scholars estimate that during Reconstruction, the turbulent period that followed the Civil War, upwards of 3,000 persons were murdered by the Ku Klux Klan and kindred groups. That's roughly the same number of Americans who died at the hands of Osama bin Laden.

In the last generation, no part of the American past has undergone a more complete scholarly reinterpretation than Reconstruction. Once portrayed as a tragic era of rampant misgovernment, Reconstruction is today seen as a noble, if flawed, experiment in interracial democracy. The work of historians, however, has largely failed to penetrate popular consciousness. Partly because of the persistence of old misconceptions, Reconstruction remains widely misunderstood. Thus, the new

———

Review of *The Day Freedom Died: The Colfax Massacre, the Supreme Court, and the Betrayal of Reconstruction*, by Charles Lane, and *The Colfax Massacre: The Untold Story of Black Power, White Terror and the Death of Reconstruction*, by LeeAnna Keith, *Washington Post Book World*, March 23, 2008.

books by LeeAnna Keith and Charles Lane are doubly welcome. Not only do they tell the story of the single most egregious act of terrorism during Reconstruction (a piece of "lost history," as Keith puts it), but they do so in vivid, compelling prose. Keith, who teaches at the Collegiate School in New York, and Lane, a journalist who covered the Supreme Court for the *Washington Post*, have immersed themselves in the relevant sources and current historical writing. Both accomplish a goal often aspired to but rarely achieved, producing works of serious scholarship accessible to a non-academic readership.

The Colfax massacre took place on Easter Sunday 1873, when a force of about 150 heavily armed whites assaulted an equal number of Blacks, many of them militia members, holed up in the courthouse at Colfax, Louisiana. After chivalrously allowing women and children to leave, they overran the outgunned defenders. Some Black men were killed trying to escape; 40 or so were taken prisoner and then executed. The final death toll remains unknown—Lane estimates between 62 and 81, Keith thinks it may have reached 150. Three whites also died.

Both authors offer gripping accounts of the assault and subsequent atrocities. But overall, their books complement rather than repeat each other. While shorter, Keith's is more comprehensive, devoting more space to the history of slavery, emancipation, and Reconstruction in west-central Louisiana. She explores the brutal nature of slavery on the sugar and cotton plantations of local magnate Meredith Calhoun, one of the richest men in the United States. Calhoun seems to have been the model for Simon Legree, the cruel master in Harriet Beecher Stowe's *Uncle Tom's Cabin*. Ironically, after the war, his son William became a leading proponent of Blacks' rights, who lived openly with a Black woman, rented land to Black farmers, established a school for their children, and aligned himself with the Republican Party. All sorts of new things were possible during Reconstruction.

In his best-selling book *April 1865: The Month that Saved America* (2001), the journalist Jay Winik commended defeated Confederates for returning to peaceful pursuits after Appomattox, thus "saving" the United States from the agony of a long guerrilla war. Would that this were so. Organized violence emerged around Colfax almost as soon as the Civil War ended, targeting Black leaders, schoolteachers, freedmen who tried to acquire land, and, once Blacks won the right to vote, local officeholders. Not all the victims were Black—Delos White, a Freedmen's Bureau agent, was assassinated in 1871. What happened in Colfax was not atypical. "Murder," Keith writes laconically, "played a central role in Louisiana and throughout the region" during Reconstruction.

While Keith illuminates the massacre's historical context, Lane offers a far more detailed account of the ensuing court cases. If his story has a hero, it is J. R. Beckwith, the U.S. attorney in New Orleans, who became obsessed with bringing the perpetrators to justice. He received little assistance from his superior, Attorney General George H. Williams, who thought it would be better if the murderers simply fled the state. Beckwith persuaded a federal grand jury to indict nearly 100 men under the recently passed Enforcement Acts, which made it a federal crime to deprive citizens of constitutionally guaranteed rights. But because of local white resistance, only a handful of those charged could be arrested.

Eventually, nine men went on trial before a biracial jury. Dozens of witnesses, almost all of them Black, related what had happened at Colfax. An initial trial resulted in a hung jury; a second produced the conviction of three defendants. But Supreme Court Justice Joseph P. Bradley, acting while on circuit court duties, voided the indictment because, he insisted, most of the rights that had allegedly been violated were matters of state, not federal, authority (an important step in the Supreme Court's retreat from enforcement of the Reconstruction constitutional amendments).

Because the presiding judge courageously refused to go along with Bradley, his judicial superior, the case went to the Supreme Court. In 1876, in *U.S. v. Cruikshank*, the justices unanimously threw out the convictions. As Lane points out, nowhere in Chief Justice Morrison Waite's 5,000-word opinion did he mention the fact that dozens of Black men had been murdered in cold blood at Colfax. Cruikshank hammered a nail into the coffin of federal efforts to protect the basic rights of Black citizens in the South. Reconstruction effectively ended a year later.

This tragic story is more than ancient history. Into the twentieth century, bones turned up in Colfax when the foundations for buildings were being laid. Until recently, there stood in the town a plaque, erected in 1951, commemorating the Colfax "riot"—not massacre—and "the end of carpetbag misrule in the South." It was replaced in 2023 by a memorial listing the names of over fifty African Americans who died at Colfax. *Cruikshank*, however, survives. In 2000 Chief Justice William Rehnquist cited that decision as a precedent in overturning a conviction under the Violence Against Women Act. The Constitution, he declared, gives the states, not the federal government, the power to punish rape. Whether we realize it or not, Reconstruction and its overthrow remain part of our lives today.

WHEN THE COURT
CHOOSES THE PRESIDENT

A CCORDING TO THE Constitution the president, with the consent of the Senate, selects the members of the Supreme Court. Twice in American history, however, Supreme Court Justices have chosen the president. The first occasion was in 1877, when five Justices served on the fifteen-member Electoral Commission charged with determining the outcome of the disputed Hayes-Tilden contest. Justice Joseph P. Bradley cast the deciding vote that made Rutherford B. Hayes president. In 2000, of course, five Justices, in *Bush v. Gore*, ordered Florida to halt the recount of ballots, allowing state officials to certify that George W. Bush had carried the state and won the presidency. In both cases, William H. Rehnquist notes rather coyly in his new book, "there was profound dissatisfaction with the process on the part of the losing parties."

Rehnquist, of course, is the Chief Justice of the United States who supplied one of the five votes that made George W. Bush president. He is an unusual jurist who reads and writes history, the author of books on civil liberties in wartime and impeachments in American history. In

Review of *Centennial Crisis: The Disputed Election of 1876*, by William H. Rehnquist, *The Nation*, March 29, 2004.

Centennial Crisis, the Chief Justice turns his attention to the electoral controversy of 1876–77.

Unfortunately, this brief, curious work adds nothing to other readily available accounts of its subject. The scholarship on which Rehnquist relies is almost entirely out of date and his grasp of the complex issues of the Reconstruction era tenuous. But if *Centennial Crisis* has little value as history, it offers a revealing glimpse into the mind of the Chief Justice. For essentially, the book is an elaborate, although indirect, apologia for the Court's decision in *Bush v. Gore* and a defense of Supreme Court Justices who help to resolve extrajudicial controversies.

Rehnquist ignores virtually all modern works on the Reconstruction period, including those that deal directly with the disputed election, not to mention relevant manuscript collections. David Lincove's comprehensive annotated bibliography of Reconstruction, published in 2000, lists twenty-seven books, articles, and doctoral dissertations under the heading "Election of 1876," some of minor importance but many indispensable. Of these, Rehnquist cites only three. He relies most heavily on Paul Haworth's history of the election, published in 1906.

Rehnquist offers colorful portraits of the two presidential candidates and members of the Court, although these add nothing to what can be found in any standard biographical encyclopedia. He sometimes wanders off into irrelevancy, as when he recounts an assault on Justice Stephen J. Field in the late 1880s in which Field's bodyguard killed the assailant. He gets facts wrong, as in his account of the Great Railroad Strike of 1877, which suggests that President Hayes refused to intervene and let the strike simply peter out. The president's diary entry after he sent troops to crush the uprising is more accurate: "the strikers have been put down by *force*."

More important, Rehnquist remains locked into an antiquated view of the Reconstruction era long abandoned by scholars. He wrongly claims that Andrew Johnson tried to carry out Lincoln's "conciliatory approach" to Reconstruction only to be foiled by the Radical Republicans who dominated Congress. In fact, moderate Republicans, not

Radicals, controlled Congress throughout Reconstruction, and Johnson's plan was very much his own, not simply a replica of Lincoln's. (On the eve of his death, Lincoln had called for limited Black suffrage in the postwar South; Johnson was an inveterate racist.) What Rehnquist calls the Radicals' "Carthaginian Peace" (that is, the total subjugation of the defeated party by the victor after a war), involved the effort by moderate and radical Republicans alike to devise ways of protecting the basic civil and political rights of the former slaves. That the Chief Justice of the United States sees national protection of Blacks' rights as a punishment imposed on whites is disheartening.

Rehnquist's account of the years preceding the election of 1876 says almost nothing about the massive violence inflicted on Black southerners by the Ku Klux Klan and kindred groups. He attributes the Hamburg massacre of 1876, in which armed whites murdered a number of Black South Carolinians, to "racial hostility," rather than recognizing it as part of a reign of terror aimed at overturning Reconstruction and restoring white supremacy. In other words, he offers no assessment of what was really at stake during the electoral crisis.

Much of *Centennial Crisis* consists of a detailed account of the formation and deliberations of the Electoral Commission, authorized by Congress to determine which candidate had carried South Carolina, Florida, and Louisiana, the states on which the presidency hinged. Both parties claimed to have won these states, and rival officials dispatched conflicting electoral vote returns to Washington. With the Constitution silent as to how to resolve the dispute, Congress in January 1877 established a commission consisting of five members of the House, five senators, and five Justices of the Supreme Court. Four of the Justices were named in the bill, and they were directed to choose the fifth, expected to be David Davis, a political independent. But in the midst of the crisis, the Illinois legislature elected Davis to the U.S. Senate. Justice Joseph P. Bradley, a Republican, took his place on the Electoral Commission. With the other members evenly divided between the two parties, Bradley became the "casting vote" in a series of 8–7 rulings that gave the disputed states to Hayes and made him president.

Rehnquist narrates these events clearly, but fails to probe beneath the surface of events to explain the complex situation that developed or to interpret it effectively. He does not describe how divisions within the two parties and growing pressure from business interests for a settlement led to the establishment of the Commission in the first place. He offers no explanation for Davis's election to the Senate, leaving the reader to wonder whether it was engineered by Democrats more interested in power in Congress than Tilden's election, or Republicans who wanted to get him off the Electoral Commission. He says almost nothing of the intense negotiations that took place outside the Commission, in which Hayes's lieutenants, leading southern Democrats, and various railroad interests, hammered out a deal involving the abandonment of Reconstruction.

This "bargain of 1877" provided that Democrats who controlled the House of Representatives would not try to obstruct Hayes's inauguration; Hayes would recognize Democratic control of the disputed southern states; the basic rights of the former slaves would be guaranteed; and federal aid would be extended to a southern railroad. The deal turned out to be far more important in its long-term consequences than whether Hayes or Tilden became president. It ended an era when the federal government sought to protect the rights of Black citizens. And since southern Democrats soon reneged on their pledge to respect Blacks' constitutional rights, it marked the beginning of the long descent into segregation and disenfranchisement.

"The Negro," *The Nation* commented soon after Hayes's inauguration, "will disappear from the field of national politics. Henceforth the nation, as a nation, will have nothing more to do with him." The editors of *The Nation*, like most white Americans of that era, rejoiced in the abandonment of Reconstruction. Chief Justice Rehnquist praises the members of the Electoral Commission for enabling the country to avoid "serious disturbance" and go "about its business." He says nothing of the cost of the settlement, which did much to shape the racial system of the United States in the decades that followed.

With one eye on the Court's actions in 2000, Rehnquist ends his account by defending Justice Bradley against the "opprobrium" he endured for his "casting vote" that made Hayes president. He offers a brief survey of other instances when Supreme Court Justices have served the nation in "extrajudicial capacities." John Jay negotiated a treaty with Great Britain in 1794 while serving as Chief Justice. Justice Melville Fuller helped to arbitrate the Venezuela boundary dispute in 1897; Justice Owen Roberts headed the commission investigating the attack on Pearl Harbor, and Chief Justice Earl Warren led the probe into the assassination of President Kennedy.

Interestingly, Rehnquist says nothing about the more explicitly partisan activities of Supreme Court Justices, of which examples abound. Justice John Catron enlisted the intervention of president-elect James Buchanan to persuade another member of the Court to side with the proslavery majority in the Dred Scott decision of 1857. President Franklin D. Roosevelt regularly conferred with Justice Louis D. Brandeis on political matters, as did Lyndon Johnson with Justice Abe Fortas. These instances seem more relevant to the behavior of the Justices in 1877 and 2000 than the Venezuela boundary question. In both cases, members of the Supreme Court made political decisions.

Actually, the outcome in *Bush v. Gore* seems far less defensible than the actions of the Electoral Commission. In 1877, Justice Bradley concluded that the Commission could not possibly conduct its own detailed inquiry into local election returns and thus had no choice but to accept the findings of local election boards (all Republican) as to who had carried their states. Bradley's position, as Rehnquist argues, was certainly "reasonable." Unlike his successors in 2000, Bradley did not invent a new constitutional principle (equal procedures in the counting of ballots) to reach a predetermined verdict and then add that this principle applied only in the specific case at hand. Bradley seems to have tried to rise above the immediate political situation, unlike Justice Antonin Scalia, who in 2000 insisted that the Court needed to ensure "public acceptance" of a Bush presidency. It is unlikely that Bradley would have gone duck-hunting with a litigant before the Court.

Rehnquist acknowledges that the Justices who accepted assignment to the Electoral Commission in 1877 "may have tarnished the reputation of the Court." This book will do nothing to rehabilitate the reputations of the five Justices, including himself, irreparably "tarnished" by their actions in 2000.

PART III

Jim Crow America

AMERICAN FREEDOM

ARLIER THIS YEAR, Randy McNally, the Speaker of the
Tennessee Senate, issued a proclamation declaring April 2023
Confederate History Month. He urged "citizens from across
the state" to remember their ancestors' "heroic struggle" for "individual freedom." Even though parts of Tennessee strongly supported the
Union, observers outside the state may find it incongruous to identify
a war fought to preserve slavery with the ideal of freedom. The historian Jefferson Cowie, who teaches at Vanderbilt University, in the
heart of Tennessee, probably is not surprised. His new book, *Freedom's
Dominion*, seeks to explain why so many Americans, especially but not
exclusively in the South, have understood freedom as an entitlement
restricted to white persons. Cowie insists that "white freedom" has long
entailed the power to dominate others, especially non-whites, without
interference from the national government. The fear that white freedom is under assault by Blacks, or immigrants, or a far-away national
government, helps to explain why in the last election Donald Trump
carried Tennessee in a landslide, winning 60 percent of the vote and all

---

Review of *Freedom's Dominion: A Saga of White Resistance to Federal
Power*, by Jefferson Cowie, *London Review of Books*, June 1, 2023.

but three of the state's ninety-five counties. In many parts of the United States, every month is Confederate History Month.

Since the election of Ronald Reagan, historians have struggled to explain why so many members of the white working class have abandoned their loyalty to the Democratic Party of Franklin D. Roosevelt and vote for candidates whose policies, including tax cuts lavished on the rich, hostility to trade unions, and an embrace of economic globalization, contradicted these voters' economic self-interest. In perhaps the most widely read such book, *What's the Matter with Kansas?* (2004), Thomas Frank argued that the upheavals of the 1960s generated fears and resentments that allowed issues such as abortion rights and racial equity to eclipse economic ones, producing deep fissures within the house of labor. Cowie's book is both an ambitious history lesson and a contribution to this ongoing discussion, recently reinvigorated by working-class support for Trump.

In his previous works, including *Capital Moves* (1999), an account of the obsessive quest for cheap labor at home and abroad by RCA, a manufacturer of radios and television sets, and *Stayin' Alive* (2010), which drew on images of workers in popular culture to argue that organized labor is no longer a self-conscious power in American life, Cowie displayed an ability to weave class, culture, politics, and ideology into a seamless narrative and to connect local histories with national and global events. The same qualities are evident in *Freedom's Dominion*. The book sweeps over more than two centuries of American history, seeking to explain the evolution and enduring power of a racially inflected understanding of freedom.

The oldest of clichés and the most inspiring of human aspirations, the idea of freedom is fundamental to Americans' sense of themselves as individuals and as a nation. "Every man in the street, white, black, red or yellow," wrote the statesman Ralph Bunche, knows that this is "the land of the free . . . [and] the cradle of liberty." Cowie's account builds on Tyler E. Stovall's 2021 book *White Freedom*, which argued that the crystallization of the modern notion of freedom as a natural right of mankind at the same time as slavery was rapidly expanding in the Atlantic world led to the ideal of freedom becoming increasingly "racialized." "Oppression and freedom are not opposites," Cowie writes, nor is a rhetorical commitment to liberty incompatible with intense insistence on the right of those who enjoy freedom to enslave others.

To trace the symbiotic relationship between freedom and racial domination, Cowie focuses on four eras in the history of a place most of his readers have probably never heard of—Barbour County, located in southeastern Alabama. It seems counterintuitive to pick a county located in the pre–Civil War Cotton Kingdom, and later the site of rigid racial segregation, to epitomize the historical evolution of American freedom. Many readers may recoil from the idea that the United States is Barbour County writ large. Why not choose New York City, a quintessentially American melting pot of peoples, or a county in California, to illustrate the freedom dream of individual mobility and economic opportunity? What about somewhere in the Midwestern "heartland," where American values—family, religion, and hard work—supposedly flourish? But Cowie insists that Barbour's history exemplifies the rise of the idea of freedom as a white prerogative. And Barbour has another attraction—it is the birthplace of George Wallace, one of the most influential political figures of the twentieth century, who struck electoral gold by claiming that an alliance of the federal government and the civil rights movement was undermining the freedom of whites. Cowie uses Barbour to relate how a "racialized, domineering version of American freedom" became increasingly linked to "anti-statism"—hostility to federal intervention in local affairs.

Fear of an autocratic central state goes back at least as far as the revolutionary era. When the U.S. Constitution was adopted, significantly strengthening the existing national government, a considerable number of Americans, known as Anti-Federalists, warned of impending tyranny. To mollify them, the Bill of Rights was added to the Constitution, protecting Americans' essential liberties against abuses of national power. Initially, however, no clear connection existed between freedom, whiteness, and fear of centralized authority. (A large majority of the presidents and Supreme Court justices between the Revolution and

Civil War, after all, were southern slaveholders or, as opponents called them, "northern men with southern principles"; the national government did not pose a threat to their interests.) Cowie identifies conflicts in the 1830s between the Creek nation, whose lands included most of Barbour County, and a small army of white settlers who flooded into the region, as a key moment in the development of a definition of freedom as "racialized anti-statism." Local and state governments aided and abetted the intruders, but at first officials in Washington sided with the Indians, who had signed treaties with the federal government ceding much of their land but guaranteeing the rest in perpetuity. Even President Andrew Jackson, whose career, Cowie writes, revealed a "merciless hostility" to the Native American population, insisted that states' rights must yield to national authority and treaties must be obeyed. Jackson threatened to dispatch troops to Alabama to drive out whites who had illegally settled on Creek land.

Half a century earlier, in the Proclamation of 1763, the imperial government in London had tried to establish peace between indigenous peoples and colonial settlers by barring whites from acquiring land west of the Appalachian mountains. The resentment caused by this edict helped to inspire the movement for American independence. The Earl of Dunmore, the governor of colonial Virginia, later notorious for arming slaves to fight on the British side during the War of Independence, complained that Americans "do not conceive that government has any right to forbid their taking possession" of Indian land. But even the bellicose Jackson could not overcome the combined power of white settlers, land speculators, and local courts that consistently ruled in favor of those Cowie calls "land thieves." Jackson's effort to protect the Indians accomplished nothing except to persuade many whites that the federal government posed a threat to their freedom, defined in part as access to ownership of land. Ironically, the eventual triumph of white settlers required a powerful exercise of national authority—the removal beyond the Mississippi River of tens of thousands of Native Americans, including many Creeks, in the Trail of Tears. After the Indians had been displaced, cotton plantations worked by slaves replaced Native communities in the states of the Lower South. Some of the resulting wealth, Cowie points out, is visible today in the mansions that dot the streets of Eufaula, Barbour County's largest city.

In his second section, Cowie examines how the sectional crisis that produced the Civil War, emancipation, and Reconstruction ended up powerfully reinforcing white Alabamans' view of the federal government as a threat to their ability to rule over the region's Black population. During the 1850s, white residents of Barbour County became increasingly insistent on being left alone to manage their own affairs, including ownership of slaves, without national interference. When Abraham Lincoln, who had pledged to halt the westward expansion of slavery, was elected president in 1860, they doubled down on the idea that the national government was their enemy and moved to create a new nation, a slave owners' republic. In the end, the mobilization of national power was crucial in bringing about what southern whites considered a loss of freedom: the end of slavery, the ouster of the old ruling class from local power, and the establishment of the first biracial democratic governments in American history. Constitutional amendments guaranteed the end of slavery, Black citizenship, the equal protection of the laws regardless of race, and, for Black men, the right to vote. Each amendment ended with a clause empowering the federal government to enforce its provisions—a promise (or threat) of future national action. Unfortunately, as Sidney Andrews, a northern journalist who visited the South in 1865, observed, "the whites seem wholly unable to comprehend that freedom for the Negro means the same thing as freedom for them." To white citizens of Barbour, the expansion of freedom for Blacks meant its diminution for whites. The white population resolved to overturn Reconstruction, first by political mobilization, then by violence.

If the Civil War proved anything, declared Supreme Court Justice Samuel F. Miller in 1873, it was that those who believed a strong federal government posed a danger to liberty "were in error." But the enjoyment of freedom by former slaves depended on outside power. For a time, such power was forthcoming. In the early 1870s, President Grant sent troops to South Carolina and federal marshals to Alabama to protect former slaves. The national willingness to intervene with force, however, soon waned, and the violent overthrow of Reconstruction followed, a process whites called Redemption, or the restoration of "home rule."

With the end of Reconstruction, Cowie turns to his third section, the period of "Federal Power in Repose." The amended Constitution remained in place but its provisions became dead letters as far as Blacks were concerned. No longer fearing federal intervention, southern states enacted measures to solidify white power. To illustrate the practical consequences of national inaction, Cowie provides a detailed description of the convict lease system that subjected countless Blacks convicted of petty crimes to involuntary servitude. Cowie makes clear, however, that the reestablishment of "white freedom" did not erase class differences within the white population. While the rest of the country moved forward economically, the planters and merchants who governed Alabama and other southern states adopted a low-wage developmental model, which impoverished many whites as well as African Americans. Like other parts of the South, Barbour County in the late nineteenth century witnessed the rise of the People's Party, or Populists, a direct challenge to elite domination. For a time, some white Populists even advocated that poor Black and white farmers join forces for mutual economic benefit. After crushing the Populists with the same combination of fraud, violence, and appeals to white solidarity that had overturned Reconstruction, Alabama's leaders in 1901 pushed through a new state constitution that disenfranchised nearly all Black voters, making future interracial political cooperation impossible.

Readers may wonder whether "repose" is the right way to describe the status of the federal government in the era between Reconstruction and the New Deal. Certainly, those years witnessed the abdication of national responsibility for protecting the rights of Black citizens. But Cowie's local focus creates problems. The role of the federal government has always been more contested than Cowie suggests. Antistatism may be the dominant outlook, but there is another tradition in which the national government actively promotes economic growth and the interests of business. Its roots go back as far as Alexander Hamilton's Federalist Party in the early republic. National power may have disappeared from Barbour, but elsewhere it was very much in evidence, especially when the interests of corporations, closely tied to the nationally dominant Republican Party, were at stake. More than once, labor uprisings were met by the intervention of federal troops. Indeed, some of the same soldiers who were ordered to end engagement in southern politics as part of the Bargain of 1877 that ended Reconstruction were deployed in the North to suppress a national railroad strike. Meanwhile, the army was battling Indians in the West, bent on opening their lands to exploitation by railroads, mining companies, and farmers. Native Americans did not think the federal government was in "repose." And the Supreme Court invalidated numerous state laws that sought to regulate the conditions of labor. This employment of national power to protect corporate interests inspired reformers to conceive of new ways the federal government might utilize its power. The Populists called for the nationalization of the railroads and government control of the credit system to help ease the plight of small farmers. Progressives in both major parties supported an expansion of federal economic regulation. National power seemed a more reliable shield for corporate interests than local "home rule."

In a previous book, *The Great Exception* (2017), Cowie portrays the New Deal, which brought into being an administrative state and a national safety net, as a detour from the main trajectory of American history, in which anti-statism is the default position. But this fails to explain why the New Deal coalition for decades enjoyed widespread support throughout the country as Americans looked to the federal government for economic relief. To be sure, white freedom still reigned in the South. But FDR actively promoted a definition of freedom as economic security for ordinary Americans guaranteed by the federal government, implicitly offering a contrast to the notion that national power was the embodiment of tyranny.

Finally, Cowie turns to the era of the modern civil rights movement and the ensuing backlash. Some participants called these years the Second Reconstruction, a successor to the time when federal power was turned against the southern racial system. With its freedom rides, freedom songs, and insistent cry "freedom now," freedom became the movement's rallying cry. Many white southerners adopted their own equation of the era with Reconstruction, warning that federal civil rights legislation violated local freedom. Despite the courage of the mass protesters, Black political rights, Cowie writes, still depended on federal enforcement. And the more the national government intervened, the more whites associated it with a loss of freedom. Cowie outlines how in Barbour white officials sought to undermine Blacks' newly regained political rights via gerrymandering, manipulation of voting qualifications, harassment of those who went to the polls, and other subterfuges. At one point, white Eufaulans came up with a plan to avoid school integration by having the city's Housing Authority employ the power of eminent domain—funded, ironically, by federal slum clearance grants—to seize the homes of African Americans living in proximity to whites. Once the city was segregated residentially, school district lines could follow without explicit mention of race. When this plan did not work, the Eufaula school board cancelled non-academic events to prevent Black and white students from socializing. Not until 1991 did the city's high school hold its first integrated prom. All this was defended in the name of freedom.

Legally speaking, the backlash failed. Federal laws and court rulings dismantled de jure segregation and southern Blacks regained the right to vote. But in the Democratic primaries of 1964 and an independent run for president four years later, Barbour's favorite son, Governor George Wallace, brought the politics of white freedom to the rest of the nation. Wallace began his career as a supporter of Big Jim Folsom, an imposing figure known as "the little man's big friend." Folsom spoke the language of economic populism, castigating the elite that controlled state politics while calling vaguely for fair treatment of the state's Blacks. But sensing that resistance to civil rights was eclipsing economic issues, Wallace shifted his focus to maintaining white supremacy. After losing the gubernatorial election of 1958 to the even more racist John Patterson, Wallace vowed never to allow himself to be outdone in playing the race card. He was elected governor in 1962, the first of four terms in that office. In his inaugural address, Wallace exclaimed, "segregation now, segregation tomorrow, and segregation forever." The centerpiece of his speech, however, was not segregation but freedom, a word he used twenty-five times. With a keen sense of political theater, Wallace created an indelible television image by personally blocking a doorway at the registration building of the University of Alabama to prevent the court-ordered admission of the institution's first Black students. Then he withdrew and the students entered. But Wallace had made himself a national standard-bearer for white freedom.

Earlier than many other politicians, Wallace realized that support for his outlook was not confined to the South. In the Newtonian physics of American politics, any action designed to improve the condition of Black Americans called forth an equal and opposite reaction. In 1964, the year that Lyndon Johnson, who had identified himself with the civil rights movement, won an overwhelming national victory, the voters of California approved by an equally large margin a referendum prohibiting the state government from promoting housing integration. Wallace received an enthusiastic reception from ethnic working-class voters in cities like Milwaukee with his message that freedom was under assault. His campaigns offered a harbinger of a conservatism in which, in the name of freedom, racists united with business-oriented opponents of New Deal economic policies. While Wallace's dream of using white resentment as a ticket to the White House failed to materialize, his campaigns cast a long shadow over American politics. In the South, Wallace helped to catalyze a remarkable transformation of political alignments. White voters en masse abandoned the Democratic Party, which had controlled the region since the end of Reconstruction, for the once-despised Republicans. The "Wallace factor," Cowie insists, "became the key variable for understanding the future of American politics." Shortly before his death in 1998, Wallace reminisced: "Nixon, Reagan, Clinton. Welfare reform. Crime. Big government. They [are] all saying now what I was saying then." Trump, of course, can be added to this list.

Cowie makes a convincing case for the enduring power of the idea that freedom, however defined, is a white entitlement. It is worth remembering, however, that not all hostility to the federal government can be explained by racism. As the historian Anne Kornhouser showed in *Debating the American State* (2015), even as the New Deal was being launched, some liberal reformers echoed conservatives' concerns about the implications for political democracy of government by unelected experts. In 1971, the lawyer Lewis Powell Jr., later appointed to the Supreme Court by Nixon, wrote an influential memorandum for the U.S. Chamber of Commerce urging corporate executives to enlist in what he described as an ideological war in which freedom, defined as free market economics, was "under broad attack," especially on college campuses. The Powell Memorandum inspired the creation of an array of conservative think tanks ready to do their part in the battle of ideas. Nowhere did it mention race; Powell was addressing elites, not mobilizing voters. But the prospect of an alliance between anti-government activists bent on repealing the New Deal and Wallace's electoral base proved too alluring for conservatives to resist. The result was a Faustian political bargain exemplified by Nixon's "southern strategy," Reagan's decision to launch his presidential campaign in Philadelphia, Mississippi, where three civil rights workers had been murdered, and the infamous 1988 political advertisement by George H. W. Bush identifying his Democratic opponent Michael Dukakis with Willie Horton, a dangerous Black criminal. Today's corporate Republicans who find Trump's inflammatory appeals to white grievances and his demagogic hostility to the "deep state" distasteful have never acknowledged that they themselves helped lay the groundwork for his political ascent.

Cowie begins his book by calling for the idea of white freedom to be replaced by "a vigorous, federally enforced model of American citizenship" that will "fight the many incarnations of freedom to dominate." His own narrative, however, suggests that this is not likely to happen soon. More than half a century after he stood in the schoolhouse door, the ghost of George Wallace still haunts American politics.

THE RIGHT TO
DISCRIMINATE

ANYONE WITH EVEN a passing interest in the history of American politics knows about the election of 1964, when Lyndon B. Johnson's landslide victory over Barry Goldwater ushered in the Great Society, the high tide of modern American liberalism. How many, however, have heard of the electoral battle in California that same year over Proposition 14, an amendment to the state constitution that repealed a recently enacted law barring racial discrimination in the sale of housing and prohibited the state from enacting any such law or regulation in the future. On the same day that Johnson carried California by 1.3 million votes, Proposition 14 passed by an even more decisive margin, 2.1 million. The state's Supreme Court quickly ruled that Proposition 14 violated the federal constitution. But its overwhelming passage revealed that millions of white Americans took for granted the right to live in racially exclusive communities. The triumph of Proposition 14 undercuts the widespread misconception that white backlash against the civil rights revolution arose when the non-violent,

———

Review of *Freedom to Discriminate: How Realtors Conspired to Segregate Housing and Divide America,* by Gene Slater, *Los Angeles Review of Books*, September 26, 2021.

interracial campaign for racial justice took a turn to urban rioting and Black separatism. It occurred almost a year before the Watts uprising of 1965 and, as Martin Luther King Jr. remarked, "before anyone shouted Black Power."

In *The Right to Discriminate*, Gene Slater, who has spent four decades as a consultant to states and municipalities on housing policy, makes a powerful case that California's real estate brokers not only originated a system of residential segregation that became a model for the entire nation, but effectively mobilized support for Proposition 14 by invoking the central idea in America's political vocabulary, freedom. The issue, they insisted, was not race but white property owners' "freedom of association," or, more simply, "freedom of choice." They described government enforcement of the right of Blacks to purchase a home as reverse discrimination against whites. Providing a template for opposition to an overbearing liberal state, Slater argues, the successful campaign for Proposition 14 laid the foundation for the rise of modern American conservatism.

Slater's book amply demonstrates that housing segregation is not simply the "natural" outcome of homeowners' desire to live among people like themselves. It had to be created and continually reinforced. This insight will come as no surprise to those familiar with an extensive literature that chronicles a long history of deliberately discriminatory policies by entities both public and private. A key work in launching this cottage industry, Kenneth T. Jackson's *Crabgrass Frontier* (1985), shocked admirers of FDR by showing that the Federal Housing Administration (FHA), created during the New Deal to encourage home ownership, systematically promoted residential segregation. Other historians have explored the role of banks, credit agencies, and urban renewal efforts in the creation of segregated neighborhoods and communities.

To these works Slater adds a valuable perspective by emphasizing the crucial role of realtors, by whom he means not everyone who tried to sell a house or plot of land, but a much smaller group—licensed members of local and state real estate associations. Drawing on research in the records of real estate boards as well as realtors' campaigns to prevent the enactment of open housing legislation, Slater offers a compelling account of how a country where in the early twentieth century most urban neighborhoods were racially mixed was transformed into one in which segregation characterized nearly every metropolitan area. His focus is on California, the country's largest real estate market and home to half the country's realtors, but he insists that where the Golden State led, the rest of the country followed.

Because the Supreme Court in 1916 invalidated a Louisville ordinance requiring that neighborhoods be segregated by race as a violation of the Fourteenth Amendment's guarantee of equal protection of the laws, most housing discrimination was implemented by private groups and individuals. In California, this meant brokers refusing to show potential buyers properties in mixed areas and homeowners signing written covenants prohibiting the sale of a house except to members of the "Caucasian race." Although this category eventually expanded to include some Mexicans and Asian Americans, the barriers against Blacks remained impenetrable. By 1960, after a decade of massive migration from the South to cities of the North and West, over 90 percent of the country's residential neighborhoods excluded Blacks. Residential segregation produced profound differences between the races in the quality of education, the nature of policing, the availability of well-paying jobs, and the siting of environmentally destructive facilities. Slater points out more than once that while realtors' propaganda insisted that the presence of Black families reduced all homeowners' property values, the opposite was often the case since with limited market choice, minorities actually paid higher prices than whites for equivalent properties. Blacks' limited ability to purchase a home made it almost impossible for them to accumulate resources that could be passed on to subsequent generations. Today, the median wealth of white families—with the house usually the largest asset—is ten times that of Black families.

Ironically, Slater shows, the promotion of housing segregation originated as part of a broader effort by California realtors to upgrade the image of their profession. In the early twentieth century, real estate brokers had a reputation, often well-deserved, as scoundrels who cheated honest buyers by misrepresenting the value of plots of land and houses. To counteract this image, realtors established boards that restricted membership to licensed brokers who pledged to follow strict rules. The boards promised to police their own ranks and drive out dishonest operators. They created a system of multiple listings, in which members of the organization had access to each other's roster of available properties, giving buyers far more choice than if they dealt with a single, non-licensed broker. They pressed for the passage of zoning laws so that a homeowner would not wake up one day to find an industrial establishment being constructed next door.

As part of their effort to guarantee the future stability of residential neighborhoods, realtors promoted residential segregation as what Slater calls a "marketing tool" that ostensibly would protect the value of an owner's investment by barring sales of homes nearby to undesirable persons. They denied licenses to Black real estate brokers, since access to multiple listings might enable them to sell a house in a white neighborhood to a minority purchaser. In order to maintain segregation, in other words, brokers themselves had to be separated by race. As late as 1960, Slater relates, the country's 80,000 licensed realtors did not include a single African American.

By the 1930s, the profession's image had improved so much that government bodies such as the FHA and Home Owners' Loan Corporation allowed realtors to shape their policies. The FHA refused to make loans or insure home mortgages except in racially homogenous communities. The presence of even a single Black family in a mostly white neighborhood led to the area being redlined—marked in red on FHA maps as unworthy of loans. FHA officials insisted that their decisions were based purely on an area's economic viability, not race, so did not violate the constitutional ban on racially discriminatory governmental actions. The FHA financed one-third of all the mortgages in the United States between 1930 and 1960; less than 2 percent went to racial minorities. Thus, non-whites found themselves trapped in over-

crowded urban ghettoes, excluded from the post–World War II suburban boom. In the 1950s, not a single Black family resided among the
60,000 inhabitants of the newly created suburb of Levittown, Pennsylvania, or the 70,000 in its sister town on Long Island. The system was
self-reinforcing. Once racial minorities were confined to a few neighborhoods, these became associated with unemployment and crime,
making white homeowners elsewhere even more determined to keep
non-whites out of their communities.

In California, Slater shows, the "central tool" for maintaining residential segregation was the racial covenant, inserted into deeds by
realtors and enforced by individual homeowners, neighborhood associations, and, if necessary, the courts. In the 1950s, of 325,000 homes
sold in the Bay Area only fifty had deeds or contracts that lacked such
covenants. In turn-of-the-century Los Angeles, the small Black population, along with Japanese and Mexicans, lived scattered across the
city in racially mixed working-class communities. But racial segregation soon became the norm. Watts, a mixed neighborhood as late as
World War II, by 1960 had become 95 percent Black. As new communities proliferated, they advertised their "permanent race restrictions"
as a means of attracting white residents. Of course, as Slater points out,
realtors could not have spread covenants so widely if they did not reflect
existing prejudices.

While Slater places most of the responsibility for implementing residential segregation on realtors, he makes clear that other actors played
a part, including, for many decades, the state and federal judiciaries.
Almost as soon as the Fourteenth Amendment was ratified in 1868,
the U.S. Supreme Court began to undermine it. The justices quickly
adopted the view that the Amendment's promise of equal protection of
the laws did not apply to discrimination by private individuals or businesses. On the basis of this "state action" doctrine, the Court in 1883
declared unconstitutional the Civil Rights Act of 1875, which barred
racial discrimination by transport companies and public accommodations. In 1919, California's Supreme Court ruled that while public
authorities could not prevent the purchase of a home on racial grounds,

this did not prevent private parties such as developers, real estate agents, and community associations from establishing rules about who could live in it. Thus, a Black family that purchased a home covered by a racial covenant could be prevented from moving in. Of course these covenants limited the rights not only of minorities but of white home owners, who were prevented from seeking the highest price for their property if that meant selling to a non-white purchaser. But few whites seemed to complain about this loss of market freedom.

In 1948, with overt expressions of racism having been discredited by the fight against Nazi tyranny and its theories of a master race, the Supreme Court declared racial covenants, including occupancy bans, legally unenforceable. Courts could not penalize property owners who signed such documents and then violated them. But the decision did not actually ban racial covenants and they continued to be attached to housing deeds.

Not until 1968, in the wake of King's assassination, did Congress pass a national Fair Housing Act. A few months later, the Supreme Court flatly declared all racial discrimination in housing, whether by public officials or private homeowners and brokers, illegal. This marked the end of the state action doctrine as far as housing was concerned. The Justices accomplished this turnabout by relying on the Thirteenth Amendment, which had irrevocably abolished slavery a century earlier, and the Civil Rights Act of 1866, a long unenforced Reconstruction law enacted over Andrew Johnson's veto under that amendment's authority. Among other things, the law mandated equal rights regardless of race in the acquisition and disposal of property. The entire way realtors had conducted their business, Slater notes, the Court now deemed a stigma that arose from slavery and therefore illegal as a violation of its abolition. After decades of bitter opposition to open housing, the National Association of Real Estate Boards solemnly informed its members that they would have to recognize that "the Negro in America" was "a free man." The court's reliance on the Thirteenth Amendment opened the door to legal challenges to all sorts of racial inequalities as "badges and incidents" of slavery. But after Richard Nixon's election as president in 1968, the Court turned in a conservative direction. In the half century since then, almost no Thirteenth Amendment–based jurisprudence has followed.

Deeply researched and clearly written, *Freedom to Discriminate* offers a persuasive account of realtors' key role in maintaining housing segregation. More problematic is the book's companion theme of how realtors, according to Slater, invented a discourse centered on freedom that served as a model for conservative politics down to the present day. Freedom, of course, is the central term in American political language.

Slater, unfortunately, does not delve very deeply into the historical origins of the realtors' invocation of freedom to defend Proposition 14. Realtors may have honed the idea that the right to exercise choice in a free market was the essence of freedom, but they hardly invented it. This notion dated back as least as far as the "liberty of contract" jurisprudence of the late-nineteenth-century Supreme Court, in which the Justices overturned state laws regulating business practices and labor conditions as violations of the "freedom" of property owners and employers. It was also central to Republican opposition to the New Deal and post–World War II efforts to overturn it.

Nor did realtors invent what Slater calls "freedom to exclude." Tyler Stovall's *White Freedom* shows that in the United States the idea of freedom has long been linked to white racial identity. Certainly, racial exclusiveness was one element of the California dream that drew millions of white newcomers to the state. California in the late nineteenth century pioneered the policy of Chinese exclusion, on the grounds that immigrants from China were "coolies" whose supposed willingness to work for starvation wages undermined the prospects of free white labor. The state's Alien Land Act of 1913 forbade immigrants ineligible for naturalized citizenship (that is, Asians), from purchasing agricultural property. The realtors' contention that expanding the rights of Blacks takes freedom away from whites, prominently featured in the campaign for Proposition 14, also has deep roots in American history.

Andrew Johnson invoked it to justify his veto of the Civil Rights Bill in 1866: "the distinction of race and color is by the bill made to operate in favor of the colored and against the white race."

Perhaps because of its very ubiquity, freedom is an idea whose meaning is always in flux. (One of the more remarkable developments of the past two years has been its expansion to include the right to infect one's fellow citizens with a deadly virus.) It seems ahistorical to argue, as Slater does, that realtors' "redefinition of freedom" became the "model for American conservatism as a whole." Today's conservative understandings of freedom have many antecedents among business groups, Cold Warriors, anti-government ideologues, and opponents of the civil rights movement, among others. And the political rise of the Right had many causes, not simply a cynical, racially exclusionary definition of freedom.

How much has changed since the Supreme Court outlawed housing discrimination? The civil rights revolution created a large Black middle and professional class with the economic resources to purchase homes in suburbs and upscale urban neighborhoods if allowed to do so. At the same time, recently arrived immigrants from Asia, Africa, and Latin America have moved directly to previously homogenous small cities and rural areas rather than to the large urban centers favored by their predecessors. In the past decade the vast majority of the counties in the United States have become more diverse demographically. Nonetheless, study after study has shown that real estate agents still steer Black home buyers to a much smaller number of neighborhoods than whites of equivalent means. According to recently released census figures, Levittown, Pennsylvania, is 76 percent white today, but still only 6 percent Black. Levittown, Long Island, is two-thirds white and 1 percent Black. In both towns, Asians and Hispanics, apparently less "objectionable" as neighbors, comprise most of the remainder. House patterns do change, although slowly. Slater writes that today, "segregation of African Americans remains almost as intense as it was fifty years ago." Unfortunately, he does not try to bring the detailed analysis up to the present.

During his campaign for reelection in 2020, Donald Trump (whose father's housing developments in New York City notoriously excluded Black tenants) promised to abandon the enforcement of housing discrimination laws so that adherents of the "Suburban Lifestyle Dream" would no longer be "bothered" by the federal government. Slater makes clear that this "dream" has long had a racial dimension, thanks in part to realtors, who powerfully shaped the America in which we live.

LAND AND FREEDOM IN THE AFTERMATH OF SLAVERY

ETWEEN 1910 AND 1930, over one million Black Americans moved from the rural South to industrial cities north of the Mason-Dixon line. Refugees fleeing grinding poverty, political disenfranchisement, inadequate education, and the ever-present threat of violence (a comprehensive system of white supremacy known by the shorthand Jim Crow), they found employment at the bottom rungs of the burgeoning industrial economy. Despite pervasive prejudice in the North and a not always friendly welcome, the migrants spoke of a second emancipation, of crossing over Jordan to the Promised Land of freedom.

The Great Migration, as it came to be called, produced the modern urban ghettoes of New York, Philadelphia, Chicago, and other cities, which epitomized African American life in the twentieth century as surely as the southern farm and plantation had in the nineteenth. It inspired innumerable responses from artists, including novels, blues ballads, Broadway shows, and The Migration Series, a collection of sixty small canvases by the black painter Jacob Lawrence. This popu-

Review of *A Mind to Stay: White Plantation, Black Homeland*, by Sydney Nathans, *London Review of Books*, June 29, 2017.

lation upheaval has been the subject of numerous scholarly treatments, most recently Isabel Wilkerson's evocative best-seller, *The Warmth of Other Suns*, and Ira Berlin's *The Making of African America*, which reconceptualizes the Black experience within the framework of four historic migrations (the other three being the forced removal of slaves from Africa to North America; the "second middle passage" that uprooted massive numbers for the journey from older states such as Virginia to the cotton kingdom of the Lower South; and the arrival in the last quarter-century of hundreds of thousands of immigrants from Africa). Population movements have been a defining feature of African American life.

The fact is, however, that more Blacks chose to remain in the South than embark on the Great Migration, and that far less attention has been paid to them. *A Mind to Stay*, by Sydney Nathans, an emeritus professor of history at Duke University, deals with one small slice of that population. The book, truly a life's work (Nathans began the interviews that led him to reconstruct this story four decades ago) is a marvelous example of how "microhistory," based on a deep immersion in local sources, can illuminate broad historical patterns. It also suggests some of the limitations of this increasingly popular genre of historical analysis.

A Mind to Stay spans nearly two centuries of history. The first part, which begins in the antebellum period, focuses on the experiences of "two Pauls"—Paul Cameron, the son of Duncan Cameron, one of the largest slaveowners in North Carolina, and his slave Paul Hargress (originally named Hargis after a previous owner)—and their families. Duncan Cameron prided himself on his paternalistic regard for his human property. He tried not to separate family members when buying or selling slaves, and relied on incentives to elicit efficient labor—for example, credits slaves could use at a local store to purchase cloth, whiskey, and other goods—rather than violence. (On the other hand, slaves who tried to run away received severe whippings.) After an unsuccessful stint as a lawyer, Paul Cameron took over management of the plantation while his father concentrated on running a local bank. It took the younger Cameron a while to develop his own system of discipline. "He acquired a reputation," Nathans writes, as an owner "who whipped his workers just to show them who was master."

In 1844, like innumerable other planters in the Upper South, where tobacco and wheat were the main crops, Paul Cameron purchased a plantation in Alabama, part of the booming cotton kingdom. He acquired 1,600 acres of land for $30,000 borrowed from his father, an immense sum at a time when the income of an urban workingman was around $300 per year. Cameron had no intention of moving himself; he sent 144 of his slaves from North Carolina to Alabama and hired an overseer to manage the plantation (which helps to explain the voluminous correspondence that makes a book like this possible). Like his father, he made an effort to keep families intact, but inevitably some of those transported left behind loved ones.

Because of the world market's insatiable demand for cotton, the key raw material of the industrial revolution, many cotton planters acquired fortunes. Paul Cameron was not among them. Almost at once, he complained that he had been cheated. The land was not nearly as fertile as he had been led to believe. Moreover, his slaves, no doubt resenting the forced removal from their homes, proved recalcitrant workers. Cotton was a far more demanding crop than wheat or tobacco, and the overseer reported constant battles over the pace of work. In the 1850s, Cameron purchased another plantation, in Mississippi. But the Alabama place never proved as profitable as he had hoped.

Four of the slaves sent to Alabama were Paul Hargis, his brother, and their two sisters. Their parents and another brother remained in North Carolina. Unfortunately, while the Cameron Family Papers comprise one of the largest manuscript collections at the University of North Carolina's Southern Historical Collection—some 33,000 pieces of correspondence, business papers, tax records, and all sorts of other documents—only what Nathans calls "shards of evidence" exist about the Hargis siblings' lives as slaves. Nathans is inevitably reduced to speculating about their experiences and aspirations. Juxtaposing the two Pauls is an effective narrative device, and the Hargis descendants dominate the twentieth-century part of the story. But it has the unfortunate result of casting all the other slaves into the shadows; apart from a handful of individuals, we learn very little about them.

One thing we do know is that when Cameron purchased his Mississippi plantation and moved thirty-five slaves there from Alabama, the extended Hargis family, now with spouses and children, were not among them. Relatively speaking, they were fortunate. In Mississippi, faced with the back-breaking task of clearing the land and then producing as much cotton as possible, all semblance of paternalism disappeared. To be sure, the overseer hired Irish laborers to do the dangerous work of draining the boggy soil, not wanting to risk the lives of valuable slaves. But to maximize production, he gave each slave a daily quota for picking cotton; those who failed to meet the target received a whipping. In his recent book, *The Half Has Never Been Told*, Edward Baptist has identified this "whipping system" as a pervasive means of increasing the productivity of labor in the cotton fields. But neither of Cameron's holdings resembled the ultra-efficient and immensely profitable enterprises Baptist claims cotton plantations had become by the mid-nineteenth century. More often than not, crops did not live up to expectations. Baptist portrays resistance as virtually impossible, but in 1860 a "slowdown" by Cameron's slaves in Mississippi forced the overseer to reduce the daily quotas. In early 1861, a slave, Zack, who had been whipped for not meeting his quota, attacked the overseer with an axe. He was tried, convicted, and sentenced to hang. But by then, a new cloud loomed on Cameron's horizon—the outbreak of civil war.

As numerous works of history have demonstrated, the war thoroughly disrupted the slave system. Cameron's plantations were no exception. In 1862, Union soldiers entered the Mississippi Valley. Fearing his slaves would run off to the federal army, Cameron moved them—111 in all—to his Alabama plantation. Slaves there, according to the overseer, quickly learned of Lincoln's Emancipation Proclamation and became more difficult to control. Meanwhile, the Confederacy requisitioned some of Cameron's slaves to help build a railroad. "We are in the midst of a terrible revolution," Cameron wrote to his son. In

1864, when federal troops approached the Alabama cotton belt, Cameron hurriedly brought sixty-five slaves back to North Carolina, among them Paul Hargis.

As on numerous southern plantations, the end of slavery was succeeded by "an unfolding insurgency" on Cameron's holdings, a bitter struggle between former master and former slave over access to land and control of labor. The freed people on the North Carolina plantation, Cameron's wife complained, were "indisposed to work" (that is, they refused to work as if they were still slaves). They were insolent and set their own pace of labor. "They are armed and so am I," the overseer reported. Many ex-slaves soon struck out on their own. Paul Hargis, however, continued to labor for Cameron in North Carolina. We know Cameron's responses to the end of slavery, but can only infer why Hargis remained. He had been relatively privileged as a slave; perhaps he was grateful. He seems to have had a closer connection to Cameron than most of the other slaves. In 1866, when he registered his marriage with the Freedmen's Bureau, he even changed his last name to Cameron.

The following year, frustrated by his inability to control his former slaves, Cameron evicted them all from his North Carolina plantation and rented the land to white tenants. Paul Hargis Cameron and his wife headed west, to reunite with their relatives on the Alabama plantation. When he arrived, he changed his name back to Hargis. Unfortunately for all concerned, a series of disastrous crops followed the end of slavery in the Lower South. Labor conflict, incessant rain, and the advent of the "army worm" that devoured the growing crop, combined to devastate cotton output. Cameron tried various means of adjusting. In 1868 the land was worked by "squads" consisting of family members. Although there was a white plantation manager, the squads pretty much directed their own labor. Many ex-slaves eventually left the plantation but the extended Hargis clan remained.

Paul Cameron had long wanted to get rid of the Alabama plantation. In 1874, in the wake of the economic depression that followed the Panic of 1873, he sold it in eight plots to a dozen of his former slaves. The purchasers had to put no money down, and could pay over five years, in cotton or cash as they desired. It remains unclear exactly why Cameron sold the land to Blacks—not a common practice in the postwar South—and offered such lenient terms. To be sure, land values had plummeted because of the depression, and white buyers were difficult to find. Perhaps the remnants of Cameron family paternalism still lingered. In any event, Paul Hargis and his brother Jim together purchased 100 acres for $800. "The Cameron plantation," Nathans writes, "became their foothold in freedom." At this point, halfway through the book, Paul Cameron disappears from the narrative, and the focus turns to the Hargis family.

In the aftermath of slavery, freedpeople throughout the South demanded access to land. When General William T. Sherman met with a group of Black ministers in Savannah in January 1865, he asked what would enable the emancipated slaves to live as free people. They answered, "give us land." Sherman proceeded to set aside a portion of coastal South Carolina and Georgia for the exclusive settlement of Black families, but Andrew Johnson, the deeply racist southern Unionist who became president after Lincoln's assassination, ordered it returned to the former owners. A few northern radicals, most notably Congressman Thaddeus Stevens of Pennsylvania, advocated confiscating the land of Confederate planters and distributing it in forty-acre plots to the former slaves, with anything left over sold to help pay off the national debt. The phrase "forty acres and a mule," encapsulating the Black desire for land, reverberated throughout the postwar South. The hoped-for land distribution never materialized. But over time, a substantial number of Blacks managed to acquire small plots for their families. Paul and Jim Hargis remained on their farm and held onto it tenaciously. As Nathans points out, in subsequent years they pledged all sorts of property as security for loans from local merchants—crops, cows, horses, wagons—but almost never the land itself. They kept it for the rest of their lives.

Not everything was harmonious on the Black-owned farms carved from the Cameron plantation. To support himself in old age, Paul Hargress (who changed the spelling of his surname around the turn of the century, presumably to sever the link with slavery represented by Hargis, the name of his first owner), deeded parts of his land to nine relatives, on condition that they each pay him ten dollars a year—a kind of private pension system. But many of them did not fulfill their promises and recriminations followed. Moreover, some Hargress family members resented non-blood farmers living nearby. Ned Forrest Hargress, reputedly the son of a slave woman raped by Confederate general Nathan Bedford Forrest as the Civil War drew to a close, inherited some of Paul Hargress's land. (Ned had taken his surname after working for many years for Hargress.) At some point, according to family lore, a group marched to his farm to try to evict him, shouting, "We are full-blooded Africans and we are here to claim our land."

Obviously, in an agricultural society it is better to own land than not. Compared with renters (who paid for the use of land) and sharecroppers (who received part of the crop as payment for their labor at the end of the year), land owners enjoyed a modicum of economic independence. But land was hardly a panacea for Blacks' economic plight. Land is not the only scarce factor of production; access to credit is also crucial. Landowners had to borrow from local planters and merchants to get through the year, and often found that they remained in debt after marketing their crops. Renters and sharecroppers had more freedom of movement; if dissatisfied with the employer they could move on. As Nathans points out, in the 1920s renters on nearby plantations seemed to enjoy a higher standard of living than Hargress's descendants. Land locked owners into a declining part of the American economy. Genuine economic opportunity lay in the industrial North, as those who took part in the Great Migration, including many thousands from Alabama, realized.

Nonetheless, events during the 1930s illustrated the vulnerability of those who did not own land. As the price of cotton collapsed during the Great Depression, the administration of Franklin D. Roosevelt devised a plan to stabilize agricultural income by paying farmers to cut back on production. Some of the money was supposed to be passed along to now idled renters and sharecroppers. But many planters simply evicted their work force and kept it all for themselves. In 1939, moreover, a plantation next to Cameron's was sold, and the new owner turned to raising cattle, expelling the Black tenants. Land ownership, even in dire circumstances, offered a bit of economic security.

In the decades that followed, the federal government favored agribusiness over small farming and refused to offer Black farm owners loans and other support on the same basis as whites. Like the Black experience under the New Deal, this sorry history illustrates how outside forces powerfully affect the lives of local communities. Microhistory, however, seems to have difficulty integrating the local and national stories. Nathans alludes only briefly to major political developments that affected Black life in Alabama. The Civil War was followed by a bitter struggle over the terms of Reconstruction, as the effort to unify the nation and come to terms with the end of slavery was called. Southern whites, abetted by President Andrew Johnson, sought to relegate Blacks to the status of plantation laborers with few if any civil and political rights. Republicans in Congress, alarmed that the results of the war were being overturned, rewrote the laws and Constitution to guarantee equality before the law regardless of race. In 1867, Black men throughout the South for the first time acquired the right to vote and hold office. A wave of local political mobilization followed. The overseer on Cameron's land reported that he could not stop the former slaves from abandoning work to attend political gatherings.

After a few years of a remarkable experiment in interracial democracy, Reconstruction in Alabama came to an end, the victim of a violent counterrevolution spearheaded by the Ku Klux Klan and kindred organizations. White supremacy resumed. In the 1890s, Alabama Populists made an effort to unite farmers, white and Black, in a new political coalition. After their defeat, new laws rescinded Blacks' right to vote almost entirely. Nathans notes these events, but not how they may have affected life on the Cameron land, or strategies of the Black purchasers for holding on to their farms. It remains unclear how much the closing off of political participation influenced the decision to move to the North. Nathans notes that an oral tradition developed among the freedpeople and their descendants in which the years immediately following slavery were recalled as "hallelujah times." But without a look at events at the state and national levels, it is difficult to understand why.

Paul Hargress died in 1918 at the age of 91. The main protagonist of the twentieth-century part of the narrative is Alice Hargress, born in 1914, who married the grandson of Ned Forrest Hargress. *A Mind to Stay* begins with her participation in a voting rights demonstration in Greensboro, Alabama, in 1965, not long after the more famous confrontation in nearby Selma, where the violent assault by police on peaceful marchers shocked the world. Alice Hargress, whom Nathans interviewed on numerous occasions, was not a radical, although in the years before 1965 she had persisted in trying to register to vote and had become one of the few Blacks in her area who eventually succeeded. She told her family that because "whites have the power," direct confrontation would be suicidal. The way to get ahead was through developing an unimpeachable character and striving to excel. "You got to know more than them white children if you want to get anything," she told her offspring. But she joined the movement, faced tear gas, and spent three days in jail. She and the others were part of a struggle that led directly to passage of the Voting Rights Act of 1965.

By then, an even larger exodus of Blacks that began in World War II and extended into the 1960s had led more people north than the Great Migration. The number of southern Black farmers, 150,000 as late as 1965, continued to shrink: there are only around 40,000 in the entire region. When Nathans met Alice Hargress, none of her eight children and numerous grandchildren was living in Alabama. They had dispersed to Detroit, Los Angeles, and other cities. (One of her grandsons would work as a cook for President Barack Obama at Camp David.) But Alice Hargress held onto the land she and her husband had inherited. She called it "heir land," meaning that any member of the extended family who encountered difficulty in the North would have a place to which to return.

Ned Forrest Hargress, born in 1865, died at 99, two months before Lyndon Johnson signed the Voting Rights Act. His entire adult life took place under the shadow of Jim Crow, and he never once was allowed to cast a ballot. Alice Hargress died in 2014, three weeks shy of her one hundredth birthday; she lived to experience the civil rights revolution. In some ways, life in Alabama has changed enormously, yet political and economic power remain in the hands of whites.

"We're a long way from being free," Lewis Black, a voting rights organizer, told Nathans in 1981. Too many still are.

A BLACK DYNASTY AND
ITS FATE

I T IS A revealing commentary on the history of American democracy
that of the nearly two thousand men and women who have served in
the U.S. Senate since the founding of the republic, only twelve, as
of 2024, have been Black. Remarkably, the first two were elected from
Mississippi during the Reconstruction era that followed the Civil War.
Hiram Revels served for a few weeks in 1870 and then returned to relative obscurity as an educator. Blanche K. Bruce, who held his seat from
1875 to 1881, amassed a small fortune and founded what Lawrence Otis
Graham calls "America's first true Black dynasty."

In this flawed but fascinating study, Graham, a Black attorney and
author of *Our Kind of People*, a best-seller about the Black upper class,
tells the story of three generations of the Bruce family. It is a poignant
tale of struggle, accomplishment, and weakness—and an illuminating
account of American racism.

Graham's cast of characters begins with Bruce and his wife Josephine, the Senator and Socialite of the book's title. Born a slave in Vir-

Review of *The Senator and the Socialite: The True Story of America's
First Black Dynasty*, by Lawrence O. Graham, *Washington Post Book
World*, July 2, 2006.

ginia in 1841, the son of his owner, Bruce escaped during the Civil War, studied at Oberlin College, and made his way to Mississippi, where he rose quickly in politics and purchased a plantation. His beautiful, light-skinned wife Josephine, whom he married in 1878, came from Cleveland's tiny Black upper class. After his Senate term expired, Bruce and his wife remained in Washington, where he held patronage posts, acquired a large townhouse and summer home, and presided over Black high society.

The second generation of Bruces enjoyed privileged lives far removed from those of most Americans, white or Black. The son, Roscoe, attended Phillips Exeter Academy and Harvard. He worked for a time as head of academic education at Tuskegee Institute, and served as superintendent of Black schools in Washington and manager of the Dunbar Apartments, a Harlem housing complex built by John D. Rockefeller Jr. His talented wife, Clara, attended Radcliffe and Boston University Law School, where she became the first woman anywhere to edit a law review. The third generation, also named Roscoe and Clara, followed in their parents' footsteps to Harvard and Radcliffe, the country's most elite institutions of higher learning.

Graham does not shy from describing the costs of these accomplishments, among them the Bruces' complete dissociation from the rest of Black America. On the Bruce plantation in Mississippi, Black sharecroppers lived in "flimsy wooden shacks" and labored in the same oppressive conditions as tenants on white-owned estates. Roscoe Bruce, Sr. found the exuberant mode of worship of lower-class Tuskegee students "disgusting."

That Roscoe Bruce worked at Tuskegee is not coincidental, for the family shared its founder Booker T. Washington's philosophy of accommodation and his reliance on connections with wealthy white patrons. Blanche Bruce said little in the Senate as white violence stripped his people of their rights. While attending Harvard, his son spied for Washington on Boston's "anti-Bookerite" Black radicals. Even though he himself had received an elite academic education, Roscoe Bruce tried to introduce Washington's philosophy of industrial train-

188 • OUR FRAGILE FREEDOMS

ing in the District of Columbia's Black schools, causing an uproar among Black parents proud of their children's educational attainments. When a scandal erupted because Bruce allowed a white man to take nude photographs of Black high school students, allegedly as part of a study of physical differences between the races, he was forced to resign. Only when it came to their own family did the Bruces turn militant. In 1923, Harvard President A. Lawrence Lowell barred the college's six Black freshmen, including Roscoe Jr., from living in freshman dormitories. Roscoe Sr. organized a national campaign that forced Lowell to rescind his order.

An indefatigable researcher in primary sources, Graham sometimes seems unaware of current scholarship. The opening chapters present a confusing picture of Reconstruction politics because Graham uses the word "liberal" in its modern sense of racial egalitarianism rather than its nineteenth-century meaning of belief in limited government and laissez-faire economics. Contrary to his account, those who called themselves liberal Republicans opposed Reconstruction.

Nonetheless, *The Senator and the Socialite* offers a compelling portrait of the Bruce family's rise, inner dynamics, and downfall. In 1936, Roscoe Sr. lost his job when Rockefeller sold the Dunbar apartments. His children lacked the drive and self-discipline of their forebears. The younger Clara failed to complete her studies at Radcliffe and eloped with a Black actor. Roscoe Jr. embezzled money from an apartment complex he managed in New Jersey and then arranged a phony burglary to explain the absence of the funds. He served eighteen months in prison and the legal costs bankrupted the family.

Problems in the third generation of privileged families are standard grist for gossip columnists. But the Black elite faced greater obstacles to recovery and had fewer resources and connections to fall back on than their white counterparts. No New York law firm would hire a Black female attorney like Clara Bruce. In their hour of need, the elite whites the Bruces had cultivated for decades abandoned them, refusing repeated requests for assistance. Roscoe Sr. and his wife were reduced to living for a time on welfare. Many of their relatives, including the younger Clara and her actor husband, avoided racism by passing as white. Today, Graham reports, most descendants of Senator Bruce live as white persons—an ironic but in some ways understandable end to a Black dynasty to which Jim Crow America never offered a secure place.

RACE, RIGHTS, AND
THE LAW

D URING ITS HEYDAY in the 1960s the civil rights movement
caused deep divisions in American society. More recently it
has been absorbed into a whiggish narrative of progress in
which a system resting on white supremacy was superseded by one that,
while hardly perfect, is considerably closer to the ideal of equal justice
under law. Participants in what is sometimes called the "freedom struggle" included courageous activists who put their lives on the line in the
Jim Crow South and a cadre of civil rights attorneys, exemplified by
Charles Hamilton Houston and Thurgood Marshall of the NAACP,
who in a series of landmark cases persuaded the federal courts that the
legal system institutionalized around 1900 in the southern states violated the constitutional rights of Black Americans.

Before this triumph of the rule of law, according to what Dylan
Penningroth calls the "master narrative of civil rights," Black southerners had little faith in the legal system and did their best to avoid
contact with it. This makes intuitive sense. Why would African

---

Review of *Before the Movement: The Hidden History of Black Civil
Rights*, by Dylan C. Penningroth, *New York Review of Books*, April 4,
2024.

Americans believe they could achieve fair results in courts dedicated to upholding white supremacy? Better to steer clear of southern courtrooms entirely.

Penningroth believes that current scholars' understanding of the emergence of the civil rights movement rests on a series of misconceptions about Black Americans' "legal lives." He sets out to demolish them. Even during the days of slavery, he insists, they knew a lot more about legal principles than one might imagine. From experience and observation, they developed what Penningroth calls "goat sense" (following the coinage of the Black tenant farmer Ned Cobb, the protagonist of the 1974 best-seller *All God's Dangers*)—a working knowledge of legal rules and concepts.

Far from avoiding the courts, they utilized all the legal tools at their disposal. From the late nineteenth century to the era of the civil rights movement, he writes, "Black people poured out their family stories" in legal cases, exhibiting a "wary faith" that the courts would uphold their claims to what he calls the mundane "rights of everyday use"— rights that derived from ownership of property, the signing of contracts, the "associational privileges" of membership in Black churches, and legal claims, such as inheritance, acquired through marriage. Rather than heroic freedom fighters courageously confronting repression or victims avoiding the courts at all costs, Black Americans emerge in this telling as ordinary folk using the law to help make the best of difficult circumstances.

Penningroth's conclusions emerge from an epic research agenda in which he and his students examined some 14,000 legal cases, identifying 1,500 with Black litigants, most but not all in the South. These were civil litigations, matters of private law whose documentary records long lay unexamined in local courthouses. As has lately become common among historians, Penningroth intersperses his account with his own family's experiences from the time of slavery to the twentieth century's Great Migration as a point of departure and reference.

Before the Movement begins with a revealing incident involving Penningroth's enslaved ancestor Jackson Holcomb, who owned a small boat in Virginia. In the final days of the Civil War, Holcomb successfully demanded payment to ferry Confederate soldiers fleeing the Union army across the Appomattox River. Legally speaking, the boat and everything else Holcomb claimed as property belonged to his enslaver. But the desperate Confederates did not challenge his ownership of a boat or his right to charge a fee for transporting individuals across the river. Whatever the letter of the law, custom throughout the slave South accepted that slaves could acquire property of their own.

Penningroth devotes particular attention to the widespread practice of allowing slaves to till small garden plots on which they grew crops for sale at local markets. He acknowledges that for slaves, cultivating "garden patches" in what was supposed to be their free time was a form of "superexploitation"—the owner shifting to the laborers themselves part of the responsibility for providing food for enslaved laborers and their families. Nevertheless he views such plots as the basis of an "informal economy" that allowed numerous slaves to earn income that would finance the acquisition of land after the Civil War.

Over time, privileges won by slaves morphed into customs, and customs into rights. While slavery existed, property ownership by slaves was not enforceable in court. That would change in 1871, in the midst of Reconstruction, when Congress established the Southern Claims Commission, charged with compensating former southern Unionists, slaves included, for property appropriated by the army during the war.

Something similar had transpired a few years earlier with regard to Black families. Slave marriages had no standing in law, but enslaved men and women married anyway and local communities, white and Black, recognized the existence of their unions, though this did not prevent their disruption by sale. Although Penningroth does not draw attention to it, in March 1865 Abraham Lincoln signed a law freeing the immediate families of Black Union soldiers. Slaves' family ties suddenly acquired legal standing in the eyes of the federal government. One consequence was that the widows of Black veterans became entitled to federal pensions. As for Jackson Holcomb, in the years after his encounter with fleeing Confederates, he married, purchased land, and paid his property taxes. He appreciated the importance of adhering to legal rules.

In order to make sense of the vast archive he and his students have created, Penningroth divides his history into four parts—slavery, Reconstruction, Jim Crow, and the "movement era." For each he delineates how Black citizens used the law and how their efforts helped to produce an evolution in the concept of civil rights itself. Many readers may find the first chapter, "The Privileges of Slavery," surprising. Penningroth freely grants the incongruity of the idea. But he shows that throughout the South, slaves were able to wring concessions from their owners and to create customary entitlements that over time evolved into rights recognized by "community opinion."

"Slaves owned property in every legal sense of the word," he writes, "except that no court would protect their ownership as a right." Readers may well consider this a significant exception, but Penningroth makes a strong case that their experience with property ownership and trade equipped slaves to become "key players" in the South's "market economy," and that as a result many were prepared for participation in a free labor system. Emancipation, he writes, was "a much less sharp break" in the lives of the enslaved than historians have assumed. (Penningroth has a penchant for ex cathedra pronouncements like this that need more supporting evidence than he provides, and he sometimes fails to make clear which historians he is taking to task.)

Penningroth's discussion of slave property rights brings to mind the work of perhaps the post–World War II generation's leading scholar of slavery, Eugene D. Genovese. Current trends in scholarship about the Old South have somewhat diminished his posthumous reputation. The stress now is on the institution's physical brutality and its central role in the expansion of modern capitalism, calling into question Genovese's portrait of southern slavery as a paternalistic, precapitalist institution whose functioning rested on mutual concessions between owner and slave.

Genovese was interested in how ruling classes acquire legitimacy and exercise authority. Toward the beginning of his classic study *Roll,*

Jordan, Roll (1974), he included a brief section entitled "The Hegemonic Function of the Law," delineating how it serves the interests of those holding power in repressive regimes to ensure that the legal system operates with a modicum of fairness, even if it means that persons like them do not always win in court. The belief that the courts actually dispense justice can help to obscure vast imbalances of power. Like Penningroth, Genovese wrote of rights based on custom enjoyed by slaves.

In the late nineteenth century, thanks to the laws and constitutional amendments enacted during Reconstruction, Black men for the first time were serving as justices of the peace and holding other judicial offices, mostly in the South. This helps to explain why more and more Black southerners were inspired to go to court, a pattern that continued well after the advent of Jim Crow. But, Penningroth was surprised to discover, very few of the thousands of cases he examined identified the race of the individuals involved. In cases revolving around property rights, he says, it made no difference if parties were Black or white—race "had no legal meaning."

Despite the pervasive hold of white supremacy, moreover, not all white people shared the same interests. In rural areas of the South, for example, some white farmers strongly opposed the presence in their neighborhoods of Black landowners, while others welcomed their availability as temporary laborers at harvest time. Via census records and other digitized sources, Penningroth was able to identify the race of many individuals who appear in court documents, yet the legal records suggest that even in the days of Jim Crow civil law did not always operate along racial lines.

In his sections dealing with Reconstruction and the Jim Crow era, Penningroth emphasizes that the post–Civil War emergence of the Black family as the central institution in Black communities forced African Americans to familiarize themselves with the nuances of family law. Black litigants engaged in "waves of lawsuits" about divorce, the sale of property, financial support of the elderly, child custody, and other family matters. These intra-family conflicts, he writes, challenge the romantic view of the Black family as a harmonious institution guided by a communal ethos, which he claims too many historians have embraced. He also points out that, judging from lawsuits, Black churches were often riven by dissension. For example, Penningroth relates the experience of the Mount Helm Baptist Church in Mississippi, "engulfed in controversy" in 1899 when a group of parishioners sued to bar the minister from preaching because he had been performing faith healing services in the sanctuary. The state supreme court ruled in their favor. Black litigants were sometimes more willing to trust the judgment of local courts than the decisions of other family and church members.

In her memoirs, published in 1898, Elizabeth Cady Stanton recalled that Reconstruction involved "the reconsideration of the principles of our Government and the natural rights of man. The nation's heart was thrilled by prolonged debates in Congress and State legislatures, in the pulpits and public journals, and at every fireside on these vital questions." Penningroth examines how the nationwide debate she describes reconfigured Americans' grasp of the concept of civil rights. Before the war, rights were divided into three categories—civil, political, and social—and enjoyment of them varied from state to state. Civil rights encompassed those entitlements necessary for participation in a free-labor economy: signing contracts; testifying in court; owning, buying, and selling property; and suing and being sued. Even in the South, many free Black people enjoyed civil rights, but not the other two. They could own property and testify in court (although often only in cases involving other Black people), but throughout the country voting and "social" rights such as equal access to public transportation, hotels, restaurants, and places of amusement were generally restricted to white men.

In 1866, over the veto of President Andrew Johnson, Congress passed the first national civil rights act, which declared all persons born in the United States citizens by birthright, with the exception of Native Americans (considered members of their tribal sovereignties). The measure severed the connection between citizenship and race, overturning the Dred Scott decision of 1857—in which the Supreme Court under

Chief Justice Roger B. Taney limited citizenship to white Americans—and for the first time delineated the rights the former slaves were to enjoy along with white citizens, essentially civil rights (the rights of contract) but not political or social rights.

As Reconstruction progressed, African Americans and their white allies, drawing on arguments popularized by the pre-war antislavery movement, demanded full legal equality for the emancipated slaves. Increasingly, various kinds of rights merged together. Many Republicans came to include the right to vote as part of an expanded definition of civil rights (except for women). In the Fifteenth Amendment they wrote Black male suffrage into the Constitution. In 1875, shortly before the end of Reconstruction, Congress enacted the second civil rights act, which made it a crime to deny any citizen access to transportation, public accommodations, or a variety of other venues. "Civil" rights had now expanded to include what once had been considered discrete political and social prerogatives.

In 1883 the Supreme Court declared the 1875 law unconstitutional, adopting the view that the Fourteenth Amendment's guarantee of equal protection of the law regardless of race applied only to "state action"—that is, racial discrimination by public officials, not private businesses. But, Penningroth points out, the process of redefinition continued well into the twentieth century, as civil rights became more and more linked to race. By the time Congress and the Warren Court had dismantled legal Jim Crow, the right of racial minorities to be free of invidious discrimination had come to overshadow the definition of civil rights as the basic entitlements of all free persons. This transformation, he speculates, made it more difficult to persuade white Americans that the struggle for civil rights was relevant to their own daily lives.

Despite losing rights of many kinds, Black southerners in the Jim Crow era enjoyed some remarkable achievements. By 1910, Penningroth relates, more than half a million Black families had managed to acquire land, amounting to more than fifteen million acres. Yet as time went on, the way they dealt with landownership generated serious problems. Frequently, property was owned jointly by members of extended families. Any decision to sell required the agreement of all co-owners, causing deep family divisions. When individual co-owners died without a will, their portion of the land was divided into small plots among surviving children and grandchildren.

Because of the Great Migration, the disposition of landed property in the South frequently involved relatives living in the North, with whom southern family members had little or no contact. Land became the subject of intra-family lawsuits in which litigants claimed to have been cheated out of their share of what came to be known as "heir property," and elderly family members sued relatives who reneged on promises of monetary payments to help them survive old age. As land-ownership fragmented, generations of Black farmers had no choice but to master the legal complexities of such transactions. The Jim Crow era also witnessed a proliferation of Black institutions, including churches, societies for mutual relief, fraternal orders, and schools and colleges. African Americans had to learn the nuances of laws regulating the powers of corporations and associations. As with family and church disputes, they used what they learned to file lawsuits.

Finally, Penningroth turns to the "movement era." Many readers may consider his judgments in this section unduly harsh. He agrees with most current scholars that rather than being brought to the South by NAACP lawyers and other outsiders, the civil rights movement drew on a long history of local legal activism. In keeping with his emphasis on the vitality of Black traditions, he reproaches the civil rights workers from the Student Nonviolent Coordinating Committee who courageously entered the South to help secure the constitutional rights of Black citizens, for misunderstanding the local culture. Offering little direct evidence of their views, he writes that the civil rights volunteers assumed that local people had little experience with legal processes and approached the court system from behind a veil of "legal ignorance." These outsiders were under the mistaken impression, he claims, that Black southerners were "ignorant of their rights" and in need of intervention to galvanize a movement for change. Both Black and white activists, he suggests, adopted a condescending attitude toward the people they were seeking to organize; some went so far as to attribute southern Black poverty, in part, to a "plantation mentality" inherited from slavery.

Penningroth's section on this era includes a valuable discussion of the evolving status of Black attorneys. Drawing on Kenneth Mack's influential book *Representing the Race* (2012), he notes that before the mid-twentieth century most Black attorneys, like most white ones, worked as general interest practitioners who spent the majority of their time representing clients of modest means in minor local cases. At the turn of the twentieth century, African Americans filed at least 17 percent of the civil suits he examined, probably more. Such litigation did not directly challenge white supremacy—nearly all these lawsuits pitted Black people against one another. But even at the height of Jim Crow, Black travelers were able to win lawsuits for damages against railroads that had subjected them to demeaning treatment, and white judges ordered whites to pay their debts to Black creditors. Where the white South drew the line was at Black lawyers' practicing cases of legal significance. Nearly all the lawyers in these thousands of cases appear to have been white. One reason cited by Penningroth was the creation by prominent white attorneys of lily-white bar associations, racially exclusionary gateways to the profession.

Whatever the outcomes of individual lawsuits, the cases handled by Black attorneys rarely produced fees or damages sufficient to sustain a legal career. This was especially true of cases litigating civil rights, which did not produce much income for the lawyers. With the movement's legal successes this changed. For the first time, Black attorneys could make a living as civil rights lawyers, litigating cases arising from new federal statutes and regulations that prohibited racial discrimination. But this development brought significant pressure to bear on Black attorneys to represent the entire "race," not simply individual clients or their own self-interest. Complaints arose that lawyers were too aloof from Black communities, or charged fees that were unaffordable for most Black clients. Not until the 1980s, Penningroth points out, did white-controlled corporations and law firms, able to pay higher salaries than Black lawyers were used to receiving, begin to hire Black attorneys in significant numbers.

Penningroth believes that recent scholars of Black legal history have been studying the wrong cases, paying too much attention to national leaders and too little to the communities from which the movement sprang. Their focus on the great constitutional rulings of the Warren Court slights many other kinds of Black encounters with the legal system. Unlike most such works, *Before the Movement* examines very few Supreme Court rulings.

Penningroth insists that the standard narrative, what he calls "civil rights history," "has left Black people disconnected from our own legal commonsense"—that is, how ordinary people thought about the law and tried to use it in their day-to-day lives. Penningroth does not hesitate to chide previous historians for what he considers mistaken interpretations. But it is also true that his work builds on that of recent scholars such as Martha S. Jones and Laura Edwards, who, like him, have expanded the terrain of legal history to include the role of law in everyday life. Like Penningroth, they have argued that law is created not only by legislatures and courts but also by people who have limited representation within these venues yet are able nonetheless to carve out rights for themselves.

Before the Movement presents an original and provocative account of how civil law was experienced by Black citizens and how their "legal lives" changed over time. Inevitably, given the broad scope of Penningroth's investigation, important questions remain to be answered. What was the impact of segregation and widespread racial violence—pillars of the Jim Crow system—on the functioning of the law? What would the analysis of Black political ideologies and practices add to the discussion?

The long disenfranchisement of Black southerners was a national scandal that did much to shape the lives and opportunities of both Black and white Americans, as well as structures of power in the South and the nation's capital. As Frederick Douglass noted during Reconstruction, in a putative democracy, exclusion from the right to vote is more than an inconvenience—it marks the boundaries of exclusion and inclusion in the body politic. Penningroth roots nineteenth-century definitions of civil rights in that era's antislavery politics. But as the book progresses, politics mostly drops out of the picture. Perhaps this stems from Penningroth's conviction that the measure of race relations may be found in the legal system, not the ballot box, or his complaint that recent historians have imposed what he calls "the politics of the 1960s" on their accounts of the civil rights movement.

Was the movement's outcome a victory, a defeat, or something more ambiguous than either? The legal edifice of Jim Crow was dismantled and numerous embodiments of white supremacy uprooted. But a look around our society today, with its stark disparities in wealth, life expectancy, education, and other indices of individual and social well-being, suggests the transformation was incomplete. Civil rights gained a powerful foothold in the nation's laws and legal consciousness. Yet something was lost, Penningroth believes, when legal issues were turned into moral ones and civil rights became a matter of race rather than of common citizenship. Did the movement itself, as he contends, encourage the transformation of "civil rights" from entitlements that should be available to all citizens into the narrower concept of non-discrimination—a shield protecting only racial minorities and thus making it more difficult to enlist other Americans on the movement's side? On this and other questions raised by Penningroth's ambitious, stimulating, and provocative book, the jury is still out.

EVERYDAY VIOLENCE
IN THE JIM CROW SOUTH

A LITTLE OVER TWENTY years ago, the New-York Historical Society mounted "Without Sanctuary," a remarkable exhibition of photographs of lynchings in the American South. The images of mobs torturing and murdering Black citizens, some widely circulated as souvenir postcards, revealed a depravity that had long been shrouded in historical amnesia. Since then, the roughly four thousand lynchings that took place between 1880 and the 1950s have received ample public attention, including at the National Museum of African American History and Culture, which opened six years ago in Washington, D.C., and the recently established National Memorial for Peace and Justice in Montgomery, Alabama. Thanks to a recent outpouring of scholarship, novels, and films, most Americans are also aware that violence was essential to the functioning of slavery. Less widely remembered, however, is the quotidian violence that claimed many hundreds of Black lives between the end of slavery and the civil rights revolution. The horrors of Black life in the Jim Crow South have not really entered the country's historical consciousness.

Review of *By Hands Now Known: Jim Crow's Legal Executioners*, by Margaret A. Burnham, *New York Review of Books*, April 6, 2023.

Jim Crow, a shorthand for the southern racial order that followed Reconstruction, is usually equated with racial segregation, but it was far more than that. A comprehensive system of white supremacy, it also included the disenfranchisement of Black voters (thus stripping them of political power); a labor market that relegated African Americans to the lowest-paying jobs; and a code of behavior in which Blacks were required to demonstrate deference in all their interactions with whites. In the Jim Crow South, for a Black person to step outside norms of behavior established by whites could be a death sentence. Violence could erupt at any time, for any reason, or for no reason at all. The possibility of chronic, unpredictable violence loomed over everyday Black life. This "mundane, largely hidden violence" is the subject of Margaret A. Burnham's new book, *By Hands Now Known*, a work by turns shocking, moving, and thought-provoking. It merits the attention of anyone interested in the historical roots of the civil rights movement of the 1960s and, more recently, Black Lives Matter.

Over the course of a long career, Burnham has been a pioneering civil rights attorney and legal scholar. In 1977 she became the first Black woman appointed to a judgeship in Massachusetts. Today, she directs the Civil Rights and Restorative Justice Project at Northeastern University, which chronicles the history of racially motivated southern homicides between 1930 and 1970, and seeks to rescue the victims, many of whose stories have never been told, from historical oblivion. The project's detective work has uncovered over one thousand such murders. Approximately thirty are discussed in detail in this book. Often, the perpetrators were the very officials sworn to uphold the law—among them police officers, sheriffs, and coroners. Almost all the murderers escaped punishment. Complicity extended well beyond the actual perpetrators. Prosecutors were reluctant to seek indictments; all-white trial juries refused to convict; the FBI, Army, and Department of Justice almost never took action; and the Supreme Court eviscerated the constitutional amendments and laws Congress had enacted during Reconstruction that empowered federal authorities to punish violent deprivations of Blacks' constitutional rights.

The diligent research, of Burnham and students at Northeastern's law school in local records, the Black press, NAACP files, and interviews with descendants, makes those who perished more than victims, bringing to light their family relations, jobs, and educations, and the details of the encounters that ended with their deaths.

Burnham's account focuses on particularly violent locations, such as Birmingham, where the laws prohibiting homicide, she writes, "simply did not apply" to the police. Long before the 1963 confrontation between Bull Connor's dogs and fire hoses and young civil rights demonstrators that marked the high point of the mass civil rights movement, shootings of Blacks and the bombing of their homes were shockingly commonplace. Fifteen bombings took place between 1947 and 1965, mostly directed against Black families who breached the color line by seeking to move into white neighborhoods. In 1948 alone, according to the *Birmingham World*, a Black newspaper, sixteen African American men died at the hands of law enforcement officers. The strange alchemy of the city's criminal justice system transformed minor infractions that landed Black persons in jail into capital crimes. One individual murdered by the police had been imprisoned because he had had too much to drink, another because the police were searching for a prowler. In Westfield, a town near Birmingham, a female white clerk at a local store, claiming that a Black customer, William Daniel, had insulted her, called the police. When an officer arrived, he almost immediately shot and killed the alleged offender, even though, as Burnham laconically remarks, Daniel had committed no crime: "even in Alabama, there was no law against 'insulting a white woman.'"

One reason for the excessive violence in what Blacks called "Bad Birmingham" was that the region's coal and steel companies had their own private police forces that worked in tandem with municipal authorities to weaken the United Mine Workers. In 1948, the Rev. C. T. Butler, pastor of a local Baptist church, father of thirteen children, and an important figure in the union, was shot and killed by members of the Tennessee Coal, Iron, and Railroad Company's police. In a familiar pattern, the white press sought to undermine Butler's reputation, publicizing police claims that he had been "molesting" a white woman. Threatened with further killings, nearly the entire Butler family fled to Michigan.

While statistics can map the scope of racist violence, it is the individual stories uncovered by Burnham and her students that make the most powerful impact. Some truly boggle the mind. In 1941, John Jackson, a Birmingham steel worker, was waiting with other African Americans to gain access to a movie theater through the "Negro entrance." Police ordered them to clear a path for passersby. Evidently Jackson did not hear the directive and laughed at something said by his female companion. "What are you laughing at boy?" a policeman yelled. Jackson replied, "Can't I laugh?" With that, he was thrown into a patrol car, shot, and beaten by an officer. He died on the way to the station house. (In this case, very unusually for Birmingham, the culprit was dismissed from the police force.) Being in the wrong place at the wrong time could be dangerous. Much like Trayvon Martin six decades later, Robert Sands, a 15-year-old Black youth, was shot and killed as he walked through a segregated Birmingham neighborhood where he was employed by a white family. Sands's presence led a white woman to express alarm to her husband. Within minutes he shot the teenager in the back. The local prosecutor refused to assemble a grand jury to consider criminal charges.

New Orleans was another city with a violent police force, including the chief detective, John Grosch, and his brother William, also a detective. In 1930, William Grosch and another officer drove to Detroit to take custody of Wilbert Smith, who had fled New Orleans several years earlier after being charged with shooting a policeman during a traffic stop a decade earlier and had been living in Detroit until apprehended by the Motor City's police. Almost as soon as the three men reached New Orleans, the detectives fatally shot Smith. The two officers went on to beat Smith's wife and ordered her to leave the city. In this instance a grand jury was summoned, but it declined to issue indictments.

The stationing of large numbers of Black soldiers, many from the North, at segregated World War II army bases adjacent to southern cities led inexorably to violence as servicemen began to push back against racial segregation. Willie Lee Davis, a 25-year-old veteran from Georgia still wearing his army uniform, was killed by a local police chief in 1946 after a verbal dispute. Davis evidently angered his killer by refusing to obey an order, saying "I'm not your man. I'm Uncle Sam's man [now]." Uncle Sam's attorney general, Tom Clark, filed a criminal charge, but the case never went to trial. Burnham reports that at least twenty-eight active-duty Black soldiers were murdered for refusing to submit silently to Jim Crow. Hundreds more suffered gunshot wounds or imprisonment. As Thurgood Marshall complained in 1944 to the Department of Justice, "there have been numerous killings of Negro soldiers by civilians and police" but he was "not aware of a single instance of prosecution." These experiences, Burnham writes, "never made it into the sagas about the 'Greatest Generation.'"

Years before Rosa Parks refused to surrender her seat to a white passenger in Montgomery, southern buses had become racial flash points. Many communities authorized drivers to carry weapons, a recipe for homicide. In 1944, a driver ordered the soldier Booker Spicely to give up his seat on a bus traveling between Durham, North Carolina, and Camp Butner when a group of whites entered the vehicle. Spicely left the bus after remarking, "I thought I was fighting this war for democracy." As he stepped into the street the driver shot him three times, then drove away, leaving the soldier bleeding from his wounds. Refused treatment by a whites-only hospital, Spicely was admitted to a "Negro bed" at another, where he died. The War Department's response was to launch an intelligence operation to learn local Blacks' response to the murder, especially if "agitators" were encouraging them to "misconduct themselves." Tried on a charge of manslaughter, the driver was acquitted.

In 1946, in Bessemer, a center of coal mining and steel production near Birmingham, a bus driver ordered Timothy Hood, a war veteran, to adjust the "color board"—the physical marker separating black and white sections of buses, which was moved back and forth depending on who entered and exited at each stop. Hood replied, "do it yourself." A fight broke out and the driver fired five shots, wounding Hood. Shortly afterwards the local chief of police, a member of the Ku Klux Klan, arrived; he shot Hood in the head, killing him instantly. A coroner's inquest ruled the incident justifiable homicide.

Gender did not shield Black women from brutality. The first case outlined in the book involved Ollie Hunter, an "elderly Negro woman" shopping in a general store in Donaldson, Georgia. The white storekeeper ordered her to put down an item she was examining. When Hunter left the store, the storekeeper followed. He physically assaulted her on the street, causing her death. Young people were also among the victims. Willie Baxter Carlisle, an 18-year-old in central Alabama, tried, with some friends, to sneak into a dance party at a local high school. Two policemen removed them and then discovered that someone had let air out of a patrol car's tires. The officers took the teenagers to jail and beat them with a whip and rubber hose. Carlisle died two days later. This took place in 1950, by which time public acceptance of extreme police brutality had begun to wane. Acquitted of murder in a local court, the officers were sentenced to a few months in prison by a federal jury. According to Burnham, no death certificate was issued for Carlisle and his grave remains unmarked.

Most of the acts of violence related in *By Hands Now Known* were committed by law enforcement officials or by persons, such as bus drivers, performing public functions. This is significant because beginning in the late nineteenth century the Supreme Court made a shibboleth of the legal concept of "state action," according to which the federal government's ability to prosecute violations of Blacks' constitutional rights was limited to crimes committed by public officials, not by private individuals. Police officers and sheriffs were certainly state actors and the federal government could have taken legal action against them, but almost never did. The Justices also adopted a rigid understanding of states' rights and federalism, ruling as early as 1873 in the *Slaughterhouse Cases* that despite the Fourteenth Amendment, which barred states from denying to any person the equal protection of the laws, most of the constitutional rights enjoyed by Americans remained under the purview of the states, not the nation.

The Supreme Court's limited interpretation of the constitutional changes brought about during Reconstruction continued well into the twentieth century. In a ruling in a 1945 murder case the Court declared that murder and assault, even when motivated by racial bias, must be prosecuted under state, not federal laws. This case involved a sheriff, Claude Screws, and two deputies who shot and killed a Black man on a courthouse lawn in Baker County, Georgia. Screws was prosecuted and convicted in federal court, but the Supreme Court overturned the verdict. Even though Georgia authorities refused to take action against the killers, the hands of the federal government were tied. For good measure, three justices—Owen Roberts, Felix Frankfurter, and Robert Jackson—reflecting the prevailing historical orthodoxy, declared that Reconstruction legislation authorizing federal protection of Blacks' rights was motivated by a "vengeful spirit" on the part of northerners after the Civil War. For members of the Supreme Court to view expanding the rights of Blacks as a form of punishment to whites did not bode well for a more expansive understanding of the federal government's power to protect Black citizens. Overall, Burnham writes, the federal courts "rendered nearly toothless the Reconstruction-era statutes that specifically targeted racist terror." As for Screws, in 1958 he was elected to the Georgia senate.

Along with Supreme Court rulings, a combination of other circumstances help explain why so many persons guilty of heinous crimes walked away scot-free. These include the exclusion of virtually all Black southerners from jury service; the FBI's reluctance to investigate these crimes; and the power of the Jim Crow South in the Democratic Party, which made it impossible to enact federal anti-lynching legislation.

In addition, Burnham writes, federalism "fortified and insulated local regimes of racial terror." To be sure, federalism can be a double-edged sword. Before the Civil War, southerners employed the doctrine of state rights as a shield for slavery only to see northern states enact laws to prevent the return to the South of fugitives from bondage. Federalism certainly protected the Jim Crow system from national interference. Today, however, in the aftermath of the Dobbs decision, "blue" states rely on federalism to uphold a woman's right to terminate a pregnancy.

Indeed, in a surprising twist, Burnham begins *By Hands Now Known* with a chapter about northern governors who refused requests by their southern counterparts for the extradition of Blacks who managed to escape the clutches of the southern legal system. These cases underscore the importance of the fact that while it could not have existed without national complicity, Jim Crow was a regional system. The Great Migration from South to North during and after World War I created large new communities where fugitives could find refuge and where Blacks, unlike in the South, enjoyed the right to vote. Despite the enactment in 1934 of the Fugitive Felon Act, which Burnham calls a "latter-day Fugitive Slave Act," northern governors like Frank Murphy of Michigan could not ignore the demands of Black voters, and battles over extradition kept the southern legal system in the national spotlight. Scores of such cases, Burnham writes, required northern authorities to make a judgment about southern justice. In many instances they refused to comply with requests to return escapees, on the grounds that they would be lynched if extradited to the South.

The rule of law—a legal system based on principles that apply equally to all persons (including the police)—is a hallmark of civilized societies. A perversion of the rule of law in the Jim Crow South—the conviction of an innocent Black man charged with raping a white woman—is the centerpiece of everybody's favorite novel, Harper Lee's *To Kill a Mockingbird*. (In 2022, a survey of 200,000 readers of *The New York Times* named this the best book of the last century and a quarter.) Lee's hero is the white lawyer Atticus Finch, who understands that the southern racial system makes it impossible for the courts to dispense justice fairly. He associates racial bigotry with the "cruel poverty and ignorance" of the accusers, a poverty-stricken white farm family. Lee's implication is that change will come to the South through the actions of well-meaning better-off whites like Finch. There is no room in this narrative for Black activism.

In reality, as Burnham amply demonstrates, respectable whites—

public officials, newspaper reporters who deemed the murder of a Black person, as she puts it, "too trivial to report," and businessmen who profited from the availability of cheap Black labor, all helped to maintain the Jim Crow system. Judges, from local courts all the way to the Supreme Court of the United States, violated their oaths to uphold the Constitution, while members of Congress refused to enact laws against lynching. The incidents detailed in *By Hands Now Known* were not the work of prejudiced poor whites. Nor were they random occurrences or the actions of a few bad apples—entire communities were to blame for the perversion of the criminal justice system. In 1947, just as the United States was embarking on the Cold War, J. Edgar Hoover told President Truman's Committee on Civil Rights that an "iron curtain" in the American South made it impossible for the FBI to conduct adequate investigations since white residents at all levels of society refused to provide information. As Burnham makes clear, the events she chronicles must be understood as expressions of "systemic" racism (a concept whose mention can today land a teacher in some states in prison). Not long ago, admirers of Lee's novel were shocked when *Go Set a Watchman*, which she had written before *Mockingbird*, was finally published. It depicted Atticus Finch not as a heroic man of principle but as an outspoken racist who could not accept the idea of Blacks challenging Jim Crow. Of the two portrayals, this is more realistic. But it is the Finch of *To Kill a Mockingbird* who remains in the minds of readers and the celebrated film version starring Gregory Peck.

The idea of the white savior, it seems, has an enduring appeal. Yet one of Burnham's key arguments is that resistance to the systemic miscarriage of justice in the South arose primarily from Black communities. Memory itself—the efforts of relatives, friends, and neighbors of the victims to keep alive their names and stories—can be a form of resistance. Protests against misconduct by police, bus companies, and others, she shows, long preceded the 1960s civil rights revolution and today's Black Lives Matter. She devotes special attention to the legal work of the NAACP. That organization, often dismissed as hopelessly conservative, emerges here as comprising courageous activists risking their lives to seek justice for Black victims of Jim Crow violence. The NAACP's "aggressiveness" alarmed J. Edgar Hoover, who did not want the federal government to become involved in such cases. Some local NAACP leaders paid with their lives. Elbert Williams, for example, was murdered in Tennessee in 1940 after announcing a voter registration campaign. (The FBI investigated, but its inquiry focused on determining whether local Blacks were influenced by communism, not identifying Williams's assailants.)

In her final pages, Burnham raises the fraught question of reparations for the families of victims of Jim Crow violence. "An apology must be made," she writes, but more than an apology is needed. She calls for a "material remedy" for relatives, including family members, some of them still living, forced to flee the South, often leaving behind farms, shops, and other hard-won economic assets, lest they too become targets of violence.

It is unclear how best to describe the United States in the Jim Crow era, when a quasi-fascist polity was embedded within a putative democracy. Some scholars, drawing on the example of South Africa in the time of apartheid, use the term Herrenvolk democracy to describe a situation in which parts of the population enjoy full democratic rights while others are entirely excluded. The political scientist Jean L. Cohen calls these systems "hybrid regimes," while pointing out that the undemocratic enclave can exercise a significant degree of power at the national level and can accustom the larger system to authoritarian practices. On the other hand, as the civil rights revolution demonstrated, when a repressive local system comes into conflict with the interests of the national state, as eventually happened during the Cold War, it becomes vulnerable to a mass challenge from below. None of this, of course, is how Americans are accustomed to thinking about our constitutional system. *By Hands Now Known* is one of those rare books that forces us to consider in new ways the nature of our politics and society and the enduring legacy of our troubled past.

TULSA: FORGETTING AND REMEMBERING

HISTORIANS, FORENSIC ANTHROPOLOGISTS, and public officials are searching for unmarked mass burial sites. Not in Bosnia or Syria, but in the United States of America—Tulsa, Oklahoma, to be precise. The on again, off again effort to locate the remains of victims of the 1921 Tulsa Riot—now known as the Tulsa Race Massacre—is a central theme of *The Ground Breaking*, a riveting book by Scott Ellsworth, who has spent most of his adult life piecing together the story of perhaps the deadliest instance of racial violence in the country's history. (I say perhaps because the exact number of victims remains unknown.)

Ellsworth grew up in a whites-only neighborhood in segregated Tulsa. He became an award-winning journalist and writer on subjects ranging from mountain climbing to the history of basketball. But ever since setting out half a century ago to investigate whispered rumors about a racial pogrom that had taken place in his city, he has worked diligently to uncover a piece of history obscured, in both white and Black Tulsa, by a conspiracy of silence. Whites did not wish to be reminded

---

Review of *The Ground Breaking: An American City and Its Search for Justice*, by Scott Ellsworth, *London Review of Books*, September 9, 2021.

of a terrible crime; Blacks for many years talked about the massacre at home but perhaps feared that public discussion might trigger some kind of repetition. Ellsworth was astonished, as a high school student, to find in microfilm copies of old Tulsa newspapers references to a "race war" he knew nothing about. He pursued the subject in a senior thesis at Reed College in far-away Oregon and in graduate school at Duke. In 1982 he published *Death in a Promised Land*, a pioneering account that remains the starting point for anyone interested in learning about the massacre. The work did not gain a large readership, although Ellsworth tells us that it was among the books most frequently stolen each year from the Tulsa library system.

In *The Ground Breaking*, Ellsworth takes the story of his personal quest to document the massacre down to the present. Although it opens with a vivid account of what happened in Tulsa, the book is not primarily a history of those events. Part memoir, part meditation on memory and forgetting, it is a primer on how to do local research when people do not want the past to be recovered, and how to build upon survivors' recollections of decades-old history but also check them against contemporary documents. The discussion is particularly relevant today as battles over the teaching of history have moved to center stage in America's ongoing culture wars.

In the years leading up to 1921, Tulsa, once a sleepy village, was transformed into a thriving metropolis by the discovery of oil nearby. The self-proclaimed Oil Capital of the United States, where J. Paul Getty began the career that made him the world's richest man, Tulsa's population had grown 300 percent—from 18,000 to 72,000—in the previous decade. Around 10,000 residents were African Americans living in Greenwood, a flourishing neighborhood known as Black Wall Street, a title bestowed by Booker T. Washington, who promoted the idea that racial progress would come through the accumulation of wealth, not political agitation. (Whites, however, commonly referred to Greenwood as Little Africa.)

One of the paradoxical results of racial segregation was that economic exclusion opened the door for black entrepreneurship. If downtown hotels refused to accommodate Black guests, Blacks built four of their own in Greenwood, including the largest Black-owned hotel in the country. If downtown shops would not serve Black customers, Black businessmen filled the gap. Greenwood was a sprawling community that covered dozens of city blocks. It boasted lawyers and physicians—there were more Black doctors than in Tulsa today— movie theaters and restaurants, grocery and clothing stores, churches, civic associations, two newspapers, and all sorts of other enterprises and institutions, all run by and serving African Americans. To be sure, as the Black historian John Hope Franklin, who spent much of his youth in Tulsa, pointed out in his memoirs, the label Black Wall Street was a bit of a misnomer. Most of the residents worked as cooks and maids in the homes of white Tulsans, and many lived in rented rooms and shacks that lacked running water. Moreover, there were no financial institutions comparable to the Black-owned banks and insurance companies in cities like Richmond and Raleigh. But Greenwood did boast a solid middle class. If the neighborhood was separate and unequal, it was proudly Black-controlled.

The tragic events of 1921 began with a minor encounter between two teenagers that, in a normal country, would hardly have become a catalyst for violence. Dick Rowland, a Black 19-year-old who worked downtown shining shoes, bumped into an elevator operator, a white woman seventeen years of age. Perhaps he tripped. In any event she screamed and rumors spread that a black youth had assaulted a white woman in downtown Tulsa. Rowland was arrested and lodged in jail in the local courthouse. A crowd bent on immediate punishment assembled and a local newspaper published an editorial with the headline, "To Lynch Negro Tonight." (Throughout the South, lynchings were frequently advertised in advance; railroads sometimes put on extra trains to accommodate those who enjoyed witnessing extra-judicial murders.) Twice, armed Blacks, including World War I veterans, turned up at the courthouse to protect Rowland, only to be turned away by the sheriff. At this time, Tulsa was what Ellsworth calls a "lawless boom town." A young white man accused of murdering a white taxi driver had

214 • OUR FRAGILE FREEDOMS

recently been lynched. It was not difficult to imagine this happening to Rowland.

As the armed Blacks were departing for the second time a shot rang out and the all-white police force began distributing weapons to members of the rapidly growing mob. Around midnight, groups of gun-toting whites tried to enter Greenwood only to be repelled by gunfire. Hundreds of white residents began to plan for a full-scale invasion of the Black neighborhood. Early the next morning, a coordinated attack began by strategically deployed mobs. Blacks offered resistance but were overwhelmed by the attackers, who now numbered in the thousands. Not satisfied with handguns and rifles, they deployed machine guns, including one manned by members of the Oklahoma National Guard, and dropped incendiary devices from airplanes provided by Sinclair Oil Company. In the long history of racial violence in the United States, Tulsa is one of only two instances in which a Black community was assaulted from the air. The other took place in 1985 when Philadelphia police dropped a military-grade bomb on a townhouse occupied by members of the Black group MOVE, resulting in the death of eleven people and a fire that consumed over sixty buildings.

The carnage in Tulsa continued for hours. Homes, churches, businesses, and a hospital, school, and library were looted and set ablaze. Black men, women, and children were gunned down in the street. Thousands of persons—a considerable majority of Tulsa's Black population—were rounded up and interned at the city's baseball stadium, convention hall, and other sites. Others fled the city on foot. Only the arrival of state police dispatched by the governor in Oklahoma City, one hundred miles away, brought the massacre to an end. The police arrested Blacks still on the streets and told whites to go home. By the time the carnage ended, some 1,500 buildings had been destroyed and most of Greenwood's residents were homeless. Photographs of the community after the assault bring to mind images of Columbia, South Carolina, after General William T. Sherman's troops passed through toward the conclusion of the Civil War, or portions of Berlin at the end of World War II. As to the death toll, current estimates range between one hundred and three hundred persons. The head of a Red Cross unit that distributed relief in Greenwood (the first time the organization acted in response to a man-made disaster rather than a natural one) recorded more than 10,000 people homeless, 183 hospitalized with gunshot wounds or burns, 222 families with the father "missing or dead," and 87 "with no mother." Survivors later recalled seeing trucks loaded with bodies heading to burial sites in unknown locations. Rowland was not one of the victims. Somehow, he escaped during the chaos.

One might think it impossible to erase from historical memory an event of this magnitude. But Tulsa tried its best. Ellsworth discovered that police reports and National Guard records had been systematically destroyed and other documents removed from the state archives. Some news articles were simply cut out of surviving copies of local newspapers in the University of Tulsa library. Shortly after the violence ended, Ellsworth learned, the city's police chief ordered his men to confiscate any images of the destruction in the possession of Tulsa's photography studios. As the years passed, Oklahoma history textbooks made no mention of the massacre. A teacher who moved to the city in 1950 was warned on pain of dismissal not to mention the events of 1921 in class.

Most of *The Ground Breaking* deals with Ellsworth's decades-long effort to bring this history to light. He is careful to give credit to Black survivors who shared their experiences and to a younger generation, such as the Black journalist-turned-politician Don Ross, whose newspaper articles published in the wake of the 1960s civil rights revolution helped break the conspiracy of silence. Ross was instrumental in the legislature's creation, in 1997, of the Commission to Study the Tulsa Race Riot, for which Ellsworth and John Hope Franklin served as consultants. Ellsworth notes how eagerly white residents sought to avoid any imputation of blame as the story of the massacre emerged from obscurity. The president of the Tulsa County Historical Society told him there had been no white rioters—they were all "Mexicans and Indians."

Ellsworth's personal story is compelling. But there is a cost to focusing so intently on his own experience. Ellsworth mentions only in passing that Tulsa was not the only city to experience a "race riot" in the years during and immediately following World War I—violent racial confrontations took place in East St. Louis, Chicago, Washington, and other cities. These years, in addition, witnessed radical uprisings inspired, in part, by the Russian Revolution—the Seattle general strike of 1919, for example—and an ensuing Red Scare, when the full force of the federal government was brought to bear on the IWW, Socialist Party, and other groups deemed "un-American." Repression and lack of respect for judicial processes were part of the Zeitgeist.

Given the scale and destructiveness, the Tulsa massacre may defy rational explanation. But it needs to be placed in the context of Oklahoma's unique history and long tradition of racism. Before becoming a state in 1907, Oklahoma was known as Indian Territory, inhabited by Native American tribes of long standing, as well as those removed from the East in the 1830s in the notorious Trail of Tears, and western indigenous peoples later forced to resettle there by the federal government. Racial dynamics were complicated. Some tribes owned slaves and sided with the South during the Civil War. After the conflict ended, the federal government required them to abolish slavery and to recognize the freed people as equal tribal citizens. This was bitterly resisted by some Native American groups; to this day they continue to fight to exclude Black members. Indian nations were also forced to provide their former slaves with land, the only slaveowners required to do so.

The late nineteenth century brought thousands of white settlers, large numbers of them from the South, in the famous Oklahoma "land rush" that followed passage of the Dawes Act of 1887, which broke up Native Americans' collective tribal land holdings into plots allocated to individual families, with the rest opened to white newcomers. Indians' former slaves were eligible for allotments. They chose land near other Blacks, forming the basis for the emergence of numerous small all-Black towns in the late nineteenth and early twentieth centuries. To the consternation of many white Oklahomans these towns attracted growing numbers of refugees from the Jim Crow South, where Blacks were being systematically stripped of their rights.

Today, Oklahoma is the nation's most solidly Republican state, the only one in which Democrats failed to win a single county in the past four presidential elections. Donald Trump carried it twice by over 30 percentage points. It is where Timothy McVeigh in 1995 detonated a bomb at the federal office building in Oklahoma City, killing 168 people and alerting the country to the danger of right-wing terrorism. It was not always so. During the early statehood period, Oklahoma was home to a vibrant socialist movement. Eugene V. Debs, the Socialist Party's presidential candidate, received one-sixth of the vote in the state in 1912, a percentage exceeded only in Nevada. (In 1920, when Debs ran again, he came in first in a straw poll of inmates in the Oklahoma state penitentiary.)

Statehood in 1907 seemed to give free rein to anti-Black sentiment. The first law enacted by the new state legislature imposed racial segregation on railroads and public accommodations. Oklahoma also moved to disenfranchise Black voters through literacy tests and other requirements, the only state to do so that had not been part of the Confederacy. This history forms the background to the events of 1921. Then there was old-fashioned greed. Many whites resented the fact that Greenwood, located not far from the burgeoning downtown, occupied valuable real estate that, in their opinion, should not belong to Blacks. The "Negro settlement," declared the mayor after the massacre, should be moved to a more distant location. But one gets the impression that what really infuriated whites was the neighborhood's prosperity and Blacks' willingness to fight to defend it. As has often been the case with lynchings and "race riots," Black success, not Black poverty or supposed criminality, inspired white violence. The presence of armed Black men seems to have infuriated white Tulsans. Many white Americans have never accepted the idea that the Constitution's Second Amendment, guaranteeing the right to "bear arms," applies to Blacks as well as themselves.

Some white Tulsans offered refuge in their homes to Blacks fleeing the massacre. But overall, few appear to have experienced second thoughts about the injustice of racism. No one was punished for riot, arson, or murder. Insurance companies refused to pay claims for property destruction on the grounds that their policies did not cover losses caused by riots. The city enacted an ordinance, later invalidated by the state Supreme Court, that aimed to prevent Blacks from rebuilding Greenwood. In the 1920s, the Ku Klux Klan grew rapidly in Oklahoma; for a time, it controlled the state government. Yet against all odds, Greenwood rose from the ashes. By the 1940s, the neighborhood's business district was larger than before the massacre. But in the 1960s, Greenwood entered a long period of decline, caused by adversaries as devastating in the long run as white mobs—modern capitalism and federal highway construction. When racial integration finally came to Tulsa's downtown shopping district, small Black-owned neighborhood businesses found it impossible to compete with less expensive national chain stores. Then, in a pattern repeated in other cities, the federal government routed an eight-lane interstate highway right through the center of Greenwood, bifurcating the community. (President Biden's proposed federal budget includes funds to "reconnect" neighborhoods throughout the country severed years ago by such highways.) Many African Americans still live in Greenwood but a recent report by Human Rights Watch details stark racial inequalities in Tulsa in life expectancy, employment, and other indices of social well-being. Meanwhile, Greenwood is now the home of an independent bookstore, a restaurant, and a museum celebrating the life of the (white) songwriter Woody Guthrie, harbingers, perhaps, of impending gentrification. Greenwood does have perhaps the only public space in the nation named for a Black historian—the John Hope Franklin Reconciliation Park.

Reconciliation, however, remains hard to come by. The commission established in 1997 began the search for unmarked graves and, in its final report, advocated that the city and state pay reparations to surviving victims and establish college scholarships for Black Tulsa youths. But both the city and state refused to consider such expenditures. Whatever one's view of the now hotly debated idea of reparations for slavery, in Tulsa the case for tangible public accountability seems overwhelming, given that city officials and police and the state's National Guard took part in the massacre or did nothing to stop it. Almost all the wealth accumulated by a generation of Blacks was wiped away, with consequences that affect their descendants to this day.

Today, thanks in large measure to Ellsworth, the Tulsa Race Massacre is not only widely known but has become embedded in popular culture. In 2019, the Alvin Ailey dance company premiered *Greenwood* by the prominent Black choreographer Donald Byrd; more recently, the television series *Watchman* included a re-creation of the events of 1921. Amazon lists over two dozen books about the massacre and one can buy tee-shirts emblazoned with the words "Black Wall Street—Never Forget." The massacre's one hundredth anniversary was marked by a visit to the city by Biden and testimony before a congressional committee by the three living survivors.

Oklahoma's public schools have begun teaching about the 1921 massacre. How long this will last is anyone's guess, as Oklahoma is among the states that have recently approved laws and regulations aimed at preventing teaching about racism. Having realized that no political advantage is to be gained by railing against Biden's popular policies relating to economic relief and infrastructure development, Republicans have sought other ways of whipping up their base. First, they mobilized against a supposed influx of transgender athletes in women's sports. Then they latched onto Critical Race Theory, an obscure academic sub-discipline that seeks to identify the ways racism is embedded in American institutions. In the past few months, the supposed need to prevent students from being indoctrinated by Critical Race Theory has become an all-purpose excuse for efforts by Republican lawmakers to prevent teachers from discussing racism at all. Florida, for example, banned teaching that "racism is not merely the product of prejudice, but . . . is embedded in American society." Teachers in Oklahoma and other states may soon be breaking the law if they talk about the history of American racism. Perhaps we will witness an updated version of the Scopes Trial of 1925, when a Tennessee instructor was convicted of violating state law by teaching Darwin's theory of evolution. To be sure, what the authors of these measures are really after is not jails full of schoolteachers, but educational self-censorship. Who wants to become the protagonist in a modern-day Scopes Trial? It is a lot simpler to teach a sanitized version of the American past.

Gore Vidal famously called the country the United States of Amnesia. Even Vidal, who liked to think of himself as a consummate cynic, could hardly have imagined that amnesia would one day become a legal mandate. Ellsworth deserves our thanks for his lifetime of effort to bring to light the history of the Tulsa Race Massacre. Meanwhile, the search for unmarked graves continues.

PART IV

The Movement

REPORTING THE
MOVEMENT

"HISTORY," OBSERVED JAMES Baldwin, "does not refer merely, or even principally, to the past. On the contrary...history is literally present in all that we do." The civil rights movement is a compelling illustration of Baldwin's insight. Today, with the birthday of Martin Luther King Jr. a national holiday, colleges and thoroughfares named after Malcolm X, and Rosa Parks chosen by *Time* magazine as one of the twentieth century's 100 most important persons, the movement has achieved iconic status in our historical self-consciousness.

Reporting Civil Rights is a good starting point for anyone who wonders how the press reported on the movement. Weighing in at nearly 2,000 pages, this two-volume addition to the Library of America includes nearly 200 examples of American journalism—daily reporting, investigative accounts, opinion pieces, and memoirs—about the struggle for racial justice. It begins in 1941 with A. Philip Randolph's call for a March on Washington to protest discrimination in the rap-

———

Review of *Reporting Civil Rights*, ed. Clayborne Carson et al., *Los Angeles Times Book Review*, March 9, 2003.

idly expanding war industries, and ends with a reflection on the extent and limits of racial change in Mississippi, written in 1973.

The editors—historians Claiborne Carson and David Garrow, former *Atlanta Constitution* editor Bill Kovach, and journalism professor Carol Polsgrove—do not, unfortunately, discuss the criteria of selection. Some of their choices seem questionable. Martin Luther King Jr.'s *Letter from Birmingham Jail* is a magnificent statement of the movement's moral outlook, but it hardly qualifies as journalism. Nor does Tom Wolfe's famous essay, "Mau-Mauing the Flak Catchers," a brilliant, sardonic work of the imagination rather than an account of actual events.

Nonetheless, the editors are to be commended for scouring the era's newspapers and magazines and for including numerous pieces by writers unknown today alongside familiar names like Anthony Lewis, David Halberstam, and Joan Didion. They present accounts of the struggle's familiar high points—Montgomery, Birmingham, Selma. But they also devote considerable space to less-well-known parts of the story, such as the bus boycott in Tallahassee that followed the Montgomery campaign, and demonstrations in places like Danville and St. Augustine. They make clear that the movement rested not only on national leaders like King, around whom the media tended to congregate, but even more on grassroots people of extraordinary courage who refused to bend to sometimes savage retribution.

The editors have been especially successful in mining the often-neglected Black press, which published some of the best reporting on the movement. They include a harrowing 1942 piece by L. O. Swinger from the *Atlanta Daily World* about the police beating of Morehouse College professor Hugh M. Gloster. His offense was to ask a train conductor if Blacks in an overcrowded Negro car could move into the all-but-empty adjoining coach. One of the most moving pieces in the collection is James D. Williams's stark account in the *Baltimore Afro-American* of the funeral of a young victim of the 1963 Birmingham church bombing.

Black reporters seem to have had a style and method different from their white counterparts. Reporting for the New York *Amsterdam News* about white anxiety caused by the impending arrival of James Meredith at the University of Mississippi, James L. Hicks writes: "Meredith literally rocked and rolled this town out of its senses ... They acted as if this young lone Negro youth was a man from Mars." Among the collection's most hilarious pieces is a 1961 account by George Collins, a reporter for the *Baltimore Afro-American*, of posing as a diplomat from the nonexistent African nation of Goban and seeking to eat in Maryland restaurants. Dressed in African attire and declaiming on the virtues of Goban's "betel nut," Collins and a colleague are treated with unfailing courtesy. As far as Blacks are concerned, Collins concludes, in Maryland "everybody eats but Americans."

Taken together, the 200 pieces offer a gripping account of a momentous epoch in American history. And while the editors, in keeping with the series format, do not provide an introductory essay, the volumes make a compelling case that the modern civil rights movement began not in the mid-1950s with the Brown desegregation decision and Montgomery bus boycott, but during World War II. The war reconfigured the nation's racial map by drawing hundreds of thousands of Blacks out of the segregated South into the army and industrial employment in the North and West. The contradiction between the Roosevelt administration's rhetoric promising a postwar world based on the Four Freedoms and the reality of racial violence, segregation, and disenfranchisement inspired a new Black militancy. The early selections in *Reporting Civil Rights* remind us that like the 1960s, World War II was a time of freedom rides, sit-ins, and urban race riots.

"The segregation question," writes Lucille Milner in a 1944 exposé of military Jim Crow, "will be a burning postwar issue." The rest of the first volume traces the movement down to 1963, when demonstrations involving tens of thousands of protesters swept across the South and President Kennedy committed the federal government to enforcing the civil rights of Black citizens.

If the movement's first phase produced a clear set of objectives and a series of coherent if sometimes competitive organizations—SCLC, SNCC, CORE, etc.—the second witnessed political fragmentation and, after 1965, few significant victories. The second volume opens with the 1963 March on Washington. This was the high-water mark of the non-violent civil rights movement. But even at this point, signs of future divisions abounded. Marlene Nadle, riding a bus to Washington to report for New York's *Village Voice*, encounters young Black radicals who tell her: "Get out of our organization. We don't need any white liberals to patronize us." Writing in the Paris periodical, *Présence Africaine*, Black activist Michael Thelwall speaks of the March as a "fiasco," because it abandoned plans for a sit-in at the Capitol in favor of staging "a mass protest against injustice without offending anyone."

Soon, Black Power replaces the integrationist vision and non-violence is succeeded by urban rebellion. The second volume ends on a bittersweet note with Alice Walker's 1973 piece about returning to live in Jackson, Mississippi, after ten years in the North. Blacks now vote, and the schools, restaurants, and hotels are integrated. The "white" and "colored" signs are gone and so is the climate of fear that so recently "shrouded Mississippi." But the movement, too, has passed into history.

In some ways, of course, the most influential reporting on civil rights appeared not in print media but on television. Nothing in these volumes has the visceral impact of the images, broadcast around the world, of Bull Connor's police attacking Birmingham demonstrators with fire hoses and dogs, or Sheriff Jim Clark's forces assaulting non-violent marchers on Selma's Pettus bridge. But *Reporting Civil Rights* proves that sometimes a word can be worth a thousand pictures.

The best pieces do what television never seems able to—offer in-depth accounts that illuminate complex local situations. The volumes are filled with memorable pieces of journalistic writing. Among them is Murray Kempton's article describing the end of Ernest Green's senior year at Little Rock's Central High School, which began with troops escorting him to classes in defiance of a howling mob. Kempton quotes the inscriptions written by white classmates in Green's yearbook, ranging from "I enjoyed having home room with you," to "I really admire you, Ernest. I doubt if I could have done half so well had the circumstances been reversed." An essay by John Hersey from the *Saturday Evening Post* in 1964 brings into vivid relief the life of Varshall Pleas, a Black farmer near Athens, Mississippi. Hersey brilliantly illuminates Pleas's struggle to make ends meet, his aspirations for his children, and his growing commitment to the movement. Other highlights include a long account by George McMillan in *Collier's* of "The Ordeal of Bobby Cain," which details the daily courage of a youth who in 1956 became the first Black student in a school in Clinton, Tennessee, far from the national media limelight. John Lowell brings to life the intensity of the 1967 Detroit uprising by interviewing National Guardsmen about strategies for fighting snipers. "It was as though the Viet Cong," Lowell observes, "had infiltrated the riot-blackened streets."

Another superb piece is Calvin Hernton's wickedly funny essay from 1966 on how Black actors in Hollywood movies never seem to be portrayed in sexual situations for fear of offending white Americans obsessed with Black sexuality. "Why can't Sidney Poitier, since he is such a superb actor, make love in the movies?" Hernton asks. To see Poitier kiss a Black woman, he answers, would lead to revulsion among white patrons. To see him kiss a white woman "would have caused a riot on Broadway and a slaughter in Alabama."

Journalism, the saying goes, is the first draft of history. As instant historical analysis, some of the reporting stands up remarkably well. In *The New Republic*, Thomas Sancton succinctly explains the reasons for the outburst of Black militancy during World War II: "The swift tides of war and race conflict sweeping through all countries of the world have caused . . . the ascendancy of aggressive Negro leadership." When the sit-ins begin in 1960, Claude Sitton of *The New York Times* recognizes that they reflect both a "growing dissatisfaction over the slow pace of desegregation" and "a shift of leadership to younger, more militant Negroes."

Two contributors to *The Nation* consistently provide analysis that goes beyond the headlines. One, Howard Zinn, was then a history professor at Spelman, an elite Black women's college. Whether describing the radicalization of the "young ladies" of Spelman or comparing Kennedy and Abraham Lincoln as "reluctant emancipators," Zinn's pieces offer an unusually high level of historical awareness. The other *Nation* writer is Dan Wakefield, whose report from Mississippi on the acquittal of Emmett Till's murderers undercuts the common misconception that racism emanates mainly from lower-class whites. The local White Citizens' Council, Wakefield notes, is composed of eminently respectable men—lawyers, bankers, and school officials. "Their shirts aren't red [a reference to the Red Shirts, violent white supremacists of the late nineteenth to early twentieth centuries] and they don't wear sheets."

In another piece, Wakefield notes that segregation is not simply a system of separating Blacks and whites, but is designed to maintain "the continuance of cheap labor in the South," a "major lure" in attracting northern industry. His pieces highlight a glaring weakness of much civil rights journalism—its neglect of what might be called the political economy of racism. With a few exceptions, reporters tend to see the movement as primarily a moral issue, a dilemma for national policy, or a question of racial psychodynamics. Thus, for example, Harrison Salisbury's vivid reporting from Birmingham in 1960, describing a city "fragmented by the emotional dynamite of racism, enforced by the whip, the razor, the gun, the bomb," makes Bull Connor the villain, entirely neglecting the steel barons who did far more than Connor to shape the city's racial policies and atmosphere.

Reporting Civil Rights compounds this problem by neglecting the northern side of the movement. In the North, demands for racial justice revolved around equal access to housing and an end to job discrimination by employers and unions, not legal segregation and disenfranchisement. The North did not offer up ready-made symbols of racism like Bull Connor, and southern tactics like marches, sit-ins, and mass arrests proved ineffective in the face of a less overt but equally powerful system of racial inequality. Only a handful of pieces—for example, George Schuyler's penetrating 1949 article for *The American Mercury* describing "Jim Crow in the North"—deal with racism outside the South. Inexplicably, the editors fail to include any reporting about King's Chicago Freedom Movement of 1966, whose failure in the face of the entrenched power of Major Richard J. Daley's political machine and the ferocious opposition of white homeowners to open housing offered a preview of the movement's national decline.

This neglect is all the more striking because the marches on Washington that open the two volumes—the protest of 1941, which was called off, and the "I Have a Dream" rally of 1963—focused on economic inequality as much as desegregation. The call for the 1941 protest labeled American democracy "a hollow mockery" if it "will not give jobs to its toilers because of race or color." The rallying cry of the 1963 march was Jobs and Freedom, and its demands included not simply the passage of the civil rights bill then before Congress but a public works program to reduce unemployment, an increase in the minimum wage, and a law banning racial discrimination in employment. E. W. Kenworthy's *New York Times* account of the 1963 March notes that a century earlier, the Emancipation Proclamation had enjoined former slaves to "labor faithfully for reasonable wages," something still unavailable to them. His is one of only a handful of pieces that brings to center stage what Hunter Thompson, in *The Reporter* in 1963, calls "segregation's second front" of jobs, housing, and an entrenched white power structure.

Overall, these volumes offer a revealing portrait of how journalists during the civil rights era pursued their craft. It was an overwhelmingly male profession—only a handful of pieces here are by women reporters. Its practitioners displayed considerable physical and moral courage. Reporters were beaten while covering the Freedom Rides and one was killed in the Oxford, Mississippi, riots of 1962. They prided themselves on being where the action was. "When I heard about the rioting on the radio," writes Lez Edmond in *Ramparts* in 1964, "I grabbed my tape recorder and I got into Harlem, deep in, quick." They were participant journalists, who developed "a sort of proprietary feeling about the Movement," as Pat Watters put it in 1969.

The editors' selections reinforce this flattering self-portrait. But there is another, less pretty side to the story, largely ignored in these volumes.

Where are the pieces from national publications like the *Wall Street Journal* and *Time*, warning that the 1963 March on Washington was certain to set back the cause of civil rights? Where is the voice of anti–civil rights journalism, the articles, for example, in *The National Review* during the 1950s that referred to whites as "the advanced race" and defended Black disenfranchisement on the grounds that "the claims of civilization supersede those of universal suffrage"? Where is the southern segregationist press, which consistently misrepresented the movement and stirred up or extenuated violence against it?

Reporting Civil Rights includes selections from liberal white southern editors—Ralph McGill of the *Atlanta Constitution* calling on the "good people" of the South to unite against the Klan, Hodding Carter explaining how he decided to add "Mrs." before the names of married Black women in his Mississippi newspaper. But the massive abdication of journalistic responsibility by much of the southern press is only hinted at via the complaints of civil rights activists. Only indirectly do we learn that during the Montgomery bus boycott the *Montgomery Advertiser* printed nothing about the wholesale arrest and harassment of Black participants, or that it later called civil rights leader Ralph Abernathy an "unprincipled and unspeakable bum." Or that the *Athens Courier* published the names of Blacks who attempted to register to vote so that they could be singled out for economic retribution, and the "entire Mississippi press" concentrated its reports on how civil rights workers "smelled" and "stank," as if their odor was what inspired violence against them.

In a revealing 1962 piece, John Herbers, a southern-born journalist reporting on Mississippi for UPI, notes that local newspapers refused to print anything that might embarrass the state or discourage outside investment. "There is," Herbers writes, "a need for a new approach in reporting the kind of social change that is going on in the South today." Most newspapers, however, "seem content to continue under the old formulas." This, too, is part of the story of reporting civil rights, but it remains unrepresented in these volumes.

Today, we live in the post–civil rights era. In unprecedented numbers, Blacks now work alongside whites in offices and on factory floors and sit together in college classrooms (although public schools are increasingly segregated). Sidney Poitier can kiss anyone he wants in the movies. Journalism, too, has changed. *The Nation* and *New Republic* survive, but there are fewer and fewer venues for serious reportorial essays. The rise of the Internet has not replaced *Look*, *Collier's*, *The Reporter*, *Ramparts*, and other now-defunct magazines where some of the best essays in these volumes were published.

This is a pity, because a new generation of journalists needs to make sense of issues that mostly eluded their predecessors. In the 1970s and 1980s, just as Jim Crow finally ended in many workplaces and unions, deindustrialization devastated the Black working class. Today, the Black rate of unemployment remains double that of whites, and millions of Black children live in poverty. The widespread incarceration of Black men, an issue all but ignored until the late 1960s, has had devastating effects on Black families and communities. Blacks today are entitled to vote, but with states denying the franchise to those in prison or on probation, or barring ex-felons for life, hundreds of thousands of Black men cannot cast a ballot.

In 1965, reporting on the Selma campaign, the freelance writer George B. Leonard observed that the civil rights movement was attempting to bring about an unprecedented revolution in laws, practices, and "the hearts of men." "If we can pull this one off," he added, "then what is impossible for us?" Did we pull it off? Half a century later, the answer remains uncertain.

THE DOUBLE V

I N AMERICAN POPULAR memory, the Second World War remains the "good war," fought, to borrow the title of Tom Brokaw's 1998 best-seller, by the "greatest generation." It is remembered as a time of national unity that not only destroyed tyrannies overseas but assimilated young men from all regions and ethnic backgrounds into a shared American identity. The war in Vietnam, by contrast, is widely viewed as a needless contest fought by an army that fell apart while experiencing the aftershocks of social divisions at home. Its legacy, reinforced by misbegotten wars in Iraq and Afghanistan, is the "Vietnam syndrome"—a reluctance among political leaders and the broader public to become involved in combat in faraway places.

Two new books challenge these ideas. After reading Matthew F. Delmont's *Half American*, the greatest generation, or at least its white component, seems considerably diminished. Although more than a million African Americans served in the armed forces during the Second

Review of *Half American: The Epic Story of African Americans Fighting World War II at Home and Abroad*, by Matthew F. Delmont, and *An Army Afire: How the US Army Confronted Its Racial Crisis in the Vietnam Era*, by Beth Bailey, *London Review of Books*, March 2, 2023.

World War, the default soldier in representations of the war is almost always white. When one directs attention to the Black experience, Delmont writes, "nearly everything" about that war looks different. What, for example, was the conflict's purpose? FDR's claim that it was being fought to ensure universal enjoyment of the Four Freedoms (freedom of speech and religion, freedom from want and from fear) rang hollow for many African Americans denied basic civil and political rights at home. Delmont's title is taken from a letter by a Black cafeteria worker in Wichita, Kansas, to the *Pittsburgh Courier*, a leading Black newspaper, just after the attack on Pearl Harbor. "Should I sacrifice my life," he wondered, "to live half American?" The *Courier* used the letter to launch the campaign for a "Double V"—victory over fascism abroad and Jim Crow at home.

Delmont employs an impressive variety of sources—diaries, letters, newspapers, military and government documents—to explore the deep-seated racism of the armed forces and the emergence during the Second World War of a militant movement for racial justice. Beth Bailey's focus in *An Army Afire* is somewhat different. A professor of history at the University of Kansas and director of its Center for Military, War and Society Studies, Bailey paints a sympathetic portrait of the army's struggle to adjust to the radical social changes sweeping the United States, to which the military could hardly remain immune.

African Americans have served in every significant war conducted by the United States. But they almost always had to fight for the right to fight. During the War of Independence, the Continental Army initially excluded Blacks, a policy reversed only when the British offered freedom to slaves who enlisted in their ranks. Between the American Revolution and the Civil War, Black men were almost entirely barred from the militia and regular army, although during the War of 1812 Andrew Jackson called on Louisiana's free Black militia, a legacy of French rule, to help defeat the British at the Battle of New Orleans. Jackson, who owned many slaves, issued an address condemning the exclusion of Blacks from the army as a "mistaken policy" and praising the Black soldiers as "sons of freedom."

African Americans were employed from the start as laborers in Civil War army camps. But Abraham Lincoln waited until almost two years into the war to authorize the enlistment of Black combat soldiers. (This was one provision of the Emancipation Proclamation.) By the end of the war, some 200,000 Black men had served in the Union army and navy. Confined to segregated units commanded by often racist white officers and initially paid less than their white counterparts, their experience was anything but equal to that of whites. Their presence helped to ensure that Union victory would mean the end of slavery and recognition of Black citizenship, but within a few decades, many of the rights won in the war's aftermath had been rescinded. White America's attitude, the Black poet Paul Laurence Dunbar wrote in 1898, seemed to be: "Negroes, you may fight for us, but you may not vote for us."

Service in the First World War also brought little lasting improvement in the Black condition. In *The Crisis*, the monthly publication of the NAACP, W. E. B. Du Bois urged Black men to enlist as soldiers to make real the promise of equality. Those who tried to heed his advice, however, found that the army didn't want them. Blacks were eventually called on for military service in Europe, but with them went warnings by American authorities to make sure Black soldiers didn't assault French women. These troops returned to a nation wracked by "race riots" and an upsurge in lynchings; some of the victims were soldiers still in uniform. The army's attitude towards enlisting Black soldiers had not changed. A report for the Army War College in 1925, complete with a pseudo-scientific discussion comparing the size of Black and white craniums, concluded that African Americans lacked the courage and intelligence to succeed in combat.

When the United States instituted its first peacetime draft in 1940, local draft boards, composed almost entirely of whites, turned away in large numbers Blacks who registered. The Marines and Army Air Corps didn't accept Black members at all, and the navy restricted them to menial work as messmen, cooking and cleaning for white officers. One group of Blacks in the navy described themselves in a letter to the *Pittsburgh Courier* as "sea-going bellhops, chambermaids and dishwashers." The army adopted a strict literacy standard, motivated in part, as the secretary of war, Henry L. Stimson, noted in his diary, by a desire to "keep down the number of colored troops." (Given the inadequacy of southern public education, the literacy requirement also excluded a considerable number of whites. My father, Jack D. Foner, later the author of a history of Blacks in the military, spent part of the war teaching draftees, mostly from the South, to read and write. I still remember his pleasure after the war at receiving letters from former students thanking him for the difference literacy had made in their lives.)

It didn't take long for the Roosevelt administration to recognize the absurdity of turning away men willing to join the armed forces. As preparations for war accelerated, the government ordered all branches of military service to establish Black units, while continuing the policy of segregation. Colonel Benjamin O. Davis, the highest-ranking Black man in the army, was soon promoted to brigadier general (he remained the only African American general for the rest of the conflict). These changes led to a rise in Black enlistment. But Black draftees were often sent to training camps in the Jim Crow South, where they encountered segregated public facilities, contempt from fellow soldiers, officers, and civilians, and occasional violence. At Camp Van Dorn in Mississippi, one Black unit was required to work on the nearby farm of a local politician. At least twenty-eight Black soldiers were murdered in the southern states during the war, with the perpetrators almost always going unpunished. Complaints by Black members of the armed forces inundated the press and NAACP. Their letters home said they would be safer in the war zone than in the American South.

Some Black units achieved fame during the war. In the Air Corps, the Tuskegee Airmen, named for the segregated air base in Alabama where they trained, broke the color bar. But it took them two years—far longer than white aviators—to be deployed to Europe. There, the white head of their combat group, convinced that Blacks lacked the capacity for aerial warfare, at first kept them hundreds of miles from the battle zone. But the Airmen went on to play a key role in the Battle of Anzio, shooting down a dozen enemy planes. In the last two years of the war, some Black soldiers were able to take part in ground combat, including D-Day and the Battle of the Bulge in Europe, and the bloody island-hopping campaigns in the Pacific theater. The vast majority of Black troops, however, remained confined to work as construction and transportation crews, stevedores, engineers, and the like. Delmont also discusses the Black members of the Women's Army Corps, some of whom served as nurses and as members of the much-admired armed forces postal service. But many others, including college graduates and schoolteachers, were consigned to work as cleaners.

Delmont makes a strong case that the unheralded work to which Blacks were assigned proved essential to Allied victory. Without the labor of thousands of Black troops removing mines, repairing railroad tracks, and delivering food, ammunition, fuel, and other supplies, the army could not have functioned following the Normandy landing. But Black soldiers continued to encounter overt racism. When Black engineers were dispatched to construct a vital military highway across Alaska, Brigadier General Simon Bolivar Buckner Jr. warned that they would "interbreed" with the indigenous population and produce an "objectionable race of mongrels."

Delmont shows that from the moment the United States entered the war, the treatment of Blacks in the military was a major source of controversy. The Black press demanded the integration of the armed forces. Military commanders strongly resisted, claiming that white soldiers would resent being in close proximity to Blacks. At a meeting of Black editors with War Department officials the day after Pearl Harbor, one of the military participants announced: "The army is not a sociological laboratory." The army deployed this line throughout the war to evade responsibility for its resistance to integration, claiming it had no choice but to abide by Jim Crow laws and mores, even on army bases outside of local jurisdiction. In fact, by not taking action to protect soldiers who were victims of racist violence and other forms of mistreatment on and off military bases; by directing Black soldiers to ride at the rear of southern buses and in Jim Crow railroad cars; and by doing, Delmont writes, "everything they could to enforce American segregation" in Europe after the war, the army did more than simply abide by the Jim Crow system—it actively bolstered it. Its policies affected millions of people at home and overseas. The military transposed racist policies from the South to military camps in other parts of the country. The result, as Delmont says, was to put a "federal stamp of approval on the South's system of racial apartheid."

A. Philip Randolph, the Black labor leader and civil rights activist, described Washington, D.C., as not only the capital of the United States but also the capital of "Dixie." Roosevelt and Congress were largely indifferent to Black demands for equality in the army and civilian life. While Blacks were fighting for the Double V, the federal government's recruitment posters promoted the idea that military success would restore the pre-war world, grounded in traditions of work, family, and, implicitly, segregation. (Senator James Eastland of Mississippi was quite candid about this: on the Senate floor he declared that white soldiers were "fighting to maintain white supremacy.")

Eastland was one of the members of Congress who, as the historian Ira Katznelson has written, exercised a "southern veto" over New Deal legislation. They ensured that measures such as the Social Security Act excluded agricultural and domestic workers—that is, nearly all employed Blacks. They also made certain that the GI Bill of 1944 (the ticket to a college education, home ownership, and well-paid jobs for millions of white veterans) was administered at the local level. This meant that Black veterans were largely excluded from the government-secured home loans that enabled their white counterparts to join the postwar suburban middle class. In the South, Black veterans could use federal benefits only to attend segregated colleges. Most, including those who had acquired valuable skills in the army, were shunted into menial employment. Delmont presents some astonishing statistics. Of 3,200 government-secured home loans issued to veterans in Mississippi in 1947, only two went to Blacks. In New York and New Jersey, with 67,000 such mortgages, Black veterans received fewer than one hundred. These policies considerably widened the wealth gap between Black and white families, which persists to this day. Even at the height of the civil rights movement, the power in Congress of segregationist southerners such as Richard Russell, the chair of the Senate Armed Services Committee, and Carl Vinson, his counterpart in the House of Representatives, made efforts to purge the military of racism all the more difficult.

In 1941, Randolph's threat to organize a March on Washington to protest against discrimination in defense employment forced Roosevelt to create the Fair Employment Practices Committee. The FEPC, however, lacked enforcement power and was effectively disbanded midway through the war. And when employers hired or promoted African Americans, "hate strikes" sometimes followed. In the summer of 1943, some 25,000 white workers walked off the job in Detroit to protest against the promotion of three Black men at a Packard plant making military vehicles. Roy Wilkins of the NAACP remarked that whites would rather lose the war than "give up the luxury of race prejudice."

Army leaders insisted that treating Black and white soldiers equally would have a deleterious effect on military efficiency. In fact, policies rooted in racism were counterproductive and often had dire consequences. The army and Red Cross segregated blood plasma, even while acknowledging that no scientific reason existed to do so, meaning men wounded in combat might die unnecessarily if only the "wrong" blood was available. Time and money were wasted constructing duplicate facilities. Confining Blacks to the position of messmen in the navy and making it almost impossible for Black soldiers to rise to the rank of officer deprived the military of skills that could have contributed far more effectively to the war effort.

The wartime battle for equitable treatment by the armed forces and in defense industries was part of what is sometimes seen as the birth of the modern civil rights movement. The experience of fighting against Nazism changed America's intellectual climate. Gunnar Myrdal's *An American Dilemma*, published in 1944, laid out for a large readership the extent of racism in the United States. By the end of the war, the previously small NAACP had grown to half a million members. The wartime movement for racial justice linked Black activists with white progressives and used tactics that would become familiar in the 1960s: sit-ins, boycotts, litigation, even armed self-defense. And in 1948, President Truman, employing his constitutional power as the military's commander in chief to make an end run around Congress, ordered the armed forces to embrace "equality of treatment and opportunity" regardless of race, religion, and national origin. His executive order didn't use the words "integration" or "segregation," but within a few years, Black soldiers were fighting alongside white in the Korean War, as they have in every war since.

The transition, however, was anything but smooth. Beth Bailey's title, *An Army Afire*, evokes the widely held image of the Vietnam War army as fraught with divisions between Black and white soldiers, and between young draftees and clueless officers. By the late 1960s, many Americans had in fact come to see the military as a model of racial progress. The army itself promoted this narrative, especially after the draft ended in 1973, forcing it to recruit thousands of volunteers each month. In a historic reversal, Black leaders no longer fought for the right to fight. Instead, they charged that in Vietnam Black soldiers were over-represented among frontline combat troops and therefore suffered disproportionate casualties, a claim that Bailey offers statistics to reject. Re-enlistment rates were considerably higher for Blacks than other soldiers. Until 1968, newspapers reported little tension between Black and white troops. Everything seemed to change that year, a time, at home, of assassinations, urban uprisings, a full-scale generational rebellion, and demands for Black Power. In Vietnam, the army experienced fights within military units and even instances of enlisted men turning their weapons on officers.

Like their counterparts on the home front, Bailey writes, "young Black soldiers were angry." And they were more likely than in the past to complain about indignities and maltreatment—Ku Klux Klan graffiti in bathrooms, the use of racial epithets by white soldiers, the low number of Black officers, off-base discrimination. But now, reflecting cultural currents swirling on the home front, Black soldiers demanded direct recognition by the armed forces. They wore Afro hair styles and read books on Black history. In a 1969 speech, secretary of the army Stanley R. Resor said that the army needed to move beyond efforts to be "race-blind." "The Negro soldier," he added, "is different from his counterpart of ten years ago." In a (probably unwitting) echo of W. E. B. Du Bois's reference in *The Souls of Black Folk* to Black "double consciousness," Resor continued: "A Negro in uniform does not cease to be a Negro and become a soldier instead. He becomes a Negro soldier."

Insubordination in the army was rife. Both Black and white troops displayed peace symbols on their uniforms. But unrest was greatest among Black soldiers. In August 1968, forty-three refused orders to stand by for riot duty at the Democratic National Convention in Chicago. The same year, two hundred Black prisoners seized control of the army jail at Long Binh, South Vietnam. Part of the facility remained under inmates' control for three weeks. They burned buildings, dressed in makeshift dashikis and played improvised "African drums." They represented, one army chaplain claimed, "the hard core of Black Power." *Time* magazine described the situation in Vietnam as a "war within the war."

Bailey, however, is less interested in warfare than in the way the military responded to what she calls "the problem of race." At first, the army seemed unwilling to recognize that such a problem existed. In October 1968, a Black major, Lavell Merritt, walked into a press conference in Saigon and distributed a statement accusing the army of being a "citadel of racism." Military officers investigated him—not the army—and concluded that he had "an obsessive preoccupation with matters pertaining to racial discrimination." Major Merritt was retired, ending twenty years of service. The incident, Bailey argues, showed that the army was simply unprepared to confront rising tensions in its ranks. Lt. Col. James S. White, a Black officer, addressed a gathering of journalists in Saigon. "The army," he said, "has a race problem because American society has a race problem." This may strike readers of Bailey's book as an excuse rather than an explanation, an evasion of responsibility for the long history of military racism. Often, it seemed, army officials saw the problem as a failure of communication: older officers needed to learn how to deal with the new generation of young African Americans.

Bailey writes that once persuaded that a problem existed (which often took a while), the army's practice was usually to conduct investigations, issue reports, hold innumerable meetings, and try its best to maintain morale and discipline in the ranks. This was the pattern followed in Vietnam. Bailey describes various efforts to understand and deal with the growing crisis. In 1970, Major Avrom Carl Segal, a psychiatrist from Philadelphia and chief of mental health services at Fort Benning, Georgia, organized focus groups and group therapy sessions for his battalion. To help improve communication, the army insisted that all soldiers attend lectures on Black history. It even screened a documentary, *Black and White: Uptight*, which Bailey describes as "unflinching in its condemnation of white racism." The army made training in "race relations" mandatory in its educational system.

Many Black soldiers were interviewed by army officials about their experiences. A remarkable number of responses had to do with culture and fashion, including many complaints about army regulations that prohibited Afro hairstyles. A 1969 report by John Kester, a member of the Judge Advocate General's Corps, noted that young soldiers hated having to have their hair cut "much shorter" than "fashionable civilian men." "The modern young man," he wrote, "is extremely jealous of his individuality . . . He regards hairstyle as an expression of himself." The army changed its regulations to allow Afros as "an assertion of manhood" and racial pride. It even paid to bring a barber from San Diego to military bases overseas to train local stylists. But such leniency raised questions. What about those white soldiers who, in good 1960s fashion, preferred long, shaggy hair? Or those who displayed the Confederate flag, claiming it was nothing more than an expression of regional pride? Bailey concludes that the army's efforts to allow soldiers to express their "individuality" in an institution normally aiming at uniformity caused more trouble than it was worth.

Many army officers were committed to rooting out racism and making military integration work. Some were willing to stand up to the president. In 1971, as part of his "southern strategy," Richard Nixon ordered West Point to construct a monument to graduates who had fought for the Confederacy. There were now 119 Black cadets at the military academy and each of them signed a "manifesto" opposing the idea and condemning racism at the institution, including the low number of Black officers and teachers. West Point's superintendent opposed Nixon's plan, the academy's alumni association refused to finance it, and the president abandoned it.

Among the more surprising heroes in Bailey's account is the defense secretary, Robert S. McNamara, mostly remembered today as a leading architect of the Vietnam War. A lifelong member of the NAACP, McNamara commissioned a study that found many examples of off-base discrimination against Black soldiers stationed in Korea and West Germany. He insisted that members of the armed forces must not be subjected to "the hate and prejudice that parades under the pomposity of racial superiority." McNamara ordered military commanders, in effect, to treat housing and places of entertainment that discriminated against Blacks as if they were venues where soldiers might contract venereal disease. That is, he banned anyone in the army from frequenting them. Army leaders objected to this use of economic sanctions to combat racism, warning that the military would seem like an occupying force if it moved too far beyond "local community attitudes." But McNamara persisted.

Bailey's account of the way the army responded to the growing crisis is original and informative. When it comes to actually describing the crisis, however, difficulties arise. She adopts the army's own vocabulary, characterizing the subject of her book as the "struggle to solve the problem of race." This language, no doubt unintentionally, seems to suggest that the "problem" was the presence of Black people in the armed forces. The real problem, however, wasn't "race"—a concept with no scientific validity—or "race relations," but a long history of racism in the military. However one defines the "problem," Bailey views the army's response as "surprisingly creative." She argues that a complex institution tried to do its best under difficult circumstances: "commitment, innovation and success" marked its efforts, she writes. The army revised training and education and implemented programs to increase the number of Black officers. Coupled with an easing of social conflict at home, these initiatives led to an ebbing of the army's crisis.

Today, the military is perhaps the largest integrated institution in the United States. The Department of Defense conducts "diversity training" exercises. Confederate flags are banned from military installations, and the names of bases, and even streets on bases, that have long honored Confederate leaders are in the process of being changed. Twelve percent of active-duty officers are Black. The army now welcomes female and gay soldiers. Senator Ted Cruz of Texas has complained that today's military has been "emasculated."

The military has made progress, but a long history of entrenched racism can be difficult to overcome. A recent lawsuit charges that the Department of Veterans' Affairs still administers benefits such as disability payments in a discriminatory manner, rejecting applications from Black veterans at a considerably higher rate than those of whites. There is a similar disparity in the punishment of soldiers convicted of the same kinds of offense in military courts, with Blacks receiving a higher number of dishonorable discharges. The Pentagon itself has issued warnings about an alarming increase within the armed forces of members of white supremacist organizations. The military has not yet solved its "problem."

THE REAL ROSA PARKS

O N DECEMBER 1, 1955, Rosa Parks, a 42-year-old Black
woman who had just completed her day's work as a tailor's
assistant in a department store in Montgomery, Alabama,
was arrested for refusing to surrender her seat on a city bus to a white
passenger, as required by municipal law. The incident sparked a year-
long bus boycott, the beginning of the modern phase of the civil rights
revolution. And it made Parks, the "seamstress with tired feet," an
international symbol of ordinary Black Americans' determination to
resist the daily injustices and indignities of the Jim Crow South.

Today, with the birthday of Martin Luther King Jr. a national holiday and Alabama cities like Birmingham, Selma, and Montgomery
competing to attract tourists by highlighting their role in the struggle
for racial justice, Rosa Parks has become a national icon second only
to King himself. Highways, city streets, and subway stations have been
named in her honor. In the 1990s, Parks was awarded a congressional
medal and invited to sit beside the First Lady during a State of the
Union address by President Bill Clinton. In December 2000, at the

---

Review of *Mine Eyes Have Seen the Glory: The Life of Rosa Parks*, by
Douglas Brinkley, *London Review of Books*, May 10, 2001.

street corner where she was arrested, Montgomery's city fathers opened the Rosa Parks Library and Museum, complete with a sculpture of Parks in her bus seat with space for visitors to have their pictures taken sitting alongside her bronze replica.

Douglas Brinkley's *Mine Eyes Have Seen the Glory* is the first serious biography of Parks. It is also part of a new series of brief lives of famous individuals. What makes the series distinctive is not only brevity, but that the books are written by authors not previously known for expertise on the individuals whose lives they examine. The "concept," as the series editor, James Atlas, explained to me a few years ago, is to produce books that airline passengers can read on a flight from New York to San Francisco and finish before they reach the Golden Gate. Given the entertainment options available at 35,000 feet this is not an exacting standard. Most of the books, including Brinkley's, have more than met it.

A historian whose previous work has concentrated on presidential politics and American foreign relations, Brinkley faced a difficult challenge in approaching the life of Parks, and not only because this is his first book on the struggle for racial justice. Despite her status as the "mother of the civil rights movement," as a world-historical figure Parks ranks somewhat below Joan of Arc, Mozart, Leonardo da Vinci, and Mao, who also figure in the series. Parks is important because of her connection with a mass movement, yet the series format does not lend itself to a life-and-times approach. Brinkley is a skilled writer who has combed the archives for information about Parks and the society in which she lived, and he succeeds in placing her life before the bus boycott in its political and social context. But her subsequent career and the fate of the movement she helped to inspire are treated in cursory fashion.

Born in Alabama in 1913, Parks grew up in a world of racial segregation and periodic lynchings, when a deep economic gulf existed between the races and the Ku Klux Klan was on the rise. The daughter of a schoolteacher and a carpenter—her father abandoned the family when she was young—Parks was raised by her grandparents.

She sought solace from the deprivations of poverty and racism in the Black church. The young Parks prayed regularly, read the Bible daily, and while imbibing the principle of turning the other cheek, coupled Christian forgiveness with a determination to stand up for her rights. From her grandfather, an admirer of Marcus Garvey, she learned the lessons of racial pride and self-discipline, principles reinforced at the Montgomery Industrial School for Girls, a segregated institution founded after the Civil War by northern missionaries. She attended the school for a few years until the Klan ran the headmaster out of town and forced it to close.

Today, it is easy to forget that the civil rights revolution came as a great surprise. Those like Gunnar Myrdal, author of the influential 1944 study *An American Dilemma*, who saw that the South's racial system could not survive indefinitely, expected the challenge to develop in the North, where Blacks had far greater latitude for political organization. One virtue of studying Parks's early life is that it makes clear the extent to which the revolution arose out of earlier local struggles for racial justice that have been largely forgotten. Although Brinkley does not quite put it this way, these earlier struggles were catalyzed during the 1930s and World War Two by a broad left-wing movement of Communists, trade unionists, and social reformers, operating in an uneasy coalition with the NAACP. This was the world in which Parks matured.

Her politicization began during the 1930s, when she married Raymond Parks, one of the founding members of the Montgomery branch of the NAACP and an avid reader of Black periodicals like the *Chicago Defender*, *Pittsburgh Courier*, and *The Crisis*—the last a brilliant chronicle of Black achievements and oppression edited by W. E. B. Du Bois. Beginning in 1933, she took part in meetings to protest the trials of the Scottsboro Boys, nine Black youths falsely accused of rape and sentenced first to death and later to long prison terms in a series of trials that revealed Alabama justice to the world as a travesty. Largely through the efforts of the American Communist Party, the case became an international cause célèbre. In 1943, Parks joined the NAACP and, as the only woman at her first meeting, was appointed secretary. For the next decade, while living with her husband and infirm mother in a Montgomery housing project and earning money as a seamstress, Parks organized the files and maintained the correspondence of E. D. Nixon, the NAACP's charismatic and militant local leader and a member of the Brotherhood of Sleeping Car Porters, which was led by the civil rights pioneer A. Philip Randolph.

Brinkley rightly points out that historians of the movement have ignored the full story of Parks's life as an "authentic grass-roots activist." Her image as a simple seamstress—so inspiring to Blacks and non-threatening to whites—obscured the fact that she was well-informed about racial politics and enjoyed a wide range of experience. When in 1943 Nixon founded the Alabama Voters' League to challenge the disenfranchisement of Blacks, Parks tried to register to vote, only to be barred because she had supposedly failed a literacy test. Unlike other rejected aspirants, she persevered and on her third attempt became one of very few Montgomery African Americans added to the voter rolls—but only after she had paid a hefty poll tax.

At the time, Parks was working at Maxwell Air Force base near Montgomery. On the base, buses were integrated, but in the city Blacks were constantly treated with discourtesy by white drivers and forced to give up their seats if whites needed them. In 1943, when she boarded a bus through the front door, the driver, James F. Blake, brusquely ordered her to leave and re-enter through the rear. Parks was so disturbed by her treatment that she resolved never again to ride a bus driven by Blake, a pledge she kept for twelve years. Ironically, the bus on which her historic act of defiance took place in 1955 was driven by the same James F. Blake.

In 1954, Parks obtained work as a seamstress for Clifford and Virginia Durr, prominent white supporters of racial justice whose commitment to this and other left-wing causes, including the presidential campaign of Henry Wallace in 1948, had led to their ostracism by Montgomery society. The Durrs arranged for her to attend a training session at the Highlander Folk School in Tennessee, a meeting ground for labor and civil rights radicals, where activists were trained and political issues and strategies discussed in a fully integrated setting. Many of the local leaders of the civil rights movement passed through Highlander.

Thus, when Rosa Parks refused to give up her seat, she was more than the simple lady with tired feet canonized in the press. "The only tired I was," she wrote in her memoir, "was tired of giving in." She was well aware that their treatment on city buses was a deeply felt grievance among Montgomery's Black population and that local Black leaders were actively seeking an incident to launch a boycott. Jo Ann Robinson, a professor of English at the all-Black Alabama State University, had publicly threatened city officials with a boycott in 1954. In March 1955, Claudette Colvin, a 15-year-old high school junior, had refused to give up her seat to a white passenger. Nixon and the NAACP moved to organize a boycott, only to call it off at the last moment when they discovered that Colvin was several months pregnant. Parks, however, was the perfect plaintiff—a demure, married, God-fearing woman about whom no one seemed to have a bad word.

We will never know precisely why Parks refused to leave her seat when ordered to do so. Her decision was not premeditated but neither was it completely spontaneous. Perhaps it was because an all-white jury in Mississippi had just acquitted the murderers of Emmett Till, a Black teenager who had allegedly whistled at a white woman. Perhaps the reason was that she had inadvertently boarded a bus driven by the same driver who had evicted her twelve years earlier. Parks knew that talk of a boycott was in the air. In any event, in the wake of her arrest the boycott began.

Brinkley ably introduces the cast of characters who organized this remarkable episode—Nixon, Robinson, the talented Black lawyer Fred Gray, the Reverend Ralph Abernathy, and, of course, 25-year-old Martin Luther King Jr., who had recently come to Montgomery to serve as minister of the Dexter Avenue Baptist Church and whose elevation to spokesman for the movement launched his career as a national figure while annoying many of the city's long-time civil rights leaders. The boycott was a complete success. For thirteen months, Black maids, janitors,

teachers, and students walked to their destinations or rode an informal network of private taxis. Eventually, the Supreme Court declared
bus segregation statutes unconstitutional. The Montgomery boycott
launched what came to be known simply as "the Movement"—a non-
violent crusade, based in the Black churches of the South, that eventually toppled the legal edifice of segregation.

After the boycott, Parks slipped into the background. In 1957, dis-
mayed by the persistent death threats directed at herself and her
husband, she and her family moved to Detroit. From here, the book
becomes extremely sketchy. Events cascade forward with little real
explanation or evaluation—the sit-ins, the March on Washington,
Selma, Black Power, the Detroit riot of 1967, the assassination of King.
Brinkley claims that by the mid-1960s, Parks had become "a tough-
minded, free-thinking feminist who had grown impatient with grad-
ualist approaches." But he offers little detail to substantiate this claim,
other than her admiration for Malcolm X. Parks certainly remained
active in the civil rights struggle and in the 1980s picketed in Washington as part of the anti-apartheid movement. In 1994 she became a
national symbol of a different kind when she was robbed in her Detroit
home by a young Black intruder. She died in 2013 at the age of 94.

Within the constraints of the series, Brinkley has done justice to
his subject. The same cannot be said for the publisher. Presumably to
avoid frightening off those potential airline readers, the book has no
notes and no index. Perhaps worse, there are no illustrations. Brinkley vividly describes well-known photographs of Parks, including
one published on the front page of *The New York Times* when she was
arrested as part of a crackdown on boycott leaders by city officials. He
writes of the "haunting Alabama photographs of African Americans
during the Great Depression" taken by the Swiss journalist Annemarie
Schwarzenback, which "offer a marvelous visual record of the world in
which Rosa Parks grew up." But what these images actually depict is left
to the reader's imagination.

Despite Brinkley's heroic effort to make us understand Parks as a
seasoned activist and part of a popular movement, her older image

remains more saleable. What does the publisher put on the back cover to promote the book? "When in 1955 Rosa Parks, a Black seamstress, refused to surrender her seat to a white passenger in Montgomery, Alabama, she changed the course of history." Like King, frozen in historical memory on the steps of the Lincoln Memorial delivering his "I Have a Dream" speech, Parks is forever the simple woman with tired feet who singlehandedly brought down segregation.

Today, Montgomery is integrated, and Blacks vote in the same proportions as whites. But a startling gap in income, life expectancy, and education continues to divide the races. The housing project in which Parks lived still stands, located on the renamed Rosa L. Parks Avenue. But squalor has overtaken these once well-maintained if segregated houses, and random gunfire can sometimes be heard at night. The story of Rosa Parks underscores how far America has come since the days of Jim Crow, and how far it still has to go.

RIDING FOR FREEDOM

WITHOUT THE HEROISM of thousands of unsung grass-roots activists, the civil rights movement would never have accomplished what it did. In *Freedom Riders*, Raymond Arsenault rescues from obscurity the men and women who, at great personal risk, rode public buses into the Deep South to challenge segregation in interstate travel. Drawing on personal papers, FBI files, and interviews with more than 200 participants in the rides, Arsenault brings vividly to life a defining moment in modern American history.

Freedom Riders begins not on May 4, 1961, when thirteen Black and white volunteers boarded two buses in Washington bound for New Orleans, but seventeen years earlier, when Irene Morgan, an African American woman who worked for an aircraft manufacturer, in an act of defiance that anticipated Rosa Parks's, refused to give up her seat to a white passenger on a bus traveling from Virginia to Maryland. Convicted of violating local segregation laws, she appealed all the way to the Supreme Court, which ruled in 1946 that segregated seating on interstate buses violated the Constitution.

———

Review of *Freedom Riders: 1961 and the Struggle for Racial Justice*, by Raymond Arsenault, *New York Times Book Review*, March 19, 2006.

In 1947, the Congress of Racial Equality, or CORE, an obscure civil rights group founded a few years earlier by Christian pacifists, organized the Journey of Reconciliation to test compliance with the Court's ruling. As Arsenault notes, the Freedom Rides represented the latest front in a battle that had begun many decades earlier. Before the Civil War, Black activists in the North fought against their exclusion from streetcars and railroad carriages. During Reconstruction, a number of southern states enacted laws requiring the integration of public transportation, and in the late nineteenth century Black travelers, often successfully, brought lawsuits demanding damages for being denied equal treatment on railroads and coastal vessels.

In most parts of the world, a bus journey would hardly have attracted attention. In the Jim Crow South of 1961, the Freedom Riders encountered shocking violence that deeply embarrassed the Kennedy administration. The trip through the upper South went off peacefully, but outside Anniston, Alabama, a mob set one of the buses on fire. The riders were lucky to escape with their lives. In Birmingham, police officers gave Klan members fifteen minutes to assault the riders at the bus station before intervening. The result was what Arsenault calls "one of the bloodiest afternoons in Birmingham's history."

Further violence was inflicted on a second group of riders in Montgomery, where John Seigenthaler, the president's personal representative, suffered a fractured skull and several broken ribs. It took a small army of policemen and National Guard troops to escort the bus from Montgomery to Jackson, Mississippi, where the Freedom Riders were promptly arrested for breach of the peace and attempting to incite a riot. Some spent time at the infamous Parchman Farm, a prison plantation the historian David Oshinsky called "synonymous . . . with brutality."

Arsenault relates the story of the first Freedom Ride and the more than sixty that followed in dramatic, often moving detail. He reminds us of the personal courage and organizational ability of forgotten catalysts of the movement such as Diane Nash, a Black student leader in Nashville who helped to mobilize new groups of Freedom Riders upon hearing of the first beatings.

As its title suggests, the book focuses above all on the riders themselves. Future scholars will be grateful for the appendix, which provides brief biographical information on more than 400 of them. Unfortunately, apart from a table showing that they were overwhelmingly young (three-quarters were under 30), mostly male, and almost equally divided between Black and white, this information remains unanalyzed. "Diversity," Arsenault writes, "was the hallmark of the Freedom Rides." The first group illustrates his point—it included a Wall Street stockbroker, a veteran unionist from Michigan, a folk singer from New York, a former Navy captain, and a Nashville theology student (John Lewis, who went on to become a movement leader and member of Congress). But "diversity" is a description, not an interpretation. One wishes for a more detailed account of the riders' political backgrounds, organizational connections, and later experiences.

As Arsenault makes clear, the Freedom Rides revealed the pathology of the Jim Crow South. This was a society not simply of violent mobs but of judges who flagrantly disregarded the Constitution, police officers who conspired with criminals, and doctors who refused to treat the injured. Southern newspapers almost universally condemned the riders as "hate mongers" and outside agitators (even though about half had been born and raised in the South). Not that the national press acquitted itself much better. The *New York Times* reporter Claude Sitton produced some of the best coverage in the country. But the paper's editorials, while defending the right to travel, called on the riders to halt their "courageous . . . but nonetheless provocative action."

Most remarkable was the supine response of the Kennedy administration. Before assuming the presidency, John F. Kennedy had evinced little interest in civil rights. Once in the White House, he viewed the Freedom Rides as an unwelcome distraction from his main concern—the Cold War. Kennedy's first impulse was to try to keep details of the violence out of the press. In the midst of the crisis, he delivered a special address to Congress. Remembered today for its pledge to put a man on the moon, it dealt primarily with international affairs, identifying the "southern half of the globe" as "the great battleground for the expansion of freedom today." It made no mention of the battle for freedom then being fought in the southern United States.

The attorney general, Robert F. Kennedy, comes off rather better. Initially as impatient with the riders as his brother, Robert Kennedy became emotionally committed to their cause. It was he who petitioned the Interstate Commerce Commission to ban segregation in interstate bus travel. The result was an order that brought the Freedom Rides to a triumphant end.

Overall, the administration's response calls into question a staple of recent writing on the civil rights movement—that the Cold War created a favorable environment for racial change. Certainly, the photographs that flashed across the world embarrassed the White House. But the conflict with the Soviets also inspired deep distrust of any movement that included critics of American foreign policy. After a telephone conversation in which he urged Martin Luther King Jr. to restrain the riders, Robert Kennedy remarked to an aide, "I wonder whether they have the best interest of their country at heart."

The Cold War did not produce a significant change in federal policy. That, as both the Freedom Riders and King knew, required a social movement. Indeed, of the civil rights leaders touched on in this book, King comes across as the most supportive of young activists. We sometimes forget how young King himself was at this time. Only 32 in 1961, he was closer in age to the riders than to the older civil rights establishment. In his conversation with Robert Kennedy, King refused to heed an appeal for moderation: "I am different from my father. I feel the need of being free now." This impatience for freedom, acted out by the courageous young Freedom Riders, helped propel a reluctant America at least part of the way down the road to racial justice.

A GREAT AMERICAN

I N MARCH 1968, only a few days before his assassination, Martin Luther King Jr. visited Long Beach, a suburb of New York City, at the invitation of a local NAACP leader. Like many suburbs at that time, Long Beach was effectively a segregated community, with an African American population living in a tiny ghetto and working in the homes of local white families. I grew up in Long Beach, but by 1968 had moved to the city. My parents, however, still lived there, and my outspoken mother arranged to see the city manager, a non-partisan administrator who exercised the authority normally enjoyed by an elected mayor. "A great American is visiting Long Beach," she declared, urging the manager to hold a reception for King at City Hall. He refused: "He's a troublemaker and we don't want him here."

Not surprisingly, this minor incident goes unmentioned in Jonathan Eig's new biography of King. But it illustrates a theme to which Eig returns several times. People of every political persuasion now claim King as a forebear. But during his lifetime, King and the civil rights movement aroused considerable opposition, and not only in the South.

Review of *King: The Life of Martin Luther King,* by Jonathan Eig, *London Review of Books,* October 5, 2023.

The government sought to destroy King's reputation. With the authorization of John F. Kennedy and Lyndon Johnson, the FBI listened in on his phone calls with close associates and planted informers in his circle. Convinced the civil rights movement was a communist plot, J. Edgar Hoover's G-men gathered recordings of his trysts with women and mailed them to his house, accompanied by an unsigned letter suggesting that he take his own life.

An accomplished biographer, Eig's previous subjects include Muhammad Ali, Al Capone, and the baseball stars Jackie Robinson and Lou Gehrig. He is an indefatigable researcher, and *King* is based on a vast array of material, old and new, including documents collected by previous historians of the civil rights movement, thousands of pages of recently released FBI intercepts, more than two hundred interviews, and previously unknown audio tapes recorded by King's wife, Coretta, after his death. Does all this produce a strikingly new portrait of King? Not really: the trajectory of his life is, in the end, familiar. But Eig offers affecting accounts of the Montgomery bus boycott, which made King a national figure, the confrontation in the streets of Birmingham between young Black demonstrators and Bull Connor's dogs and fire hoses, and the march for voting rights from Selma to Montgomery. Eig's admiration for King is obvious, but he is not reluctant to point out failures, such as the Chicago Freedom Movement and the Poor People's Campaign, which sought to expand the civil rights movement to address poverty among Americans of all races.

Eig's style is journalistic, with brief paragraphs driving the narrative forward. This structure sometimes seems at odds, however, with the book's aspiration to present a full portrait of King; it makes it hard for Eig to provide analysis of the movement's historical background or King's own ideas. But he avoids pitfalls to which some previous writers have succumbed, such as drawing too stark a contrast between a "good," racially integrated, non-violent movement led by King and a subsequent "bad" one when Black Power became the order of the day and urban uprisings alienated many previously sympathetic whites. Eig makes clear that King was masterful in appealing for support from white Americans. But he resists the temptation to portray the movement as fulfilling the immanent logic of an American creed of liberty and equality established at the nation's founding. (For this latter approach, see *The 1776 Report*, a brief account of American history issued in the waning days of the Trump administration, which claims that the establishment of the American nation "planted the seeds" of the abolition of slavery and equal citizenship rights for Blacks.) Eig demonstrates that neither the movement's emergence nor its successes were preordained. They required both King's leadership and the mobilization of thousands of courageous men and women who risked their lives to bring down Jim Crow.

King was born in Atlanta in 1929, the son of Martin "Daddy" King, a prominent Baptist minister who grew up in poverty in rural Georgia and through hard work and self-discipline managed to join Atlanta's Black middle class. The elder King established strong connections with the city's white power brokers—so strong, in fact, that even while speaking out against racism he urged parishioners, including the ten-year-old Martin, dressed as a slave, to take part in a gala celebration for the 1939 premiere of the film *Gone with the Wind*. Daddy King "fought for social change," Eig writes, but "urged his followers to be patient." King Jr., who after some resistance acceded to his father's pressure to follow him into the ministry, attended the segregated Morehouse College in Atlanta, Crozer Theological Seminary, a small institution in Pennsylvania, and Boston University, where he earned his PhD. At Morehouse, King was inspired by the lectures of the college president, Benjamin Mays, who urged students to challenge segregation and was strongly influenced by the Social Gospel movement popularized by the theologian Walter Rauschenbusch, who in the late nineteenth century had argued that the fight for social justice was a religious duty. King Jr. was a serious student of philosophy and theology, drawing on the writings of Gandhi and Henry David Thoreau to develop a powerful justification for disobedience to unjust laws. At a time when only 2 percent of the Black population had graduated from college, King exemplified the "talented tenth" to whom W. E. B. Du Bois looked for racial leadership.

In 1954, King became minister of the Dexter Avenue Baptist Church in Montgomery, Alabama, a rigidly segregated city that Eig describes as "a bastion of the Ku Klux Klan." When King arrived, local leaders were already campaigning for improvements in the Black condition. But in 1955, Montgomery became the site of a bus boycott that lasted a year and inspired advocates of social change throughout the United States. Partly because he was new to the city and hadn't been involved in factional fighting among Black leaders, King was asked to lead the boycott. Eig makes the useful point that thanks to housing segregation, the solidly middle-class King family had no choice but to live among maids and sanitation workers, giving him, perhaps for the first time, experience of the Black working class.

In a speech delivered to an overflow crowd at the Holt Street Baptist Church in Montgomery, King struck a prophetic note, telling his audience of ordinary African Americans that the Constitution and Christian morality were on their side and that their moral superiority over the white perpetrators of violence was their greatest strength. "If you will protest courageously and yet with dignity and Christian love, when the history books are written in future generations, the historians will have to pause and say: "There lived a great people—a Black people—who injected new meaning and dignity into the veins of civilization." King's oratory, combined with the commitment of Montgomery's Black residents, who walked for a year rather than ride the segregated buses, eventually led to a Supreme Court decision requiring the integration of public transportation. King was catapulted to national prominence. For the rest of his life, he travelled the country lecturing, leading demonstrations, raising funds, and recruiting participants to the civil rights movement. In 1960, when the sit-ins launched a wave of protests throughout the South, leadership passed to a younger generation of Black activists. But the press never stopped equating King with the movement, to the annoyance of many of his associates.

The path from Montgomery to the Civil Rights Act of 1964, the Voting Rights Act a year later, and the Fair Housing Act of 1968— the movement's legislative triumphs—was anything but smooth. Eig points out that in 1964, a decade after the Supreme Court declared racial segregation of public schools unconstitutional, only 1 percent of white children in the South attended school alongside Blacks. Later in the 1960s, when King brought the movement to Chicago, his marchers were met by rioters carrying "White Power" signs. The fate of the Chicago Freedom Movement revealed some of the strengths and weaknesses of King's leadership. He mobilized Blacks and white allies with memorable speeches and earned his followers' respect both for his deep religious convictions and for being willing to suffer the same treatment they endured. He was jailed more than two dozen times and had a bomb explode at his Montgomery home.

But King was never a strong administrator and the result, according to Eig, was "organizational chaos." King refused to listen when colleagues warned that the movement lacked the resources to launch a campaign against urban poverty, slum housing, and other manifestations of economic inequality. He battled exhaustion from ceaseless travels and suffered bouts of self-doubt and depression. Eig discusses two of King's less praiseworthy traits. One was a weakness for plagiarism, which began in high school and was evident in his doctoral dissertation, though Eig points out that his supervisors at Boston University should have caught King's appropriation of language from well-known works of theology and philosophy. Without excusing what he calls his subject's "bad habit," Eig notes that King's plagiarism reflected his haphazard research method of copying information onto notecards without recording the source, then incorporating the material directly into his text. "Sampling"—borrowing particularly effective passages from the sermons of other ministers—wasn't uncommon among Baptist preachers.

More serious is King's history of extra-marital relationships, some brief, some long term. The FBI's wiretaps of King's phone calls and surveillance of his travel reveal the extent of such liaisons. Hoover was obsessed with King's sex life, though his preoccupation seems to have had as much to do with prurience as national security. He delighted in sharing salacious information from the recordings with select members of Congress as well as Kennedy and Johnson (who weren't exactly choirboys when it came to infidelity). The most serious accusation against King is that he was present in a hotel room where a woman was raped by one of his associates. This charge appears in a summary of phone recordings written by William C. Sullivan, one of Hoover's lieutenants. Experts on King's career have questioned the reliability of Sullivan's account. Like Hoover, Sullivan was committed to "completely discredit[ing] King as the leader of the Negro people." A judge has ordered the recordings closed until 2027, when scholars can evaluate the truthfulness of Sullivan's report.

Eig takes a matter-of-fact approach in discussing King's liaisons. He points out that King—charming, powerful, and widely respected—attracted interest from many women, but rightly focuses on the impact of King's behavior on his wife, who was aware of at least some of the affairs. Eig devotes more attention to Coretta Scott King than previous biographers, emphasizing that she was an anti-racist radical in her own right. It tells us something about life in the Jim Crow South that although she was the daughter of a successful Black businessman, she grew up in a home in rural Alabama without running water or electricity and was forced to walk five miles each day to attend school while white children traveled by bus.

Coretta attended Antioch College in Ohio, where she became involved in political activism. In 1948, as a student delegate, she attended the national convention of the Progressive Party, whose presidential candidate, Henry Wallace, advocated for racial justice and challenged the Truman administration's emerging Cold War foreign policy. In 1952, during their courtship, she gave King a copy of Edward Bellamy's influential socialist novel *Looking Backward* (1888). She was a talented singer and attended the New England Conservatory in Boston. (Ironically, in accordance with the Supreme Court's "separate but equal" doctrine, the government of Alabama partly paid her tuition since the state did not make such training available to Black students.) With four children at home and her husband almost always absent, a professional career was impossible, but she sometimes gave fundraising performances. King admired her intellect and frequently consulted her on matters of strategy. Yet she later wrote that he thought women's main roles were as mothers and housewives. The movement had no dearth of talented, strong-willed women activists, including the grassroots organizer Ella Baker and Jo Ann Robinson, a Montgomery college professor and a key organizer of the bus boycott. But its top echelons were almost entirely male. Every speaker at the 1963 March on Washington was a man.

In 1957, Black ministers formed the Southern Christian Leadership Conference (SCLC), with King at its head, to co-ordinate protests against segregation throughout the South. But as state and local governments embarked on a path of "massive resistance" to integration, the pace of progress slowed and the phrase "white backlash" began to appear in the press. Resistance stiffened as the 1960s progressed. "King came under attack from all sides," Eig writes. After the 1966 march demanding open housing in Chicago was targeted by rioters, King said: "I think the people of Mississippi ought to come to Chicago to learn how to hate."

The Chicago campaign and the Poor People's Movement that followed are often seen as marking a shift in King's priorities from racial to economic equality. But King had long recognized how closely these issues were intertwined and had often spoken of the need for "economic justice." Despite racial discrimination by many unions, King saw the labor movement as Blacks' greatest potential ally. In 1959, he lent his name to organizing efforts by Local 1199, the Drug, Hospital and Health Care Employees' Union in New York City, whose members at the time earned a meagre thirty dollars a week. "Whatever I can do, call on me," he told the union's executive secretary, my uncle Moe Foner.

Sometimes King spoke of eliminating the "physical ghetto" altogether. It is often forgotten that the March on Washington was a joint venture of the civil rights movement and liberal labor unions, and that its demands included a massive public works program to provide the poor of all races with "Jobs and Freedom"—the event's official title. In the mid-1960s, King and the veteran activist Bayard Rustin proposed a Bill of Rights for the Disadvantaged that would eradicate poverty by guaranteeing full employment and a universal basic income. Portions of the left had been promoting such policies since FDR proposed a Bill of Economic Rights in 1944. When King delivered his Riverside Church speech of 1967, calling for an end to the war in Vietnam, he not only spoke in unusually heated language about the U.S. government—the "greatest purveyor of violence in the world"—but also warned that the conflict was draining resources from the struggle against what he elsewhere called the country's "tragic inequalities."

Eig notes that as a college student, King expressed interest in "democratic socialism." Before their marriage he wrote to Coretta that "I am much more socialistic in my economic theory than capitalistic." But Eig doesn't do enough to elucidate King's economic ideas. It's true that the anti-poverty campaigns of the last years of his life were grounded in Christian morality as much as economic analysis. It might be best to view him as seeking ways to extend to African Americans the principles of the Social Gospel, most of whose advocates had ignored the Black condition even as they called for equality of wealth and power. King insisted that "genuine equality" meant "economic equality." Such comments reinforced Hoover's conviction that King was "the most dangerous Negro" in the United States.

One of the things Hoover found alarming was the presence among King's close advisers of Stanley Levison, a New York lawyer and businessman who had once been a member of the Communist Party. Hoover passed warnings about Levison to Robert Kennedy, who urged King to sever their connection. Neither Hoover nor Kennedy knew much about African American history. If they had, they wouldn't have found the presence in the movement of a former communist surprising. Since the 1930s, the party had been one of the few predominantly white organizations to make racial justice a major concern. Levison had spent many hours helping to get SCLC off the ground. (He also prepared King's annual tax returns.) Rather than conspiring to overthrow the government, Levison often pushed King in a moderate direction. He warned him that white Americans were willing to support some changes in the social order, but not "revolution," and argued against shifting movement resources to the Poor People's Campaign. Levison criticized the Riverside Church speech for lacking focus and urged King to "remain basically a civil rights leader and not a peace leader." (This didn't prevent Hoover from informing Johnson that Levison had written the speech for King.) Despite his voluminous research, Eig doesn't take advantage of recent books by Martha Biondi, Glenda Gilmore, Michael Honey, and others who delineate the role of communists in civil rights struggles without embracing Hoover's fantasy that the movement was directed from Moscow. None of these historians is cited in Eig's text or notes.

Nor does Eig touch on the last major speech before King's death, delivered in 1968 in New York City at a celebration of the centenary of Du Bois's birth. King paid tribute to Du Bois's *Black Reconstruction in America*, calling it a "monumental achievement." The book had dismantled the racist representation of the post–Civil War years as a period of misgovernment that demonstrated the supposed inability of Blacks to take part in American democracy. Du Bois, King declared, "exemplified Black power in achievement and he organized Black power in action," language that reminds us of the often-ignored overlap between King's views and those of younger Black militants. King forthrightly rejected Cold War ideology. Du Bois, King noted, was "a communist in his later years . . . a genius [who] chose to be a communist," and his career demonstrated the absurdity of "our irrational obsessive anti-communism."

King's Du Bois speech came at a time when his own view of American history was changing. Previously he had rarely discussed Reconstruction. Now he saw that era, not the Revolution or even emancipation, as a crucial moment of hope for Black Americans, "their most important and creative period of history." The continuing distortion of the period by historians raised a troubling question. King had long identified the movement with core American values inherited from the nation's founding. But what, in fact, were the nation's deepest values? All men are created equal? Or something more sinister, exemplified by Reconstruction's violent overthrow? King had originally believed, he told the journalist David Halberstam, that American society could be reformed through many small changes. Now, he said, he felt "quite differently." "I think you've got to have a reconstruction of the entire society, a revolution of values." Was the movement the fulfilment of American values, or their repudiation?

According to Monuments Lab, an organization that keeps track of such things, King today ranks fourth, after Lincoln, Washington, and Columbus, among individuals with public monuments in the United States. But the price of King's deification in recent years has been the absorption of the civil rights movement into a consensual, feel-good portrait of American history. King, Eig warns us, has been "defanged." On Martin Luther King Jr. Day, we don't hear the voice of the radical King, the ally of the labor movement and critic of economic inequality and war. His great speech at the March on Washington is all but reduced to a single sentence: "I have a dream that my four little children will one day live in a nation where they will not be judged by the color of their skin, but by the content of their character." Conservatives have long quoted this to enlist King retroactively in the campaign to end affirmative action. In fact, in his final book, *Where Do We Go from Here?* (1967), King, while acknowledging that "special treatment" for Blacks seemed in conflict with the principle of "equal treatment of people according to their individual merits," embraced affirmative action. Why? History—the long history of racism, resulting in the widespread exclusion of Black Americans from economic opportunities and positions of political influence and power—supplied the answer. After doing "something special against the Negro for hundreds of years," the United States had an obligation to "do something special for him." It is a pity that in 2023 six members of the Supreme Court, in a case involving affirmative action in college admissions, made it clear that they do not agree. It is still more lamentable that because of recent laws barring the teaching of "divisive" subjects, the history of racism—without which King's life is incomprehensible—is being driven out of American classrooms.

KING'S DREAM AT 60

A LITTLE OVER SIXTY years ago, Martin Luther King Jr. delivered the most celebrated speech in modern American history. The date was August 28, 1963, the occasion the March on Washington for Jobs and Freedom, the place the Lincoln Memorial. We remember the speech largely for its memorable metaphors—"the whirlwinds of revolt," "the tranquilizing drug of gradualism"—and for the urgency of King's "dream" of a future America that had moved beyond the tyranny of race. King achieved a delicate balance between hope and despair, between anger at the Black condition and reassurance to other Americans that they had nothing to fear from the civil rights movement. All Americans would benefit from the dismantling of the decades-old structures of Jim Crow.

It is easy to forget how thoroughly American King's "I Have a Dream" speech was. He wrapped himself, and the movement he had come to personify, in the mantle of core American values discernable in the most cherished documents of the national experience. In a little over 1,500 words, he managed to invoke the Emancipation Proclamation, the Declaration of Independence, and the patriotic song *Amer-*

The Nation, August 28, 2023.

ica, interspersed with the language and cadences of the Bible. When he first used the words "I have a dream," he immediately added that it was "deeply rooted in the American dream." It would be difficult to make the civil rights movement less threatening to white fellow citizens. King managed to make his call for a radical restructuring of American life familiar, indeed almost conservative.

King's speech built on a tradition dating back to the American Revolution, when Black critics of the racial order chastised the country for not living up to its professed ideals, while at the same time claiming those ideals as their own. During the struggle for independence, Black petitioners cited the ideology of liberty to demand their own freedom. In pamphlets, sermons, and manifestos they insisted that, as one petition put it, "every principle from which America has acted" demanded the abolition of slavery. In the pre–Civil War decades, Black abolitionists and their white allies seized on Jefferson's timeless pronouncement that "all men are created equal" as a weapon for abolition. Gatherings of free African Americans called themselves "conventions of colored citizens," claiming a status enjoyed by white Americans but which the federal government denied to them. If white Americans could enjoy citizenship by birthright, the same principle should extend to African Americans born in the United States.

Perhaps the most striking instance of condemning national hypocrisy while claiming the benefits of liberty was Frederick Douglass's 1852 speech "The Meaning of July Fourth for the Negro." Douglass excoriated Americans who celebrated Independence Day while subjecting millions of their countrymen to bondage. Yet he did not repudiate the founders or their handiwork. Far from it: Douglass laid claim to the founders' legacy. They were "brave men," he declared, "great men," and the Constitution they had fashioned was "a glorious liberty document" that, properly interpreted, would bring an end to slavery. Indeed, Douglass implied, since the Declaration of Independence identified liberty as a universal entitlement of mankind, Blacks—whether free or enslaved—who rejected the idea that liberty could be confined to one race were the real inheritors of the American Revolution.

King's "I Have a Dream" speech utilized some of the same rhetorical strategies. Like Douglass, King insisted that the nation had tragically strayed from the principles bequeathed by the founders. King emphasized that (like abolitionism) the movement for racial justice was itself interracial. He noted that many whites had participated in civil rights demonstrations, sometimes suffering imprisonment or worse, and had traveled to Washington for this occasion. Along with calls for enactment of the Civil Rights Bill then languishing in Congress, the marchers' demands—the Jobs and Freedom of the March on Washington's title—would benefit Americans of all races: "their freedom is inextricably bound to our freedom." Black equality was not a threat to whites.

King also sought to allay widespread fears that the march would result in violence. He urged Blacks to conduct their struggle "on the high plane of dignity and discipline" and explicitly rejected "distrust of all white people." Yet, despite his uplifting tone, King did not eschew sharp, even angry language. Just as Douglass had accused the nation of "crimes that would disgrace a nation of savages," King spoke of "the unspeakable horrors of police brutality," language that may surprise those who encounter the speech today knowing only the words "I have a dream." Today, we remember the language that embodied hope— King's dream—but not his description of the stark realities of Black life. At one point King seemed to abandon reassurance altogether in favor of a not-so-veiled threat: "There will be neither rest nor tranquility in America until the Negro is granted his citizenship rights."

In effect, King was asking white Americans to decide whether they wished to align themselves with resistance, often violent, to social change, or act in accord with constitutional principles. In many ways, the same choice confronts us today.

WHATEVER HAPPENED TO INTEGRATION?

I NTEGRATION, THE IDEAL that once inspired an interracial mass movement to dream of a better America, has lately fallen into disuse or disfavor. Books continue to appear with the word in their titles, but most seem resigned to integration's failure, treating it as an ongoing "ordeal" or seeking to allocate blame for the nation's departure from integrationist ideals. Many leftists feel that as a political goal, integration fails to address deeply rooted economic inequalities. Many African Americans criticize it for implying the dismantling of a distinctive Black culture and identity. Those who still claim to favor the idea of integration often reduce it to a matter of "color-blind" laws and social practices.

This special issue of *The Nation* hopes to rekindle critical discussion of integration by examining whether it remains, thirty years after the end of the civil rights era, a desirable goal and a viable political strategy. The essays that follow do not claim to cover every aspect of the subject, or to represent all points of view in today's political spectrum. We conceive this issue as a discussion within *The Nation*'s extended family, focused on a series of questions essential to a modern assessment

—

Introduction, Special Issue of *The Nation*, December 14, 1998.

of integration—in what historical context did the idea of integration emerge, what do its present status and future prospects appear to be, what relevance does it have to contemporary Black politics, and how ought liberals and the left regard integration today?

Although race relations in America have increasingly moved away from the bipolar categories of Black and white, this issue focuses on the experience of African Americans, not only because the idea of integration has historically been associated with them, but because the Black condition has always been a unique litmus test of how fully American society lives up to its professed creed of equal rights and opportunities for all.

As the essays make clear, there is no single definition or understanding of integration. Some writers see integration as a worthy goal in and of itself; to others, it is a means toward other ends, such as racial justice or Black empowerment. Some see integration as a dream of humane interpersonal relations, to be worked out through daily interactions in neighborhoods and families. To others, integration in practice has proven to be an avenue of social mobility for those located at the center of powerful institutions, with little relevance to the majority of African Americans. Other essays adopt different positions. But all agree that the time has come for a fresh consideration of integration, as a political program, moral ideal, and social agenda.

Any assessment of integration must begin by acknowledging both the enormous changes in race relations of the past thirty years, and how much remains to be accomplished to fulfill the goals of the civil rights struggle. Nearly one hundred years ago, W. E. B. Du Bois identified the "color line" as the main problem confronting the new century. Today, as Daryl Scott observes, the color line is in a "shambles." Thanks to the movement itself and to a generation of affirmative action policies by public and private institutions, realms of American life from sports to politics, from corporate board rooms to university classrooms, have achieved an unprecedented racial diversity. The ranks of the Black middle class have expanded enormously in these years and African Americans occupy positions of genuine authority inconceivable only a few decades ago.

Why, then, do so many Americans feel that integration has failed? Partly because the historical gap between Black and white in employment, income, and family wealth remains intractable. Our prisons overflow with Black inmates, and a large part of the Black population (including millions of Black children) remain mired in poverty. As Douglas Massey and Mary Fisher explain, one reason for the high incidence of poverty among African Americans is that housing patterns remain nearly as segregated as ever—the product of a long history of discriminatory policies by government, real estate developers, insurance companies, and banks, and of millions of individual choices by white homeowners. This "hyper segregation" affects Black Americans far more powerfully than other racial minorities, and helps account for the fact that nearly a half-century after Brown, large numbers of Black and white children attend school in racial isolation.

Is "integration" an adequate response to these social realities? To answer this question, one must recall, as Judith Stein points out, that while the struggle for racial justice in America is very old, the language of integration is a relatively recent innovation. The two men widely considered the most prominent spokesmen for the integrationist strand in Black thought—Frederick Douglass and W. E. B. Du Bois—rarely if ever used the word. When the modern civil rights movement was born during and immediately after World War II, its watchword was "Negro rights," not integration, and its theme was not simply the dismantling of segregation, but concrete improvements in Black Americans' jobs, housing, political power, and treatment by the police and judicial systems.

Integration did not become the rallying cry of the movement for racial justice until the 1950s and 1960s. The demand for integration proved a potent weapon for mobilizing Americans of all races to break down the walls of legalized segregation. But it tended to encourage a view of race relations as essentially a matter of interpersonal dynamics and to identify segregation—often understood as an abstraction—not concrete deprivations such as inadequate income, jobs, housing, and education, as the main problem confronting the Black population.

As with other "keywords" of our political language, such as freedom and independence, the definition of integration often hinges on the understanding of its opposite, segregation. If one sees this as essentially a system of classifying and separating people by race, it is easy to equate "color-blindness" with integration and racial justice. Once one realizes that segregation was only one part of a complex system of white supremacy each of whose elements—including political disenfranchisement, economic deprivation, and social inequality—reinforced the others, then the demand for integration implies a broader program for a far-reaching transformation of American society.

Indeed, even in the heyday of the civil rights movement, many proponents of integration persistently drew attention to the inequalities in employment, education, and housing left intact after the dismantling of legal segregation, and proposed a variety of strategies, some "color-blind," some race-based, to attack them. Martin Luther King Jr. called for a "Bill of Rights for the Disadvantaged" to mobilize the nation's resources to abolish the scourge of economic deprivation, and for what would come to be called affirmative action ("special treatment" for Blacks, he called it) to address the unique plight of the Black poor. He did not see one as a substitute for the other or either as violating the goal of integration. Indeed, by the mid-1960s, addressing economic deprivation in American society had become central to King's understanding of integration.

We do not believe that the left should cede the language of integration to conservatives or to those who understand race relations as a psychodrama rather than a system of unequal access to economic resources and political power. Three years ago, an editorial in this magazine reaffirmed the radicalness of integration, on the premise that an end to the deep inequalities that afflict our society and, on a more personal level, brotherly and sisterly personal relations between persons of all races, can only be achieved in a society of genuine equality. The need remains as great as ever for the left to formulate a political program, including but not limited to integration, to continue in the post–civil rights era the long struggle for racial justice.

PART V

An Imperfect Democracy

THE ELECTORAL
COLLEGE

E VERY FOUR YEARS Americans wake up to the fact that a president can be elected despite receiving fewer votes than another candidate. Until 2000 the electorate couldn't be blamed for being unaware of this possibility, because it hadn't happened since 1888. But in 2000 George W. Bush squeaked into office with a five-vote majority in the electoral college even though Al Gore outpolled him by half a million votes. Then in 2016 Hillary Clinton received nearly three million more votes than Donald Trump but still lost by a substantial margin—304 to 227—among the electors. Ask a man or woman in the street why this system of electing a president was adopted and how it works and you will almost certainly draw a blank. It's complicated, but the main point to bear in mind is that the president is elected indirectly. To be sure, on election day Americans think they're casting a ballot for their preferred candidate. But, technically, what they're doing is voting for electors pledged to support that candidate. The electors

---

Review of *Why Do We Still Have the Electoral College?* by Alexander Keyssar, and *Let the People Pick the President: The Case for Abolishing the Electoral College*, by Jesse Wegman, *London Review of Books*, May 21, 2020.

vote a month or so later and in almost all cases choose the candidate who carried their state. No matter who won the national popular vote, the electors have the final say.

The United States prides itself on providing a global model of democratic government. But of the nearly two hundred sovereign states that make up the United Nations it is difficult to think of another that elects its chief executive as Americans do. Even countries with constitutions explicitly modeled on ours have not thought the electoral college worthy of emulation. Liberia, established as a settlement for manumitted slaves, closely followed the American example in its constitution, but opted for direct election of the president "by the people." The post–World War Two constitutions of West Germany and Japan, their drafting strongly influenced by the American occupying authorities, did not adopt this system. The electoral college (an odd name for an institution whose members only assemble once every four years, and not together but in the fifty state capitals) certainly makes the U.S. exceptional.

How the president should be elected was one of the most divisive issues to confront the constitutional convention of 1787. The delegates agreed that the new nation must be a republic, which ruled out a hereditary head of state. Some favored selection by the legislature, the method used in parliamentary systems, but others feared this would make the president dependent on Congress. The most democratic option, of course, was election by the people (or at least the minority of the population eligible to vote in each state, generally white men with property), but most of the framers believed unrestrained democracy was as dangerous as tyranny. Placing prominent men of "discernment" between the electorate and the final outcome, Alexander Hamilton insisted, would hold popular passions in check and prevent a demagogue, perhaps beholden to a foreign government, rising to power. James Madison had a more self-interested objection to popular election. The Constitution had already increased the political power of the South, where slaves made up 40 percent or more of the population, thanks to a clause adding three-fifths of the slave population to the number of free inhabitants when using population to allocate the seats given to each state in the House of Representatives. Since the slave population would have no impact on the outcome, warned Madison, a Virginia slaveowner, a popular vote for president would deprive the South of "influence in the election on the score of the Negroes."

The electoral college system was adopted shortly before the convention's deliberations ended, and it has remained almost unchanged ever since. Each state was given the right to choose electors by a method it determined, which ended up meaning either selection by the state legislature, or by popular vote. The number of electors in each state was equivalent to that state's delegation in Congress—two senators plus however many members it had in the House. The candidate who received a majority of the electoral vote would become president, and the one who came second would become vice president. If no one won a majority, the House of Representatives, with each state casting one vote, would select the president from among the top finishers. Thus, the electoral college imported into the election of the president two undemocratic features from elsewhere in the Constitution—the allocation of two senators to each state regardless of population, and the three-fifths clause enhancing the white South's political power—and added a third, the provision that in the event of a final election by the House, each state, large or small, would have the same influence on the outcome.

The Constitution's framers neither anticipated nor desired the rise of political parties, which they saw as divisive institutions that elevated factional interests above the common good. But parties quickly emerged anyway and caused havoc in the electoral system. Ever since, instead of men of local prominence and independent judgment, each party has nominated as candidates for elector minor functionaries who can be relied on to vote for their party's presidential candidate. The electors are not supposed to think for themselves. Not one voter in a thousand can name any of them past or present.

In 1788 and 1792, the state legislatures in most cases chose the electors, and they unanimously chose George Washington as president. After that, trouble began. Initially, each elector cast two votes without differentiating between president and vice president, because it was assumed that candidates would compete as individuals, not as representatives of political parties, and that the two most qualified would occupy the two highest offices. In 1796 this resulted in the winning candidate, John Adams of the Federalist Party, ending up tied with Thomas Jefferson, leader of the opposition Republicans (not to be confused with today's Republican Party), as vice president. Four years later, the Republican ticket consisted of Jefferson for president and Aaron Burr for vice. They outpolled Adams and his running mate, Charles Pinckney, but in order for Jefferson to become president, one or more Republican electors had to avoid voting for Burr so that he would end up in second place, and thus as vice president. The electors failed to get the message. Jefferson and Burr ended up with 73 electoral votes each, sending the contest to the House of Representatives. Burr schemed to become president with Federalist assistance. Only after 35 indecisive ballots did Hamilton, who disliked Jefferson but thought Burr incorrigibly dishonest, convince enough Federalists to abstain to allow Jefferson to be elected. This set in motion a train of events that culminated in the 1804 duel in which Burr took Hamilton's life. It also led to the adoption of the Twelfth Amendment, requiring electors to vote separately for president and vice president, in recognition of the fact that candidates were already running as party tickets and would continue to do so.

The framers had assumed that the House of Representatives would decide most elections because in a vast, diverse nation it would be difficult for any candidate to win a majority of the electoral vote. But after presidential elections became party contests, nearly all produced a clear winner. After 1800, the only time the House chose the president was in 1824, when the party system was temporarily in disarray. John Quincy Adams, who had come second to Andrew Jackson in both the popular and electoral votes, struck a deal with Henry Clay, who came fourth, giving Adams a majority of the House votes. Adams then named Clay his secretary of state. What Jackson's supporters called the "corrupt bargain" was precisely the kind of political maneuvering the framers had hoped to avoid.

Almost from the beginning, there were efforts to game the electoral college system. In the early republic, states switched back and forth between popular and legislative selection of electors, using whichever method seemed to favor their candidate. (When the legislature chose the electors, the majority party could simply assign the state's electoral vote to its preferred candidate, forgoing the inconvenience of an actual election.) In 1836, the Whig Party ran four regional candidates for president, in the hope that together they would prevent the Democratic candidate, Martin Van Buren, from winning a majority of the electoral votes (they didn't succeed). In 1864 and 1876, Congress admitted a thinly populated territory (Nevada, then Colorado) as a state shortly before election day to bolster the Republican candidate's electoral vote. The Constitution, moreover, failed to explain what should happen if the result in a state was contested. This transpired in 1876, when disputed returns from three southern states made it impossible to know who had been elected president. After months of political crisis, Congress appointed a fifteen-member electoral commission to determine the outcome—a procedure with no basis in the Constitution. Rutherford B. Hayes, a Republican, became president and as part of the "bargain of 1877" his party agreed to recognize Democratic control of the disputed state governments. This marked the end of Reconstruction in the South.

By the 1830s, "democracy" had lost its pejorative implications and every state except South Carolina was choosing its electors by popular vote. Alongside this development came the tradition, not required by the Constitution, that the candidate who carried a state received all of its electoral votes. Sometimes called the "general ticket," the winner-takes-all system in the electoral college has been nearly ubiquitous for almost two centuries—today only Maine and Nebraska allocate some of their electors by results in congressional districts. (In 2008, Barack Obama carried a Nebraska district, winning one of that solidly Republican state's five electoral votes.) Winner-takes-all maximizes a state's impact on the outcome, but also makes more likely a mismatch between the winner of the popular vote and the electoral vote. A candidate can carry a dozen or so large states by small margins and capture the presidency while trailing far behind in the popular vote. This is what happened in the momentous four-candidate election of 1860. Abraham Lincoln received virtually no popular votes in the slave states and only 40 percent nationally. But by carrying the entire North, he captured an electoral vote majority. Indeed, if the popular votes of the other candidates had been combined and given to one of them, Lincoln would still have become president even though 60 percent of the electorate opposed him.

Winner-takes-all discourages the emergence of third-party candidates unless they have a regional base. In 1992, Ross Perot, running as an independent, received nearly twenty million votes (19 percent of the total), but no electoral votes since his popular vote was spread out among the states and he failed to carry a state. It also has a powerful effect on the way that presidential campaigns are conducted. For reasons ranging from tradition to demography and ideology, the winner in most states is predictable well before election day. Neither candidate sees much point in campaigning in reliably "red" or "blue" states, since even a loss by a narrow margin translates into no electoral votes. As a result, the contest is confined to half a dozen or so "swing" or "battleground" states that both candidates have a realistic chance of carrying. In 2016, two-thirds of the campaign events held by Clinton and Trump took place in only six states. Today, the swing states include Arizona, Michigan, North Carolina, and Pennsylvania. Voters who live in places like my home, the Democratic stronghold of New York, are essentially ignored. To be sure, I have the luxury of being able to "throw my vote away" on a minority party candidate, knowing that this will not affect the electoral vote tally. (Things would be different if I lived in Arizona.) Not surprisingly, voter turnout is higher in battleground states, where each vote really matters.

For most of American history, the electoral college system has enhanced the political power of white southerners. Without the votes of the extra electors that resulted from the addition of three-fifths of the South's slaves to the population calculation, for example, Jefferson would not have defeated John Adams in 1800. In the late nineteenth century, the southern states systematically stripped the right to vote from Black citizens in flagrant violation of the Fifteenth Amendment, enacted during Reconstruction, which outlawed denial of the franchise on the grounds of race. But this did not affect these states' representation in the House. Ironically, the abolition of slavery increased southern political power because the entire Black population, not just three-fifths of it, was now counted in the allocation of House seats and electoral votes. Like the three-fifths clause, disenfranchisement allowed the white South to benefit politically from the presence of the Black population while denying it any semblance of democratic rights. For much of the twentieth century, the southern states resembled a series of rotten boroughs, whose tiny electorates wielded disproportionate power in Congress and in the election of the president. (According to the Fourteenth Amendment, states that deprive significant numbers of citizens of the right to vote are supposed to lose a portion of their congressional representation and electors. But this penalty has never been enforced.)

Given its undemocratic nature and long history of dysfunction and racial bias, it isn't surprising that almost from the start proposals began to circulate about changing the way electors were chosen, or even doing away with the electoral college entirely. Over time, more than eight hundred such amendments have been introduced in Congress. Amending the Constitution is a daunting task, requiring the approval of two-thirds of Congress and three-quarters of the states. But it has nevertheless been accomplished twenty-seven times, effecting changes that have significantly democratized American politics: extending the right to vote to African Americans, women, and 18-year-olds; shifting the election of senators from legislatures to voters; barring the imposition of poll taxes, and allocating electoral votes to residents of Washington, D.C. But the stark fact is that with the exception of the Twelfth Amendment, which only tweaked the system, the strange way we elect the president has survived intact for over two centuries. These two books try to explain why.

Alexander Keyssar's *Why Do We Still Have the Electoral College?* examines efforts to change or abolish the system. Keyssar is the author of *The Right to Vote*, which twenty years after its publication remains the standard account of the history of suffrage in the United States. His new book is comprehensive and full of historical insight. Even specialists in political and constitutional history will encounter surprises. But in telling this story it's impossible to avoid repetition. Madison described the debates about the presidency at the constitutional convention as "tedious and reiterated," a comment that can be applied to the entire history of efforts at electoral college reform. The problem is exacerbated by the book's partly chronological, partly thematic structure.

As Keyssar shows, the most common proposal has been for proportional allocation of each state's electoral votes. Such proposals typically give one elector to the winner in each of a state's congressional districts, as Maine and Nebraska currently do, with two more chosen statewide. Election by congressional district would obviate the main problem of the winner-takes-all system, which is the effective disenfranchisement of millions of voters whose ballots do not translate into electoral votes. It would undoubtedly increase the number of contested states and thus voter turnout. Allocating electors by congressional district, however, would introduce the problem of gerrymandering into the election of the president. In almost every state, legislatures draw district lines. And ever since the early days of the republic, the dominant party has drawn them so as to maximize its electoral prospects. Today, thanks to sophisticated computer analysis of voting returns, politicians can effectively choose their voters rather than the other way round. Redistricting takes place every decade, when the census determines how many members of the House each state will be given. The 2010 elections gave Republicans control of a majority of state governments, and they proceeded radically to redraw district lines to enhance the power of their party. In such circumstances, the district system would not eliminate the possibility of the loser of the popular vote becoming president. If electors had been allocated by congressional district in 2012, Mitt Romney would have been elected even though he trailed Obama by five million popular votes.

To avoid this problem, Henry Cabot Lodge, the Republican senator from Massachusetts, proposed in the 1940s that each state's electoral votes should be automatically distributed in proportion to the popular vote in that state, with a national run-off if no candidate received 40 percent overall. Race played a major and somewhat paradoxical part in the debate. Lodge hoped that his plan would enable the Republicans to pick up electoral votes in the then solidly Democratic South, especially if Black people regained the right to vote there. Nonetheless, some southern Democrats initially supported the measure, believing it would weaken the power of Black voters in the urban North. The massive migration of African Americans from the South to northern industrial cities, where they enjoyed the right to vote, coupled with a continuing shift in their allegiance away from the party of Lincoln, had changed the political configuration of states like New York, Illinois, and Michigan. "There are enough Negroes in New York City," proclaimed Ed Lee Gossett, a congressman from Texas who introduced Lodge's measure in the House, to determine the electoral vote of the entire state. "With all due deference to our many fine Jewish citizens," Gossett added, the same was true of them. In February 1950, the Senate approved Lodge's proposal, the first time in more than a century that either chamber had passed a constitutional amendment to change the way we elect the president. But the proposal died in the House. Liberals, as well as Black and Jewish organizations, became convinced that it would weaken the power of Democratic urban enclaves in the North without affecting the South's ability to prevent Black voting.

Only in the mid-twentieth century, Keyssar shows, did a national popular vote become the preferred alternative for the electoral college's detractors. Thanks to the civil rights revolution of the 1960s, southern Blacks finally regained suffrage, weakening the advantage the electoral system gave to white voters there. Then, in 1968, George Wallace, a pioneer of white backlash politics, won forty-six electoral votes as an independent candidate. Wallace didn't succeed in throwing the election into the House, where he hoped to influence the outcome, but the prospect of this happening in future led to an upsurge of support for replacing the electoral college with a popular vote for president. The leading proponent in Congress was Senator Birch Bayh, a liberal Democrat from Indiana. But support for his proposal transcended party and ideological lines. President Nixon endorsed it, along with the U.S. Chamber of Commerce, the League of Women Voters, and the American Bar Association. A Gallup poll found that 81 percent of respondents favored the change.

Bayh's amendment passed the House in 1969. More than half the votes against it came from southern Democrats who hoped that the enfranchisement of Blacks could somehow be reversed. In the Senate, three segregationists—Strom Thurmond of South Carolina, James Eastland of Mississippi, and Sam Ervin of North Carolina—mobilized opposition. (Ervin's role may surprise those who remember him only for his principled part in the Nixon impeachment investigation. But before that he was mostly known as an outspoken opponent of racial integration.) As with the Lodge amendment, Black leaders outside the South joined the campaign against reform, fearing a diminution of their political influence in the northern industrial states. The Senate failed to break a filibuster and the amendment died.

Keyssar opens his book with a warning not to expect an analysis of current debates or a clear prescription for change. For these, one can turn to *Let the People Pick the President* by Jesse Wegman. Wegman is a fluid writer who manages to make constitutional debates and the history of political parties lively, even amusing. His account skims much of the history related by Keyssar but offers a sustained argument in favor of the latest proposal to replace the electoral college, the National Popular Vote Interstate Compact. States that sign up pledge that their electors will cast their ballots for the winner of the national popular vote, regardless of which states he or she carries. The compact will go into effect when states with a combined 270 electoral votes—a majority of the electoral college—have joined. The advantage of this plan is that it avoids the laborious process of constitutional amendment. As of today, fifteen states and the District of Columbia, representing 196 electoral votes, have joined, so there is still a long way to go.

Wegman devotes considerable space to debunking misconceptions about the electoral college. The most common is that the system benefits small states, because, since they start with the two votes representing their senators, they have more influence on the outcome in proportion to their population than if a president were elected directly. This belief is a major obstacle to winning over the three-quarters of the states required to change the Constitution. Wegman argues persuasively that the winner-takes-all system negates the small-state advantage. It makes much more sense for candidates to focus on populous states when winning them by even a narrow margin yields an electoral vote bonanza. In 2000, Bush's majority of 537 votes out of six million cast in Florida gave him all of the state's twenty-five electoral votes.

What is to be done? Keyssar refers briefly to the compact but does not seem to consider it a viable alternative. It carries a whiff of duplicity—many citizens would be outraged if a candidate who failed to carry their state nonetheless received its electoral votes. Whatever the plan's shortcomings, however, it would encourage both parties to maximize turnout in every state and ensure that whoever wins the popular vote becomes president. But the hyper-partisanship of current U.S. politics makes agreement on any proposal for change unlikely. All the states that have endorsed the compact are Democratic strongholds, not surprisingly, since the party's candidates have won the popular vote in six of the last seven presidential elections. For the same reason, Republicans are convinced that the current system favors them. The two most recent Republican national platforms oppose any change in the electoral college system.

These books deserve a wide readership. But the electoral college is only one symptom of a far deeper problem. American democracy is sick in ways that go well beyond how the president is chosen. The symptoms include widespread efforts in Republican states to suppress the right to vote and to rig elections, employing such tactics as onerous identification requirements, partisan gerrymandering, and the removal of many thousands of citizens from the voting rolls for trivial reasons. A partisan Supreme Court, in addition, has allowed unlimited corporate spending on campaigns and abrogated key parts of the Voting Rights Act of 1965, which restored Black suffrage in the South. These problems will not be solved by allowing the people to elect the president, but that would be a valuable first step. Rooted in distrust of ordinary citizens and, like so many other features of American life, in the institution of slavery, the electoral college is a relic of a past the United States should have long ago abandoned.

POLITICAL WARS OF THE GILDED AGE

I N "THE FOUR Lost Men," an elegiac short story written in the 1930s about his dying father's recollections of life in post–Civil War America, Thomas Wolfe memorably conjured up the era's presidents: "My father spoke then of the strange, lost, time-far, dead Americans . . . the proud, vacant, time-strange, and bewhiskered visages of Garfield, Arthur, Harrison and Hayes . . . Who was Garfield, martyred man, and who had ever seen him in the streets of life? . . . Who had heard the casual and familiar tones of Chester Arthur? And where was Harrison? Where was Hayes? Which had the whiskers, which the burnsides: which was which? Were they not lost?"

Wolfe's words are frequently quoted to illustrate the seeming irrelevance of national politics in America's Gilded Age, when it did not seem to matter who occupied the White House. Can anyone today identify a single accomplishment of Benjamin Harrison or Chester A. Arthur? Who can explain in plain English what the heated battle over the "free coinage of silver at 16 to 1" was all about? Jon Grinspan does not cite Wolfe in his new book, *The Age of Acrimony*, but it is easy to

---

Review of *The Age of Acrimony: How Americans Fought to Fix Their Democracy, 1865–1915*, by Jon Grinspan, *The Nation*, June 1, 2021.

imagine him doing so. Not, however, to underscore the pointlessness of Gilded Age politics, but as evidence of late-nineteenth-century Americans' intense identification with the two major parties. Wolfe's four lost men may have lacked charisma and accomplished almost nothing while in office, but, Grinspan argues, Americans were far more passionately invested in national politics then than they are today. And if you think our current moment of hyper-partisanship, political polarization, abusive language, widespread efforts to suppress the right to vote, and violent clashes over electoral outcomes is unprecedented, think again. As far back as the 1790s opponents called George Washington a British agent and Thomas Jefferson a lackey of revolutionary France. In the decades before the Civil War, not a session of Congress passed without punches being exchanged between members of Congress and knives and pistols being drawn in the Capitol. But the high point of this kind of acrimonious politics came in the Gilded Age.

A curator of political history at the National Museum of American History in Washington, D.C., Grinspan draws on an impressive array of memoirs, letters, and scholarly works. Thanks to his position in a history museum he is intimately familiar with the material culture of politics, and he directs the reader to the "incredible variety of campaign paraphernalia"—the banners, placards, broadsides, buttons, and other artifacts on display during political campaigns. The result is a compelling portrait of the central place of national politics in Americans' lives and how this began to change around the turn of the twentieth century.

The word "democracy" does not appear in the Declaration of Independence or the Constitution. The founders thought that unrestrained democracy was as dangerous as tyranny. To keep popular enthusiasms under control they included numerous undemocratic features in our frame of government, including an electoral college to choose the president, a Senate elected by state legislatures, not the people, and a Supreme Court whose members served for life. But by the 1830s, as Alexis de Tocqueville discovered when he visited the United States, the idea of democracy (for white men) had become a defining feature of American life. Union victory in the Civil War reinforced democratic sentiments. Many Americans believed that the advent of a "pure democracy," purged of slavery and racial injustice and confidently addressing the dislocations caused by a rapidly industrializing economy was at hand. Instead, Grinspan argues, Gilded Age political campaigns subordinated substance to mass spectacle, with huge nightly parades of torch-bearing partisans, incessant political rallies, and spellbinding oratory laced with scurrilous attacks on opponents. In saloons and on urban streetcars, Americans engaged in fistfights over politics. On election day, armed men employed by local political machines tried to prevent supporters of the opposing party from casting ballots.

Presidential elections between the Civil War and the end of the nineteenth century, Grinspan writes, were "the loudest, roughest political campaigns in our history." One magazine described them as "the theater, the opera, the baseball game, the intellectual gymnasium, almost the church, rolled into one." The campaign of 1884, which pitted Republican James G. Blaine against Democrat Grover Cleveland, wrote one contemporary, was "the dirtiest, most disgusting and disgraceful our nation has ever known." Republicans dwelled on the fact that Cleveland had fathered an illegitimate child, Democrats on Blaine's record of financial malfeasance. Yet no matter how mediocre or corrupt, political leaders were revered by their followers. Who today would call a presidential candidate the Plumed Knight, as Blaine was known in 1884?

Despite, or because of, the raucousness of politics, voter turnout was extraordinarily high. The election of 1876, remembered today for the bargain that made Rutherford B. Hayes president and ended Reconstruction, brought to the polls 82 percent of eligible voters, the highest participation rate in American history. Eight and a half million men voted in 1876, nearly as many persons as visited the great Centennial exposition in Philadelphia that year during its entire six-month existence. Turnout would have been even higher had violent white supremacists not prevented numerous African Americans in the South from casting ballots. (Had Blacks' voting rights been secure, the result of the "disputed election" would not have been disputed; Hayes would have handily won several southern states and, with them, the election.)

When they got into office, Grinspan writes, politicians behaved as if they belonged to "organized crime syndicates" more interested in distributing the spoils of office than addressing the nation's problems. Before the war, large numbers of congressmen (including Abraham Lincoln) served one term and then returned to their districts. Now, they "hung around." Politics had become a full-time profession and officials spent much of their time dispensing patronage to local supporters. With the size of the federal bureaucracy greatly enhanced as a result of the Civil War, there were plenty of positions to distribute. As to significant legislation, little materialized. One reason for both the intensity of political competition and the lack of substantive accomplishment was that parties were so closely divided. In three of the five presidential elections between 1876 and 1892 the candidates were separated by less than 1 percent of the electorate. Twice the candidate who received the most popular votes lost in the electoral college. No president between Grant and McKinley was reelected. Only for brief periods did the same party control Congress and the presidency.

In the 1870s, a group of political reformers emerged who self-consciously styled themselves the "Best Men." Disgusted by the spectacle of campaigning, high levels of spending and taxation by urban political machines, and their own lack of political influence, they struggled to find ways to make American public life less vulgar. It was easy enough to blame corrupt politicians for the degradation of politics. But increasingly, writes Grinspan, reformers blamed democracy itself. The problem was that too many people were voting, especially lower-class Americans—immigrants in the large cities, Blacks in the Reconstruction South—easily swayed by demagogues. The real dividing line in Gilded Age politics, he insists, was not issues such as the currency, the tariff, or the rights of the former slaves, but politics itself—those who benefitted from democracy and those who wanted to curtail it.

One of the most influential statements of the latter outlook came from the pen of the historian Francis Parkman, in an 1879 essay entitled "The Failure of Universal Suffrage." The honest middle class, Parkman wrote, found itself trapped between "an ignorant proletariat and a half-taught plutocracy." But while Parkman disdained the rapaciousness of the era's robber barons, he made clear that the lower classes posed the greater danger. Democracy, Parkman complained, transferred power "from superior to inferior types of men," resulting in the reign of "organized ignorance." One solution to what Parkman called the problem of "promiscuous suffrage" was to limit the number of people voting. During the 1870s, Samuel J. Tilden, the Democratic presidential candidate in 1876, headed a commission that proposed a new city charter for New York that imposed a hefty property qualification to take part in elections for the Board of Finance. Voters overwhelmingly rejected it— people generally do not willingly disenfranchise themselves.

Reformers, Grinspan notes, hoped that civil service reform—basing government employment on passing an examination rather than having a connection with a political boss—would "finally separate politics from government." Unfortunately, this reform, implemented in 1883 in the wake of President James A. Garfield's assassination by a man universally described as a disappointed office-seeker, did as much to weaken democracy as to purify it. Political appointees had been expected to pay a portion of their salaries to their party—this was how both major parties financed themselves. Now, forced to look elsewhere for funds, the parties increasingly turned to corporations and the wealthy. "Men who already had money stepped in to bankroll campaigns," Grinspan writes. We still live with the consequences.

Beginning in the 1890s, an unusual alliance emerged between conservative businessmen bent on limiting the power of ordinary voters and middle-class reformers hoping to rescue politics from the politicians. No longer simply criticizing from the sidelines, those who hoped to transform democracy became directly engaged in politics, challenging the power of political bosses and reducing the size of the electorate. The changes were most extreme in the South, where white supremacist Democrats disenfranchised nearly all Black voters, as well as a substantial number of poorer whites, via poll taxes, literacy tests, and "good character" requirements.

Elsewhere, Grinspan writes, "respectable reform shifted its focus from who should vote to how." In the nineteenth century voting was a quasi-public act. Political parties issued printed ballots to their supporters, and crowds milling around the election site could see which one each voter deposited in the ballot box. The widespread adoption of the secret ballot and, soon afterwards, curtained mechanical voting machines, transformed voting into a private act. Combined with new laws that barred providing assistance to voters, especially the illiterate, the secret ballot effectively disenfranchised a considerable number of Americans. Meanwhile, electoral campaigns became more restrained, more "educational," with formal lectures and the distribution of innumerable pamphlets and broadsides taking the place of rowdy physical confrontations. No longer did the weeks before election day witness daily torchlight parades. That day was orderly, even dull. Politics, Grinspan writes, moved indoors—people discussed it at home but did not fight about political differences in the streets.

By the early twentieth century, what Grinspan calls an "incredible transformation of American politics" had taken place. One result of "the withering of partisanship and the cooling of political passion" was a precipitous decline in voter participation. In 1924, for the first time in American history, less than half the eligible voters cast ballots. To be sure, the ratification in 1920 of the Nineteenth Amendment enfranchising women represented the greatest expansion of democracy in the nation's history. But, Grinspan writes, women "got to play in the game only after most of the fun was gone." The age of acrimony had been superseded by an age of political civility, but at a cost—the ability of large numbers of lower-class Americans to influence the decisions that shaped their lives.

Running like a bright thread through the book is the story of William D. Kelley and his remarkable daughter Florence, whose careers, taken together, lasted nearly a full century and illustrated the changes Grinspan describes. The elder Kelley, a long-serving member of Congress from Philadelphia, was a leading Radical Republican during the Civil War era. Because of his monomaniacal advocacy of the protective tariff as the key to prosperity, he became known as Pig Iron Kelley. Florence Kelley, essentially educated at home via her father's massive library, went on to attend Cornell University and, after being denied entrance by the University of Pennsylvania because of her sex, decamped to the University of Zürich, where she fell in with a cadre of socialist exiles from Russia, marrying one of them. Returning to the United States and abandoning her physically abusive husband, Florence Kelley moved to Chicago, where she was appointed inspector of factories for Illinois, making her one of the most powerful women in the nation. Subsequently, she founded the National Consumers League, which sought to mobilize women's purchasing power in the burgeoning mass consumption economy to fight child labor and the exploitation of female factory workers.

Pig Iron Kelley exemplified the strength and limits of traditional politics. Grinspan devotes a little too much space to his deep, resonant diction. It didn't much matter what Kelley stood for, Grinspan writes, "so long as enough people in Pennsylvania's Fourth congressional district liked his voice." Politics was a show, with success deriving from the ability to campaign, not govern. Like her father, Florence Kelley was certainly political, but she exemplified how much could be accomplished via the deployment of expertise, outside of partisan politics.

A gifted writer, Grinspan tells this story in a highly engaging manner. The reader is swept along as if in the midst of one of the mass parades of the 1870s. Grinspan peppers the book with tidbits of information that illuminate larger trends, pointing out, for example, that while in the nineteenth century virtually every newspaper was affiliated with a political party, by the early twentieth fully a quarter proclaimed their political independence. He frequently reaches for novelistic effects, unexpected juxtapositions, and quotable turns of phrase. Sometimes, to be sure, style seems to overwhelm substance. Despite passing mention of the idea that membership in a mass political party provided a "tribal" sense of identity in a fractured society, we do not really learn why Americans devoted so much energy and emotion to political campaigns, and why they voted as they did. We learn a great deal about the mechanisms of politics, but far less about party ideologies. "Mostly," Grinspan writes, "each side just opposed what the other side stood for."

294 • OUR FRAGILE FREEDOMS

Grinspan demonstrates how central party politics was to American culture during the Gilded Age. But he displays a surprising impatience with the era's movements outside the national two-party system, and with the numerous historians who study them. He says little about the deep sense of social crisis in the late nineteenth century, when many Americans feared they were "standing at Armageddon" (the title of the historian Nell Irvin Painter's history of this period). He chides scholars for devoting more attention to "radical solutions" and "tiny minorities"—for example, labor unions, socialist clubs, and the Farmers'Alliance—than to the major parties. Historians, he suggests, should concentrate on the winners. They have made "great efforts to understand the Populists" and William Jennings Bryan's campaign for president in 1896, he observes, "but [William] McKinley *won*." Grinspan essentially ignores Gilded Age radicals who did attract large followings. Henry George, proponent of the "single tax" on land, whose book *Progress and Poverty* was one of the century's great best-sellers, makes a very brief appearance because he ran against Theodore Roosevelt for mayor of New York City. Edward Bellamy, whose futuristic novel *Looking Backward* inspired the creation of hundreds of socialistic Nationalist Clubs in the 1890s, goes unmentioned. So does Ida B. Wells and her crusade against lynching. These "cranks," as Grinspan calls them, may not have overturned the two-party system. But they did help to change the political discourse. And the era's third parties—Greenbackers, Populists, local labor parties—placed on the political agenda the rapidly expanding gap between rich and poor, and pioneered the graduated income tax, public regulation of corporations, and other initiatives that would later come to fruition.

At the other end of the social scale, the book contains no mention of financiers such as J. P. Morgan who, at the turn of the twentieth century, remade American capitalism by creating the monopolistic corporations that would dominate the economy for many decades. The years straddling 1900 were not only a moment of political transition, as Grinspan demonstrates, but of other changes in American life. This was when the United States, thanks to the Spanish-American War, acquired an overseas empire; the Jim Crow system became firmly entrenched in the South; the Census Bureau announced the closing of the frontier; and conservative jurisprudence took hold on the Supreme Court, as the Justices ignored the abrogation of Black Americans' constitutional rights while shielding corporations from public regulation. Of course, it would be unfair to criticize an author for not producing a book he did not set out to write. But changes in the functioning of democracy cannot be understood in isolation from these transformative developments.

Nonetheless, *The Age of Acrimony* speaks directly to our current moment. It reminds us that American democracy is a terrain of conflict, forever a work in progress.

THE OLDEST MASS PARTY

"I'M NOT A member of an organized political party," the American comedian Will Rogers declared. "I'm a Democrat." When Rogers made this remark, in the early 1930s, the party was just emerging from a decade of disorganization and defeat. Riven by divisions over Prohibition, immigration, religion, and the Ku Klux Klan, Democrats had suffered staggering losses in the presidential elections of the 1920s. In 1924, the party's nominating convention required more than a hundred rounds of voting even to agree on a presidential candidate. Then, with the election of Franklin D. Roosevelt in 1932, there was a remarkable reversal of fortunes. For decades afterwards, the party almost always controlled Congress and the presidency. But the winning political coalition forged by FDR was shattered in the 1960s and 1970s, and under Richard Nixon and Ronald Reagan American politics took a conservative turn. Democrats are still divided over how to respond.

In *What It Took to Win*, Michael Kazin traces the history over the past two centuries of what he calls "the oldest mass party in the world." Kazin has been engaged with Democratic politics since 1960, when, at

---

Review of *What It Took to Win: A History of the Democratic Party*, by Michael Kazin, *London Review of Books*, May 12, 2022.

the age of twelve, he sported a large campaign button for John F. Kennedy. Until recently he was a co-editor of *Dissent*, which prides itself on being the nation's oldest democratic socialist magazine. His previous books include *The Populist Persuasion* (1995), an illuminating analysis which predated the recent emergence of populist movements in the U.S. and abroad; *American Dreamers* (2011) about the twentieth-century Left; and a biography of William Jennings Bryan, published in 2006, which attempted to rescue its protagonist from what E. P. Thompson in a different context called "the enormous condescension of posterity." (Condescension regarding Bryan emanates from secular urban liberals who know him only from his condemnation of the theory of evolution in the notorious Scopes Trial of 1925, not his efforts in support of small farmers and urban laborers or his opposition to American imperialism.)

Until recently, Democrats celebrated Thomas Jefferson as the party's founder, though the author of the Declaration of Independence has fallen into disfavor among many Americans because of his ownership of slaves. But as Kazin makes clear, the party of the early republic that elected Jefferson to two terms as president was an alliance of local notables, not a mass organization. The Democratic Party's true father is Martin Van Buren, the son of a tavern keeper and the only president who grew up speaking a language other than English (Dutch). In the 1820s, Van Buren made the party a powerful electoral machine complete with a network of local newspapers, regular nominating conventions, a "spoils system" whereby party functionaries were rewarded with government jobs, and, in Andrew Jackson, a charismatic leader.

The intense competition between Democrats and their rivals—the Whigs, and then Republicans—galvanized popular participation in politics. Political leaders became folk heroes, with nicknames like the Great Compromiser (Henry Clay), the Godlike Daniel (Daniel Webster), the Great Commoner (Bryan), the Plumed Knight (James G. Blaine) and, most popular of them all, Old Hickory (Jackson). The central event of Jackson's eight years as president (1829–37) was his war against the Bank of the United States, a private corporation chartered by Congress whose powers made it the closest thing to an American central bank until the creation of the Federal Reserve system in 1913. The Bank War tied the Democratic Party's destiny to what Kazin calls "moral capitalism," the belief that government should serve the interests of ordinary Americans, not business elites. Kazin draws a straight line from Jackson's destruction of the Bank to such later Democratic achievements as the progressive income tax and the Wagner Act of 1935, which guaranteed workers the right of collective bargaining.

But as Kazin acknowledges, during the Jacksonian era and for at least a century afterwards, Democrats adhered to another principle: white supremacy. In the years leading up to the Civil War, northern Democrats welcomed immigrants to the U.S. but persistently sought to restrict the rights of free Black Americans. Their southern counterparts were slavery's staunchest defenders. In a letter often quoted by historians, Van Buren explained that the party he created rested on an alliance between the well-to-do planters of the South and the "plain Republicans"—farmers, artisans, factory workers—of the North. In such a coalition, ideological consistency was impossible. Generally, Democrats favored states' rights and limited government, but when it came to opening new land in the South to slavery they supported a vigorous exercise of national power, including the forced removal of tens of thousands of Native Americans from their ancestral homelands. Of course, in a sprawling, heterogeneous country major political parties will always be coalitions of diverse interests and outlooks. By uniting people from all parts of the nation in a common endeavor, mid-nineteenth-century parties helped hold together a society fractured by the issue of slavery. It is more than a coincidence that when the Democratic Party broke into two sectional factions in 1860, the dissolution of the Union soon followed.

During the Civil War, northern and southern Democrats faced each other on the battlefield. But even while fighting for the Union, most northern Democrats strenuously opposed emancipation. And in the postwar era of Reconstruction, the party was reunited by its opposition, often violent, to Republican-sponsored laws and constitutional amendments that attempted to make equal citizens of the four million former slaves. One can at least credit the Democrats with candor. In the presidential election of 1868, the party distributed campaign material emblazoned with the motto "This Is a White Man's Country; Let White Men Rule." After Reconstruction ended, southern Democrats moved to make the slogan a reality, creating, with the acquiescence of the North, a new system of racial inequality, Jim Crow, that nullified southern Blacks' civil and political rights.

The elimination of Black voting produced the Solid South, long a fixture of American politics. Between 1880 and 1924, the Republican presidential candidate only once carried a state of the old Confederacy (Tennessee in 1920). This didn't matter in most elections, since the Civil War had made Republicans the "natural" majority party in the North, where most of the voting population lived. But Kazin doesn't sufficiently emphasize the fact that the disenfranchisement of Black southerners, a significant component of the American working class, skewed the entire political system to the right, to the detriment not only of African Americans but also of the "ordinary" whites the Democratic Party claimed to represent.

Kazin sees Bryan's unsuccessful campaigns for president—in 1896, 1900, and 1908—as harbingers of a fundamental shift in Democratic politics. In his first run Bryan was endorsed by the insurgent People's Party—the original Populists—and subscribed to their belief that significant social change required using public authority to redistribute private wealth and to regulate the banks and industrial corporations that now dominated the American economy. Bryan's radicalism appealed to farmers, but he failed to make inroads among industrial workers or a middle class alarmed by his repudiation of the gold standard. (In one of the most celebrated political speeches in American history, Bryan warned against "crucify[ing] mankind upon a cross of gold.") His next two campaigns also ended in defeat. But Woodrow Wilson, who strengthened antitrust legislation, instituted an income tax on wealthy Americans, subjected banks to regulation, and expanded the rights of labor, carried the party forward in the direction Bryan had laid out. However, neither Bryan nor Wilson, the first post–Civil War president born in the South, evinced any interest in racial justice.

Today, when the parties have in effect switched identities with regard to race, it is worth recalling how long Democrats took the Jim Crow system for granted. As late as 1952, the party's presidential candidate, Adlai Stevenson of Illinois, chose an arch-segregationist as his vice-presidential running mate: Senator John Sparkman of Alabama, who regularly voted against civil rights bills. There was no protest from the liberal academics and writers who idolized Stevenson. Even FDR, fearful of alienating the white South, failed to object when Congress, where southern Democrats controlled key committees, allowed states to set the rules for popular programs such as Social Security, federal home mortgages, and the GI Bill, leading to gross inequities for African Americans. Social Security, the centerpiece of Roosevelt's New Deal, initially excluded agricultural and domestic laborers, the vast majority of the Black working class.

Beginning during the First World War, however, the migration of Blacks from the South, where most could not vote, to northern cities, where they could, slowly reshaped the map of party politics. Desperately in need of even the limited New Deal benefits available to them, Black voters in the 1930s began to shift their allegiance from the party of Lincoln to the Democrats, a transition completed in 1964 when Republicans nominated Senator Barry Goldwater, who had voted against that year's landmark Civil Rights Act, as their presidential candidate. Since then, Black voters have been the Democratic Party's most loyal supporters. As Kazin points out, a new Democratic coalition came into being, uniting urban African Americans, small farmers, industrial workers, and liberal reformers, many of them activist women such as Frances Perkins, Roosevelt's labor secretary and a pioneer in promoting legislation to improve conditions for female factory workers.

Central to what came to be called the New Deal coalition were the militant labor unions that emerged in the 1930s and were closely tied at local and national levels to the Democratic Party. Kazin understands that political success requires organization as well as popular policies and charismatic leaders. This makes his book surprisingly sympathetic to Irish-dominated political machines such as New York City's Tammany Hall. The machines got out the vote. So did the industrial unions. Unlike Tammany, unions also pushed Roosevelt and congressional Democrats to the left. Without the pressure they brought, the so-called Second New Deal of the mid-1930s would have been far less radical. Left-leaning unions—autoworkers, hospital workers, steelworkers— would also play a significant role in the civil rights movement. The unions' precipitous decline over the past two generations has produced a gaping hole in the political landscape that Democrats have not been able to fill. Despite an upsurge of militancy, many of labor's recent successes have taken place among highly educated groups such as museum curators and adjunct faculty in colleges and universities. This reflects both the changing nature of contemporary work and a broader realignment within the Democratic Party away from its earlier industrial base.

The Second World War, when the government condemned Nazi race theory yet accommodated segregation at home, laid bare the contradictions inherent in the Democratic coalition. The war gave rise to the modern civil rights movement as well as a cadre of Democratic leaders, Black and white, anxious to dismantle segregation. In 1947, the Truman administration produced a report, *To Secure These Rights*, which made clear the deep inequalities confronting Blacks in every area of American life. The following year, the Democratic nominating convention adopted a civil rights plank in its national platform, inspiring a walkout by southern delegates and the formation of a States' Rights Party, whose presidential candidate, Strom Thurmond of South Carolina, carried four Deep South states.

The Democrats' embrace of Black rights, Kazin notes, was a "time bomb." When the bomb detonated two decades later it blew apart the New Deal coalition. Under pressure from the civil rights movement, Lyndon Johnson secured the passage of laws that dismantled the Jim Crow system, restored the right to vote in the South, and expanded the social safety net to include the previously neglected. Johnson, on signing the Civil Rights Act, supposedly declared: "I think we just delivered the South to the Republican Party." He probably never said those words, but Republicans soon devised a "southern strategy" that fed on white resentment over the civil rights revolution. The strategy's appeal proved to be national. Racial backlash would pay political dividends for Nixon, Reagan, and eventually Trump, as well as scores of local Republican candidates. Today, when people speak of the Solid South, it is Republicans they have in mind.

Further cracks quickly appeared in the Democratic coalition, sparked by the Vietnam War, second wave feminism, and an immigration law that remade the nation's racial and ethnic composition by opening the door to newcomers from Latin America, the Caribbean, East and South Asia, and Africa. The Democrats' problems were compounded by the difficulty of devising a response to the massive job losses caused by deindustrialization. The party experienced what Kazin calls "a quarter century of frustration and internal division." "The opportunity was lost," he writes, "to forge a new coalition of working and lower-middle-class people of all races." Many Democratic leaders concluded that the path to success lay in embracing a milder version of Reaganism. When in 1996 Bill Clinton declared that "the era of big government is over," he was both channeling Reagan and repudiating the Democratic Party's modern tradition of viewing the federal government as an active agent in promoting a more equitable capitalism.

Like many progressives, Kazin sees Obama's presidency as another missed opportunity. Coming into office on a wave of enthusiasm, especially among Black voters and the young, Obama "committed one of the cardinal errors in politics: he dispirited and demobilized his base." The financial crisis that began in 2008 put economic inequality squarely on the political agenda. Activists who hoped to empower the "99 percent" looked not to the Democratic Party, however, but to Occupy Wall Street, a movement outside the party system. Obama resisted demands to restructure the banking system, infuriating those who believed that Wall Street should pay a price for its role in the financial collapse. The result was political disaster. In 2010, Republican voters were mobilized by the extreme right-wing Tea Party, while large numbers of Democrats stayed at home. The Republicans gained control of Congress and significantly increased their power in state legislatures. They quickly took advantage of the opportunity to redraw election district lines after the decennial U.S. census, locking in a partisan advantage in contests for local and state officials as well as the House of Representatives. In some states extreme gerrymandering dating from 2010 still constitutes a nearly impregnable barrier to Democratic political success.

Reports of the party's demise may be exaggerated. The Democratic presidential candidate has won the popular vote in seven of the last eight elections (though thanks to the funhouse American electoral system this has translated into just five presidential terms). Regarding the Democrats' long-term political health, the narrowness of Biden's victory in 2020 was worrisome. Key components of the current Democratic coalition—Hispanics, Blacks, white women—gave Trump a higher percentage of their votes than they had four years earlier. Particularly alarming was the increase in Trump's support among Hispanics. Democrats were so overjoyed at defeating Trump that for a time they failed to notice that the election returns called into question the demographic determinism which in recent years has led many Democrats to assume that the growth of what is now the country's largest racial minority will soon translate into an enduring electoral majority for the party. Counterintuitively, Biden's victory hinged on his success in attracting increased support, especially in suburban districts, from that much maligned group, white men.

Today, the Democratic Party commands the allegiance of affluent voters in economically thriving metropolitan areas; members of racial minorities, most of them working class; and a majority of women. Meanwhile, the Republicans have succeeded in solidifying their position in rural and small-town America, much of it still suffering from long-term economic decline. Individual elements of the Democratic agenda remain popular—including, in a remarkable turnaround, Obamacare, enacted in 2010 over unanimous Republican opposition. But the stark fact remains that a party that long prided itself on speaking for ordinary Americans has lost the loyalty of white working-class voters. Matters are made worse by the structure of the political system itself, including an electoral college and Senate that privilege rural voters over urban, new laws in Republican states that erect barriers to voting by minorities and the poor, and a Supreme Court which for the foreseeable future will remain under the control of conservative partisans.

All sorts of strategies are being devised for improving the Democrats' fortunes. But the cure depends on the diagnosis. Is the party too progressive or too corporate? Too tied to "identity politics" or too nostalgic for the New Deal? Some diagnosticians advise Democrats to concentrate on wooing suburban moderates; others recommend doubling down on the existing base with a massive effort to register members of minority groups. Kazin urges the party to heed what he sees as a lesson of history. The Democrats have succeeded, he writes, when they have enacted policies, such as Medicare in the 1960s, that demonstrably serve all segments of the working and middle class, so that they are not seen by white voters as primarily benefitting racial minorities. Universal programs, Kazin believes, will generate universal support.

Forging a new electoral majority by mobilizing working people across lines of race, ethnicity, and geography is, however, easier said than done. Especially when large numbers of white workers embrace their own version of identity politics, which places the blame for the crisis of economically declining communities not on corporations that have shifted employment to low-wage sites overseas but on immigration, while condemning changes in the racial and gender landscape and taking aim at an array of imaginary culture war targets including secularists undermining religion and teachers indoctrinating students with "politically correct" ideas.

Kazin does see some cause for optimism. He singles out what happened in 2020 in the swing state of Nevada, where the largely Hispanic Culinary Workers Union (whose members include not only kitchen laborers but workers of every description in the giant hotels of Las Vegas) mobilized voters effectively and carried the state for Biden. These workers did not have to choose between class and ethnicity—the identities reinforced one another. Whether Democratic success in Nevada offers a model for other states remains to be seen. Las Vegas is one of the most unionized cities in the country, partly because it is a one-industry town (tourism) whose many thousands of hotel desk clerks, bartenders, maids, and construction workers can't be replaced by outsourcing.

Whatever the result of coming elections, Kazin's account of the party's history will remain essential reading for those hoping to chart its future.

THE FIRST BLACK
PRESIDENT

THEY SAY IT is better to be lucky than smart—and better still
to be both. Barack Obama is undoubtedly smart. But his rise to
the presidency was also marked by instances, large and small,
of good luck. Obama was fortunate to come of age in the aftermath of
the civil rights revolution, when elite educational institutions, including Columbia College, where he received his undergraduate degree,
and Harvard University, where he studied law, were actively recruiting
Black students after many decades of racial exclusion. He had the ambition and talent to take full advantage of these opportunities. Fortune
smiled on his early political campaigns. When he ran for the U.S. Senate in Illinois in 2004, his main opponent in the Democratic primary
saw his candidacy derailed when his wife went to court alleging domestic abuse. In the election that followed, Obama's Republican adversary
withdrew when it was alleged that he had forced his wife to accompany
him to sex clubs.

Obama was also lucky when he first ran for president. A few weeks
before the election of 2008, the global financial crisis struck, not only

Review of *A Promised Land*, by Barack Obama, *Times Literary Supplement*, December 4, 2020.

inspiring a widespread desire for political change but revealing that Obama's opponent, Senator John McCain, had virtually no grasp of economics. Obama was also fortunate, given the currents that have since been tapped into, that McCain was a decent man who did not seek to whip up racial resentment against a Black candidate whose middle name was Hussein. How long ago 2008 now seems, when McCain gracefully conceded defeat and commentators spoke of Obama's victory as the dawn of a "postracial" era. And when it comes to Obama's hopes for a positive historical reputation, he could not have chosen a better successor. The contrast between Donald Trump and Obama confirms the "law of American presidents" devised by the late British scholar of American history, J. R. Pole: every president makes his predecessor look good.

Americans do not choose their leaders based on literary talent. One of Andrew Jackson's campaign slogans in the election of 1828 was: "Vote for Jackson, who can fight, not John Quincy Adams, who can write." But after four years of Trump, many people evidently want to read something more elevated than a cascade of insulting tweets. Thus, Obama's *A Promised Land*, a long, elegantly written memoir of his first two years in the White House, appears at precisely the right moment. A one-man economic stimulus plan for a publishing and bookselling industry battered by the pandemic, Obama has seen his volume's global first print run exceed five million copies. Books about Trump sell; books by Obama sell even better.

Nineteenth-century presidents did not generally write books chronicling their time in office. (The first to do so was James Buchanan, on whose watch the nation splintered in 1861. His memoir was mostly devoted to blaming everyone but himself for the Civil War.) More recently, nearly every former president has felt the need to set pen to paper, usually, though not in Obama's case, with the help of ghostwriters. *A Promised Land* is certainly among the most impressive contributions to this minor genre. The book begins with a brief overview of the author's upbringing—as discussed at greater length in his earlier memoir, *Dreams from My Father* (1995)—and his career before reaching the presidency. It ends in May 2011, two years and four months after his inauguration, with a vivid account of the commando raid that killed Osama bin Laden. Obama comes across as literary, tolerant, and dignified. A gifted writer, he maintains the reader's interest for over 700 pages.

A Promised Land alternates between long discussions of public policy, foreign and domestic, and revealing descriptions of family life in the White House. On the latter subject Obama is quite candid. (Perhaps too candid—his daughter Malia may not appreciate her father's reference to her "body mass index" having "increased somewhat" when discussing Michelle Obama's efforts as first lady to combat childhood obesity.) Obama does not try to sugar-coat the toll his political career exacted on his wife. "This isn't what I signed up for," Michelle tells him during his term in the Illinois legislature, when she was constantly left alone with their two young children. She later declares that she hates politics and does not want him to run for higher office, adding that she probably won't even vote for him. The book contains many small but touching private moments. Obama, for example, suggests to the two White House butlers, both African Americans, that it is not necessary for them to wear formal attire when serving dinner to the family. One replies, "We just want to make sure you're treated like every other president."

When Obama deals with major policy issues, his inner professor (he taught for a decade at the University of Chicago Law School) makes an appearance. Each discussion opens with a lucid, well-informed history lesson establishing the context—for example, the evolution of the Senate filibuster; efforts, beginning with Theodore Roosevelt, to enact universal health insurance; the origins of the Israeli–Palestinian conflict—and then proceeds to a detailed account of how decisions were made. Obama frequently adopts a self-deprecating tone (when informed that he has been awarded the Nobel Peace Prize, he remarks, "for what?"), but he is not given to introspection. Rather than view past events from the vantage point of the present, the book keeps the reader firmly in the moments it is describing.

In his 2008 presidential campaign, Obama managed to attract what he calls a giant "grassroots infantry," for whom he became "a vessel for a million different dreams." This was a mixed blessing. As the former Czech leader Václav Havel tells him during one of Obama's trips to Europe as president, "You've been cursed with people's high expectations." Indeed, much of *A Promised Land* is framed as an answer to progressives within Obama's own party, who came to view his presidency as a missed opportunity for far-reaching change. In a recently published biography of one of Obama's heroes, Abraham Lincoln, the historian David S. Reynolds describes the Great Emancipator as a "principled centrist" who adhered to high-minded ideals but understood the limits of the politically possible. This is how Obama portrays himself—as an idealist who promised "Change We Can Believe In" but sought a middle ground between Left and Right. He emphasizes the powerful barriers to the exercise of presidential power, especially in domestic matters, erected by the American constitutional system. Addressed in part to young people who want to change the world, the book demonstrates how hard that is to do, even from the White House.

But more than this, Obama frequently returns to the tension between a social outlook he imbibed from his activist mother, reinforced when he worked as a community organizer in Chicago, and the pull of realpolitik. He writes that he has drawn inspiration from the civil rights and antiwar movements of the 1960s, in which his mother took part, as well as from other crusades for structural change, such as the battles for women's suffrage, labor rights, and the abolition of slavery. A surprising omission from this list is Reconstruction, the period after the Civil War when emancipated slaves demanded, and for a time enjoyed, the full rights of American citizens. That era has direct relevance to Obama's own career. It was during Reconstruction that Hiram Revels of Mississippi became the first Black senator in American history. A century and a half later, Obama became only the fifth. (There have now been twelve.) Obama is well aware that the nation's history has more than its share of "conquest and subjugation, a racial caste system and rapacious capitalism." Yet while his heroes are the critics and reformers—he singles out Nelson Mandela, Mahatma Gandhi, and Martin Luther King Jr.—he still embraces the egalitarian "promise" of America.

The shift from an idealist committed to structural change to a pragmatist began almost as soon as Obama became president, with his appointment of a team of economic advisers closely tied to the banking institutions and neoliberal policies that had helped to bring about the financial crisis in the first place. The demobilization of the grassroots movement that had put him in the White House soon followed. Had that movement survived, it might have provided a counter to the right-wing (and often nakedly racist) populism of the Tea Party, which emerged in 2009 to combat Obama's economic and healthcare initiatives.

Obama frequently expresses irritation in these memoirs with progressive Democrats who pressed for what he considers unattainable initiatives, such as single-payer universal health insurance and the nationalization or breakup of the largest banks. He refers to their "carping" and "grumbling," their "starry-eyed plans," even while noting that he had "some sympathy with the Left's indictment of the status quo." He tells us that before his inauguration he perused books on Franklin D. Roosevelt's celebrated first 100 days in office, to see how FDR responded to public demands for bold action at a time of economic crisis. Yet Obama's economic stimulus legislation ended up being far smaller than most economists believed necessary. And his administration seemed to spend more energy bailing out banks and other large financial institutions than assisting homeowners facing foreclosure, or Americans who had lost their jobs.

His task, Obama writes, was not to remake the economic order but to prevent an even worse disaster. In this he succeeded. But Obama has to acknowledge that the bailouts seriously damaged his popularity, a situation exacerbated by the behavior of bankers reluctant to give up their lavish bonuses even as the economy collapsed. In one of the rare instances of the author questioning his original policy decisions, Obama now wonders about the wisdom of his emphasis on restoring the pre-crisis system without tackling many of its structural flaws, about whether he should have been "bolder." He does not provide an answer.

The presidency, Obama writes, revealed his true political character: "I was a reformer, conservative in temperament if not in vision."

This sensibility informs not only economic policy but also Obama's lengthy account of the passage of the Affordable Care Act (universally known as Obamacare), a complex measure that significantly expanded access to healthcare but left the giant insurance companies intact. Once again, he resents what he considers the utopian outlook of those members of his own party who favor a single-payer system that does away with private insurance entirely, or at least offers a "public option"—a government plan that would compete with private insurers, forcing them to lower their prices. Of course, utopian thinking comes in many forms. Obama's dream of restoring an imagined golden age of bipartisan cooperation turned out to be at least as unrealistic as the ideas of his critics. Republicans, it turned out, had no interest in working with him; almost unanimously, they opposed any form of government-sponsored health insurance. At this point, Democrats and their independent allies enjoyed a majority in both Houses of Congress. But in the Senate, which requires sixty senators to end a filibuster, there were no votes to spare. Thus, and for one of the few times in his presidency, Obama engaged in old-fashioned horse trading, first making concessions to drug companies, hospitals, and insurance firms, then cutting deals with wavering Democrats and the few Republicans who could be persuaded to vote yes.

Obamacare may well be Obama's most enduring domestic achievement. But, as he laconically notes, the way it was enacted was not exactly "the new brand of politics I'd promised on the campaign trail." Today, it is quite popular. But initially Republicans were able to rouse a large portion of the public against it. With his approval ratings falling, Obama embarked on a national speaking tour in the autumn of 2010. But, he acknowledges, in part because of the emergence of the Tea Party, he "failed to rally the nation." The result was a devastating setback for Democrats in the congressional elections, with Republicans capturing control of the House of Representatives—a recipe for political gridlock in the remaining six years of Obama's presidency.

If Obama is disturbed by criticism from within his own ranks, he is truly angered by the increasing prominence in the Republican Party of what he calls a "politics of racial resentment." Tea Party rallies sometimes featured posters of Obama as an animal or an African witch doctor. Increasing numbers of Republicans seemed to find his very presence in the White House illegitimate. And of course Trump launched his successful run for the presidency with the false allegation that Obama was not U.S.-born and therefore not eligible to be president.

Obama does not directly address how being the first African American to occupy the White House constrained his choices as president, but in one way or another this theme is implicit throughout the book. To be sure, well before he assumed office Obama walked a fine line between reassuring people of all races and ethnic groups that he spoke for them, and forging a special relationship with Black America. He seems to have assumed that many Americans would accept a Black president so long as he was not "angry." During the 2008 campaign, he said very little explicitly about race. He rejected, he writes, criticism from Black activists who wanted him to take "the most uncompromising positions." They saw Obama's campaign as a way to raise public consciousness; he wanted to win. He felt obliged to repudiate the Reverend Jeremiah Wright, the pastor at the Chicago church the Obama family attended, after Wright's fiery speeches denouncing the U.S. as incurably racist became known. In his "race" speech responding to Wright, Obama characteristically sought a middle ground, laying out the historical basis for Black grievances, while suggesting that white fears and resentments also had legitimate roots. The speech succeeded in its aim of pushing race from the political center stage to the wings. But the equivalence Obama suggested between Black responses to centuries of inequality and white resentment over charges of pervasive racism seemed, at best, historically tone deaf.

When it comes to foreign policy, Obama again finds himself torn between idealism and pragmatism. He entered the presidency with a reputation as a peacemaker because of a brief speech in 2003 condemning the Iraq War. He made clear he was not opposed to "all wars," just "stupid" ones, and distinguished sharply between Iraq and the war in Afghanistan, of which he approved. By the time he became president, plans for the withdrawal of American combat forces from Iraq were well underway. But Obama had to decide what to do about Afghanistan. He offers revealing accounts of how military leaders tried to persuade him to commit tens of thousands of additional troops to that conflict. Because of what he calls her "hawkish instincts," Secretary of State Hillary Clinton almost always favored the military's requests, while Vice President Joe Biden usually opposed them. Regarding Iraq, Obama notes, "decision makers in Washington consistently failed to level with the American people." He does not mention *The Afghanistan Papers*, published a few years ago in the *Washington Post*, which detailed the shocking history of how the Bush, Obama, and Trump administrations consistently misled the public about America's longest war, citing progress when there was none and altering data to present the rosiest possible picture.

A Promised Land deals with a little over a quarter of Obama's time in office. Ahead lies a second volume, which will have to confront several issues omitted from this book but already controversial during these first two years, including the policies of Obama's Secretary of Education, Arne Duncan, who sought to link the allocation of federal aid to public schools to students' scores on standardized tests. And, of course, new questions came to the fore, among them the rise and fall of demands for gun control after mass shootings; the emergence of Occupy Wall Street; and Black Lives Matter. The next volume will have to deal with immigration policy, all but ignored here, including the reasons why Obama's administration deported far more undocumented immigrants than Trump's, despite the latter's nativist fulminations. Then there will be the foreign policy successes and failures, from Obama's attempt to forge better relations with Cuba to the negotiation of an international agreement to curtail Iran's progress towards developing nuclear weapons. And it will certainly be interesting to see how Obama explains the election of his successor, who seemed to devote his entire four years in office to undoing everything Obama had accomplished.

FREE SPEECH AND ITS
HISTORY

ASK AMERICANS TO enumerate their civil liberties and they
instinctively turn to freedom of speech and the press. Many
assume that these freedoms have been enjoyed more or less
continuously since 1791, when the Bill of Rights was ratified. In fact,
for much of our history numerous legal and extralegal obstacles have
confronted dissenters hoping to publicize their views, hold meetings,
picket, and distribute literature. Consciousness of the importance of
free speech developed gradually and unevenly. In *Perilous Times*, Geoffrey R. Stone offers a compelling account of a crucial part—but only a
part—of this checkered history.

Stone's focus is free speech in wartime, and it is not a happy story.
Time and again, war has led to serious restrictions on civil liberties.
The book examines six historical moments during which the government tried to punish individuals for their beliefs—the "quasi-war" with
France of the late 1790s; the Civil War; World War I; World War II;
the Cold War; and Vietnam. For each episode, Stone sketches the cast
of characters involved in free-speech cases and provides detailed exam-

----

Review of *Perilous Times: Free Speech in Wartime from 1798 to the War
on Terrorism*, by Geoffrey R. Stone, *The Nation*, December 6, 2004.

314

ination of debates over the proper limits on civil liberties. A professor at the University of Chicago Law School, Stone makes his sympathies clear at the outset: "dissent in wartime can be the highest form of patriotism." Governments, unfortunately, rarely see it that way.

Each of Stone's episodes bears lessons for the present. He begins in 1798, when the administration of John Adams, faced with the threat of war with France and a growing Jeffersonian opposition at home, moved to silence political dissent. The Alien Act allowed the president to deport foreigners he deemed dangerous. The Sedition Act essentially made it illegal to criticize the government. Most of the seventeen people indicted under the provisions of the latter law were Jeffersonian editors, including Matthew Lyon, a Vermont congressman who published a newspaper with the compelling title *Scourge of Aristocracy and Repository of Important Political Truths.* Lyon was found guilty and received a $1,000 fine and a four-month jail sentence.

Unlike the recent USA Patriot Act, the Sedition Act was actually read and debated in Congress. Federalists, drawing on an old tradition of English law that defined "prior restraint" as the greatest threat to a free press, insisted that since the act eschewed pre-publication censorship and allowed truth as a defense, it did not violate the First Amendment. Jeffersonians insisted that for the government to punish the expression of ideas was a step toward tyranny. Jefferson's election in 1800 put a stop for more than a century to federal legislation criminalizing political dissent.

Stone then jumps to the Civil War, offering a careful examination of Abraham Lincoln's arguments for suspending the writ of habeas corpus and allowing military tribunals to try civilians outside war zones. He notes the damage to civil liberties but makes clear that Lincoln took pains to mitigate the excessive actions of subordinates. Not all of his successors were so scrupulous.

During World War I Woodrow Wilson, as assured of the righteousness of his crusade to remake the world as any member of the Bush administration during the Iraq War, insisted that people he deemed disloyal had "sacrificed their right to civil liberties." Stone points out that when Congress passed the Espionage Act of 1917, the first national law to punish political speech since 1798, it rejected some of Wilson's extreme proposals, including a provision authorizing the government to censor the press and punish "disaffection." But by 1918, when Congress approved the Sedition Act, such caution had evaporated. That law forbade writing or making any statement that brought the government into "disrepute."

In the wake of World War I, the arrest of numerous Americans for speeches and publications critical of the war effort forced the Supreme Court for the first time to deal with free-speech issues. In its initial decisions, Stone relates, it dealt the concept of civil liberties a devastating blow. In 1919 it upheld the convictions of Charles Schenck, who distributed leaflets urging political action against the draft, and Eugene V. Debs, the country's leading socialist, for a speech condemning American involvement in the war. Debs was convicted. In the decision, Justice Oliver Wendell Holmes declared that the First Amendment did not prevent Congress from prohibiting speech that presented a "clear and present danger" of inspiring illegal action.

During World War II, the administration of Franklin D. Roosevelt actively promoted freedom of expression as one of the key differences between American liberty and Nazi tyranny. Freedom of speech took its place as one of the Four Freedoms Roosevelt promised to extend to the entire world after peace arrived. This time, the Supreme Court, Stone writes, "played a cautiously speech-protective role," overturning, for example, the conviction of Jehovah's Witnesses who refused to salute the American flag. (It also, however, upheld the internment of more than 100,000 Japanese Americans, the greatest violation of civil liberties in American history other than slavery.)

The progress of free expression proved tentative and partial. The Cold War witnessed a "steady erosion" of support for civil liberties. Stone strongly criticizes President Harry S. Truman for establishing a series of tribunals at which government employees were asked to respond to ill-defined charges of disloyalty (which often included union activism and support for civil rights) by unnamed informants.

Truman hoped the program would insulate him from Republican criticism. In fact, writes Stone, his actions "laid the foundation" for the ensuing "anti-Communist hysteria."

At first, in the words of Justice William O. Douglas, the Supreme Court ran "with the hounds," affirming the conviction of Eugene Dennis and other communist leaders for the vaguely defined charge of "conspiring to advocate the overthrow of government." Stone's analysis of the Dennis case underscores the dangers that exist when judges succumb to the temper of the times or defer unquestioningly to the president's judgment as to whether a threat to national security actually exists. Not until 1957, after the Senate had censured Joe McCarthy, did the Supreme Court finally put an end to the prosecution of communists, and it soon went on to eviscerate federal and state loyalty programs.

During the Vietnam War, the last of Stone's episodes, the Court demonstrated how far it had traveled from World War I. In 1968 it did uphold the conviction of a war protester for burning his draft card, rejecting the claim that this action should be considered symbolic speech. But in the *Pentagon Papers* case it allowed the publication of classified government documents whose release was certain to affect the war effort—quite a change from the World War I jailing of dissenters who circulated innocuous antiwar leaflets. Government efforts against dissent hardly ceased, but apart from a few unsuccessful conspiracy indictments, they now took the form of FBI disruption of antiwar and civil rights groups rather than the prosecution of dissenters.

Overall, *Perilous Times* tells a story every American should know, and tells it well. The book provides an almost encyclopedic account of the evolution of legal doctrine concerning dissent, and perhaps the best available analysis of the legal questions relating to free speech in wartime. Why, then, did I experience a growing feeling of unease as I read through the volume? The reason lies in Stone's myopic definition of both free speech and the threats to it. *Perilous Times* reflects the strengths and limitations of a certain kind of law school history—a history that revolves around federal laws and constitutional cases, and whose heroes are jurists and lawyers. Stone's understanding of free speech flows from the First Amendment, which defends our civil liberties against violations by Congress (subsequently interpreted by the courts as including all agencies of government). The amendment does not prohibit the suppression of free speech by private individuals and institutions, and thus Stone devotes little attention to the way non- governmental actors have affected freedom of expression. Employers can fire people because of their political beliefs, and consolidated media can decide what views do not deserve to be printed or circulated online, without violating the First Amendment.

This focus on repression by government explains why Stone chose to study free speech only during wars. In peacetime, which, according to his calculation, represents 80 percent of our history, "the United States does not punish individuals for challenging government policies." Stone's account leaves the impression that respect for freedom of expression is the "default" position of American society, upset from time to time by wartime hysteria. History does not bear this out.

A broader view of the subject would include the numerous violations that have occurred in peacetime, sometimes by the federal, state, and local governments, often by private parties. Stone, for example, states that between 1800 and the Civil War, the federal government "did not attempt to silence criticism of national leaders or policies"—ignoring the state-level prosecutions for seditious libel that continued long after the national Sedition Act expired in 1801. Even on its own terms, the statement is factually incorrect. In the 1830s the House of Representatives' "gag rule" prohibited the consideration of antislavery petitions, and the administration of Andrew Jackson allowed southern mobs to remove abolitionist materials from the mails. Indeed, Stone's formulation ignores the centrality of the slavery controversy to the growth of civil liberties. In response to the disruption of their meetings and the killing of an abolitionist editor, critics of slavery elevated freedom of expression to a central place in the definition of American liberty. Even though their campaign occurred in peacetime, it forms an essential part of the history of free speech.

Similarly, in the twentieth century grave threats to civil liberties have come from local governments and private groups, and "normal" times have seen their share of repression. While Stone mentions the depredations of organizations like the American Protective League, which rounded up suspected draft dodgers during World War I, and the widespread blacklisting by employers during the McCarthy period, he devotes little attention to their actions since they did not raise a constitutional question. He deals with Japanese internment but says nothing about other ways racism has affected the suppression of free speech, including the lynching of Blacks who spoke out against the South's racial order, and numerous state and local efforts to suppress the NAACP.

Stone highlights the bravery of federal judges Charles Amidon, George Bourquin, and Learned Hand, who challenged the hysteria of World War I by dismissing indictments of war critics. But other, equally heroic battlers for free speech go unmentioned—anarchists who combated state "criminal syndicalism" laws; the Industrial Workers of the World (IWW), which campaigned against local ordinances that limited public speaking; birth-control advocates who fought for the right to distribute information about reproduction and contraception in the face of national and local obscenity laws; immigrants who resisted state laws that prohibited teaching in a language other than English.

Most of these struggles never got to the Supreme Court, so they do not form part of the history of constitutional law. But they helped to shape a civil liberties consciousness that eventually influenced congressional policies and court decisions. For example, the exposure during the 1930s of the violent methods used by employers to combat unionization played a crucial role in making the federal government for the first time a protector of freedom of expression. With its restrictions on employers' antiunion activities, the Wagner Act of 1935 was, among other things, a landmark in the development of free speech.

Many readers will be disappointed that Stone devotes only a handful of pages to the free-speech implications of the "war on terrorism." But he makes it clear that the lessons of history are not encouraging. "The United States," he writes, "has a long and unfortunate history of overreacting to the dangers of wartime." American political leaders have frequently blurred the line between treason and dissent, raised the specter of internal subversion, and inflamed public fears for partisan purposes.

The history of free expression—in peacetime as well as war—underscores the fragility of civil liberties in the face of assertive patriotism. Not long after the attacks of September 11, the journalist Jay Winik argued in the *Wall Street Journal* that since restraints on civil liberties in earlier wars had no lasting effect, we should not be concerned about parallel actions today—"when our nation is again secure, so too will be our principles." Stone's account offers a powerful rebuke to such complacency. The episodes he relates did indeed have enduring consequences. World War I repression destroyed the IWW, the Socialist Party, and much of the mainstream labor movement. McCarthyism dealt a severe blow to all sorts of movements for social change and severely limited the acceptable boundaries of political criticism among intellectuals.

Given that the "craving for security at any price" has more than once led to public acquiescence in restraints on civil liberties, Stone insists on the necessity of having in government people with a commitment to civil liberties. Too often in our country's history, no such person has been present.

AMERICAN ANARCHISTS

W ITH ITS ECONOMIC instability, mass immigration, corrupting influence of money on politics, and ever-increasing gap between the rich and everyone else, our current era bears more than a slight resemblance to the late nineteenth and early twentieth centuries, widely known as the Gilded Age. There are also striking differences. Back then, larger-than-life radical organizers—Eugene V. Debs, Emma Goldman, Bill Haywood, and others—traversed the country, calling on the working class to rise up against its oppressors. Today's critics of the capitalist order such as Bernie Sanders and Elizabeth Warren seem tame by comparison.

In her time, Lucy Parsons was as celebrated a radical orator as Debs and the others. Born a slave in Virginia in 1851, she lived into the 1940s, witnessing vast transformations in the American economic and political order but also the persistent exploitation of American workers. She became a prolific writer and speaker on behalf of anarchism, free speech, and labor organization. But she has been largely forgotten, or treated as

---

Review of *Goddess of Anarchy: The Life and Times of Lucy Parsons, American Radical*, by Jacqueline Jones, *New York Review of Books*, December 21, 2017.

an afterthought compared with her husband, Albert, an anarchist executed after Chicago's Haymarket bombing of 1886. Thanks to *Goddess of Anarchy*, Jacqueline Jones's new biography, readers finally have a penetrating account of Parsons's long, remarkable life.

One of the most influential historians of her generation, Jones is the author of books that sweep across centuries. Her previous works include a pioneering history of Black women's work in America, a study of the evolution of the underclass, an account of four centuries of Black and white labor, and a history of "the myth of race" from the colonial era to the present. Again and again, Jones returns to the complex connections between racial and class inequality in American history.

Jones makes clear that Lucy Parsons deserves attention apart from her martyred husband. Originally named Lucia, she was removed with other slaves to Texas by her owner (probably also her father, Jones believes) during the Civil War to prevent them from seeking refuge with the Union army. Educated after becoming free at a school established by a northern teacher, she fell in love with Albert Parsons, the descendant of early New England settlers, whose father had moved to Alabama in the 1830s. (Parsons had enlisted on the Confederate side and managed to survive four years of bloody fighting.) During Reconstruction, when Congress rewrote laws and the Constitution to grant legal and political equality to the emancipated slaves, Parsons embraced these radical changes. He moved to Texas, where his brother ran a newspaper, and became one of the few white leaders of the state's predominantly Black Republican Party. (Most of the other white members in Texas were German immigrants who had remained loyal to the Union and suffered severe reprisals under the Confederacy.)

Albert Parsons worked as a journalist, political operative, and officer of the state militia as it sought to put down violence against Blacks. He emerged as a spellbinding speaker, addressing crowds of up to a thousand freed people. Reconstruction was a violent time, and nowhere as violent as in Texas, where armed bands committed many atrocities against former slaves and their allies. The life of a Republican leader was hardly secure, and Albert's became even more dangerous when he and

Lucia wed in 1872—interracial marriages were frowned upon, to say the least, by white Texans. Albert was assaulted, shot at, and threatened with lynching.

Soon after white supremacist Democrats regained control of the state government in 1873, the couple left for Chicago. En route, in good American fashion, Lucia reinvented herself. Passing for white has always been an option for light-skinned Blacks. Lucy's dark complexion made this impossible; she did, however, try to shed the stigma of slave origins. She changed her name to Lucy and henceforth described her ancestry as Mexican and Indian (although on his birth certificate her son, born in 1879, was identified as "Negro").

Chicago in the 1870s was home to a militant labor movement, and the site of bread riots and mass strikes. Albert Parsons joined the small Socialist Labor Party and picked up where he had left off as a public speaker, quickly making the transitions from denouncing the southern planter class to assailing northern capitalists and from condemning chattel slavery to demanding the abolition of wage slavery. "My enemies in the southern states consisted of those who oppressed the Black slave," he proclaimed. "My enemies in the North are among those who would perpetuate the slavery of the wage workers."

During the national railroad strike of 1877, thousands of demonstrators clashed on Chicago's streets with police and armed veterans' organizations, leaving over thirty workers dead. Afterward, Parsons lost his job as a printer and was blacklisted. Lucy, an accomplished seamstress, supported the two of them by establishing a clothing shop. That same year, Albert Parsons ran for local office as a socialist and did so for the next three years. But he received only a tiny number of votes. This lack of electoral success, combined with the labor militancy he witnessed in 1877, convinced him and his wife that violent upheaval, not the ballot box, was the path to social transformation. The two renounced the electoral system and joined the city's anarchist movement.

Anarchists in Chicago were almost entirely immigrants from Germany. Jones suggests that his experience working with Germans in Texas made Parsons comfortable with their Chicago counterparts.

As a descendant of colonial Puritans and virtually the anarchists' only English-speaking orator, Parsons was especially valuable to the movement—his presence proved that anarchism was not simply a foreign import.

Meanwhile, Lucy Parsons engaged in a program of self-education, attending weekly anarchist meetings and devouring radical books and newspapers. She soon established herself as a talented writer and lecturer. Her article "A Word to Tramps" in *The Alarm*, a periodical edited by her husband, became a widely reproduced "staple of anarchist propaganda." In another piece, "Communistic Monopoly," she joined numerous other radical writers of the era—Edward Bellamy the most famous—who made their point by transporting a character to a future utopia. Unlike Bellamy's authoritarian socialism, in Lucy's model of the good society small local associations governed the economy and polity.

As American-born anarchists, Albert and Lucy Parsons were a minority within a minority. Their outlook, however, had more in common with that of their German associates than with other native-born anarchists, whose views represented an extreme version of unfettered individualism, a common American value. European anarchists tended to be more collectivist in orientation. Their ideology, sometimes called anarcho-syndicalism, envisioned labor unions, not liberated individuals, taking over the functions of government. While many Chicago Germans denounced existing unions as hopelessly reformist, Lucy worked with the Chicago Working Women's Union and Albert with the Knights of Labor and the Chicago Eight-Hour League.

One issue on which the couple fully agreed with other anarchists was their forthright advocacy of violence. They hailed dynamite, invented by Alfred Nobel in the 1860s, as the great equalizer in the class struggle. Dynamite would even the odds between a weak and fractured working class and the economic and political elite (which time and again proved quite willing to use violence to promote its own interests). Johann Most, the leading anarchist in Germany, preached the propaganda of the deed. Acts of violence, he maintained, would awaken class consciousness and inspire a working-class uprising. He urged his followers to plant bombs not only in government buildings but, among other places, in ballrooms and churches of the rich.

Albert and Lucy Parsons, too, celebrated violence. Lucy urged tramps to "learn the use of explosives." Albert advised members of one audience to "buy a Colt's navy revolver, a Winchester rifle, and ten pounds of dynamite." *The Alarm* published articles on how to make dynamite bombs. Despite their heated rhetoric, Albert and Lucy do not seem to have committed any acts of violence themselves. But others did. In Europe, Irish revolutionaries planted dynamite bombs in London, and anarchists assassinated Tsar Alexander II of Russia and King Umberto I of Italy. In 1901 an anarchist assassinated President William McKinley. In 1910 the McNamara brothers, two radical unionists, bombed the *Los Angeles Times* building. An anarchist was probably responsible for the Wall Street bombing of 1920.

Today, in the wake of Timothy McVeigh and Osama bin Laden, loose talk celebrating violence seems rather less exhilarating than in the Parsonses' era. Jones makes it clear that she believes their advocacy of violence was "largely harmless." Few workers seem to have taken it seriously. A local newspaper, reporting on one of Chicago's Sunday labor picnics, noted that after speakers harangued the crowd to arm themselves, listeners did—with beer. Jones points out that the Parsonses' language was entirely counterproductive, needlessly frightening law-abiding citizens and allowing authorities to tar all radicals with the brush of armed insurrection.

To explain why the couple insisted on using such shocking language, Jones develops an elaborate scenario in which a symbiotic relationship developed between the Parsonses, the mainstream press, and the police. Albert and Lucy knew that advocacy of violence would attract attention the tiny anarchist movement could not otherwise enjoy. Reporters eagerly recounted their fiery speeches and interviews because such articles sold newspapers. Albert seems to have known the identity of undercover police agents who attended anarchist meetings. When they were present, he spoke even more vividly of violent class warfare so that their reports would rattle the city's establishment. Meanwhile, his language justified the city's pouring more and more public money into what would later be called its Red Squad. This interpretation seems too conspiratorial to be entirely persuasive. Another possibility is that the Parsonses believed what they were saying and how they said it.

The turning point in Lucy's life was her husband's trial and execution. On May 4, 1886, a mass rally took place at Haymarket Square to protest the killing of four men when police opened fire during an altercation between strikers and strikebreakers at the giant McCormick agricultural machinery factory. Albert delivered one of the rally's speeches, after which he and Lucy repaired to a local saloon. As the gathering was winding down, someone threw a dynamite bomb, killing a policeman. At least ten other people later succumbed to injuries, some from gunshots fired by the police.

Eight prominent anarchists (five immigrants from Germany, one from England, an American of German descent, and Albert Parsons) were put on trial for murder and conspiracy. The proceedings were notably unfair, beginning with the decision to try all eight together. Only two of the men had been present when the bomb was thrown, and Parsons had not even attended the meeting the evening before when the rally was planned. The judge openly displayed bias against the defendants and spent part of his time flirting with female admirers in the audience. The prosecutor told the jury to convict because anarchy itself was on trial. For his part, Albert Parsons claimed, falsely, that he had brought his two young children to the rally, supposedly proving that he did not anticipate violence. All eight men were convicted. After fruitless appeals, four, including Parsons, were hanged. Having survived the Civil War and the violence of Reconstruction Texas, Parsons went to his death in Illinois for a crime he did not commit.

With her husband in jail (where he received a steady stream of visitors, some bringing food, cigars, and other gifts), Lucy Parsons came into her own. She embarked on speaking tours to raise money for the expensive appeals process. She spoke at union halls and saloons, and at highly respectable venues such as Cooper Institute in New York City. She insisted on her husband's innocence but refused to renounce her views (she began her speeches by proclaiming, "I am an anarchist"). In interviews Lucy repeated the tale that she had been born in Texas of Mexican and Native American ancestry. The mainstream press reviled her as "a sanguinary Amazon." Reporters obsessed over the exotic appearance of this "dusky representative of anarchy," dwelling in detail on her coloring, hair, and elegant clothing (she did not present herself as an unkempt rabble-rouser). But working-class audiences, whether they agreed with her anarchist views or not, saw her as a symbol of the judicial system's class bias, and she succeeded in raising significant sums of money. Albert would long be remembered as a working-class martyr. John Brown, Joe Hill, Sacco and Vanzetti, Julius and Ethel Rosenberg, and Albert Parsons—execution elevated all of them to a fame that transcended their particular political views and the crimes they did or did not commit.

Lucy Parsons lived for over half a century after her husband's execution. For years she pursued her career as an anarchist speaker and writer. She became a prominent figure in Chicago's vibrant reform culture, in which groups of all kinds, from labor radicals to Christian socialists and settlement house workers, debated ways to ameliorate the dire conditions of the urban working class. As Jones relates, middle-class reformers proved remarkably willing to listen to a radical like Lucy Parsons. She even spoke before the ultra-respectable Friendship Liberal League and New Century Club. Parsons became a stalwart advocate of free speech, engaging in frequent battles with the Chicago police, who tried to prevent her from lecturing and displaying anarchist flags. In the early twentieth century she joined the free-speech fights of the Industrial Workers of the World. These battles remind us how much our civil liberties owe to radicals—abolitionists, anarchists, free lovers, labor agitators, Black militants—all of whom had to fight for the right to disseminate their ideas without official persecution.

Despite her husband's fate, Lucy Parsons did not retreat from the advocacy of violence. "Rivers of blood," she said in one speech, would have to flow before social justice could be achieved. By the early twentieth century, however, she seemed a relic of an earlier era. Anarchism was changing as urban intellectuals and bohemians claimed the label for themselves. These new recruits did not idealize violence and were more interested in shattering social taboos, especially with regard to sex, than liberating the working class. Parsons did not find this stance appealing. Not that she was sexually conventional. A few months after Albert's execution she began living with a younger man, and other lovers followed. But open advocacy of sexual freedom offended her. Women, she said, "love the names of father, home and children too well" to embrace the idea of free love. When Emma Goldman published her autobiography in 1931, Parsons, now eighty, criticized the "sex stuff" in the book and wondered why Goldman felt it necessary to identify fifteen of her lovers.

There is much to praise in *Goddess of Anarchy*, including Jones's thorough research, which has laid to rest uncertainty about Parson's origins, and the ways the book illuminates the rapidly changing economic and political circumstances in which Parsons operated. A work that could easily have descended into a confusing litany of tiny organizations, short-lived publications, and endless speaking tours retains clarity and coherence throughout. Lucy Parsons finally receives her due as a pioneering radical. As Jones points out, Parsons was hardly the only flamboyant and enthralling woman orator of the industrial era—one thinks also of Goldman, the Populist Mary Ellen Lease, and the labor radicals Mother Jones and Elizabeth Gurley Flynn. But she was the only woman of color; indeed, it is probable that no other non-white person of the era except Frederick Douglass addressed as many Americans. Jones takes Lucy Parsons seriously as a speaker and writer, rather than reducing her to an adjunct of her husband.

Ultimately, however, the portrait is not sympathetic. As Jones makes clear, Parsons pursued her goals, personal and political, with "ruthlessness." Jones chides both Albert and Lucy for thinking of the working class as an abstraction, ignoring deep divisions along lines of ethnicity, religion, race, and craft, as well as the fact that most workers valued their democratic rights and did not view the ballot box as a trap.

Candid criticism is always preferable to hagiography. Jones, however, sometimes seems to measure both Parsons against an ahistorical ideal—the radical attuned to the intersections of race and class, the nuances of political strategy, and the impact of language, whose private life reflected his or her political principles. Not surprisingly, by this standard Lucy is found wanting. So would almost any human being. The great Debs enjoyed racist humor. Goldman preached free love but flew into rages of jealousy over the womanizing of her lover, Ben Reitman. "Did she live life as an anarchist?" Jones asks of Parsons. The answer is no: Parsons failed to pursue the "playful" kind of life other anarchists aspired to, or to break openly with "stifling social conventions." She did not lead a non-conformist personal life, especially when it came to sexual behavior.

A scholar deeply committed to revealing the history of racial inequality, Jones frequently takes Albert and Lucy Parsons to task for their "pronounced indifference to the plight of African-American laborers," in both the South and Chicago. Blacks were the most downtrodden sector of the working class, but the Parsonses said almost nothing about the particular exploitation—disenfranchisement, segregation, lynching, etc.—to which they were subjected. American radicals, Jones writes, should be judged by "a single dominant standard": the degree to which they participate in a struggle against racism. Lucy Parsons fails this test, politically and personally. Indeed, the book's most serious charge is that she refused to embrace her identity as a Black woman and former slave. Parsons, Jones believes, should have spoken for her race.

It is difficult today to appreciate that earlier generations may not always have been as preoccupied with race as we are. The Parsonses assumed that the liberation of the working class would benefit Blacks as much as whites. In one article, Lucy wrote about the plight of southern Blacks, but attributed it mainly to poverty, not racial oppression. This analysis is open to criticism, but it was one adopted by Debs and many other white radicals. At various points in our history, moreover, Black activists and social critics have also challenged the primacy of race. As Jonathan Holloway shows in *Confronting the Veil* (2003), this was the position of Abram Harris Jr., E. Franklin Frazier, and Ralph Bunche in important writings of the 1920s and 1930s.

The vexed question of the intersection of race and class has no single answer. But it seems misguided for Jones to conclude that Albert's "indifference" to racial inequality in Chicago proves that his courageous efforts on behalf of African Americans in Reconstruction Texas were "purely opportunistic," or to criticize Lucy for going to great lengths to deny her "African heritage" (an intellectual and political concept less widely discussed in the context of Jim Crow than today).

Political commitment is a choice, not an obligation. Throughout American history, some people of all backgrounds, like Lucy Parsons, have found it liberating to be part of an international movement with a universalist vision of social change, rather than seeing themselves primarily as members of a group apart. Then and now, DNA is not necessarily political destiny.

THE WAR ON CIVIL
LIBERTIES

W ITH THE EXCEPTION of the Second World War,
every military conflict in which the United States has
taken part has generated an antiwar movement. During
the American Revolution, numerous Loyalists preferred continued
British rule to independence. New Englanders opposed the War of
1812; most Whigs denounced the Mexican-American War launched
by the Democratic president James K. Polk; and both the Union
and the Confederacy were internally divided during the Civil War.
More recently, the wars in Vietnam, Iraq, and Afghanistan split
the country. At the same time, wars often create an atmosphere of
hyper-patriotism, leading to the equation of dissent with treason
and to the severe treatment of critics. During the struggle for independence, many Loyalists were driven into exile. Both sides in the
Civil War arrested critics and suppressed antiwar newspapers. But by
far the most extreme wartime violations of civil liberties (with the
major exception of Japanese-American internment during the Second

---

Review of *American Midnight: The Great War, A Violent Peace, and
Democracy's Forgotten Crisis*, by Adam Hochschild, *The Nation*, February 20/27, 2023.

World War) took place during World War I. This is the subject of Adam Hochschild's latest book, *American Midnight*.

Adam Hochschild is one of the few historians whose works regularly appear on best-seller lists, a tribute to his lucid writing style, careful research, and unusual choice of subject matter. Most historians who reach an audience outside the academy focus on inspirational figures like the founding fathers or formidable achievements such as the building of the transcontinental railroad. Hochschild, on the other hand, writes about villains and rebels. His best-known book, *King Leopold's Ghost*, is an account of the Belgian monarch's violent exploitation of the Congo, one of the worst crimes against humanity in a continent that has suffered far too many of them. When Hochschild writes about more admirable figures, his heroes are activists and reformers: British antislavery campaigners in *Bury the Chains*; the birth control advocate and socialist Rose Pastor Stokes in *Rebel Cinderella*; the Americans who fought in the Spanish Civil War in *Spain in Our Hearts*.

American Midnight does not lack for heroic figures. But as Hochschild notes at the outset, the book presents a tale of "mass imprisonments, torture, vigilante violence, censorship, killings of Black Americans." It will certainly not enhance the reputation of President Woodrow Wilson or that of early twentieth-century liberalism more broadly, nor will it reinforce the widely held idea that Americans possess an exceptional devotion to liberty.

Hochschild relates how, when the United States joined the conflict against Germany and its allies in 1917, "war fever swept the land." Some examples of the widespread paranoia seem absurd: hamburgers became "liberty sandwiches," frankfurters "hot dogs." (The latter name stuck, unlike the rechristening of French fries as "freedom fries" in 2003, after France refused to support the Iraq War.) The German Hospital and Dispensary in New York City changed its name to Lenox Hill Hospital (even though the nearby terrain is quite flat.) In New Haven, Connecticut, volunteers manned an anti-aircraft gun around the clock, oblivious to the fact that Germany had no aircraft capable of reaching the United States. Neighbors accused Karl Muck, the German-born conductor of the Boston Symphony Orchestra, of radioing military information to enemy submarines from his vacation home on the coast of Maine. Anecdotes like these have long enlivened history classrooms. But Hochschild also details the brutal treatment of conscientious objectors subjected to various forms of torture in military prison camps, including the infamous "water cure" the Army employed in the Philippines, nowadays known as waterboarding.

In 1917 and 1918, Wilson and Congress codified this patriotic fervor in the Espionage and Sedition Acts. These laws had nothing to do with espionage as the term is commonly understood (and Hochschild points out that hardly any German spies were actually apprehended). The former criminalized almost any utterance that might interfere with the war effort. The latter outlawed saying or printing anything that cast "disrepute" on the country's "form of government." States supplemented these measures with their own laws and decrees, including banning speaking on the telephone in German or advocating "a change in industrial ownership." It is difficult to say how many people were arrested under these statutes, but the number certainly reached into the thousands.

Meanwhile, private organizations such as the Knights of Liberty and the American Protective League took the law into their own hands. The APL investigated the "disloyal" by, among other methods, purloining documents, and it swept up thousands of Americans in "slacker raids," in which men were accosted on the streets, in hotels, and in railway stations and required to produce draft cards. If a person did not have one, he would be dragged off to prison. Throughout the country, individuals who refused to buy war bonds were tarred and feathered and paraded through their communities. German Americans everywhere came under suspicion of disloyalty, as did members of other immigrant groups. In the years before the war, southern and eastern Europeans had immigrated to the United States in unprecedented numbers, sometimes bringing political radicalism with them, and they too found themselves in the crosshairs of nativism.

The atmosphere of intolerance opened the door to settling scores that predated the war. Long anxious to rid the nation of the Industrial Workers of the World, business leaders and local and national officials seized on the organization's outspoken opposition to the war to crush it. All sorts of atrocities were committed against IWW members, from Frank Little, an organizer lynched in Montana, to more than 1,000 striking copper miners in Bisbee, Arizona, who were rounded up by police and a small private army hired by the Phelps Dodge company, then driven into the desert and left to fend for themselves. Local police routinely raided the IWW's offices without a warrant. In 1918, over 100 "Wobblies" were indicted for conspiracy to violate the Espionage and Sedition Acts, resulting in the largest civilian criminal trial in American history. Every defendant was found guilty and received a jail sentence.

Hochschild brings this history to life by introducing the reader to a diverse cast of characters, some well-known, many unfamiliar even to scholars. His protagonists include Ralph Van Deman, who oversaw the surveillance of Americans deemed unpatriotic. Having honed his skills in the Philippines by keeping track of opponents of American annexation, Van Deman became head of the newly created Army Intelligence branch—the first time, according to Hochschild, that the U.S. army spied on American civilians. One of Van Deman's men was among the first to tap Americans' telephones. The surveillance reports in government archives also allow Hochschild to highlight the exploits of Louis Walsh, a militant labor activist in Pittsburgh who was actually Leo Wendell, a paid government agent who sent a "blizzard" of paperwork to the Bureau of Investigation, the FBI's forerunner. Wendell boasted of joining "prominent Reds" in stirring up violence, providing a justification for further repression.

The Espionage Act empowered the Post Office to exclude from the mail publications that undermined the war effort. Postmaster General Albert S. Burleson interpreted this as authorization to go after any published expression of dissent. In the first year of American participation in the war, Burleson banned forty-four periodicals. He also suppressed single issues of other publications. Issues of *The Gaelic American*, a supporter of Irish independence, were barred for fear of offending our British ally. Burleson particularly targeted the Socialist Party press, which consisted of numerous small local newspapers—a powerful blow against the party's efforts to communicate with its membership. His first target, though, was a small Texas paper, *The Rebel*, whose "crime" had less to do with the war than with having published an exposé of how Burleson had replaced Mexican and white tenant farmers with convict laborers on a cotton plantation his wife had inherited. The crusade against unorthodox opinion continued after the armistice. Even as the Paris Peace Conference deliberated in 1919, the *New York World* commented, Burleson acted as if "the war is either just beginning or is still going on."

To ensure that Americans received the right kind of news, not the "false statements" criminalized by the Espionage Act, the federal government launched a massive wartime propaganda campaign, spearheaded by the newly created Committee on Public Information. Headed by the journalist George Creel, the CPI flooded the country with publications, films, and posters. It mobilized journalists, academics, and artists to produce pro-war works, as well as some 75,000 "Four Minute Men" trained to deliver brief speeches at venues including churches, movie theaters, and county fairs. In previous wars, such propaganda had been disseminated by non-governmental organizations. But Wilson decided that patriotism was too important to be left to the private sector. Much of Creel's output whipped up hatred of Germans as barbaric "Huns." But he also put forth a vision of the country's future strongly influenced by the era's Progressive movement, a postwar world in which democracy would be extended into the workplace and the vast gap between rich and poor ameliorated. This wartime rhetoric was one contributor to an upsurge of radicalism after the conflict ended, when it became apparent that no such changes were in the offing. Creel's success at shaping wartime public opinion, Hochschild remarks, launched the symbiotic relationship between advertising and politics so visible today. It alarmed observers like the political commentator Walter Lippmann, who in a series of writings in the 1920s

lamented that while democracy required an independent-minded cit-
izenry, the war experience demonstrated that public opinion could be
shaped and manipulated by the authorities.

Then there was Wilson's attorney general, A. Mitchell Palmer.
Obsessed with deporting radical immigrants, the "fighting Quaker," as
the press called him, launched what came to be known as the Palmer
Raids, which lasted from November 1919 into the following year. By
this point, the First World War was over, but not the Wilson administration's war on the American left. Thousands of people—critics of
the war and suspected socialists and anarchists—were arrested, mostly
without a warrant. Many who had recently immigrated and not become
citizens were deported. The Palmer Raids dealt a serious blow to the
Left, and they were followed by one of the most conservative decades
in U.S. history.

American Midnight does introduce the reader to more praiseworthy
figures. Hochschild devotes considerable attention to the great anarchist and feminist orator Emma Goldman, who spent much of the war
in prison for conspiracy to interfere with the draft and was deported
a year after the arrival of peace as an undesirable alien. In contrast
to Burleson, Palmer, and the enigmatic Wilson, whom Hochschild
describes as simultaneously an "inspirational idealist" and a "nativist
autocrat," a few government officials remained committed to constitutional principles. If the book has a hero, it is Louis F. Post, the assistant secretary of labor, who ran the Labor Department in the spring
of 1920 when his boss was away because of family illness. Post's career
embodied much of the nineteenth-century radical tradition. His forebears were abolitionists, and he himself participated in Reconstruction
in the South. Post was an ardent follower of Henry George, the popular late-nineteenth-century economist who proposed a "single tax" on
land to combat economic inequality. For a time, Post edited a magazine
that opposed America's war in the Philippines, denounced the power
of big business, and called for unrestricted immigration. He directed
the Labor Department for only six months, but in that time he invalidated thousands of deportation orders that lacked the proper paper-

work. He released numerous immigrants being held, ironically, at Ellis Island, normally considered an entry point into the United States but now housing persons awaiting expulsion from the country. Post refused to be intimidated when a congressional committee held hearings about his actions.

One individual who doesn't quite get the attention he deserves is Eugene V. Debs, the most prominent leader of the Socialist Party, which on the eve of the war was a major presence in parts of the United States, with 150,000 dues-paying members and a thriving local press. The party controlled the local government in many working-class communities, sent elected members to Congress, and won almost one million votes for Debs in the presidential election of 1912. Compared with the colorful IWW, with its *Little Red Songbook* and its rallying cry of "One Big Union," the Socialists seem boringly respectable, which perhaps accounts for their relative neglect here. But they arguably had a greater impact on American life. The Socialist Party was the largest organization to oppose America's entry into the war.

Debs was arrested in 1918 after delivering a speech in Canton, Ohio, critical of the draft. He received a sentence of ten years in prison for violating the Espionage Act. Before his sentencing, he delivered a brief speech to the jury that remains a classic vindication of freedom of expression. "I look upon the Espionage Law as a despotic enactment in flagrant conflict with democratic principles and with the spirit of free institutions," Debs declared. He traced the right to criticize the government from Thomas Paine to the abolitionists and women's suffrage leaders. While Wilson and his administration proclaimed themselves the creators of a new, liberal world order, Debs asked, "Isn't it strange that we Socialists stand almost alone today in upholding and defending the Constitution of the United States?" After the war ended, Wilson rebuffed appeals for Debs's release. "I will never consent to the pardon of this man," he declared. It was left to his successor, Warren G. Harding, a conservative Republican, to free Debs from prison in 1921.

Hochschild presents a vivid account of this turbulent time. But he does not really explain one of its many disturbing features: why so many

Progressive-era intellectuals failed to raise their voices against the suppression of free speech. Many, in fact, enlisted in the CPI's propaganda campaign. Although the Progressive movement, which envisioned government as an embodiment of democratic purpose, is sometimes viewed as a precursor of the New Deal and the Great Society, it differed from them in a crucial respect: Civil liberties were not among the Progressives' major concerns. Many saw the lone person standing up to authority as an example of excessive individualism, which they identified as a cause of many of the nation's problems. They believed that the expansion of federal power required by the war would enable their movement to fulfill many of its goals for social reconstruction, from the public regulation of business to the creation of social welfare programs, and they also hoped that the mobilization of America for war would help integrate recent immigrants into a more harmonious and more equal society.

Hochschild says nothing about one of the most memorable exchanges of these years, the debate over American participation in the war between the prominent intellectual John Dewey and the brilliant young writer Randolph Bourne. Hailing the "social possibilities" created by the conflict, Dewey urged Progressives to support American involvement. In response, Bourne ridiculed the idea that forward-looking thinkers could guide the conflict according to their own "liberal purposes." It was far more likely, he wrote, that the war would empower the "least democratic forces in American life." War, Bourne famously declared, "is the health of the state," and as such a threat to individual liberty.

Despite the clear words of the First Amendment, the Supreme Court offered no assistance to those seeking to defend civil liberties. Early in 1919, the justices unanimously sustained the conviction of the Socialist Party's Charles T. Schenck for violating the Espionage Act by distributing leaflets opposing the draft. A week later, it upheld Debs's conviction. The same result followed in the case of Jacob Abrams and four others jailed for distributing publications opposing U.S. intervention in the Russian Civil War. This time, however, Justices Oliver Wendell

Holmes and Louis Brandeis dissented. The next year, 1920, saw the formation of the American Civil Liberties Union by an impressive group of believers in free speech, including Jane Addams, Roger N. Baldwin, Helen Keller, and Oswald Garrison Villard, the editor of *The Nation*. The ACLU would wage a long battle to invigorate the First Amendment. Its efforts were initially stymied, its own pamphlets defending civil liberties barred from the mail. But the excesses of wartime repression were finally beginning to generate opposition.

How can we explain the "explosion of martial ferocity" in a country where respect for the free individual is supposedly the culture's bedrock? Hochschild doesn't offer a single explanation, but he directs the reader's attention to a number of factors—historical, material, political, and psychological—that "fed the violence." They include nativism, which made it easy to identify radical ideas with immigrants; the "brutal habits" (which is to say, a penchant for torture) picked up by the military in the Philippine-American War; and the long-standing hostility of business leaders to trade unions and socialists. He notes that Palmer sought the Democratic Party's presidential nomination in 1920, hoping to ride the hysteria he had helped create all the way to the White House. Hochschild also suggests that American men felt uneasy at a time when "the balance of power between the sexes" was changing, with women rapidly moving into the work force and the campaign for women's suffrage reaching its culmination. War offered a way to reinvigorate an endangered masculinity. As Lippmann observed, World War I created a situation in which all sorts of preexisting prejudices and fears could be acted out, a perfect storm in which "hatreds and violence . . . turned against all kinds of imaginary enemies."

One additional element should be noted: As Black Americans streamed out of the South to take up jobs suddenly available in northern industry because the war cut off European immigration, "race riots" broke out in East St. Louis, Chicago, Tulsa, and other cities. Protests by Blacks who came to realize that Wilson's rhetoric about democracy did not apply to the American South were met with an upsurge in lynchings. Some of the victims were soldiers still in uniform. W. E. B.

Du Bois had urged Black men to enlist in the armed forces to stake a claim to equal citizenship. Instead, as he put it, "the forces of hell" had been unleashed "in our own land."

Wilson's deep-seated racism has been the subject of much discussion in the past few years. Princeton University recently removed his name from its School of International and Public Affairs. (This step was taken almost entirely because of his racial views; there was little discussion of the wartime suppression of civil liberties.) Wilson grew up in Columbia, South Carolina, during Reconstruction, a time of major gains for African Americans but also a campaign of violence by the Ku Klux Klan and kindred organizations. He shared the prevailing disdain among white southerners for the enfranchisement of Black voters during Reconstruction and embraced the Jim Crow system that followed. One of his initiatives as president was to segregate the civil service in Washington, D.C.

It is striking how many southerners held high positions in the Wilson administration. Wilson's closest adviser, Col. Edward House, was from Texas; his physician, Dr. Cary Grayson, and Wilson's wife, Edith, who together effectively ran the government after Wilson suffered a severe stroke in 1919, were from Virginia. Creel's grandfather was a Missouri slaveowner. The father and grandfather of Postmaster General Burleson served in the Confederate army, and Burleson believed that "offensive Negro papers" were among the country's most dangerous publications. At home and abroad, Wilson's rhetorical commitment to democracy stopped at the color line. The promise of a postwar liberal world order outlined in Wilson's Fourteen Points did not apply to the colonized peoples of Asia and Africa or to the American South. One would hardly anticipate respect for the rule of law, or for basic constitutional rights, from an administration with so many members who had roots in the Confederacy and the Jim Crow South.

Hochschild ends this powerful and disturbing history on a surprisingly optimistic note. The very excesses of the World War I era, he writes, "gave Americans a greater appreciation of the Bill of Rights." It is true that in subsequent wars the government did not censor newspapers, arrest thousands of critics, or engage in the sadistic torture of prisoners (at least those incarcerated in the United States). But the echoes of the World War I era survive. The Espionage Act remains on the books. The wartime hunt for radicals created the modern FBI and launched the systematic surveillance of political activity that continues to this day. The demonization of immigrants, disdain for democracy, and penchant for labeling political opponents as unpatriotic are all features of our current moment. One conclusion we might glean from Hochschild's history lesson is the fragility of our freedoms.

CHICAGO, 1968

I T IS NO secret that the news media are in crisis, with troubling
implications for American democracy. Jobs for reporters are
scarce, partly because local newspapers are fast disappearing; in
many communities, local government proceeds with no journalistic
oversight at all. News has largely migrated from print to cable television and the Internet. Until a few years ago, Starbucks sold local
and national newspapers at its eight thousand–plus locations in the
United States, but it has abandoned the practice for lack of demand.
Most young people get the news from social media such as TikTok,
Facebook, and Instagram. News websites do attract many visitors,
and nightly news broadcasts on the TV networks still enjoy large
audiences, but these are not adequate replacements for in-depth print
reporting. Not long ago, every other rider on the New York City subway seemed to be reading a physical newspaper. Now they gaze at
their phones, and not, in most cases, for the day's news.

These developments have unavoidable financial consequences.

———

Review of *When the News Broke: Chicago 1968 and the Polarizing of
America*, by Heather Hendershot, *New York Review of Books*, September 21, 2023.

No one has discovered an economic model—other than a paywall, something viable for only a handful of national newspapers—to support serious political journalism. In the nineteenth century, newspapers were generally financed by political parties, in the twentieth by advertising, now considerably diminished. Both sources of funds might be preferable to relying on the long-term commitment of billionaire publishers like Jeff Bezos (owner of the *Washington Post*) or online ads, which create the temptation to shore up income by maximizing clicks via the use of outrageous language, and are subject to algorithms that drive people to sites that reinforce their existing beliefs. All this makes the public-spirited dialogue necessary in a democracy impossible.

Then there is a crisis of a different kind. Newspapers have suffered from the broader decline of respect for once well-regarded institutions such as universities, now under assault as hotbeds of "woke" indoctrination. Donald Trump has gone so far as to declare the press an "enemy of the people." Few persons outside the media seem to care that the leading presidential candidates have all but given up holding news conferences or subjecting themselves to interviews with reporters.

Journalism's crisis began many years ago, but in her new book, *When the News Broke*, Heather Hendershot identifies a specific moment when broad public regard for the news media gave way to the widespread belief that it cannot be trusted. This was in August 1968, during the infamous Democratic National Convention in Chicago, a gathering remembered today for the violence directed against young demonstrators by the police and National Guard. As they faced assault on the city streets, protesters chanted, "The whole world is watching!" They knew that earlier in the 1960s, televised images of violence against demonstrators in Birmingham, Selma, and other cities had galvanized public support for the civil rights movement. But this time, Hendershot says, violence in the streets had a different result. A large majority of TV viewers sided with the police and excoriated the networks for liberal bias.

Hendershot, who teaches film and media at the Massachusetts Institute of Technology, presents a vivid account of the events in Chicago, chronicling the actions of a cast of characters that includes TV reporters, demonstrators, and Mayor Richard J. Daley. The last of the old-time city bosses, Daley was so desperate to use the convention to enhance his own reputation that he had a picture of his smiling face attached to every telephone in a hotel that housed reporters and on billboards on the way into town from the airport, and ordered fences constructed to block views of Chicago's slums. To ensure that television conveyed the image of a Democratic Party unified in enthusiasm for its nominee for president, Hubert Humphrey, Daley had counterfeit tickets distributed to some five thousand machine operatives. Arriving at sessions early, they filled the seats in the galleries, roaring their approval when Humphrey's name was mentioned, and leaving little room for supporters of other candidates. (Nearly a century earlier, Abraham Lincoln's campaign managers pulled off the same trick at the Republican National Convention of 1860, which also met in Chicago.)

Thousands of young people representing various elements of Sixties radical politics descended on Chicago. They included members of Students for a Democratic Society, energized by opposition to the war in Vietnam. Their hero and Humphrey's chief rival for the nomination was Minnesota senator Eugene McCarthy, a politician who seemed to prefer discussing philosophy to wooing voters but whose opposition to the war had inspired a small army of students, including the present reviewer, to campaign on his behalf in the New Hampshire primary. There were hippies anticipating a rock concert and other, less lawful forms of stimulation, and Yippies, members of the Youth International Party, whose leaders included Abbie Hoffman, a self-proclaimed cultural revolutionary who believed that generational conflict had the same potential for disrupting the status quo as class conflict had in the 1930s. Like Martin Luther King Jr., Hoffman realized that television's penetration of all levels of American society offered radicals the opportunity to reach a mass audience with carefully staged actions that dramatized injustice. One group was not strongly represented in the streets of Chicago: African Americans. They knew firsthand how well the city police deserved their reputation for brutality. When Daley spoke of the police adopting a "shoot to kill" approach to disorder, their experience taught that he was not kidding.

For readers of a certain age, Hendershot's account of what transpired in the Chicago convention hall and the city's streets will rouse dramatic memories. On Sunday, August 25, the night before the convention opened, demonstrators gathered in Lincoln Park, adjacent to one of the city's most affluent neighborhoods. They hoped to remain there all night, but the city imposed a curfew, and police used clubs to clear the park. Late the next evening, removing their ID badges, police officers used mace and tear gas to do it again, beating journalists in the bargain. Then came the third day, when the convention heard speeches supporting various candidates and nominated Humphrey for president. Meanwhile, thousands of police and members of the National Guard assaulted a crowd of protesters from Grant Park trying to march south on Michigan Avenue, opposite the Conrad Hilton in downtown Chicago, driving them against the giant windows of the hotel's Haymarket bar. Those not lacerated by broken glass suffered head injuries from police billy clubs, and McCarthy's headquarters, on an upper floor of the Hilton, was transformed into a makeshift hospital ward. The name Haymarket itself evoked another era of Chicago's violent history. In 1886, after a bomb exploded at a labor rally in Haymarket Square, the police responded with wild gunfire, killing or injuring more than a dozen people, including some of their own. Self-discipline has never been a characteristic of the Chicago police.

As news from the Hilton filtered into the convention hall, located several miles from the hotel, the week's most celebrated verbal exchange took place. Departing from his prepared speech nominating Senator George McGovern of South Dakota for president, Senator Abraham Ribicoff of Connecticut declared, "With George McGovern as president of the United States, we wouldn't have to have Gestapo tactics in the streets of Chicago!" Enraged, Daley unleashed a stream of invective at Ribicoff from the convention floor. As he was not near a microphone, few people heard his words. But self-appointed lip-readers soon deciphered them from film: "Fuck you, you Jew son of a bitch, you lousy motherfucker, go home!" (A video of the tirade is available on YouTube; interested viewers can make out some of Daley's phraseology.) On the convention's fourth and final day, a group of protesters led by the Black comedian and activist Dick Gregory attempted to march from downtown to the convention amphitheater. The peaceful march was blocked by police, after which the National Guard dispersed the crowd with tear gas.

The Chicago convention took place during one of the most chaotic years in modern history. Dramatic occurrences succeeded one another with such rapidity that society itself seemed to be unraveling. "No convention ever had such events for prelude," wrote Norman Mailer, who was there that week (though, unlike most of the reporters, he spent part of his time at the local Playboy Club). In January, North Vietnamese and Vietcong troops launched the Tet Offensive, which gave the lie to the Johnson administration's pronouncements that American victory was near. A few days later, members of the South Carolina Highway Patrol killed three unarmed Black civil rights demonstrators at the state university at Orangeburg. In March came McCarthy's strong showing in the New Hampshire primary, leading to Lyndon Johnson's abandonment of his reelection campaign. Four days later King was assassinated, setting off the greatest outbreak of urban violence in the country's history. (This was when Daley issued his "shoot to kill" order.) On April 23 students at Columbia occupied campus buildings to protest the university's involvement in military research and its plan to appropriate parts of a park in nearby Harlem to build a gymnasium. A week later, in a preview of the turmoil in Chicago, New York police violently removed the occupiers and cleared the campus by assaulting students, faculty, and bystanders. June brought the assassination of Robert F. Kennedy, who was also seeking the Democratic nomination for president.

The uprisings of 1968 were not confined to the United States. Challenges by young radicals to existing power structures swept the globe, as did authorities' violent responses. Mass antiwar demonstrations took place in London, Paris, Tokyo, and numerous other cities. In May a nationwide student walkout began in France. Unlike in the United States, millions of workers joined the striking youths, temporarily paralyzing the country. A few days before the Democratic convention assembled, Soviet tanks entered Prague, putting an end to the effort to reform Czech communism in the name of "socialism with a human face." In October, on the eve of the Mexico City Olympics, police fired into an immense crowd of unarmed students demanding greater democracy, killing hundreds. Unfortunately, Hendershot pays little attention to how the American media covered the international dimensions of 1968, thereby missing the opportunity to assess whether political polarization and distrust of the media were exacerbated in other countries as well.

Those alarmed by our current level of political discourse and the widespread dissemination of "fake news" may find it tempting to look back on the years before 1968 as a golden age of civility in the media, when journalists enjoyed widespread respect and the three television networks presented nightly news broadcasts that gave millions of Americans a shared civic experience and a reservoir of commonly accepted information. Walter Cronkite, the anchor of CBS's evening news show, was reputed to be "the most trusted man in America." When he announced after a visit to Vietnam early in 1968 that the U.S. could not win the war, President Johnson was heard remarking that if he had lost Cronkite, he had "lost middle America."

Hendershot eschews nostalgia, making it clear that news coverage before 1968 left much to be desired. For many years, especially but not exclusively in the South, the mainstream press published articles about the civil rights movement that denigrated demonstrators, defended segregation, and included the names of Black men and women who sought to register to vote, frequently resulting in economic retribution such as the loss of their jobs. By the mid-1960s, as the movement peaked, the news media became more sympathetic. But local newspaper editors remained leading figures in the southern power structure. Hendershot chastises the networks for ignoring the racism still present in the Democratic Party in 1968, before segregationists made the transition en masse to the Republicans as a result of Nixon's "southern strategy." (Until 1966 the emblem of Alabama's Democratic Party, shown in every voting booth in the state because widespread illiteracy meant many voters needed a visual representation of the party to cast a ballot, was a rooster beneath a banner with the words "White Supremacy.") The Chicago convention witnessed challenges to seating all-white delegations from several southern states; the networks paid little heed. Black newspapers covered the challenges—nearly all unsuccessful—far more effectively than the mainstream media.

Before the Chicago convention, complaints of bias in news coverage were more likely to arise from the Left than the Right. In the 1950s, much of the press reported as fact Senator Joseph McCarthy's unsubstantiated charges of Communist infiltration of the government. Until 1968 the news media displayed a remarkable credulity about official claims of military progress in Vietnam and failed to examine in any depth the rising tide of nationalism in the colonial world that helped explain the conflict. For that, one had to read niche publications such as *I. F. Stone's Weekly*, *The National Guardian*, *The Nation*, and the underground press, which had emerged as the New Left's most significant counter-institution. The *Columbia Daily Spectator*, the university's student paper, and WKCR, its radio station, did a far better job reporting on the crisis on campus in 1968 than *The New York Times*, which repeatedly downplayed police violence.

Interspersed with Hendershot's detailed description of what happened in the convention amphitheater and the streets of Chicago is a careful analysis of network coverage of the convention. It is startling to learn, given what so many people think they remember, how little TV time was actually devoted to film of police assaulting demonstrators. Cameramen filmed only seventeen minutes of footage of the violence outside the Hilton. Hendershot points out that in NBC's thirty-five hours of broadcasting, only one hour showed street protests. Today, nearly every person in the street carries a smartphone that makes it possible to record live action and immediately post photos and videos online. Such a world could not have been imagined in 1968, when film had to be developed and edited and it took an hour or more for the images to appear on the nation's television screens.

But the obstacles faced by journalists were as much political as technological. Along with the conflict in the streets, a battle raged over control of news coverage. Mayor Daley did nothing to hide his contempt for journalists. Some were physically assaulted by security guards on the convention floor and others manhandled by police on the streets. Daley tried to confine live reporting to the inside of the convention hall, and the state of technology allowed him mostly to succeed. TV cameras were bulky and difficult to maneuver when crowds and police were in motion and tear gas was in the air. Networks could not send live images from anywhere but the amphitheater—also Daley's doing. Meanwhile, electrical workers, probably egged on by the mayor, were on strike, so reporters could not gain access to additional telephone lines.

Publicity was key to the Yippies' hopes for the demonstrations. As Hoffman put it, they believed images of chaos would "fuck up" the country's self-image as a "democratic society being run very peacefully," turning viewers against the political establishment. According to Hoffman's biographer Jonah Raskin, at one planning meeting the Yippie leader Jerry Rubin said the aim was to "force a confrontation in which the establishment hits down hard"—to which Hoffman responded, "On that theory the only way that Chicago would be a success is if twenty of us got shot to death." The civil rights leader Jesse Jackson had advised demonstration organizers that if TV showed Black victims of the police, white viewers would not care, but violence against whites would make headlines. Some demonstrators shouted epithets and threw things at the police, hoping for an overreaction—of course, police are supposed to know how to ignore such provocation.

How did the chaos in the streets of Chicago affect network coverage? As Hendershot points out, the media had long normalized the idea that there were two and only two sides to every issue, with the truth lying somewhere in the middle. She shows that until well into the convention, television newsmen clung to the ideal of impartiality.

They seemed to accept Daley's claim that "troublemakers" were responsible for disorder and the police had no choice but to step in. Then, as images from the Hilton became available, the networks dropped, for the moment, the stance of neutrality. CBS aired film of the National Guard entering the hotel with fixed bayonets and gas masks, and scenes from the impromptu hospital in McCarthy's suite. It showed a National Guard soldier pointing a grenade launcher through the open car window of a woman who found herself caught in the confrontation near the Hilton and simply wanted to escape. Cronkite spoke of "naked violence in the streets" and interviewed bandaged tourists. Hendershot notes that the networks did not show the most extreme use of force, but the bloody images they did air changed the tone of the coverage. The CBS analyst Eric Sevareid declared, "This is the most disgraceful night in the history of American political conventions." On NBC, Chet Huntley gravely announced, "What we've seen requires no comment."

If the demonstrators craved publicity, they certainly received it. Network coverage of the convention enjoyed the highest ratings of any television program in 1968. But a majority did not like what they saw. This reaction is crucial to Hendershot's overall argument about when the news "broke" and divisiveness took off. She effectively uses the letters and telegrams that poured into the three networks' headquarters and public opinion polls to demonstrate that most Americans viewed protesters as "militants" or "terrorists" and network coverage as "prejudiced and one-sided." By this time, public opinion had turned against the Vietnam War. But all the same, most viewers seemed to believe that demonstrators got what they deserved.

Many Americans were fed up with a pointless war but also with Black uprisings, campus disruptions, and antiwar demonstrations. They craved order. Here was Nixon's putative silent majority, in fact anxious to articulate its fear that civic peace was disintegrating. It looked to the police, who still enjoyed a positive image in the white mainstream, to restore it. This was not true among the Black community. A public opinion survey conducted in October 1968 found that only 19 percent of white respondents thought the police had used excessive force, one third said they employed the right amount, and 25 percent said not enough. But 63 percent of Black respondents said police had used too much force.

Alarmed by the negative reactions to their coverage, TV journalists retreated to the tried-and-true method of presenting both sides. On day four, NBC became the first network to interview Chicago policemen, who predictably said that accusations against them were "completely unfounded" and that street demonstrators never accomplished anything. That day Daley, who had shunned the press, agreed to speak on camera with Cronkite. Hendershot calls the resulting interview "astonishingly terrible" and a "low point" of the anchorman's career. Cronkite allowed Daley to repeat without challenge falsehood after falsehood, including gross exaggerations of the provocations aimed at the police and the claim that injured reporters had not identified themselves as such. The mayor blithely declared that he wanted free and full coverage of the convention.

The interview ended with Cronkite's speaking of the "politeness and the genuine friendliness" of the Chicago police. Daley was later outraged when an official investigation overseen by a prominent Chicago attorney described the events of August 1968 as a "police riot." In response, he sponsored a film with the enigmatic title *What Trees Do They Plant*, which lauded police behavior and insisted the networks had gotten the story wrong. Daley marketed the film to television stations not affiliated with the networks, finding few takers. But the mayor had won a major propaganda victory, and Hoffman and the others had learned a painful lesson. TV was not the young radicals' secret weapon.

The phrase "law and order" was not widely used until Nixon's presidency, but the idea was present in Chicago's aftermath. Even Humphrey invoked it in his speech accepting the presidential nomination. "We do not want a police state," he declared. "But we need a state of law and order." "Law and order" merged legitimate fears about crime with hostility to Black activism, even though nearly all the Chicago demonstrators were white. The notion fueled Nixon's successful run for president and helped justify the transition from the war on poverty to the "wars" on crime and drugs of the 1970s and 1980s. Today it remains a mantra among Republicans. Similarly, according to Hendershot, it was after the Chicago convention that accusations of "liberal media bias" took root in the national political consciousness.

Movement activists thought that because of the televised violence they had scored a great triumph. *The New York Times* ran an article entitled "Chicago Protesters Say Police Action on Television Will 'Radicalize' Many Viewers." But the year ended with Nixon's election. His margin of less than 1 percent of the popular vote might cast doubt on the idea that televised disorder discredited the Democratic Party. Yet the southern segregationist George Wallace, running as an independent, garnered 13 percent of the vote. Simple arithmetic suggested that combining the support of Nixon and Wallace would produce a formidable political majority. People talked of revolution, wrote Todd Gitlin, an early leader of SDS and subsequently a chronicler of the history of the 1960s, but 1968 ended in counterrevolution.

Was that year, then, one of those turning points at which history failed to turn, as the historian G. M. Trevelyan described the year 1848? There is a widespread myth that the Sixties ended in 1968. But radicalism did not suddenly disappear. By the early 1970s social movements dotted the political landscape, including the second wave of feminism, gay liberation, and environmentalism, while the Black struggle continued. All survive to this day, and all have changed American life in dramatic ways. The antiwar movement did not reach its peak until 1970 when, in the aftermath of the U.S. invasion of Cambodia and the killing of four protesting students at Kent State University by members of the Ohio National Guard, a strike paralyzed campuses throughout the country. And in 1975 the war ended.

The story Hendershot tells is often riveting. Readers may wonder, however, why she says almost nothing about how newspapers, magazines, radio, and other news venues covered the convention. All sorts of media were present in Chicago, from the Black press to community radio stations and underground newspapers. TV may have reached millions of Americans instantaneously, but other coverage also deserves attention. Despite the book's success in reconstructing a seminal episode in modern American history, moreover, Hendershot's interpretive framework is not entirely persuasive. Was the Chicago convention the moment when the polarization of American political culture that persists to this day was born? Another way of putting it might be that responses to the convention reflected and magnified existing polarization. The country was already deeply divided by the war, the civil rights revolution, and the countercultural rebellion. In 1966 Ronald Reagan had been elected governor of California after a campaign that blamed student radicals for disorder. The backlash was already present in 1968, even if television exacerbated it.

When did the decade of the Sixties end? Did it end at all? We sometimes seem to be reliving those years that did so much to shape the world we live in.

THE COURT: GRAVE OF LIBERTY

THE SUPREME COURT'S recent decision refusing to interfere with extreme partisan gerrymandering not only seriously
undermines our already fragile democracy; it also brings to
mind the court's acquiescence more than a century ago in laws that
denied the right to vote to millions of Black southerners. In particular,
it is reminiscent of the court's 1903 ruling in *Giles v. Harris*, a largely
forgotten case in which the justices, as today, claimed they were not
authorized to adjudicate "political" matters.

In that case, Jackson W. Giles, the president of the Colored Men's
Suffrage Association, sued to overturn voting requirements openly
designed to disenfranchise Black voters in Alabama after the end of
Reconstruction. The state constitution of 1901 allowed registrars to
bar from voting those who lacked "good character" or did not understand "the duties and obligations of citizenship." The result was that
almost every Black voter was eliminated from the rolls, despite the fact
that the Fifteenth Amendment, ratified in 1870, prohibited states from
denying the right to vote because of race. To work around that amendment, Alabama's requirements did not explicitly mention race. But it

---

The Nation, July 29/August 5, 2019.

was clear, as Giles's complaint argued, that the state's entire registration system was racially biased.

Oliver Wendell Holmes, recently appointed to the court by Theodore Roosevelt, wrote the opinion for the majority after a 6–3 vote. Like Chief Justice John Roberts today, Holmes threw up his hands and described the Supreme Court as impotent. If "the great mass of the white population intends to keep the Blacks from voting," he wrote, there was nothing the justices could do about it. The courts were not permitted to get involved in politics. "Relief from a great political wrong" could come only from the "people of a state" through their elected officials or from Congress. He ignored the fact that the definition of the "people" of Alabama was precisely the point at issue. Holmes would go on to have a distinguished judicial career. *Giles v. Harris*, one scholar has written, "is—or should be—the most prominent stain" on his reputation. Chief Justice Roberts, take note.

Like Republicans today, the white southern press in 1903 hailed the ruling as an indication that the Supreme Court would not interfere with "a sovereign state's regulation of its elections." Some signs of discontent appeared in the North. "Is the Constitution non-enforceable?" asked one of the nation's leading newspapers, the *Springfield Republican*. "We are brought face to face with the consideration that the Constitution may be violated with impunity."

The idea that the Supreme Court does not have the authority to get involved in political matters would be laughable if the results of the current decision were not so damaging. Was not *Baker v. Carr*, the one-man-one-vote ruling of the 1960s, political? What about *Bush v. Gore* (2000), which decided the outcome of a presidential election? Roberts claims that the founders, by leaving the drawing of district lines to state legislatures, anticipated political involvement in the process. But the founders did not expect or desire the rise of political parties that sought to warp the electoral process to their advantage. As Richard Hofstadter demonstrated many years ago in *The Idea of a Party System*, the founders thought political parties were divisive institutions indifferent or hostile to the common good. They would have been appalled to see a political party use its control of districting to override the will of a state's voters.

Supreme Court decisions have practical consequences, which justices too often blithely ignore. It took well over half a century for the right to vote to be restored to Black citizens of the southern states, via the Voting Rights Act of 1965. During those years the country experienced profound social and economic changes, which the disenfranchised millions in the South had no voice in shaping. Needless to say, the right to vote is still being fought out in numerous states at this very moment. What is the difference between being denied access to the ballot box and living in a district designed so that your party is guaranteed to lose?

Our Constitution is not self-enforcing. At certain moments in our history, the Supreme Court has used its authority to protect constitutional rights when legislatures and Congress abdicate this responsibility. At other times, as one lawyer wrote in 1890, the court becomes "the grave of liberty." That seems to be where we are headed today.

AMERICAN
EXCEPTIONALISM,
AMERICAN FREEDOM

PATRIOTISM, TO QUOTE George Bernard Shaw, "is your conviction that this country is superior to all others because you were
born in it." The same may be said of American exceptionalism.

That phrase has had a highly unusual career. It seems to have originated in debates in the 1920s and 1930s among American communists over whether some unique characteristic of American society
has inhibited the transition from capitalism to socialism. It was initially employed as a term of abuse directed at those who believed—or
feared—that the United States might be exempt from the iron laws of
historical development outlined by Marx. In the 1950s, exceptionalism
became a weapon in the Cold War, suggesting a national responsibility
to lead the forces of the Free World in the containment of Soviet power.
The terrorist attack of September 11, 2001, reinvigorated the rhetoric of
exceptionalism as an all-purpose explanation for the onslaught ("they
hate us because we are free") and for a new sense of American mission,
now identified with the global war on terror.

Most recently, American exceptionalism has emerged as a political
slogan of the Tea Party and its acolytes. That President Obama "does

---

not believe in American exceptionalism" was among the numerous charges leveled against him by Republicans. Like his race and supposed lack of a birth certificate, this made Obama seem dangerously alien. In fact, as his administration's foreign policy became more and more warlike, Obama, like his predecessors, spoke of the uniqueness of the United States, a justification for our right to intervene in the affairs of nations throughout the world.

Long before the term itself existed, the idea of American exceptionalism was built into our culture. It has always been linked to the idea of freedom. The identification of the United States as a unique embodiment of liberty in a world overrun by oppression goes back to the American Revolution. Tom Paine, in his clarion call for American independence, *Common Sense*, called the country an "asylum for mankind," a place where people fleeing Old World tyranny could find freedom. Thomas Jefferson spoke of the new nation as an "empire of liberty." This seems an oxymoron, since empire suggests domination, but Jefferson's point was that unlike the empires of Europe, ours would be based on democratic self-government. Thus, American territorial expansion by definition meant the expansion of freedom and those who stood in its way (Indians, Mexicans, rival European powers) were ipso facto freedom's enemies.

Abraham Lincoln, who also embraced the idea of a unique American democratic mission, called the United States the last best hope of earth, although he thought the nation should spread freedom by example, not by invading other countries (he opposed the Mexican-American War). Throughout the nineteenth century, American exceptionalism was invoked by home-grown critics, such as abolitionists, who claimed the United States was not living up to its professed values, and by the European Left, who deployed the image of an exceptional nation where workers enjoyed political rights and economic opportunity as a weapon against the status quo in their own countries. Others (most famously the sociologist Werner Sombart) cited the high American standard of living to explain the relative weakness of socialism compared to early twentieth-century Europe.

To a considerable degree, the essence of American exceptionalism—a nation-state with a special mission to bring freedom to all mankind—depends on the "otherness" of the outside world, so often expressed in the Manichean categories of New World versus Old or free world versus slave. Yet, at the heart of the idea lies an odd contradiction. American freedom is generally held to derive from a specific national history and unique historical circumstances—the frontier, the inborn qualities of the Anglo-Saxon race, a divinely appointed mission, and so forth. Yet Americans claim for their experience and ideals universal relevance. America may be exceptional, but its exceptional role is to serve as a model for the rest of mankind. Presumably, when our self-appointed mission of promoting the worldwide spread of freedom has finally been achieved—when the world has become America writ large—the country will no longer be exceptional.

At its best, the idea of American exceptionalism carries with it healthy pride in the freedoms Americans enjoy. But overall, the insistent claim for exceptionalism goes along with national hubris and closed-mindedness, and offers an excuse for ignorance about the rest of the world. Since the United States is so exceptional, there is no point in learning about other societies, as their histories have no bearing on ours.

Historians, unfortunately, have aided and abetted this parochialism. Perhaps the most influential idea ever developed by an American historian was Frederick Jackson Turner's frontier thesis, which explained the country's supposedly unique characteristics—political democracy, self-reliant individualism—as the product of the struggle to conquer the West. Cold War intellectuals provided historical justification, differentiating "good" from "bad" revolutions. In the 1950s, historians portrayed the American Revolution as a decorous constitutional debate among the educated elite, quite different from the class-based violence of revolutionary France and Russia, or Third World revolutions led by communists (even when, as in Vietnam, they invoked the American Declaration of Independence as justification for their actions). As the historian Herbert Bolton complained many years ago, by treating the American past in isolation from the rest of the world, historians were helping to raise up "a nation of chauvinists."

Of course, the history of every country is, to some extent, unique, and the antidote to American exceptionalism is not to homogenize the entire past into a single global history. But the institutions, processes, and values that have shaped American history, among them the rise of capitalism, the spread of political democracy, the rise and fall of slavery, and international labor migrations, can only be understood in a global context. The exceptionalist paradigm homogenizes the rest of the world as having a single history, entirely different from that of the United States. Much writing on exceptionalism is based on sheer ignorance of other countries—the United States, we are told again and again (falsely) has the highest standard of living in the world, the highest rate of social mobility, the greatest racial and ethnic diversity, the most individual freedom, the least political radicalism, etc. Oddly, one genuine expression of American exceptionalism—the principle, embedded in the Fourteenth Amendment, that anyone born in the United States is automatically a citizen, regardless of the status of the parents—is now under assault by the very conservatives who so stridently proclaim their devotion to American uniqueness.

The historical and political uses and abuses of exceptionalism came together in the debate over health care reform. A century ago, as Daniel Rodgers reminds us in his book *Atlantic Crossings*, American reformers and social scientists eagerly studied European responses to the crises of urbanization and industrialization. They thought European experiences could contribute to the development of American social policy. Fast forward to 2009–10. Every advanced country in the world has some kind of national health care system. But in the American debates, no one thought to refer to their experiences, except to hurl abuse. Obamacare would bring to the United States the alleged horrors of the British National Health Service, or Canadian single-payer health insurance—abuses "known" through rumor and invective, not actual investigation. Obama's critics made a virtue of isolation and ignorance. Here is the deepest problem with American exceptionalism—the conviction that Americans have nothing to learn from the rest of the world.

LETTER TO BERNIE

D EAR SENATOR SANDERS,
        Congratulations on the tremendous success of your cam-
        paign. You have energized and inspired millions of Amer-
icans and forced the questions of economic inequality and excessive
corporate power to the center of our political discourse. These are
remarkable accomplishments.

So take the following advice as coming from an admirer. I urge you
to reconsider how you respond to the inevitable questions about what
you mean by democratic socialism and peaceful revolution. The next
time, embrace our own American radical tradition. There's nothing
wrong with Denmark; we can learn a few things from them (and vice
versa). But most Americans don't know or care much about Scandina-
via. More importantly, your response inadvertently reinforces the idea
that socialism is a foreign import. Instead, talk about our radical forebears here in the United States, for the most successful radicals have
always spoken the language of American society and appealed to some
of its deepest values.

You could begin with Tom Paine and other American revolution-

—

The Nation, November 16, 2015.

aries who strove not simply for independence from Britain but to free the new nation from the social and economic inequalities of Europe. Embrace the tradition of abolitionists, Black and white, men and women like William Lloyd Garrison, Frederick Douglass, and Abby Kelley, who, against overwhelming odds, broke through the conspiracy of silence of the two major parties on the issue of slavery and helped to create a public sentiment that led to Lincoln's election and, eventually, to emancipation. (And don't forget to mention that slaves represented by far the largest concentration of wealth in the United States on the eve of the Civil War, that slaveholders were the richest Americans of their time, and that nothing could be accomplished without confronting their economic and political power.) Refer to the long struggle for women's rights, which demanded not only the vote but also equality for women in all realms of life and in doing so challenged some of the most powerful entrenched interests in the country.

You should mention the People's Party, or Populists, and their Omaha platform of 1892, which describes a nation not unlike our own, with inequality rife and a political system in need of change, where "corruption dominates the ballot-box, the Legislatures, the Congress, and touches even the ermine of the bench . . . [and] the fruits of the toil of millions are boldly stolen to build up colossal fortunes for a few."

What about the Progressive platform of 1912, for the party that nominated Theodore Roosevelt for president, calling, among other things, for strict limits on campaign contributions, universal health insurance, vigorous federal oversight of giant corporations, and other measures that, over a century later, have yet to be realized.

Of course, every politician gives lip service to the idea of enhancing economic opportunity, but you have, rightly, emphasized that to secure this requires the active involvement of the federal government, not simply letting the free market work its supposed magic. Your antecedents include not just FDR's New Deal but also his Second Bill of Rights of 1944, inspired by the era's labor movement, which called for the government to guarantee to all Americans the rights to employment, education, medical care, a decent home, and other entitlements that are out of reach for too many today. You could point to A. Philip Randolph's Freedom Budget of 1966, which asked the federal government to address the deep economic inequalities the civil rights revolution left untouched. But beyond these and other examples, the point is that the rights we enjoy today—civil, political, economic, social—are the result of struggles of the past, not gifts from on high. That's what you mean when you say we need a citizens' revolution.

As to socialism, the term today refers not to a blueprint for a future society but to the need to rein in the excesses of capitalism, evident all around us; to empower ordinary people in a political system verging on plutocracy; and to develop policies that make opportunity real for the millions of Americans for whom it is not. This is what it meant in the days of Eugene Debs, the great labor leader and Socialist candidate for president who won almost a million votes in 1912. Debs spoke the language of what he called "political equality and economic freedom." But equally important, as Debs emphasized, socialism is as much a moral idea as an economic one—the conviction that vast inequalities of wealth, power, and opportunity are simply wrong and that ordinary people, using political power, can produce far-reaching change. It was Debs's moral fervor as much as his specific program that made him beloved by millions of Americans.

Each generation of Americans made its own contribution to an ongoing radical tradition, and you are following in their footsteps. So next time, forget about Denmark and talk about Paine, Douglass, Kelley, FDR, and Debs as forebears of a movement that can make the United States a freer society.

THE ENEMY WITHIN

J ANUARY 6, 2021, will long be remembered as the day two
strands of the American experience, both deeply embedded in our
national history, collided. One was reflected in the election of African American and Jewish senators from Georgia. This is a state that
witnessed the 1915 lynching of the Jewish factory superintendent Leo
Frank, the transformation of Tom Watson from a populist who sought
to unite poor Black and white farmers into a vicious racist and anti-
Semite, and the Atlanta Massacre of 1906, in which white mobs killed
perhaps two dozen African Americans. The election results are the culmination of a mass, interracial movement to transform a state that long
denied its Black population the right to vote into a genuine democracy.
The campaign led by Stacey Abrams and others to register new voters is
an inspiring example of the possibility of progressive change.

Yet the riot by supporters of President Trump, aimed at preventing the counting of electoral votes, reveals a darker side of the history
of American democracy. One can begin with the fact that, more than
two centuries after the adoption of the Constitution, we still select the
president through the Electoral College, an archaic system that reflects

---

The Nation, January 8, 2021.

the founders' conviction that ordinary people are not to be trusted with voting directly for president, and their desire to bolster the slaveholding South, whose political power was augmented by the three-fifths clause that gave slave states extra electoral votes based on their disenfranchised Black population. Indeed, Trump occupies the White House only because an undemocratic electoral system makes it possible to lose the popular vote and still become president. Moreover, efforts to restrict the right to vote by race, gender, or some other criteria have a long history. The idea that the people should choose their rulers, the essence of democracy, has always coexisted with the conviction that too many people—of the wrong kind—are casting ballots. Georgia's requirement that office seekers receive over 50 percent of the vote or face a runoff election, enacted in 1963 at the height of the civil rights revolution, was intended to prevent the victory of a candidate preferred by Blacks if several aspirants split the white vote.

The events of January 6 are the logical culmination of the disrespect for the rule of law nurtured by the Trump presidency, evidenced in the glorification of armed neo-fascist groups, most notoriously until now at Charlottesville, the whipping up of anti-mask and anti-lockdown riots in Michigan and other states, and the refusal to accept the clear results of the presidential election. But those familiar with American history know that the Capitol riot was hardly the first effort to overturn extralegally the results of a democratic election. The Reconstruction era and the years that followed witnessed many such events, some far more violent than the January 6 riot. Scores of members of a Black militia unit were murdered in 1873 in Colfax, Louisiana, by armed whites who seized control of the local government from elected Black officials. An uprising the following year by the White League sought to overthrow the biracial state government of Reconstruction Louisiana. In 1898, a coup by armed whites in Wilmington, North Carolina, ousted the elected biracial local government. By the early twentieth century, Black voting and office holding had essentially ended throughout the South. This is not just ancient history. As recently as 2013, the Supreme Court eviscerated key provisions of the Voting Rights Act of 1965, opening the door to widespread efforts in Republican-controlled states to suppress the ability to vote. Let's not assume that until the Capitol riot the United States was a well-functioning democracy.

Alexander H. Stephens, the Georgia political leader who served as vice president of the Confederacy, famously described the effort to create a slaveholders' republic as an embodiment of the "great truth that the Negro is not equal to the white man, that slavery . . . is his natural and normal condition." January 6 may be the first time the Confederate flag was openly displayed in the Capitol building—a shocking sight that, I hope, will never be repeated. But in his opposition to the removal of monuments to Confederate leaders and to renaming military bases on the grounds that they erase "our" history, Trump has consciously identified his presidency with the Confederacy and the white nationalism at its core.

Today, the United States spends far more on its military than any other nation. Yet the mob that stormed the Capitol consisted not of Chinese, Iranians, Russians, or other purported enemies of American democracy, but our fellow citizens. Nearly two centuries ago, in his famous Lyceum speech, Abraham Lincoln condemned growing disrespect for the rule of law as the greatest danger to American democracy. "If destruction be our lot," he declared, "we must ourselves be its author and finisher." The electoral results in Georgia offer hope for a revitalization of a democratic political culture. But now, as in Lincoln's time, the danger to American democracy ultimately lies within.

PART VI

History, Memory, Historians

THE MONUMENTS
QUESTION

To THE SURPRISE of historians themselves, history—or at least its public presentation—has become big business. The Freedom Trail—a walking tour of monuments, buildings, and historical markers—is Boston's leading tourist attraction. The History Channel is among the most successful enterprises on cable television, and attendance at historical museums and other sites is at a record high.

What account of the past does our public history convey? This is the question James Loewen sets out to answer. A former professor at the University of Vermont, Loewen is a one-man historical truth squad, best known as the author of *Lies My Teacher Told Me*, which argued that high school history texts are laced with omissions, misconceptions, and outright lies. In *Lies Across America*, based on visits to historic markers, houses, and monuments in all fifty states, Loewen comes to essentially the same conclusion about the public presentation of American history.

Friedrich Nietzsche once identified three approaches to history— the monumental, antiquarian, and critical (the last defined as "the his-

Review of *Lies Across America: What Our Historic Sites Get Wrong*, by James W. Loewen, *The Nation*, October 21, 1999.

tory that judges and condemns"). Nearly all historical monuments, of course, are meant to be flattering to their subjects; it is probably asking too much to expect them to be critical in Nietzsche's sense. But one can expect basic accuracy and honesty, and this test, as Loewen demonstrates, much of our public history fails.

Problems begin with the language commonly used to describe early American history, which suggests that the continent was uninhabited before white settlement and that only persons of English origin qualify as "civilized." Now excised from most historians' accounts of Columbus's voyages, the much-abused word "discovery" remains alive and well on historical markers, even where self-evidently inappropriate. A marker in Iowa declares that the French explorer Jean Nicolet "discovered" Okamanpadu Lake, although Indians had clearly named it well before Nicolet's arrival. A Minnesota marker credits Henry R. Schoolcraft with the "discovery" of Lake Itasca, the source of the Mississippi River, even while acknowledging that the lake was "known to Indians and traders" well before his arrival in 1832. In Gardner, Kansas, where the Oregon and Santa Fe trails diverge, a marker honors the "pioneers who brought civilization to the western half of the United States"— thus expelling from history not only Indian populations but the Spanish, who planted their civilizations in the West centuries before the advent of overland settlers.

But what really concerns Loewen is not so much misrepresentations such as these, but lies of omission. Nietzsche spoke of "creative forgetfulness" as essential to historical memory; what is not memorialized tells us as much about a society's sense of the past as what is. For Loewen, the great scandal of our public history is the treatment of slavery, the Civil War, and the country's long history of racial injustice.

Visitors to Washington, D.C., will find a national museum devoted to the Holocaust, funded annually with millions of taxpayer dollars, but almost nothing related to slavery, our home-grown crime against humanity. Tours of historic plantations, Loewen shows, ignore or sugar-coat the lives of slaves. No whips, chains, or other artifacts of discipline are on display and presentations by guides focus on the furniture, gardens, and architecture, rather than the role of slave labor in creating the wealth they represent.

At Hannibal, Missouri, whose principal industry is the commemoration of native son Mark Twain, the fact that Twain grew up in a slave society remains unmentioned, and a two-hour outdoor pageant based on *Huckleberry Finn* manages to eliminate Jim, the runaway slave on whose plight the book pivots. The slave trade, a central element of the pre–Civil War southern economy, has also disappeared from public history. In Alexandria, Virginia, the Franklin and Armfield Office bears a plaque designating it as a National Historic Landmark. That this elegant building served as headquarters for the city's largest slave dealer is conveniently forgotten.

Especially but not exclusively in the South, Civil War monuments glorify soldiers and generals who fought for southern independence, explaining their motivation by reference to the ideals of freedom, states' rights, and individual autonomy—everything, that is, but slavery, the "cornerstone" of the Confederacy according to its vice president, Alexander H. Stephens. Fort Mill, South Carolina, has a marker honoring the "faithful slaves" of the Confederate states, but one would be hard pressed to find monuments anywhere in the country to slave rebels like Denmark Vesey and Nat Turner, to the 200,000 Black soldiers and sailors who fought for the Union (or, for that matter, the thousands of white southerners who remained loyal to the nation).

As Loewen points out, most Confederate monuments were erected between 1890 and 1920 under the leadership of the United Daughters of the Confederacy as part of a conscious effort to glorify and sanitize the Confederate cause and legitimize the newly installed Jim Crow system. General Nathan B. Forrest, "one of the most vicious racists in U.S. history" as Loewen puts it, was a slave trader, founder of the Ku Klux Klan, and commander of troops who massacred Black Union soldiers after their surrender at Fort Pillow. Yet there are more statues, markers, and busts of Forrest in Tennessee than of any other figure in the state's history, including President Andrew Jackson. Only one transgression was sufficiently outrageous to disqualify Confederate leaders from the pantheon of heroes. No statue of James B. Longstreet, a far abler commander than Forrest, graces the southern countryside, and Gen. James F. Fleming is omitted from the portrait gallery of famous figures of Arkansas history in Little Rock. Their crime? Both supported Black rights during Reconstruction.

Even today, Loewen points out, Reconstruction is almost invisible in America's public history. Guides at plantations rarely mention what happened after emancipation, and there are no statues of Reconstruction governors or of the era's numerous Black political leaders.

The same pattern of evasion and misrepresentation marks post-Reconstruction racial history. Texas has nearly 12,000 historical markers—more than the rest of the country combined—but not one mentions any of the state's numerous lynchings, the Brownsville race riot of 1906, or even *Sweatt v. Painter*, the landmark civil rights case that paved the way for the Brown school desegregation decision. Scottsboro, Alabama, contains four historical markers, but none touches on the only event for which the town is famous—the 1930s trials in which nine young Black men were wrongly convicted of rape. A marker in Louisiana celebrates the life of Leander Perez for his "dedicated service to the people of Plaquemines Parish," without mentioning that he referred to Plaquemines' Blacks as "animals right out of the jungle" and fought a bitter battle against racial integration. Such forgetfulness is not confined to the South. The plaque on the statue of Orville L. Hubbard, mayor of Dearborn, Michigan, from 1942 to 1978, praises his achievements in snow removal and trash collection, but fails to take note of his outspoken and successful efforts to keep the city lily-white (when he left office, fewer than twenty of Dearborn's 90,000 inhabitants were Black).

Slavery and its legacy are not the only aspects of our history to be sanitized, romanticized, or ignored in what Loewen calls our historical "landscape of denial." American radicalism is generally excised from public history. Helen Keller's birthplace in Tuscumbria, Alabama, contains no mention of her support for labor unions, socialism, or Black rights. A marker at Finn Hall in southwestern Washington notes the weddings, athletic competitions, and other events held there by Finnish immigrants without acknowledging their socialist convictions or the name of the association that constructed the building—the "Comrades Society."

Commemorations of wars are also highly selective. Numerous plaques and statues honor those who served in the Spanish-American War; none, however, tell the story of America's brutal suppression of the Philippine movement for independence that followed. Despite the popularity of the Vietnam Memorial in Washington, D.C., America's longest war remains too controversial to mention elsewhere. The aircraft carrier U.S.S. *Intrepid*, now anchored at a Manhattan pier as a floating war memorial, saw extended duty in World War II and Vietnam. But the onboard historical presentation deals only with the ship's role in the first of these conflicts, despite complaints from some Vietnam veterans about being written out of history.

Overall, Loewen has written a devastating portrait of how American history is commemorated. The book is lively and informative, and his mini-essays correcting the errors and omissions at various sites offer valuable history lessons in themselves. Loewen does take note of recent efforts to diversify and modernize public history. Montana has introduced new markers on aspects of Indian history, and Pennsylvania recently decided to commemorate the state's African American past. But perhaps because he is so intent on exposing the deficiencies of the historical landscape, Loewen fails to give adequate attention to larger debates and changes now underway.

Loewen does not analyze the visiting experience itself, and the possibility that people attuned to newer perspectives on the past may come away from monuments and exhibits with rather different impressions than their originators intended, or may contest how history is being presented. He offers no account, for example, of the controversy over history at the Alamo, where Mexican Americans and others are challenging the representation of the fort's white defenders as champions of liberty while ignoring the expropriation of Mexican lands and the expansion of slavery that were part and parcel of the movement for Texan independence. He notes that Boston's Freedom Trail has been supplemented by a Women's History Trail, a Black Heritage Trail, and even a guide to the city's gay and lesbian history, but fails to reflect on how the quest for tourist dollars can be a spur to diversifying public history.

Loewen says nothing about the efforts of the National Parks Service, under chief historian Dwight Pitcaithley, to reevaluate the hundreds of sites under its control. Slavery may be ignored in most public presentations of history, but the Parks Service is currently developing a historical site in Natchez devoted to the experience of slaves and free Blacks in the city's history.

These developments, while salutary, do not negate the overall force of Loewen's critique. Why, one wonders, has our understanding of history changed so rapidly, but its public presentation remained so static? Ultimately, public monuments are built by those with sufficient power to determine which parts of history are worth commemorating, and what vision of history ought to be conveyed. One of Loewen's more interesting observations is that while labor history is almost entirely ignored in textbooks, it enjoys considerable presence in public monuments. Because unions possess economic power and political influence, they have been able to persuade states to erect markers commemorating strikes and confrontations between labor and the police, as well as noting mine and factory disasters.

Nonetheless, powerful forces remain resistant to change—a lesson the Smithsonian Institution learned in the 1990s when protests from veterans' organizations scuttled a proposed exhibit on the dropping of the first atomic bomb because it pointed out that military officials disagreed over the necessity for the weapon's use. Regarding the racism so powerfully embedded in our public history, what is surprising is not that monuments and markers erected a century ago reflect the views of the Jim Crow era, but how many Americans remain wedded to these representations.

Americans applauded the Muscovites who in 1991 toppled the statue of Felix Dzerzhinsky, founder of the Soviet secret police, but citizens of New Orleans who demanded the removal of the monument glorifying the White League were denounced as "Stalinists" by a leading historian in the pages of *The New York Times*. The point is not that every monument to a slaveholder ought to be dismantled, but that existing historical sites must be revised to convey a more complex and honest view of our past, and that statues of Black Civil War soldiers, slave rebels, civil rights activists, and the like should share public space with Confederate generals and Klansmen, all of them parts of America's history.

TEXTBOOK HISTORY

L IKE MOST WORKS of history, W. E. B. Du Bois's *Black Recon-struction in America* concludes with a bibliography listing pri-mary and other sources consulted by the author. Most of the groupings are unexceptional—for example, monographs, government reports, and biographies. But Du Bois's first and largest category comes as a shock to the modern reader: it consists of books by historians who believe African Americans to be "sub-human and congenitally unfitted for citizenship and the suffrage." Just before the bibliography, Du Bois includes a chapter, "The Propaganda of History," that indicts the pro-fession for abandoning scholarly objectivity in the service of "that bizarre doctrine of race that makes most men inferior to the few." This was the state of historical scholarship in the United States when *Black Reconstruction* was published, in 1935.

As part of his research, Du Bois scoured history textbooks to see what was being taught in American classrooms about Reconstruction. Students learned that the period marked the lowest point in the Amer-

———

Review of *Teaching White Supremacy: America's Democratic Ideal and the Forging of Our National Identity*, by Donald Yacovone, *New York Review of Books*, September 22, 2022.

ican saga, a time of corruption and misgovernment caused by granting the right to vote to Black men. The violence perpetrated by the Ku Klux Klan, the books related, was an understandable response by white southerners to the horrors of "Negro rule." The heroes of this narrative were the self-styled white Redeemers who restored what they called "home rule" to the South, the villains northern abolitionists who irresponsibly set North against South, bringing on a needless civil war. Du Bois was well aware that what is said in history classrooms has an impact beyond the schoolhouse. The history of Reconstruction taught throughout the country "proved" that non-white peoples are incapable of intelligent self-government.

Now, nearly a century later, Donald Yacovone has published *Teaching White Supremacy*, which follows in Du Bois's footsteps by tracing what textbooks, over the course of our history, have said about slavery, abolitionism, the Civil War, Reconstruction, and race relations more generally. Yacovone examined hundreds of texts held in the library of Harvard's Graduate School of Education, dating from the early nineteenth century to the 1980s—a heroic effort that few historians are likely to wish to emulate. Some of the authors were well-known scholars. Most will be unfamiliar even to specialists in the history of education—writers such as John Bonner, Marcius Willson, and Egbert Guernsey.

From the beginning, Yacovone concludes, American education has served "the needs of white supremacy." Well into the twentieth century, he finds, most textbooks said little about slavery or portrayed it as a mild institution that helped lift "savage" Blacks into the realm of civilization. From generation to generation the books made no mention of Blacks' role in helping to shape the nation's development. They ignored Black participation in the crusade against slavery and the Civil War and portrayed Reconstruction as a disaster caused primarily by Black incapacity. Many of these textbooks were produced by the nation's leading publishing houses—Little, Brown; Scribner's; Harper and Brothers; Macmillan; and Yale and Oxford University presses, to name just a few.

For those who have studied the evolution of American historical writing, Yacovone's account will not be unfamiliar. It is well known that in the nineteenth century the concept of race, closely linked to pseudoscientific ideas about racial superiority and inferiority, was deeply embedded in American culture, including accounts of the nation's past, and that for much of the twentieth, white southerners, through the United Daughters of the Confederacy and other organizations, successfully pressured publishers to produce textbooks that glorified the Lost Cause and condoned the nullification of the constitutional rights of Black citizens. But there are surprises as well. Beginning in Reconstruction and stretching into the early twentieth century, a number of textbooks adopted an "emancipationist" interpretation of the Civil War and its aftermath—a term Yacovone borrows from David Blight's classic work *Race and Reunion*—and pushed back strongly against racism.

Yacovone begins his narrative before the American Revolution. Even then, the idea was widespread that North America is the natural home of people defined as "white." No less a personage than Benjamin Franklin suggested in 1751 that since the number of "purely white People" in the world was very small, Britain's North American colonies ought to exclude all "Blacks and Tawneys," among whom he included the "swarthy" peoples of Europe, such as Spaniards, Italians, and, in a surprising touch, Swedes. This outlook was written into law in 1790 in the first Naturalization Act, which limited the right to become citizens to "white" immigrants.

History, closely tied to ideas about race, became part of the nation-building project. Nineteenth-century historians such as George Bancroft explained that the new nation's destiny as what Jefferson called an "empire of liberty" arose from the innate characteristics of the Anglo-Saxon race, a construct whose definition depended on exclusion—of Blacks, Native Americans, and immigrants, especially Roman Catholics. History textbooks, Yacovone shows, reflected this equation of American identity with whiteness. American history was the story of British settlement and westward expansion. The indigenous population, often referred to as "savages," was little more than an obstacle to the fulfillment of the nation's world-historical destiny of dominating the continent. As for the Black presence, textbooks said almost nothing about it other than to suggest that the nation would be better off if, whether slave or free, the Black population was "colonized" in Africa. Since textbooks ignored slavery, pupils at midcentury must have been hard-pressed to explain contemporary events like the Missouri Controversy, the Compromise of 1850, and the rise of the Republican Party.

Only a handful of textbooks, including one by the Quaker writer Mary Bothan Howitt (published in 1860), condemned slavery or pointed out that it had existed in the North as well as the South. More typical was Emma Willard, a founder of Troy Female Seminary, in New York, who wrote several textbooks, which together sold more than one million copies. "Her popularity," Yacovone writes, "cannot be overstated." While she was a leader in the movement for women's education, Willard at the same time condemned the abolitionist and women's rights movements and considered Blacks an inferior species undeserving of "political equality." (The seminary did not admit a Black student until 1948.) In a preview of changes to come, however, as the Civil War approached, she condemned the Atlantic slave trade and declared slavery "an evil so vast in its consequences" that its peaceful eradication was all but impossible.

Yacovone provides the reader a litany of white supremacist quotations from prominent nineteenth-century writers including Ralph Waldo Emerson, Walt Whitman, and Henry Adams—a kind of greatest (or worst) hits of American racism. But he devotes the most attention—an entire chapter—to a racist author and propagandist few scholars have ever heard of, John H. Van Evrie. A prolific writer and publisher of fevered books, pamphlets, and newspapers (one entitled the *Weekly Caucasian*), Van Evrie was firmly devoted to the idea that the U.S. should be the white man's country.

Van Evrie's books included *White Supremacy and Negro Subordination* (1870; the work is still available from the Confederate Reprint Company), and he popularized the term "master race," which originated before the Civil War in the writings of pro-slavery ideologues.

Having trained as a physician, he was especially interested in publicizing the pseudoscience of race, arguing, among other things, that Blacks were a species distinct from whites. In Yacovone's view, Van Evrie was "the father of white supremacy." Whether he deserves this label is open to question, given how widespread in nineteenth-century cultural and intellectual life was the notion that mankind can be divided into distinct races, each with inborn capacities and characteristics, and that races exist on a hierarchy of innate ability, with whites at the top and Blacks at the bottom. In fact, Van Evrie's version of white supremacy was somewhat eccentric. He strongly defended slavery but refused to use the word, deeming it an inaccurate description of the Black condition. He opposed the colonization movement on the grounds that the economy could not survive without Black labor, and his notion of separate Black and white creations offended believers in the literal truth of the Bible, including in the South.

The Union's triumph in the Civil War and the abolition of slavery posed an immense challenge to traditional narratives of American history. Yacovone shows how textbook writers—some of them, like Thomas Wentworth Higginson, veterans of the abolitionist movement—embraced the Reconstruction ideal of equal citizenship regardless of race. Textbooks written in the 1870s, along with revised editions of pre-war works, now placed slavery at the center of the American story. They traced the conflict over slavery to the nation's beginnings and depicted the emergence of militant abolitionism as a turning point. Antislavery radicals such as William Lloyd Garrison, previously ignored or seen as dangerous fanatics, were now depicted as men and women of high moral principle. These books assimilated the end of slavery into the preexisting narrative of national progress, as a step toward fulfilling the American mission of being a beacon of liberty for mankind.

The postwar decades also witnessed the first textbooks aimed at a Black readership, designed to be used in southern schools established by the Freedmen's Bureau and the biracial Reconstruction governments. They emphasized Blacks' contributions to American history, particularly their service in the wartime Union army. *A School History of the Negro Race in America, from 1619 to 1890* (1891) by Edward A. Johnson, a lawyer and teacher born a slave, devoted an entire chapter to Frederick Douglass, whom pre-war textbooks had ignored. Most remarkable, perhaps, was *The Nation: The Foundations of Civil Order and Political Life in the United States*, published in 1870 by Elisha Mulford, a Yale graduate who later studied in Germany. (Yacovone states that Mulford—who was born in 1833—studied with Hegel himself, although the philosopher died in 1831.) Whether because of the advent of Reconstruction or not, Mulford explicitly repudiated the identification of the U.S. with white persons. The nation, he wrote, should rest on "the rights of man," not the "rights of a race," and should embrace all those who lived within its borders.

Yacovone chides previous scholars for jumping over these post–Civil War history textbooks. But, as he is well aware, a backlash eventually set in, with emancipationist works superseded by what David Blight called the "reconciliationist" account of the Civil War, which minimized the horrors of slavery and celebrated the Lost Cause. A combination of developments contributed to this marked regression in classroom education—the acquisition of an overseas empire in the Spanish-American War; the consolidation, with the North's acquiescence, of the Jim Crow system in the South; and the spread of racist ideologies including Social Darwinism and eugenics. Meanwhile, advocates of the Lost Cause pressed southern boards of education not to assign textbooks that portrayed the Old South in unflattering terms, and northern publishers revised their textbooks accordingly.

By the 1920s and for decades afterward, Yacovone writes, textbooks depicted slavery in ways "indistinguishable from the views of John C. Calhoun." Almost universally, they portrayed it as a benign institution, an idea reinforced by pictures of happy slaves dancing to banjo music on pre-war southern plantations. (Around 1950, my mother, a high school art teacher, marched into the office of my grade school principal to complain about such an image in my third-grade textbook. The principal replied, "What difference does it make what they are taught about

382 • OUR FRAGILE FREEDOMS

slavery?") A best-selling textbook, *The Growth of the American Republic* (1930) by Samuel Eliot Morison and Henry Steele Commager, two of the country's leading historians, declared that there was "much to be said for slavery as a transitional status between barbarism and civilization." Notoriously, the book's discussion of the overall impact of the institution on its victims began, "As for Sambo . . ." With slavery white-washed, so to speak, abolitionists were portrayed as a group of mentally disturbed malcontents.

White supremacy, often assumed rather than elaborated in nineteenth-century textbooks, now became explicit. Lothrop Stoddard, a leading eugenicist best known today as the author of *The Rising Tide of Color Against the White Race* and a proponent of the "replacement theory" so avidly promoted on Fox News today, also published a history textbook, *Re-Forging America* (1927). In it he confidently proclaimed, "Nothing is more certain than that the Fathers of the Republic intended America to be a 'white man's country.'" Thomas Maitland Marshall went even further. On the first page of his 1930 textbook *American History* he defined history: "the story of the white man."

The most successful textbook of the first half of the twentieth century was written by David Muzzey, a professor at Columbia University. It faithfully repeated the arguments of what came to be called the Dunning School—named for his Columbia colleague William A. Dunning—that condemned Reconstruction as a disaster brought about by granting Black men the right to vote. Muzzey's book was widely used into the 1960s. It was the textbook in my own high school history class, its outlook faithfully echoed by our teacher, Mrs. Bertha Berryman. If memory serves, the edition of Muzzey we used did not mention a single African American by name. The Dunning School and the textbooks that replicated its portrait of Reconstruction offered white students an easy explanation for Blacks' unequal status. They had been given a chance to progress during Reconstruction. They had abused the opportunity and could hardly complain if the more capable whites surpassed them in wealth and political power. It is not surprising, given what was being taught in American schools in the 1920s, that when Robert and Helen Lynd conducted research in Muncie, Indiana, for their book *Middletown*, they found that 70 percent of high school students agreed with the statement "The white race is the best race on earth."

In the 1930s and 1940s, Columbia's anthropology department was home to Ruth Benedict, Margaret Mead, and Franz Boas, whose writings demolished the idea that races have inborn, permanently fixed capabilities. But next door, scholars in the history and political science departments continued to disseminate white-supremacist narratives. Apart from Morison, Harvard comes out somewhat better. Unlike Dunning, Edward Channing and Albert Bushnell Hart were willing to train Black scholars, including Du Bois himself and Carter G. Woodson, founder in 1916 of the *Journal of Negro History*, where Black scholars began the laborious task of challenging prevailing accounts of slavery, the Civil War, and Reconstruction. Woodson's textbook *The Negro in Our History* (1922) was widely used in Black colleges but ignored in mainstream institutions. Hart rejected the pro-Confederate revision of Civil War history and praised Thaddeus Stevens and other Radical Republicans. Even he, however, echoed the Dunning account when it came to Reconstruction.

Yacovone deserves thanks for undertaking the task of reading through all these textbooks. Unfortunately, he does not really subject the idea of white supremacy, so crucial to his narrative, to careful examination. He fails to make clear what exactly it means, whom it benefits, and how it may have changed over time. Despite his having demonstrated otherwise in his account of "emancipationist" post–Civil War textbooks, too often white supremacy appears as a timeless set of beliefs and practices that defines the entire society. As a result, the distinction between slavery and freedom sometimes fades into the background. They become simply different manifestations of an ideology equally dominant in the North and South. Indeed, a number of times Yacovone asserts that racism was more extreme and more deeply rooted in the pre–Civil War North than the slave South, where, he claims, without elaborating, white supremacy had a "patchwork quality" and

384 • OUR FRAGILE FREEDOMS

Blacks enjoyed "more freedom" than in the "nominally" free states. Not only does this make it difficult to explain why the Civil War took place, but it ignores the fact that while Blacks in the antebellum North faced numerous forms of discrimination, unlike in the South they had white allies, whose struggles to improve their condition laid the foundation for the legislation and constitutional amendments of Reconstruction.

After the end of slavery, Yacovone claims, nothing about "white perceptions of Black inferiority" changed. Abolition, he writes, "only increased the North's desire to erect walls of racial segregation." This makes it hard to understand the spate of state laws enacted in the North in the 1880s banning racial discrimination in public accommodations. As an analytical tool, moreover, the idea of a timeless white supremacy ignores differences of power within white America. I once heard the great historian C. Vann Woodward offer the following gloss on the concept: "White supremacy means that some whites are supreme over all Blacks and over some other whites."

Focusing on a few pages in sprawling books, moreover, can obscure broader questions of interpretation. Writing a textbook is an exercise in selection. One cannot cover everything. What is included depends on the book's overall interpretive approach. Charles and Mary Beard, in a textbook written in the 1920s, pretty much ignored the abolitionist movement. This reflected not only racism, certainly present in their book, but also the "Beardian" understanding of history as a series of struggles between economic classes, with political ideologies essentially masks for economic self-interest. In this view, the Civil War was a struggle for national power between southern planters (whose status as an agrarian class the Beards believed more important than the system of labor they utilized) and the industrial bourgeoisie of the North. Scholars of the 1950s disparaged the abolitionists not only because of racism but as part of the then dominant "consensus" interpretation of the nation's history, which emphasized areas of broad agreement among Americans rather than moments of internal strife.

In the past two generations, historical scholarship on slavery, antislavery, and Reconstruction has undergone a profound transformation. Most historians today see slavery as fundamental to American economic and political development, the antislavery movement as an admirable part of American society, and Reconstruction as a flawed but idealistic effort to build an egalitarian society on the ashes of slavery. A host of new sources, many of them making available the perspective of African Americans, have appeared, in such venues as the Freedmen and Southern Society Project, the Black Abolitionist Papers, Freedmen's Bureau Records, and many others. Readers of *Teaching White Supremacy* are likely to wonder how fully these sources and new interpretations are reflected in current textbooks, yet Yacovone says next to nothing about those published in the past thirty or forty years, including textbooks in use today. This is a missed opportunity.

Lately, as is well known, the teaching of history has become—not for the first time—a terrain of conflict in the ongoing culture wars. Numerous states have enacted laws or regulations banning the teaching of "divisive concepts," with the histories of slavery and racism at the top of the list. Charges—almost entirely imaginary—proliferate that teachers are seeking to make white students feel guilty for our racial past and indoctrinate the young with critical race theory, an obscure methodology mostly encountered in law schools and graduate departments. In some states teachers are breaking the law if they talk seriously about racism. It is easy to scoff at these measures, which require (in the words of a North Dakota statute) that the teaching of history be "factual and objective" while at the same time forbidding mention of the idea that racism is "systemically embedded in American society." But they pose a serious threat to academic freedom. There have always been those who wish to impose Friedrich Nietzsche's "monumental" approach on the nation's classrooms.

Perhaps an equally significant problem with history education today is that there is simply not enough of it. In the past two decades, state after state, spurred by the growing emphasis on STEM subjects and the No Child Left Behind policy of linking school funding to test scores in English and mathematics, has significantly reduced how much history is taught at all levels of public education.

Neither the historical profession nor the publishing industry has fully acknowledged its decades-long complicity in disseminating the poisonous idea that Black Americans are unfit for participation in American democracy. Meanwhile, people are still teaching history, and many are teaching it well.

TWISTING HISTORY IN
TEXAS

T
HE CHANGES TO the social studies curriculum approved by
the conservative-dominated Texas Board of Education have
attracted attention mainly because of how they may affect textbooks used in other states. Since Texas certifies texts centrally rather
than by individual school districts, publishers have a strong incentive
to alter their books to conform to its standards so as to reach the huge
Texas market. Where was Lee Harvey Oswald, after all, when he shot
John F. Kennedy? In the Texas School Book Depository—a tall Dallas
building filled with textbooks.

Most comment on the content of the new standards has focused on
the mandate that high-school students learn about leading conservative
figures and institutions of the 1980s and '90s, specifically Phyllis Schla-
fly, the Moral Majority, the Heritage Foundation, the Contract with
America, and the National Rifle Association. In fact, of course, there is
nothing wrong with teaching about modern conservatism, a key force
in recent American history. My own textbook has a chapter called "The
Triumph of Conservatism" and discusses most of the individuals and
groups mentioned above.

The Nation, April 5, 2010.

More interesting is what the new standards tell us about conservatives' overall vision of American history and society, and how they hope to instill that vision in the young. The standards run from kindergarten through high school, and certain themes obsessively recur. Judging from the updated social studies curriculum, conservatives want students to come away from a Texas education with a favorable impression of women who adhere to traditional gender roles; the Confederacy; some parts of the Constitution; capitalism; the military, and religion. They do not think students should learn about women who demanded greater equality; other parts of the Constitution; slavery, Reconstruction, and the unequal treatment of non-whites generally; environmentalists; labor unions; federal economic regulation; or foreigners.

Here are a few examples. The board has removed mention of the Declaration of the Seneca Falls Convention, the letters of John and Abigail Adams, and suffrage advocate Carrie Chapman Catt. As examples of "good citizenship" for third graders, it deleted Harriet Tubman and included Clara Barton, founder of the Red Cross, and Helen Keller (the board seems to have slipped up here—Keller was a committed socialist). The role of religion—but not the separation of church and state—receives emphasis throughout. For example, religious revivals are now listed as one of the twelve major "events and eras" from colonial days to 1877.

The changes seek to reduce or elide discussion of slavery, mentioned mainly for its "impact" on different regions and the coming of the Civil War. A reference to the Atlantic slave trade is dropped in favor of "Triangular trade." Jefferson Davis's inaugural address as president of the Confederacy will now be studied alongside Abraham Lincoln's speeches.

In grade one, Veterans Day replaces Martin Luther King Jr. Day in the list of holidays students should be familiar with. (For later grades, "building a military" has been added as one of two results of the American Revolution—the other being the creation of the

United States—an odd inclusion, given the founders' fear of a standing army.) The Double-V Campaign during World War II (Black Americans' demand that victory over the Axis powers be accompanied by victory over segregation at home) has been omitted from the high school curriculum. Japanese-American internment is now juxtaposed with "the regulation of some foreign nationals," ignoring the fact that while a few Germans and Italians were imprisoned as enemy aliens, the vast majority of people of Japanese ancestry who were interned were U.S. citizens.

Students in several grades will be required to understand the "benefits" (but none of the drawbacks) of capitalism. The economic system, however, dares not speak its name—it is referred to throughout as "free enterprise." Labor unions are conspicuous by their absence. Mankind's impact on the environment is apparently entirely benign— the curriculum mentions dams for flood control and the benefits of transportation infrastructure but none of the problems arising from the exploitation of the natural environment. Lest anyone think that Americans should not fall below a rudimentary standard of living, the kindergarten curriculum deletes food, shelter, and clothing from its list of "basic human needs."

Americans, the board seems to suggest, do not need to take much notice of the rest of the world, or of non-citizens in this country. Kindergartners no longer have to learn about "people" who have contributed to American life, only about "patriots and good citizens." High school students must evaluate the pros and cons of U.S. participation in "international organizations and treaties." In an original twist, third-grade geography students no longer have to be able to identify on a map the Amazon, the Himalayas, or (as if it were in another country) Washington, D.C. Clearly, the Texas Board of Education seeks to inculcate children with a history that celebrates the achievements of our past while ignoring its shortcomings, and that largely ignores those Americans who have struggled to make this a more equal society.

I have lectured on a number of occasions to Texas precollegiate teachers and have found them as competent, dedicated, hospitable, and open-minded as the best teachers anywhere. But if they are required to adhere to the revised curriculum, the students of our second most populous state will emerge ill prepared for life in Texas, America, and the world in the twenty-first century.

DU BOIS

I T WAS IN 1960, at his home in Brooklyn, that I last saw W. E. B. Du Bois, a friend of my parents. My younger brother and I, then teenagers, were describing how, along with hundreds of other young people, we had been picketing a Woolworth's store in New York City to demonstrate solidarity with the sit-ins, then taking place in the South. After listening to our account, Du Bois, then 92, pointed to his wife, the writer Shirley Graham, and remarked with a knowing smile, "I wanted to demonstrate too, but Shirley wouldn't let me." Age had not dimmed his passion for political action or social change.

Scholar, poet, agitator, father of pan-Africanism, founder of the NAACP, pioneer of modern sociology and African American history, Du Bois lived one of the twentieth century's most remarkable and accomplished lives. Born in Great Barrington, Massachusetts, in 1868, he grew up as the promise of equality embodied in Reconstruction was replaced by a new system of racial injustice. He died in 1963, on the eve of the March on Washington. Along the way, he thought more pro-

---

Review of *W. E. B. Du Bois: The Fight for Equality and the American Century, 1919–1963*, by David Levering Lewis, *Journal of Blacks in Higher Education*, Winter 2000/2001.

foundly than any other American about strategies for combating racism at home and colonialism abroad, and about the meaning of Black identity in America.

This volume concludes David Levering Lewis's masterful and massive biography of Du Bois. Its predecessor, winner of the Pulitzer Prize, traced his life from rural Massachusetts through study at Fisk University, a Harvard doctorate, the controversy with Booker T. Washington that made Du Bois the spokesman for militant and educated Black Americans, and the founding of the Niagara Movement and NAACP, which rekindled the abolitionist struggle for equal citizenship. It ended with World War I, when Du Bois, to the dismay of some of his admirers, called upon Black Americans to "close ranks" in the hope that participation in the war to make the world safe for democracy would produce racial democracy at home.

In this second volume, Lewis's talents as a historian are again displayed—extensive research, an elegant and discursive style reminiscent of Du Bois himself, and the ability to offer brief and incisive sketches of the remarkable cast of characters with whom Du Bois crossed paths. Sometimes, to be sure, the detailed account of events great and small threatens to overwhelm the narrative and obscure Lewis's interpretative themes. But this biography will surely stand for many years as the finest effort to come to terms with the life and times of Du Bois.

The current volume opens with the Red Summer of 1919, when the tide of revolutionary change seemed to engulf large parts of the world while in the United States lynchings, race riots, and the repudiation of the promise of democracy as far as the world's colonial peoples were concerned sparked a bitter sense of betrayal among Black Americans. In 1919, Du Bois appeared to be at the peak of his influence. *The Crisis*, the NAACP monthly he edited, covering an amazing range of subjects regarding Black America—politics, ideas, economics, society, the arts—enjoyed a monthly circulation of 100,000. Du Bois's standing as an intellectual and agitator was so great that "most Negro Americans who read seriously or listened carefully" looked to him for inspiration.

In 1921, Du Bois, who long before talk of "global studies" always placed the plight of Black Americans in an international context, was the chief organizer of the second Pan-African Congress, whose resolutions demanded independence for Europe's colonies.

Lewis is at his best in detailing Du Bois's controversies in the 1920s with Marcus Garvey and the artists of the Harlem Renaissance. Garvey, Lewis points out, was far more capable than Du Bois of mobilizing the Black masses with his slogan of Africa for the Africans and his bombastic oratory and colorful spectacles. His followers were poorer and darker than the educated Blacks who gravitated to the NAACP. Du Bois always considered him a demagogue who, with his contempt for people of mixed race, was attempting to import into the United States the sharp color divisions of his native Jamaica (even though the close correlation between high status and light skin color in Black America was hardly a secret). Never one to opt for moderation in his writing, Du Bois called Garvey "the most dangerous enemy of the Negro race in America." Garvey responded in kind.

Du Bois also turned his pen against the Harlem Renaissance. He had hailed its advent but by 1926 had withdrawn *The Crisis* from its support. He began to see its focus on art and literature as an unacceptable substitute for politics (which was why, he felt, whites were so eager to patronize Renaissance artists). Claude McKay's novel, *Home to Harlem*, with its depiction of lower-class Black life awash in sex and violence, "nauseated" him. In 1928, Du Bois published his own example of what Black art should be, the novel *Dark Princess*, about a plot by non-whites to overthrow European colonialism. While the novel seems formulaic to the modern reader, Lewis offers high praise for its incorporation of carefully developed characters from India—a first in Black American writing—and its astute portrayal of Black politicians, restless Black youth, and ambitious self-seekers of all races.

Lewis's extended treatment of *Dark Princess* is typical of this volume. Du Bois was first and foremost a public intellectual (long before that term had come into vogue). Lewis deals in some detail with Du Bois's enormous body of writing—essays, novels, works of politics, sociology, and history. There is an excellent account of his collection of essays, *Darkwater* (1920), whose tone of "apocalyptic bitterness" and prediction of an impending "fight for freedom" against imperialism captured the mood of the moment. He praises *Black Folk Then and Now* (1939), an ambitious brief world history of Black people that devoted much attention to early African civilizations and the role of slavery and the slave trade in the development of the Western Hemisphere.

Most impressive is Lewis's lengthy discussion of Du Bois's monumental work *Black Reconstruction in America,* published in 1935. He offers an excellent analysis of the preparation and substance of a book that laid the groundwork for a revolution in American historical understanding. At the time Du Bois wrote, scholars in the field viewed the enfranchisement of Black men after the Civil War as a tragic mistake that had produced a sordid era of corruption and misgovernment. In eloquent, biting prose, Du Bois challenged this interpretation head-on. His views have been vindicated by modern scholarship. Blacks emerging from slavery, he insisted, were not passive victims of manipulation by whites but active agents in shaping the era's history. Slavery was the fundamental cause of the Civil War and the status of the former slaves the central issue of the postwar years. Reconstruction was an era of remarkable progress, laying the foundation for public education in the South and enacting much progressive social legislation. Its failure was a tragedy from which the nation had yet to recover.

Some of *Black Reconstruction*'s language—the "general strike" of slaves during the Civil War, the role of the "black proletariat" in creating the era's new southern governments—reflected Du Bois's newly developed interest in Marxism, catalyzed by the Depression. While always sympathetic to the ideals of socialism, Du Bois at first held that the Bolshevik revolution had little relevance for Black Americans. He never changed his view that the idea of uniting workers along class lines was a fanciful project in the United States, where white labor enjoyed the "wages of whiteness" (a term he used in *Black Reconstruction* to describe how whites benefitted economically from the racially segmented labor market and psychologically from their higher status than Black workers).

But the Depression persuaded Du Bois, who in 1900 had described "the color line" as the main problem of the twentieth century, to see class inequality as equally central. He began to read widely in the works of Marx, Engels, and Lenin, and during the 1930s struck out on a new political course, which, Lewis writes, combined "cultural nationalism, Scandinavian cooperativism, Booker Washington, and Marx in about equal parts." Persuaded that Black America faced economic disaster and that segregation would remain a fact of life for many years to come, Du Bois insisted that there was no alternative for his people other than to organize for economic survival, building as autonomous and cooperative an economy as they could within the segregated world. Having earlier called for the creation of a Talented Tenth of educated Blacks to provide racial leadership, he now acknowledged that their emergence could not by itself alleviate the plight of twelve million impoverished African Americans. Du Bois's apparent abandonment of the goal of racial integration led to a bitter struggle within the NAACP and his departure in 1934.

Lewis's treatment of the broader context of the 1930s—when the rise of a Popular Front culture stressing racial and ethnic pluralism as central to American democracy placed racial inequality on the national political agenda for the first time since Reconstruction—is not as satisfying as his account of the previous decade. But he deals effectively with the final period of Du Bois's life. "The role of the Communist Party in the life of twentieth-century America," he remarks in an ironic understatement, "has thus far not lent itself to disinterested, balanced interpretation." Reading current literature, one would assume that nearly every American communist was a spy of some sort or blindly took orders from Stalin. Lewis offers a more nuanced account of Du Bois's drift further and further to the left, and of its consequences in Cold War America.

Impressed by the Soviet Union's stance against imperialism in Asia and Africa and the role of communists in civil rights struggles at home,

Du Bois sharply criticized the Truman administration's Cold War policies, supported the candidacy of Henry Wallace in 1948, joined Paul Robeson at the Council on African Affairs (declared a "subversive" organization by the federal government), and became chair in 1950 of the Peace Information Center, which circulated the communist-inspired Stockholm Appeal against nuclear weapons. Thanks to McCarthy-era hysteria, alliances and associations quite uncontroversial during the 1930s and World War II took on sinister implications. In 1951, at the age of 82, Du Bois was tried as an unregistered foreign agent, a charge so absurd that even at the height of the Cold War it was dismissed by the judge.

The role of Black organizations and leaders in this era is not a happy tale. Much of the Talented Tenth that he had helped to summon into being ran for cover or kept "a safe distance" from Du Bois. Invitations to speak at Black colleges were canceled, guests failed to appear at birthday celebrations. For several years, his passport was suspended. Charged with failing to uphold American democracy against Soviet tyranny, Du Bois—like Robeson—learned that this country had its own secret police, internal exiles, travel restrictions, and persons written out of history. "The colored children," he lamented, "ceased to hear my name."

As old friends peeled away, Du Bois became closer and closer to those in the communist orbit, especially Herbert Aptheker, his comrade and literary executor, without whose indefatigable work in collecting and republishing Du Bois's voluminous writings this biography would have been almost impossible (as Lewis graciously acknowledges). Eventually, Du Bois joined the party himself in 1961 and immediately departed for Ghana, where he became a citizen. He died there in 1963 even as hundreds of thousands of Americans gathered at the Lincoln Memorial in the cause of racial justice that he, more than any other individual, had symbolized and promoted.

Although this is almost exclusively a public biography, Lewis does delve on occasion into Du Bois's private life. He is straightforward—neither moralistic nor sensationalist in the manner of certain treatments of Martin Luther King Jr.—about Du Bois's numerous extramarital affairs. He certainly makes clear that Du Bois treated his long-suffering first wife Nina cavalierly and that he was not above exploiting young women's fascination with his intellect and notoriety. Yet the roots of Du Bois's behavior, the "deep-seated emotional incompleteness" that led him to pursue women with "the compulsiveness of a Casanova" is never really made clear.

If one theme unites these two volumes it is how "the race problem" shaped both Du Bois's life and America itself. Among Lewis's signal accomplishments is his refusal to paper over the extent of racism in American life. He makes clear that the disenfranchisement of millions of southern Black voters made a mockery of claims that ours was a democracy. The book is filled with poignant instances revealing how educated Black men and women found avenues for advancement, even modest jobs like teachers, librarians, or clerks in government offices, blocked at every turn. Du Bois knew all too well how white decision-makers had a veto on Black aspirations. Funding for his beloved plan for an Encyclopedia of the Negro was rejected by the Rockefeller Family's General Education Board. When the Carnegie Corporation decided that a comprehensive study of race was desirable it enlisted Gunnar Myrdal, on the grounds that only a white scholar could approach the subject in an "objective and dispassionate" way.

RAYFORD LOGAN

THIS 1997 REISSUE of *The Betrayal of the Negro from Hayes to Wilson*, a classic work of American history by Rayford Logan, provides an opportune moment to reflect on the life of one of the twentieth century's most accomplished Black scholars, and the reasons for his book's enduring significance.

Born in Washington, D.C., in 1897, Logan grew up in a poor family, far removed from the city's Black elite. The family, however, acquired social status, if not an adequate income, from his father's job as butler in the home of Frederick C. Walcott, a U.S. senator from Connecticut. Logan attended M Street (later Dunbar) High School, the most prestigious public school for Blacks in the city, whose rigorous curriculum required students to master the sciences as well as Latin and Greek. He went on to study at Williams College, graduating in 1917.

Logan soon joined the United States Army and served in France, rising to the rank of first lieutenant. He had already encountered racism in segregated Washington and at Williams, where he was barred from fraternities and eating clubs, but the racism pervasive in the army, cou-

Preface to the 1997 edition of *The Betrayal of the Negro: From Rutherford B. Hayes to Woodrow Wilson*, by Rayford W. Logan.

pled with the failure of the victorious allies to extend the principle of self-determination to colonial peoples in Africa and Asia, seems to have radicalized him. Logan soon became a pan-African activist. While he did not attend the Pan-African Congress that met in Paris in February 1919, he was elected to its permanent bureau. Like W. E. B. Du Bois, with whom he developed a lifelong acquaintance while in Paris, Logan combined the roles of activist and scholar. He remained involved in the struggle for African independence for the next four decades, and in the late 1940s would become the NAACP's principal adviser on international affairs.

After remaining in France until 1924, Logan returned to the United States. He obtained a teaching job at Virginia Union University, a Black institution in Richmond, only to be fired in 1931 for demanding that the white president be replaced by a Black one. He went on to work for Carter G. Woodson at the Association for the Study of Negro Life and History, and to teach at Atlanta University from 1933 to 1938, meanwhile earning a PhD at Harvard. His dissertation, subsequently published as a book, chronicled relations between Haiti and the United States and was a pioneering investigation of the interconnections of race and diplomacy. In 1938, Logan left Atlanta to teach at Howard University, where he remained until his retirement in 1974. Here, Logan took his place among a remarkable group of talented Black scholars, among them Alain Locke, Eric Williams, John Hope Franklin, Sterling Brown, E. Franklin Frazier, Ralph Bunche, and Charles Hamilton Houston.

Already known, in the words of the Chicago *Defender*, as a "bad Negro with a Ph.D." because of his involvement in a voter registration drive in depression-era Atlanta, Logan during World War II stood at the forefront of those Black persons directly challenging the nation's system of racial subordination. He worked closely with A. Philip Randolph in planning the 1941 March on Washington, which was called off when President Roosevelt ordered an end to job discrimination in defense industries. In 1944, he edited the pioneering volume *What the Negro Wants*, a collection of militant essays by Du Bois, Randolph, and others demanding full equality and the immediate dismantling of segregation. William T. Crouch, the liberal-minded white editor at the University of North Carolina Press, was so shocked by the book's uncompromising radicalism that he first tried to suppress it (only to be dissuaded by Logan's threat of a lawsuit) and then felt obliged to write a preface disavowing its arguments.

After the war, while continuing his political involvement, Logan began work on a study of the nation's retreat from the Reconstruction era's promise of equal citizenship. He completed the study in 1952 and, oddly enough, submitted it to North Carolina, with which he had such difficulty eight years earlier. But the manuscript was rejected. Dial, a British publisher, agreed to take up the project, but Logan was required to subsidize publication to the tune of $5,000, a not-insubstantial sum in those days. The book appeared in 1954, under the title *The Negro in American Life and Thought, The Nadir: 1877–1901*.

Logan was not the first to challenge prevailing interpretations of the end of Reconstruction and the road to reunion in late-nineteenth-century America. Three years before Logan's book appeared, C. Vann Woodward's magisterial *Origins of the New South* had shattered the smug portrait of the post-Reconstruction South as a time of progressive social change, instead depicting the region as a colonial economy replete with racial and class inequalities. Logan, however, was the first scholar to delineate in devastating detail the political, economic, and cultural story of the retreat from equality, and to provide an overall framework that still helps to guide interpretations of the era.

As far as Black Americans were concerned, Logan argued, the road to reunion was a story not of national reconciliation but of betrayal, and its human costs were "massive and . . . ugly." In the new edifice of national unity, he went on, "on the pediments of the separate wing reserved for Negroes were carved Exploitation, Disfranchisement, Segregation, Discrimination, Lynching, Contempt." But the book's power lay not so much in Logan's sense of indignation, but in the encyclopedic research that enabled him to relate in authoritative fashion the narrative of national betrayal. Looking back forty years after its publication, what remains impressive is the comprehensiveness of Logan's research and argument, and the deconstruction, as it were, of the idea of "reunion" after the Civil War to reveal its victims as well as its beneficiaries.

The book begins with a survey of the racial policies of presidents from Hayes to McKinley, demonstrating how, one after another, they turned a blind eye to the abrogation of the Fourteenth and Fifteenth Amendments by the white South. It moves on to sketch the Supreme Court's retreat from the Reconstruction ideal of racial equality, examining well-known decisions from *Slaughterhouse* to *Plessy v. Ferguson*, as well as more obscure cases involving voting rights and other issues. Logan also discussed the second-class economic citizenship that resulted from the failure of land reform during Reconstruction, and job discrimination practiced by employers and unions alike.

This first section of the book was remarkable for the scope of its approach, its synthesis of the economic and political manifestations of racial subordination. But where Logan really broke new ground was in the second part, a comprehensive analysis of the images of Blacks in newspapers, magazines, popular literature, and other cultural forums. This survey offered a devastating account of the resurgence of racism, North as well as South, in the late nineteenth century. Black people were persistently stereotyped as criminals, savages, or comic figures. They were superstitious, lazy, violent, immoral, the butt of humor, and the source of danger to civilized life. In the relentless purveying of racist iconography and literary images, in distortions of Black history and indifference to lynching, race riots, and disenfranchisement, popular culture in effect legitimated and "naturalized" the system of political and economic inequality described in the book's opening chapters.

By the end of the century, as the United States assumed the white man's burden in the Spanish-American War, racism was supreme throughout the country. This was the "nadir" of the Black experience in America, Logan wrote—an arresting idea given that slavery is usually considered the low point of African American history. Moreover, as

Logan noted sardonically, historians had completely ignored this story. The twentieth century's major works of intellectual history—Merle Curti's *The Growth of American Thought*, Henry Steele Commager's *The American Mind*, Paul Buck's *The Road to Reunion*—said nothing, Logan noted, about "the portrayal of the Negro in American mind and thought." Excluded from the rights of citizens, Blacks had been erased from the narrative of American history.

Appearing shortly before the Supreme Court outlawed racial segregation in public education, *The Negro in American Life and Thought* received a respectful reception from historical journals. In the *Mississippi Valley Historical Review*, George Tindall praised it as "an important study in the history of American society and ideas." Ulysses Lee, in the *American Historical Review*, however, criticized Logan for relying overwhelmingly on white sources. "Thought," Lee complained, seemed to mean what whites said about blacks—a fair criticism even though Logan had devoted some attention to the Black press and Black historians like George Washington Williams. Unlike subsequent scholars of Black history, Logan was more concerned to expose the depths of racism than to explore how African Americans responded to inequality. Only at the very end of the book, in a brief discussion of the rise of opposition among educated and professional Blacks around the turn of the century, did he devote attention to what he called "the roots of recovery."

Despite the generally positive reaction, the market for Black history was still in its infancy in 1954, and *The Negro in American Life and Thought* soon went out of print. Eleven years later, it was reissued in a second edition, under the new title, *The Betrayal of the Negro*. Logan now added a brief third section, taking his story down to World War I, incorporating new details but in no way altering the original story of political inequality and racist stereotypes. Nineteen sixty-five was the height of the civil rights movement. Federal laws had just outlawed discrimination in public accommodations and restored the right to vote to Black southerners. With race commanding center stage of national politics, *The Betrayal of the Negro* won a much larger audience than in its first edition, going through five additional printings before finally going out of print in 1970.

Logan retired from Howard in 1974 and died eight years later. At the end of his 1965 edition, he had written, "we American Negroes have edged forward since the end of 1953." This was a surprisingly cautious comment given the scope of changes in race relations that had swept over the country. Perhaps the depths of racism his book exposed caused Logan to doubt the permanency of the civil rights revolution. But surely, Logan could not have foreseen the resurgence, in the years following his death, of many of the same ideas that had dominated American culture at the end of the nineteenth century.

Today, legal segregation has been dismantled and many areas of our society, from workplaces to universities, are far more integrated than was conceivable a few decades ago. But in the enduring legacy of decades of discriminatory actions by federal and state authorities, private employers, realtors, educators, and a host of others, the pattern of inequality Logan explored lives on. Indeed, there are ominous parallels between the time of which Logan was writing, and our own.

The late nineteenth century was an era when Social Darwinism and the idea of racial superiority dominated intellectual discourse. Speaking for the Supreme Court in *Plessy v. Ferguson*, Justice Henry B. Brown declared that "racial instincts" were inherent in human nature and unreachable by law, and termed whites the "dominant race," statements eerily reminiscent of current arguments that races occupy a fixed position on the I.Q. scale, that whites are "civilizationally" if not genetically superior to Blacks, and that the country should preserve its racial character by limiting non-white immigration.

As in the late nineteenth century, we have witnessed a slow, steady repudiation by the Supreme Court of aggressive enforcement of civil rights laws and a narrowing of the definition of racial equality. Ironically, Justice Harlan's famous statement, "our Constitution is color-blind," hurled at the Court's *Plessy* majority as a challenge to a system of second-class citizenship mandated by law, has today been appropriated by those who oppose taking race into account under any circumstances in the effort to remedy the lingering effects of past injustice.

All this, one suspects, would not have surprised Rayford Logan. The legacy of the institutional and cultural racism of over one hundred years ago, described in such compelling detail in *The Betrayal of the Negro*, continues to haunt our troubled society.

VANN WOODWARD

D URING THE 1950S and 1960s, a generation of scholars rose to prominence in the United States with books and essays that breached the wall separating the academy and the broader public. Many were historians, including Daniel Boorstin, Richard Hofstadter, and Arthur Schlesinger Jr. Invocations of history punctuated debates over the Cold War, civil rights, and Vietnam. But none of these storied "public intellectuals" reached a larger audience or had a greater social and political impact than C. Vann Woodward, whose books and essays elucidated the nation's most enduring problem, racial inequality. Historians are frequently warned to avoid "presentism," but Woodward demonstrated that history can powerfully illuminate the world in which the scholar lives. Readers who sought to understand the civil rights revolution that dismantled the southern racial system known as Jim Crow turned to Woodward's writings. By the time he died in 1999, many of Woodward's historical findings had been challenged by younger historians, and he himself had become disaffected with trends in both the writing of history and the struggle

Review of *C. Vann Woodward: America's Historian*, by James Cobb, *London Review of Books*, October 20, 2022.

for racial justice. Yet he was widely considered, to borrow the subtitle of James Cobb's new biography, *America's Historian.*

Most historians are not very introspective and lead uneventful lives, making things difficult for the aspiring biographer. Understandably, Cobb, a historian at the University of Georgia, focuses almost entirely on Woodward's intellectual and political career. Drawing on his subject's writings and his voluminous papers at Yale, where Woodward taught from 1961 to 1977, Cobb paints a compelling portrait of a scholar impatient with the mythologies, distortions, and misguided hero worship that for most of the twentieth century inhibited candid discussion of the South's many problems.

Born in 1908 in Vanndale, a small town in Arkansas that serviced the area's cotton economy, Comer Vann Woodward was a member of a prominent local family (his birthplace bore his mother's family name). Very early, Woodward came to understand that the Jim Crow system, built on the disenfranchisement of Black voters, racial segregation, lynching, and a biased criminal justice system, made a travesty of the nation's supposed commitment to equality and democracy. Where did his rebellious outlook originate? Cobb credits the influence of his uncle and namesake Comer, who was not afraid to denounce the local Ku Klux Klan. There were other influences as well. During a year (1931–32) working on a master's degree at Columbia University, Woodward met Langston Hughes, W. E. B. Du Bois, and other African American writers and activists. In the summer of 1932, Woodward traveled to Europe; his itinerary included a visit to the Soviet Union. On his return he became involved in the defense of Angelo Herndon, a Black communist convicted of violating Georgia's nineteenth-century "insurrection" law by organizing Black and white factory workers. The Herndon case became an international cause célèbre and led to a Supreme Court ruling invalidating the statute as a violation of freedom of speech. (Woodward's experience working with communists did not escape the notice of the FBI. In 1951 he was denied security clearance for an appointment as historical advisor to the Joint Chiefs of Staff.) In the summer of 1935, Woodward came face to face with the dire poverty of tenant farmers, white and Black, while working for a New Deal agency surveying social conditions in rural Georgia.

Like any complex social system, Jim Crow required an ideological foundation. Historians, united, Woodward later wrote, in their "dedication to the present order," helped to provide it. By the 1930s, a distinctive account of history had become an orthodoxy among white southerners, endlessly reiterated in textbooks, classrooms, and public monuments. It rested on several axioms: Slavery had been a benign institution; the Confederacy a glorious Lost Cause; Reconstruction a time of misgovernment and corruption; the self-styled Redeemers who rescued the South from the supposed horrors of "Negro rule" by overthrowing Reconstruction the inheritors of the values of the Old South. A New South was emerging, historians insisted, and with it the promise of widespread prosperity. This dogma held sway even at the University of North Carolina, a center of southern liberalism, where Woodward earned his doctorate. In 1935 he wrote to a friend that he had "not gleaned a single scholarly idea from any professor." That year, however, Howard K. Beale arrived from the North and became Woodward's mentor.

Beale was a disciple of the historian Charles Beard, who taught that political ideologies were legitimations for economic interests. Beale had recently published *The Critical Year*, in which he followed Beard in viewing the Civil War not as a struggle over slavery but as a Second American Revolution that transferred political power from southern planters to northern industrialists. The era's Radical Republicans were less interested in the rights of the former slaves than in using Black votes to help fasten northern economic control on the defeated South. For the rest of his career, Woodward remained something of a Beardian. In the acknowledgments to one of his books, Woodward paid tribute to Beard as the "dean of historians."

Woodward received his doctorate in 1937. Over the next two decades he produced four books that established him as one of the most influential historical voices of his generation: *Tom Watson: Agrarian Rebel* (1938), a slightly revised version of his dissertation; *Reunion and Reaction* (1951), in which he argued in good Beardian fashion that railroad magnates were the key architects of the "bargain" that resolved the disputed election of 1876 and ended Reconstruction; *Origins of the New South* (1951), an all-out critique of the political and social order created by the Redeemers; and *The Strange Career of Jim Crow* (1955), an examination of the origins of segregation. These books demolished every important feature of the orthodox historical credo. The revered Redeemers were not the direct descendants of Old South planters but a new class of business-oriented merchants and industrialists, closely linked to the North. The state regimes they headed were as guilty of corruption as they claimed southern governments had been during Reconstruction. Contrary to received wisdom, the New South was a "stunted neocolonial economy" whose sharecropping and credit systems consigned Black and white tenant farmers alike to peonage. Even though some of Woodward's arguments inspired spirited rebuttal, these books established the agenda for generations of historians of the nineteenth-century South.

This was presentism in the service of radical social change. Woodward hoped to discredit the existing southern ruling class by exposing the "ethical bankruptcy" of the Redeemers, from whom they claimed descent. Moreover, history, he insisted, offered home-grown alternatives to Jim Crow. In his biography of Tom Watson, Woodward traced the transformation of that leader of the People's Party, or Populists, from an advocate of political and economic cooperation among Black and white small farmers to a vicious racist, the only possible route to electoral success once the region's elite had eliminated Black voting rights. In the early 1890s, Watson brought to mixed-race audiences the message that small farmers of both races shared the same economic interests and should unite in common cause. For decades, Woodward would defend the historical reputation of the People's Party, especially against the criticism of his friend Richard Hofstadter, who argued that the insurgent farmers exemplified how Americans suffering from economic decline frequently turned to conspiracy theories and cultural hatreds to understand their plight. To be sure, Woodward would later yield to critics who insisted that he had exaggerated the extent and sincerity of white Populists' appeal for Black support. "It was a book *for* the 1930s and *of* the 1930s," he explained. Today, when the Populist label is commonly used as a term of abuse, promiscuously applied to figures who share nothing in common, such as Donald Trump and Bernie Sanders, it remains striking how long Woodward insisted that far from exemplifying what Hofstadter called the "paranoid style" of American politics, the People's Party had advanced "one of the most thoroughgoing critiques of corporate America and its culture we have had."

A different road not taken was central to Woodward's argument in *The Strange Career of Jim Crow*. The timing could not have been better for this brief, lucid book that appeared not long after the Supreme Court handed down its decision in *Brown v. Board of Education* outlawing racial segregation in public schools. Today, with Brown widely viewed as the Court's most important ruling of the twentieth century, it is easy to forget how quickly the South's white leadership launched a campaign of "massive resistance" in order to preserve Jim Crow, and how many national leaders, including Adlai Stevenson, the Democratic candidate for president in 1952 and 1956, and president Dwight D. Eisenhower himself, bought into southern arguments that segregation had existed from time immemorial and would prove impossible to uproot. Woodward presented a counter-history, a usable past for the burgeoning civil rights movement.

Segregation, Woodward insisted, was a recent invention, not a timeless feature of southern life. It had not existed in the Old South (it would make little sense to try to separate the races under slavery) and was not immediately implemented after the Civil War. In fact, it was not enshrined in law until the 1890s. Before then, indeterminacy defined southern race relations. Black and white riders mingled in railroad cars and sat next to one another in restaurants, theaters, and other places of public accommodation. Why could they not do so again? The book's powerful influence, wrote the Black sociologist E. Franklin Frazier, stemmed from its present-day message: "The race problem was *made* and . . . men can *unmake* it." Ironically, this optimistic history lesson persisted even after other historians called into question important parts of Woodward's account. In revised editions of the book that appeared in 1965 and 1974 Woodward acknowledged that segregation had a longer history than he had allowed. It was already present in the pre–Civil War North, and Woodward kept pushing the date of its emergence in the South back in time, acknowledging that segregation had existed as a social reality well before being codified in law.

Woodward did not rely solely on scholarship to "unmake" the racism so deeply embedded in the academy and society at large. He worked to eradicate it within the Southern Historical Association (SHA). Cobb's account of Woodward's campaign to desegregate the group's annual meetings would be hilarious if it did not offer a reminder of the daily humiliations Black Americans experienced under Jim Crow. State law and local custom forbade venues that hosted such events from allowing Black participants to eat with white attendees or lodge in the same hotel. The 1949 meeting was held at the College of William and Mary in Virginia. Woodward arranged for John Hope Franklin, a Black historian who had just published *From Slavery to Freedom*, a pioneering survey of African American history, to deliver a paper. But where would Franklin stay and eat? At one point, Woodward facetiously suggested that Franklin bring along a "pup tent and k-rations." What if he needed to utilize a restroom? Franklin could hardly be expected to use the same primitive toilet facilities as were set aside for the College's waiters, gardeners, and other Black employees. The distinguished historian Carl Bridenbaugh offered to give Franklin a key to his own house for use when he needed to relieve himself. Franklin's participation in the meeting took place without incident. The SHA, however, quickly reverted to meeting in places where Black historians could not attend functions alongside whites. It comes as a shock to read that not until 1962 did the SHA's executive committee resolve that the organization would meet only in venues where Black and white participants were treated identically.

Strange Career marked the end of Woodward's own career as a research-based historian. His subsequent books consisted largely of previously published essays. Some of his best-known pieces tackled the fraught question of southern identity. He pointed to the irony that even as the Cold War intensified claims about American exceptionalism, the South in fact shared key historical experiences—military defeat, widespread poverty, colonial exploitation—with many other countries. The rest of the nation, he suggested, might learn something from historians of the South, including humility.

In this later phase of his career, Woodward acted as a kind of gatekeeper, using his connections and reputation to promote the advancement, via jobs, fellowships, and book reviews, of his former graduate students. Many of them, including Barbara J. Fields, James M. McPherson, Louis Harlan, and Steven Hahn, would go on to celebrated careers of their own. Most studied the nineteenth-century South; as a result, the Festscrift they produced for Woodward in 1982 has a coherence such books usually lack. To be sure, like many other "star" professors, Woodward was frequently on leave, seeking, Cobb writes, to "minimize time spent in the classroom." But he devoted time to reading and evaluating manuscripts not only for friends and students but also for historians with whom he had no personal connection. Woodward sometimes bent commonly accepted rules, writing reviews of books that originated in dissertations he himself had supervised, and suggesting to editors the names of writers, including his students, to review his own works. Cobb's account reminds us of the small size and homogeneity of the interconnected worlds of publishing, reviewing, and college teaching before the expansion of higher education in the 1960s and the advent of significant numbers of women and members of minority groups. A few prestigious journals published the same writers over and over again. Cobb counts more than 250 book reviews written by Woodward himself during the course of his career, including 50 in the *New York Review of Books* and 21 in *The New York Times*.

All this extra-curricular activity helps explain why Woodward never wrote his long-planned and eagerly awaited general history of Reconstruction. Judging from evidence in his papers, he seemed genuinely uncertain how such a book should be organized, whether he should directly engage what he called "the century-old debate" on the era, and if he should include comparison with other societies that experienced the end of slavery (a subject whose study he pioneered). As Woodward mulled over such questions, the history of Reconstruction was being rewritten, in part by his students. The old image of the period, trotted out whenever an argument was needed for why Black people should not have the right to vote, was superseded. While hardly unaware of the era's failings, younger scholars were broadly sympathetic to the impulse to remake the South after the Civil War. Abolitionists and Radical Republicans, whose professions of concern for the rights of the freed people Woodward had long viewed skeptically, were now being lionized as principled crusaders for justice. Woodward was put off by northerners who, wielding "legends of emancipation," lectured the South about its failings. Charles Sumner, among the most principled of the Radical egalitarians, Woodward wrote in 1945 in a letter to the historian William J. Carleton, "nauseates me." Woodward believed the post–Civil War northern commitment to racial equality had been weak and short-lived and that Reconstruction failed as much because of persistent northern racism as rampant southern violence.

Beginning in the 1960s, new scholarship was placing the former slaves—their aspirations, activism, and understanding of freedom—at the center of the Reconstruction story. In previous works Woodward had primarily portrayed Blacks as victims, not active historical agents, and he did not probe very deeply the shifting tides of grassroots Black leadership, which would now be a necessary part of any general history of Reconstruction. He understood why Reconstruction appealed to a new generation, but cautioned against viewing the era "as if it was in some ways a sort of Golden Age." All in all, Woodward felt uncomfortable with the directions in which the field was moving. One suspects that he was not interested in engaging in a debate with the authors of the new historiography, many of whom he had taught.

As he approached retirement, Woodward entered what one former student called his "Tory period." He found himself taking positions that surprised, even shocked, many of his admirers. While admitting that he was "embarrassed" to say so, he opposed a plan to admit women as fellows in one of Yale's colleges. To be sure, Woodward did nothing to hide his distaste for the administrations of Lyndon B. Johnson and Richard Nixon. He lent his name to public statements protesting the Vietnam War and organized a group of historians who prepared a report for the House impeachment committee on abuses of presidential power in U.S. history. Turning down an invitation to contribute to a book of essays celebrating the bicentennial of American independence in 1976, he replied, "I am, in fact, beginning to wonder what there is to celebrate."

Perhaps the most controversial moment in this phase of his career came in the mid-1970s, when Woodward orchestrated a campaign to prevent Herbert Aptheker from teaching a seminar on the life of W. E. B. Du Bois at a Yale college. The university allowed colleges, with the approval of an academic department, to offer classes taught by persons without an academic position but with other kinds of expertise. Aptheker's *Documentary History of the Negro People* was an indispensable work used in courses throughout the country. His *American Negro Slave Revolts* was the only scholarly book on that subject. He had written important journal articles on Black abolitionism and on Reconstruction, and was editor of a projected collection of Du Bois's correspondence. He was also a leading member of the American Communist Party. As such he had been blacklisted for decades by the academy. Woodward was an ardent foe of McCarthyism. In 1966, he had taken part in a panel at the Socialist Scholars Conference along with Aptheker and the Marxist historian of slavery Eugene D. Genovese. At a time when the shadow of McCarthyism still hung over the academic world, for a scholar of Woodward's standing to appear alongside Aptheker was a powerful statement that the latter was part of the fraternity of historians. It was not unlike when movie studios a few years earlier had given screen credit to Dalton Trumbo for writing the films *Exodus* and *Spartacus*, marking the beginning of the end of the Hollywood blacklist. But the Aptheker affair did not work out that way.

Woodward mobilized opposition to the proposed seminar. Aptheker's work, he insisted, was not up to Yale's standards. At his behest, the History Department declined to sponsor the course. But the Political Science Department voted to do so. Woodward brought his case to the faculty committee that approved such classes (normally a formality), which at first rejected the course and subsequently approved it. The dispute dragged on for years; in the end Aptheker did teach his seminar on Du Bois, twice. The students suffered no known adverse consequences. But Woodward's reputation for open-mindedness received a serious blow, especially among the rising generation of historians.

Aptheker was white, but Woodward's crusade against the proposed course dovetailed with his growing distaste for the shift in focus of the civil rights struggle from integration to calls for Black Power and its corollary on campus, demands for the establishment of Black Studies programs. He lashed out against multiculturalism, as well as militant students' insistence that Black professors teach the new courses on Black history. Often, as the Black historian Sterling Stuckey pointed out, Woodward seemed to conflate students' heated rhetoric with the scholarship, often outstanding, being produced in these programs. Elected president of the Organization of American Historians in 1969, Woodward devoted his presidential address to criticism of Black Studies. Coming less than a year after the assassination of Martin Luther King Jr., the title of his lecture, "Clio with Soul," seemed condescending to Black historians. He warned white scholars against aligning with this "fashionable cause," and advised the "Brother in Black" not to embrace "a mystique of skin color" or to elevate "deservedly neglected figures" such as African kings and ghetto hustlers to the status of heroes. His insinuation that universities were employing Black scholars solely on the basis of their race cost him his long friendship with John Hope Franklin, who had been hired a few years earlier by the University of Chicago.

Woodward died in 1999, hailed inside and outside the academy for his pioneering scholarship and "moral leadership" in a profession that for most of the twentieth century sorely needed it. Historical interests, of course, change over time. Today, Woodward's books, even *Strange Career*, are not widely assigned in college classes. This is unfortunate not only because of the enduring quality of his writing, but because, despite his "Tory" turn toward the end of his life, they offer an inspiring example of engaged scholarship. At his best, Woodward's work demonstrated that history enables us to pass judgment on the world around us. He employed his historical imagination to help bring down the towering edifice of Jim Crow. That is an accomplishment of which any historian would be proud.

HOFSTADTER

O VER HALF A century has now elapsed since the untimely death of Richard Hofstadter. Despite the sweeping transformation of historical scholarship during these years, his writings continue to exert a powerful influence on how scholars and general readers alike understand the American past. Since his death, the study of political ideas—the recurring theme of Hofstadter's work—has to a considerable extent been eclipsed by the histories of family life, race relations, popular culture, and a host of other social concerns. The writings of many of his contemporaries are now all but forgotten. Yet because of his penetrating intellect and sparkling literary style, Hofstadter still commands the attention of anyone who wishes to think seriously about the American past. The 1992 reissue of his first book, *Social Darwinism in American Thought*, provides an opportune moment to consider the circumstances of its composition and the reasons for its enduring influence.

Richard Hofstadter was born in 1916 in Buffalo, New York, the son of a Jewish father and a mother of German Lutheran descent. After graduating from high school in 1933, he entered the University of Buffalo,

———

Preface to the 1992 edition of *Social Darwinism in American Thought,* by Richard Hofstadter.

where he majored in philosophy and minored in history. As for so many others of his generation, Hofstadter's formative intellectual and political experience was the Great Depression. Buffalo, a major industrial center, was particularly hard hit by unemployment and social dislocation. The Depression, he later recalled, "started me thinking about the world. . . . It was as clear as day that something had to change. . . . You had to decide, in the first instance, whether you were a Marxist or an American liberal." At the university, Hofstadter gravitated toward a group of left-wing students, including the brilliant and "sometimes overpowering" (as Alfred Kazin later described her) Felice Swados, read Marx and Lenin, and joined the Young Communist League.

In 1936, on the eve of his graduation, Hofstadter and Felice were married and subsequently moved to New York City. Felice first worked for the National Maritime Union and International Ladies' Garment Workers Union and then took a job as a copy editor at *Time*, while Hofstadter enrolled in the graduate history program at Columbia University. Both became part of New York's broad radical political culture that centered on the Communist Party in the era of the Popular Front. Hofstadter would later describe himself (with some exaggeration) as "by temperament quite conservative and timid and acquiescent," and it seems that the dynamic Felice, a committed political activist, animated their engagement with radicalism. Nonetheless, politics for Hofstadter was much more than a passing fancy; he identified himself as a Marxist and in apartment discussions and in his correspondence with Felice's brother Harvey Swados, took part in the doctrinal debates between Communists, Trotskyists, Schachtmanites, and others that flourished in the world of New York's radical intelligentsia.

In 1938, Hofstadter joined the Communist Party's unit at Columbia. The decision, taken with some reluctance (he had already startled some of his friends by concluding that the Moscow purge trials were "phony"), reflected a craving for decisive action after "the hours I have spent jawing about the thing." As he explained to his brother-in-law: "I join without enthusiasm but with a sense of obligation. . . . My fundamental reason for joining is that I don't like capitalism and want to get rid of it. I am tired of talking. . . . The party is making a very profound contribution to the radicalization of the American people. . . . I prefer to go along with it now."

Hofstadter, however, did not prove to be a very committed party member. He found meetings "dull" and chafed at what he considered the party's intellectual regimentation. By February 1939 he had "quietly eased myself out." His break became irreversible in September, after the announcement of the Nazi-Soviet Pact. There followed a rapid and deep disillusionment—with the party (run by "glorified clerks"), with the Soviet Union ("essentially undemocratic"), and eventually with Marxism itself. Yet for some years, Hofstadter continued to regard himself as a radical. "I hate capitalism and everything that goes with it," he wrote Harvey Swados soon after leaving the party. Never again, however, would he devote his energies in any sustained manner to a political cause. He became more and more preoccupied with the thought that intellectuals were unlikely to find a comfortable home in any socialist society likely to emerge in his lifetime. "People like us . . . ," he wrote, "have become permanently alienated from the spirit of revolutionary movements. . . . We are not the beneficiaries of capitalism, but we will not be the beneficiaries of the socialism of the 20th century. We are the people with no place to go."

Although Hofstadter abandoned active politics after 1939, his earliest work as a historian reflected his continuing intellectual engagement with radicalism. His Columbia master's thesis, written in 1938, dealt with the plight of southern sharecroppers, a contemporary problem that had become the focus of intense organizing efforts by socialists and communists. Hofstadter showed how the benefits of New Deal agricultural policies in the cotton states flowed to large landowners, while the sharecroppers' conditions only worsened. The essay presented a devastating indictment of the Roosevelt administration for pandering to the South's undemocratic elite. Its critical evaluation of Roosevelt, a common attitude among New York radicals, would persist in Hofstadter's writings long after the political impulse that inspired the thesis had faded.

As with many others who came of age in the 1930s, Hofstadter's general intellectual approach was framed by Marxism, but in application to the American past, the iconoclastic materialism of Charles A. Beard was his greatest inspiration. "Beard was really *the* exciting influence on me," Hofstadter later remarked. Beard taught that American history had been shaped by the struggle of competing economic groups, primarily farmers, industrialists, and workers. Underlying the clashing rhetoric of political leaders lay naked self-interest; the Civil War, for example, should be understood essentially as a transfer of political power from southern agrarians to northern capitalists. Differences over the tariff had more to do with the war's origins than the debate over slavery. Hofstadter's first published essay, a "note" in a 1938 issue of the *American Historical Review*, took issue with Beard's emphasis on the tariff as a basic cause of the Civil War, while accepting the premise that economic self-interest lay at the root of political behavior. (The homestead issue, Hofstadter argued, far outweighed the tariff as a source of sectional tension.) The article inaugurated a dialogue with the Beardian tradition that shaped much of Hofstadter's subsequent career.

While Beard devoted little attention to political ideas, seeing them as mere masks for economic self-interest, Hofstadter soon became attracted to the study of American social thought. His interest was encouraged by Merle Curti, a Marxist Columbia professor with whom Hofstadter by 1939 had formed, according to Felice, a "mutual admiration society." Other than his relationship with Curti, however, Hofstadter was not particularly happy at Columbia. For three years running, he was refused financial aid. Hofstadter was gripped by a sense of unfair treatment. "The guys who got the fellowships," he complained, "are little shits who never accomplished or published anything." (None of them, one can assume, had, like Hofstadter, published in the *American Historical Review*.)

Meanwhile, having passed his comprehensive examinations, Hofstadter set out in quest of a dissertation topic. In a letter to his brother-in-law that typified Hofstadter's wry, self-deprecating sense of humor, he described the process. First, he considered writing a biography of "the old rascal Ben Wade" (the Radical Republican senator from Ohio) only to discover that Wade had destroyed most of his papers. Then he turned to Simon Cameron, Lincoln's first secretary of war, but abandoned that subject when he heard that "somebody from Indiana had been working on Cameron for 15 years." Columbia professor John A. Krout suggested a biography of Jeremiah Wadsworth, a colonial merchant who not only left abundant papers but had some admirers willing to help fund biographical research. Hofstadter, however, did not pursue the idea far—he and Felice considered Wadsworth inconsequential and kept referring to him as Jedediah Hockenpfuss. Finally, with Curti's approval, he settled on Social Darwinism. By mid-1940, he was hard at work, and two years later, at the precocious age of 26, he completed the dissertation. *Social Darwinism in American Thought* was published by the University of Pennsylvania Press in 1944.

However serendipitous the process by which he found it, Social Darwinism was the perfect subject for the young Hofstadter. It was a big topic, likely to interest a large audience, and it combined his growing interest in the history of social thought with his continuing alienation from American capitalism. It was the kind of subject, Felice wrote Harvey, "in which all his friends want to have a hand." "But in which they won't," Hofstadter added. The book focuses on the late nineteenth century and ends in 1915, the year before Hofstadter's birth. But, as he later observed, the "emotional resonances" that shaped his approach to the subject were those of his own youth, when conservatives used arguments descended from Social Darwinism to justify resistance to radical political movements and government efforts to alleviate inequality. Studying Social Darwinism helped explain "the disparity between our official individualism and the bitter facts of life as anyone could see them during the great depression."

Social Darwinism in American Thought describes the broad impact on intellectual life of the scientific writings of Charles Darwin and the growing use of such Darwinian ideas as "natural selection," "survival of the fittest," and "the struggle for existence" to reinforce conservative, laissez-faire individualism. The book begins by tracing the conquest of Darwinian ideas among American scientists and liberal Protestant theologians, a conquest so complete that by the Gilded Age "every serious thinker felt obligated to reckon with" the implications of Darwin's writings. Hofstadter then examines the "vogue" of Herbert Spencer, the English philosopher who did more than any other individual to define nineteenth-century conservatism. Spencer, of course, preceded Darwin; well before the publication of *The Origin of Species*, Spencer not only coined the term "survival of the fittest" but developed a powerful critique of all forms of state interference with the "natural" workings of society, including regulation of business and public assistance to the poor. But Spencer's followers seized upon the authority of Darwin's work to claim scientific legitimacy for their outlook, and to press home the analogy between the natural and social worlds, both of which, they claimed, evolved according to natural laws.

From Spencer, Hofstadter turns to a consideration of William Graham Sumner, the most influential American social Darwinist, whose writings glorified the competitive social order and justified existing social inequalities as the result of natural selection. Combining Darwinian ideas with the Protestant work ethic and classical economics, he condemned governmental activism, preferring instead a complete "abnegation of state power." Sumner offered defenders of the economic status quo a compelling rationale for opposing the demands of labor unions, Grangers, and others seeking to interfere with the "natural" functioning of the social order.

Despite the book's title and the deftness with which he sketches the lineaments of Social Darwinism in its opening chapters, Hofstadter actually devotes more attention to the theory's critics than its proponents. For a time, Social Darwinism reigned supreme in American thought. But beginning in the 1880s, it came under attack from many sources—clergymen shocked by the inequities of the emerging industrial order and the harshness of unbridled competition, reformers proposing to unleash state activism in the service of social equality, and intellectuals of the emerging social sciences. Hofstadter makes no effort to disguise his distaste for the Social Darwinists or his sympathy for the critics, especially the sociologists and philosophers who believed intellectuals could guide social progress (views extremely congenial to Hofstadter at the time he was writing). In the 1880s, sociologist Lester Ward pointed out that economic competition bred not simply individual advancement but giant new corporations whose economic might needed to be held in check by government, and he ridiculed the social Darwinists' "fundamental error" that "the favors of the world are distributed entirely according to merit." But Hofstadter's true heroes were the early twentieth-century Pragmatists. William James destroyed Spencer's hold on philosophical thought by pointing to the elements of psychology—sentiment, emotion, and so on—ignored in the Darwinian model and insisting that human intelligence enabled people to alter their own environment, thus rendering pointless the analogy with nature. James, however, evinced little interest in current events. Hofstadter identified more closely with John Dewey, whom he presents as a model of the socially responsible intellectual, the architect of a "new collectivism" in which an activist state attempts to guide and improve society.

By the turn of the century, Social Darwinism was in full retreat. But even as Darwinian individualism waned, Darwinian ideas continued to influence social thinking in other ways. Rather than individuals striving for advancement, the struggling units of the analogy with nature became collectives—especially nations and races. With the United States emerging as a world power from the Spanish-American War, writers like John Fiske and Albert J. Beveridge marshaled Darwinian ideas in the service of imperialism, to legitimate the worldwide subordination of "inferior" races to Anglo-Saxon hegemony. In the eugenics movement that flourished in the early years of the twentieth century, Darwinism helped to underwrite the idea that immigration of less "fit" peoples was lowering the standard of American intelligence. Fortunately, the "racist-military" phase of Social Darwinism was as thoroughly discredited by World War I, when it seemed uncomfortably akin to German militarism, as conservative individualism had been by the attacks of progressive social scientists.

When Hofstadter tries to explain the rise and fall of Social Darwinism, he falls back on the base-superstructure model shared by Marxists and Beardians in the 1930s. Hofstadter recognizes that there was nothing inevitable in the appropriation of Darwinism for conservative purposes. Marx, after all, was so impressed by *The Origin of Species*, which dethroned revealed religion and vindicated the idea of progress through ceaseless struggle (struggle among classes, in his reading, rather than individuals), that he proposed to dedicate *Capital* to Darwin—an honor the latter declined. How then to account for the ascendancy, until the 1890s, of individualist, laissez-faire Darwinism? The reason, Hofstadter writes, was that Social Darwinism served the needs of those groups that controlled the "raw, aggressive, industrial society" of the Gilded Age. Spencer, Sumner, and the other social Darwinians were telling businessmen and political leaders what they wanted to hear. Subsequently, it was not merely the penetrating criticism of Ward, Dewey, and others, but the middle class's growing disenchantment with unbridled competition, Hofstadter argues, that led it to repudiate Social Darwinism and adopt a more reform-minded social outlook in the Progressive era.

Hofstadter's concluding thoughts amount to a reaffirmation both of the Beardian approach and of his own status as a radical intellectual. The rise and fall of Social Darwinism, he writes, exemplified the "rule" that "changes in the structure of social ideas wait on general changes in economic and political life" and that ideas win wide acceptance based less on "truth and logic" than their "suitability to the intellectual needs and preconceptions of social interests." This, he adds, was "one of the great difficulties that must be faced by rational strategists of social change." Clearly, Hofstadter still viewed economic self-interest as the basis of political action, and clearly he identified with those "rational strategists of social change" who hoped to move the nation beyond Social Darwinism's legacy.

Actually, Hofstadter offered no independent analysis of either the structure of American society or the ideas of most businessmen or politicians. His effort to explain Social Darwinism's rise and fall is a kind of obiter dictum, largely confined to his brief concluding chapter. Indeed, Hofstadter later reflected that the book may have inadvertently encouraged the "intellectualist fallacy" by exaggerating the impact of ideas without placing them in the social context from which they sprang. *Social Darwinism* is a work of intellectual history, not an examination of how ideas reflect economic structures. And as such, it retains much of its vitality half a century after it was written. The book's qualities would remain hallmarks of Hofstadter's subsequent writing—among them an amazing lucidity in presenting complex ideas, the ability to sprinkle his text with apt quotes that make precisely the right point, the capacity to bring past individuals to life in telling portraits. For a dissertation, it is a work of remarkable range, drawing not only on the writings of sociologists and philosophers, but also on novels, treatises, sermons, and popular magazines to explore the debates unleashed by Darwinism. Very much a product of a particular moment in American history, it transcends the particulars of its origins to offer a compelling portrait of a critical period in the development of American thought. To the end of his life, Hofstadter's writings would center on *Social Darwinism*'s underlying themes—the evolution of social thought, the social context of ideologies, and the role of ideas in politics.

Social Darwinism has had an impact matched by few books of its generation. Hofstadter did not invent the term "Social Darwinism," which originated in Europe in the 1880s and crossed the Atlantic in the early twentieth century. But before he wrote, it was used only on rare occasions; he made it a standard shorthand for a complex of late-nineteenth-century ideas, a familiar part of the lexicon of social thought. The book demonstrates Hofstadter's ability, even in a dissertation, to move beyond the academic readership to address a broad general public. Since its appearance in a revised paperback edition in 1955 (Hofstadter left the argument unchanged but added an author's note and made several hundred "purely stylistic" alterations), it has sold more than 200,000 copies.

Although, thanks to Hofstadter, Social Darwinism has earned a permanent place in the vocabulary of intellectual history, his analysis has not escaped criticism. While few scholars have challenged Hofstadter's account of the main currents of late-nineteenth-century American thought, some have cast doubt on the extent of Darwin's influence on both laissez-faire conservatives and their liberal and radical critics. Soon after Hofstadter's revised edition appeared, Irvin G. Wyllie published an influential essay disputing Darwin's impact on American businessmen. Entrepreneurs, he found, justified the accumulation of wealth not by appealing to a vision of ruthless competition in which the success of some meant the ruin of others but by reference to hard work, Christian philanthropy, and the conviction that the creation of wealth benefitted society as a whole.

Since Hofstadter had devoted little attention to businessmen, apart from Andrew Carnegie, Wyllie's findings did not significantly affect the book's main argument. More damaging was the criticism advanced by Robert C. Bannister, who argued that Hofstadter had greatly exaggerated Darwin's influence on social thinkers themselves. Remarkably few late-nineteenth-century writers, Bannister found, either invoked Darwin's authority, referred directly to biological evolution, or used Darwinian terminology such as survival of the fittest and the struggle for existence. The roots of their thought lay elsewhere, in classical economics and a preoccupation with defending property rights and limiting the power of the state. They were more likely to appeal to the authority of Adam Smith than Darwin, more likely to be influenced by contemporary events such as the 1877 railroad strike, than by analogies to biological evolution. In fact, Bannister concluded, Social Darwinism existed mainly as an "epithet," a label devised by advocates of a reforming state to stigmatize laissez-faire conservatism.

Hofstadter, to be sure, never claimed that Darwin created Gilded Age individualism; rather, he wrote, Darwinian categories supplemented an existing vocabulary derived from laissez-faire economics. Moreover, Bannister's definition of Social Darwinism, requiring explicit use of Darwinian language, ignores less direct influences on social thought and more subtle adaptations of scientific reasoning. Toward the end of his life, Hofstadter praised his critic for careful reading of sources, but went on to suggest that "intellectual history, even as made by men who try to be rational and who try to regard distinctions, proceeds by more gross distinctions than you are aware of." This was a fairly devastating critique of Bannister's approach (which, to his credit, Bannister included in the introduction to his own book). Nonetheless, Bannister's basic point struck home. Today, writers who examine Gilded Age conservatism are likely to locate its primary sources in realms other than Darwinism. Spencer's influence, it is true, still looms large; some have even suggested that the body of thought Hofstadter described ought to be called Social Spencerism, not Social Darwinism.

This, however, would be a mistake, for if Hofstadter perhaps exaggerated Darwin's influence, he was certainly correct in identifying a commitment to developing a science of society as all but ubiquitous among late-nineteenth- and early-twentieth-century intellectuals. Darwin's writings helped to catalyze this belief, which became a major point of self-definition and self-justification for intellectuals at a time when, through the rise of social science, their role in American society was becoming institutionalized. Hofstadter's central insight—that analogies with science helped to shape the way Americans perceived and interpreted issues from the differences between races and classes to the implications of state intervention in the economy—remains the starting point for serious investigations of American thought during the Gilded Age.

Inevitably, *Social Darwinism* now seems in some ways dated. Today, in the wake of the "new social history," historians are more cognizant of the many groups that make up American society and no longer write confidently, as Hofstadter did, of a single "public mind." But the most striking difference between Hofstadter's cast of mind and that of our own time lies in his resolute conviction that Social Darwinism was an unfortunate but thankfully closed chapter in the history of social thought. Hofstadter wrote from the certainty that Social Darwinism was demonstrably wrong, that biological analogies are "utterly useless" in understanding human society, that this episode had all been some kind of "ghastly mistake."

"A resurgence of social Darwinism . . . ," Hofstadter did note, was "always a possibility so long as there is a strong element of predacity in society." But he could hardly have foreseen the resurrection in the 1980s and 1990s of biological explanations for human development and of the Social Darwinist mentality, if not the name itself: that government should not intervene to affect the "natural" workings of the economy, that the distribution of rewards within society reflects individual merit rather than historical circumstances, that the plight of the less fortunate, whether individuals or races, arises from their own failings. Had he lived to see Social Darwinism's recrudescence, Hofstadter would certainly have noted how two previously distinct strands of this ideology have merged in today's conservatism—the laissez-faire individualism of a William Graham Sumner (who, it should be noted, condemned the imperial state with the same vigor he applied to government intervention in the economy) and the militarist and racist Darwinism of the early twentieth century.

If *Social Darwinism* announced Hofstadter as one of the most promising scholars of his generation, his second work, *The American Political Tradition*, published in 1948, propelled him to the very forefront of his profession. Since its appearance, this brilliant series of portraits of prominent Americans from the founding fathers through Jefferson, Jackson, Lincoln, and FDR has been a standard work in both college and high school history classes and has been read by millions outside the academy. Hofstadter's insight was that virtually all his subjects held essentially the same underlying beliefs. Instead of persistent conflict (whether between agrarians and industrialists, capital and labor, or Democrats and Republicans), American history was characterized by broad agreement on fundamentals, particularly the virtues of individual liberty, private property, and capitalist enterprise. In *Social Darwinism*, he had observed that Spencer's doctrines came to America "long after individualism had become a national tradition." Now he appeared to be saying that the subject of his first book *was* the American political tradition.

With its emphasis on the ways an ideological consensus had shaped American development, *The American Political Tradition* in many ways marked Hofstadter's break with the Beardian and Marxist traditions. Along with Daniel Boorstin's *The Genius of American Politics*, and Louis Hartz's *The Liberal Tradition in America* (both published a few years afterwards), Hofstadter's second book came to be seen as the foundation of the "consensus history" of the 1950s. But Hofstadter's writing never devolved into the uncritical celebration of the American experience that characterized much "consensus" writing. As Arthur Schlesinger Jr. observed in a 1969 essay, there was a basic difference between *The American Political Tradition* and works like Boorstin's: "For Hofstadter [and, Schlesinger might have added, Hartz] perceived the consensus from a radical perspective, from the outside, and deplored it; while Boorstin perceived it from the inside and celebrated it." As a courtesy, Schlesinger sent Hofstadter a draft of the essay. In the margin opposite this sentence, Hofstadter, who never felt entirely comfortable with the consensus label, scribbled: "Thank you."

Hofstadter had abandoned Beard's analysis of American development, but he retained his mentor's iconoclastic, debunking spirit. In Hofstadter's hands, Jefferson became a political chameleon, Jackson an exponent of liberal capitalism, Lincoln a mythmaker, and Roosevelt a pragmatic opportunist. And the domination of individualism and capitalism in American life produced not a benign freedom from "European" ideological conflicts, but a form of intellectual and political bankruptcy, an inability to think in original ways about the modern world. If the book has a hero, it is abolitionist Wendell Phillips, the only figure in *The American Political Tradition* never to hold political office. As in *Social Darwinism*, Hofstadter seemed to identify most of all with the engaged, reformist intellectual. It is indeed ironic that one of the most devastating indictments of American political culture ever written should have become the introduction to American history for two generations of students. One scholar at the time even sought to develop an alternative book of essays on America's greatest presidents precisely in order to counteract the "confusion and disillusionment" he feared Hofstadter was sowing among undergraduates.

"All my books," Hofstadter wrote in the 1960s, "have been, in a certain sense, topical in their inspiration. That is to say, I have always begun with a concern with some present reality." His first two books, he went on, "refract the experiences of the depression era and the New Deal." In the 1950s, a different "reality" shaped Hofstadter's writing—the Cold War and McCarthyism. Having remarried after the death of his first wife in 1945, Hofstadter assumed a teaching position at Columbia and again found himself part of New York's intellectual world. But this was very different from the radical days of the 1930s. He had "grown a great deal more conservative in the past few years," Hofstadter wrote Merle Curti, then teaching at Wisconsin, in 1953. Unlike many New York intellectuals, including a number of his friends, Hofstadter never made a career of anticommunism. Nor did he embrace neoconservatism, join the Congress for Cultural Freedom, or become an uncritical apologist for the Cold War. He was repelled by McCarthyism (although he declined Curti's invitation to condemn publicly the firing of communist professors at the University of Washington). After supporting with "immense enthusiasm" Adlai Stevenson's campaign for the White House in 1952, Hofstadter retreated altogether from politics. "I can no longer describe myself as a radical, though I don't consider myself to be a conservative either," he wrote Harvey Swados a decade after Stevenson's defeat. "I suppose the truth is, although my interests are still very political, I none the less have no politics."

What Hofstadter did have was a growing sense of the fragility of intellectual freedom and social comity. His next book was *The Development of Academic Freedom in the United States*, written in collaboration with his Columbia colleague Walter P. Metzger and published in 1955. As with other intellectuals, his sensibility was strongly reinforced by the Holocaust in Europe and the advent of McCarthyism at home. Hofstadter understood McCarthyism not as a thrust for political advantage among conservatives seeking to undo the legacy of the

New Deal, but as the outgrowth of a deep-seated anti-intellectualism and provincialism in the American population. The result was to reinforce a distrust of mass politics that had been simmering ever since he left the Communist Party in 1939. This attitude was reinforced by his search for new ways of understanding political behavior. Reared on the assumption that politics essentially reflects economic interest, he now became fascinated with alternative explanations of political conduct—status anxieties, irrational hatreds, paranoia. Influenced by the popularity of Freudianism among New York intellectuals of the 1950s and by his close friendships with the sociologist C. Wright Mills and literary critics Lionel Trilling and Alfred Kazin, Hofstadter became more and more sensitive to the importance of symbolic conduct, unconscious motivation, and, as he wrote in *The Age of Reform* (1955), the "complexities in our history which our conventional images of the past have not yet caught."

Hofstadter applied these insights to the history of American political culture in a remarkable series of books that made plain his growing conservatism and his sense of alienation from what he called America's periodic "fits of moral crusading." *The Age of Reform* offered an interpretation of Populism and Progressivism "from the perspective of our own time." In his master's essay, Hofstadter had thoroughly sympathized with the struggles of the South's downtrodden tenant farmers. Now, he portrayed the Populists of the late nineteenth century as small entrepreneurs standing against the inevitable tide of economic development. He saw them as taking refuge in a nostalgic agrarian myth or lashing out against imagined enemies from British bankers to Jews in a precursor to "modern authoritarian movements." (Interestingly, this interpretation still bore the mark of the traditional Marxist critique of petty bourgeois social movements; the American Marxist thinker Daniel DeLeon had said much the same thing about the Populists in the 1890s.)

In *Social Darwinism*, William Graham Sumner and the capitalist plutocracy of the Gilded Age had emerged as the main threats to American democracy; while noting the underside of Progressivism—

its racism and Anglo-Saxonism—Hofstadter seemed to embrace its demand for state activism against social injustice. In *The Age of Reform*, he depicted the Progressives as a displaced bourgeoisie seeking in political reform a way to overcome their decline in status. Rather than a precursor of the New Deal, as it was commonly seen, Progressivism, with its infatuation with the idea of pure democracy, was the source of some of "our most troublesome contemporary delusions" about politics. A similar sensibility informed Hofstadter's next two books. In *Anti-Intellectualism in American Life* (1963), he identified an American heartland "filled with people who are often fundamentalist in religion, nativist in prejudice, isolationist in foreign policy, and conservative in economics" as a persistent danger to intellectual life. *In The Paranoid Style in American Politics* (1965), he suggested that a common irrationality characterized popular enthusiasms of both the right and the left throughout American history.

The Age of Reform and *Anti-Intellectualism* won Hofstadter his two Pulitzer Prizes. And today's politics certainly provide examples of paranoia and intolerance. But both books, ironically, today seem more dated than his earlier books. Since the rise of the new social history, it has become impossible to study mass movements without immersing oneself in local primary sources, rather than relying on the kind of imaginative reading of published works at which Hofstadter excelled. These books seemed to wed him to a consensus vision that deemed the American political system fundamentally sound and its critics essentially irrational.

Hofstadter's, however, was too protean an intellect to remain satisfied for long with the consensus framework. As social turmoil engulfed the country in the mid-1960s, Hofstadter remained as prolific as ever, but his underlying assumptions shifted again. In *The Progressive Historians* (1968), he attempted to come to terms once and for all with Beard and his generation. Their portrait of an America racked by perennial conflict, he noted, was overdrawn, but by the same token, the consensus outlook could hardly explain the American Revolution, Civil War, or other key periods of discord in the nation's past (including, by implication, the 1960s). *American Violence* (1970), a documentary volume edited with his graduate student Michael Wallace, offered a chilling record of political and social turbulence that utterly contradicted the consensus vision of a nation placidly evolving without serious disagreements. Finally, in *America at 1750*, the first volume in a proposed three-part narrative history of the nation, Hofstadter offered a portrait that brilliantly took account of the paradoxical coexistence of individual freedom and opportunity and widespread social injustice and human bondage in the colonial era. The book remained unfinished at the time of his death from leukemia in 1971, offering only a tantalizing suggestion of what his full account of the American past might have been.

For all his accomplishments, Hofstadter was utterly without pretension, always unintimidating, never too busy to talk about one's work. He did not try to impose his own interests or views on his students—far from it. If no "Hofstadter school" emerged from Columbia, it is because he had no desire to create one. Indeed, it often seemed during the 1960s that his graduate students, many of whom were actively involved in the civil rights and antiwar movements, were having as much influence on his evolving interests and outlook as he on theirs.

It would not be strictly true to call Hofstadter a great teacher. Writing was his passion, and he did not share the love of the classroom that marks the truly exceptional instructor. Hofstadter disliked the lecture podium intensely and almost seemed to go out of his way to make his lectures unappealing, perhaps to drive away some of the large numbers who inevitably registered for his courses. He was at his best in small seminars and individual consultations, and when criticizing written work. Here his erudition, open-mindedness, and desire to help each student do the best work of which he or she was capable came to the fore.

Despite his death at the young age of 54, Hofstadter left a prolific body of work, remarkable for its originality and readability, and his capacity to range over the length and breadth of American history. From *Social Darwinism* to *America at 1750*, his writings stand as a model of what historical scholarship at its finest can aspire to achieve.

AMERICAN MYTH

I T HARDLY QUALIFIES as news nowadays that the United States, the world's foremost economic and military power, suffers from a political and cultural malaise. Americans are deeply skeptical of once well-regarded institutions such as colleges, the media, and the public health system, and do not trust the functioning of democratic politics. Entrenched inequality characterizes the economy, and intense polarization between the parties makes addressing long-term problems such as climate change all but impossible. The crisis, however, the historian Richard Slotkin argues in *A Great Disorder: National Myth and the Battle for America*, is essentially cultural rather than economic or political. Among the contributors to the steadily intensifying "culture wars" between "red" and "blue" states and rural and urban communities, Slotkin identifies the banking crisis of 2008–2009, the Covid pandemic, and changes in the racial and ethnic makeup of the American population. But to these familiar culprits he adds a deeper problem—a lack of unifying "national myths" that embody shared views of the country's history and future. "The loss of a common national

Review of *A Great Disorder: National Myth and the Battle for America*, by Richard Slotkin, *London Review of Books*, June 20, 2024.

story," Slotkin writes at the outset, is "central to the contemporary crisis." Once, myths that sought to explain American history and chart a path to the future helped to bind the country together. Today, they are absorbed into the culture wars, reflecting divergent understandings of foundational American values and clashing definitions of who constitute "real" Americans. Is it just a coincidence that one of last summer's most popular films was entitled *Civil War*?

My dictionary defines "myth" as both a popular tradition that embodies core social values and "an unfounded or false" idea. The word hints at intentional distortion of the truth. But truth is more or less beside the point in Slotkin's discussion of myths. He is neither asking Americans to embrace demonstrable falsehoods as a way of restoring a lost sense of national unity nor demanding that unifying narratives embody only verifiable facts about the country's past. "As I use the term," he writes, "myths are the stories—true, untrue, half-true—that provide an otherwise loosely affiliated people with models of patriotic action and material with which to think of a common future." Such common beliefs are more important in the United States than elsewhere since compared with other nations the country lacks traditional underpinnings of patriotic nationalism such as a common ethnocultural identity, a long-established history, and a powerful and threatening neighbor. In a more unified nation, people of different political persuasions would seize upon commonly held myths as ready-made paradigms that help make sense of events. In *A Great Disorder*, Slotkin explores the emergence and evolution of the "foundational" myths that have helped define American culture.

Slotkin is a prolific historian, best known for his trilogy of books on the "Myth of the Frontier" (he always capitalizes the names of the myths he analyzes)—*Regeneration Through Violence: The Mythology of the American Frontier, 1600–1860* (1973); *The Fatal Environment: The Myth of the Frontier in the Age of Industrialization 1800–1890* (1985); and *Gunfighter Nation: The Myth of the Frontier in Twentieth-Century America* (1992). Unusually, he has also written accounts of Civil War battles that have won praise for their command of military strategy. As his book titles suggest, Slotkin is particularly interested in how the frontier experience helped to shape American identity, citing, for example, a tendency to settle differences by violence. Over the course of the country's history the conquest of the West was widely understood as a battle between civilization and barbarism. "Savage war"—the nation's way of conducting combat via massacres that did not spare women, children, and non-combatants—came to be seen as unavoidable. As Frederick Douglass pointed out, however, it was not always easy to discern which side was which. In view of the horrors of slavery, Douglass declared in his 1852 speech on the meaning of the Fourth of July to Black Americans, the United States could be said to be "guilty of crimes that would disgrace a nation of savages."

Slotkin's current book is a sequel to and extension of his earlier trilogy. The Myth of the Frontier remains central to his account, but other myths make an appearance, among them the Myth of the Founders, the belief that the American nation was created by a unique generation of statesmen, who produced a governing structure that enabled the United States to balance liberty and order while mostly avoiding the ideological conflicts experienced by European nations. Impressively, Slotkin brings his discussion of national myths all the way to the present, where he explores the visions of America's history and future delineated by the current radical right.

In this latest volume, Slotkin devotes more attention than in the past to the division of the United States into distinct societies based on slave and free labor and how national myths failed to prevent the country from plunging into internecine warfare. Each region, he shows, developed sectionally based variants of the Myths of the Frontier and Founding, making it difficult for these myths to play their role of smoothing over the nation's internal differences. The Civil War, he writes, "above all was a culture war," and Slotkin presents a persuasive discussion of the part played by a clash of regional cultures in helping to bring about the conflict. Pre–Civil War southern culture, Slotkin writes, rested primarily on racism, which he describes as "the division of Black and White into different orders of humanity." What did this mean for the Myth of the Founding, which, as an aspiration if not in actual practice took as its basic premise Jefferson's words in the Declaration of Independence: "all men are created equal"? Eventually, Slotkin argues, leaders of the slave South concluded that Jefferson had simply been wrong, a conviction made plain by Confederate vice president Alexander H. Stephens in his famous "cornerstone speech" of 1861, which insisted that inequality, not equality, was a "law of nature" and the foundation of social order. Another expression of this revised Myth of the Founding could be found in the Supreme Court's 1857 Dred Scott decision, which, Slotkin points out, claimed to be an exercise in what today is called judicial "originalism." Chief Justice Roger B. Taney's infamous pronouncement in Dred Scott that Black persons had "no rights which the white man is bound to respect," purported to reflect the founders' racial views at the time the Constitution was written.

White southerners' efforts to redefine the Myth of the Founding along proslavery lines opened the door for the emergence of an antislavery movement that claimed its own descent from the revolutionary generation. To drive home this point Slotkin offers the examples of Frederick Douglass and Abraham Lincoln. In his 1852 speech, Douglass chastised the nation for failing to live up to the founders' egalitarian creed. Almost a decade later, in the midst of the Civil War, Lincoln began the Gettysburg Address by claiming that the founders had intended the nation to embody "the proposition that all men are created equal."

The Civil War, Slotkin writes, gave birth to no fewer than three distinct myths—the Myth of Liberation, embodied in slave emancipation; the Myth of White Reunion, which depicted the war as a battle of brother against brother in which both sides could retrospectively take pride; and the Lost Cause, a glorification of the Old South and a legitimation of the system of segregation and disenfranchisement put in place, with northern acquiescence, in the 1890s. During Reconstruction the United States embarked on a remarkable, if short-lived, experiment in interracial democracy, an attempt to remake the body politic so as to bring to fruition the Myth of Liberation. Reconstruction's violent overthrow put an end to this effort. The Lost Cause soon became deeply entrenched in American culture, North as well as South. As Slotkin points out, the Myths of the Frontier and the Lost Cause were "mutually reinforcing." Both were premised on the necessity of rule by white Americans over non-white peoples, at home and overseas.

More than in his previous books, Slotkin in *A Great Disorder* sees national myths as contested, evolving, and sometimes self-contradictory. Thus the nationwide dissemination of the Lost Cause in the late nineteenth and early twentieth centuries left space for the emergence of a more egalitarian vision. This, however, did not take hold until during and after the Second World War. Before then, the New Deal gained widespread support for the unifying idea of government promotion of economic security for ordinary Americans. But, Slotkin writes, partly because of the strength of southern segregationists in the Democratic Party it failed to produce a myth powerful enough to overcome the idea that the nation was meant to be a "White man's republic," which had exerted a strong hold on American culture since the Gilded Age and Progressive era. Numerous developments in addition to the overthrow of Reconstruction contributed to this racialization of nationhood, among them widespread revulsion against the influx of immigrants from southern and eastern Europe supposedly unfit for participation in American democracy; the final military defeat of the Plains Indians; and the acquisition of an overseas American empire as a result of the Spanish-American War. The list of "savage" enemies who posed a danger to society came to include not only immigrants, Indians, and emancipated slaves, but workers who engaged in strikes and, improbably, advocates of women's suffrage.

Slotkin points to three crises of the years 1876 and 1877—the abandonment of the last southern Reconstruction governments, a national railroad strike, and the annihilation of General George Armstrong Custer and his men by warriors of the Lakota Sioux and other Native American nations (popularly known as Custer's Last Stand). Each was seen as a battle in which more primitive people stood in the way of national progress. Increasingly, divisions along the lines of class, race, and gender now defined American "ethnonationalism." Although the conquest of the West was a collective endeavor, Slotkin discerns an individualist underpinning to the Myth of the Frontier. As evidence, he turns to Hollywood, highlighting films and television series in which a lone gunman imposes order on a chaotic community, echoing, perhaps, the self-appointed global role of the United States during much of the twentieth century. (These echoes of the Myth of the Frontier in popular culture include the 1950s movies *High Noon* and *Shane*, and the television series *The Lone Ranger* and *Have Gun, Will Travel*.)

In Slotkin's account, after a long period in which it shaped national identity, the racist "ethnonationalism" of the late nineteenth and early twentieth centuries gave way to an egalitarian Myth of the Good War. Partly to heighten the distinction between the United States and Nazi tyranny, partly as a way of generating support for the war among the descendants of recent immigrants, the federal government promoted the idea that the United States stood for pluralism and democracy. Racism was the enemy's philosophy and Allied victory would lead to a peace in which FDR's Four Freedoms were enjoyed throughout the world. The Myth of the Good War received its most influential articulation, according to Slotkin, in what he calls platoon movies. These depicted multicultural American fighting units as harmonious cross sections of society. The platoons' members represented the diverse nationalities that made up the American population, among them Irish Americans, Italian Americans, Jews, and Blacks (even though the army, and indeed society at large, remained rigidly segregated). But however much these movies were divorced from reality, Slotkin believes that they promoted racial and religious toleration and helped lay the groundwork for the emergence of the Myth of the Movement, an outgrowth of the triumph of the non-violent civil rights revolution and the mobilization of other groups inspired by its success. According to this myth, the nation's purpose lay not so much in what had been accomplished as in the agendas based on different versions of equality that remained to be fulfilled. In official rhetoric and Hollywood's myth-making machine, tolerance succeeded white supremacy as the defining quality of American culture and politics.

Meanwhile, during the Cold War, the Myth of the Frontier was refashioned, so that the frontier was now seen as a gateway to world power and economic abundance. (John F. Kennedy's reference to a New Frontier in his 1960 speech accepting the Democratic nomination for president carried this implication.) The myth of a West dominated by small family farms (Jefferson's vision of the future) had already given way to the idea that the region was home to what Slotkin calls "bonanza capitalism," the possibility of instant riches derived from successive gold rushes, a burgeoning oil industry, and railroad construction. Slotkin makes the interesting point that the eastern press reported on Custer's Last Stand by invoking the ready-made paradigm of a battle for the defense of civilization, leaving virtually unmentioned the corporate economic interests that had drawn the army into the Black Hills where Custer met his death—railroad development and the discovery of gold on land guaranteed in perpetuity to indigenous peoples. As always, the Myth of the West carried with it intimations of violence. Slotkin does not beat about the bush—he calls Indian removal an example of "ethnic cleansing."

Slotkin, of course, is hardly the first to identify the presence of the frontier and westward expansion more generally as key dynamics in the evolution of American culture. Over a century ago, the historian Frederick Jackson Turner insisted that the experience of exerting control over the frontier fundamentally shaped the American character. I vividly recall Richard Hofstadter's remark in a graduate seminar at Columbia University that Turner's "frontier thesis" was the only truly original idea ever developed by a historian of the United States. (Hofstadter, however, a confirmed urbanite, did not think much of what he called the western "agrarian myth," which he identified with less than praiseworthy elements of American culture including anti-Semitism and a penchant for conspiratorial thinking.) But Slotkin's West is different from Turner's. Those influenced by the latter often left the impression—sometimes expressed in quasi-sexual imagery—that the

West was an empty space waiting to be conquered and exploited. Compare with Slotkin's trilogy—for example, the titles of influential works on this theme such as *Virgin Land* by Henry Nash Smith, and Perry Miller's *Errand into the Wilderness*. Slotkin makes clear that the conquest of the West resulted from violence, not persuasion.

In the Cold War years, many scholars aligned with the emerging discipline of American Studies sought to ascertain what was distinctive about American culture and history. Daniel Boorstin pointed to a pragmatic temperament that led Americans to eschew ideological debates and get down to the business of scientific and economic advancement. Louis Hartz and Hofstadter wrote about an all-encompassing liberal consensus. Boorstin celebrated that consensus; both Hofstadter and Hartz deplored it, believing it made it impossible for the society to develop new ideas.

Scholars of American Studies anticipated Slotkin in pointing to the importance of "symbols and myths" in the shaping of American culture and in homing in on the West as the foundation of American development. What makes American Studies distinctive is the wide range of source material it deploys, including films, novels, music, artifacts of popular culture, and the like. As in other disciplines, the Vietnam war and civil rights movement threw into question the quest for a single "American Mind" (the title of an influential book by the historian Henry Steele Commager.) The field fragmented, as society itself seemed to be doing. Under these circumstances, younger, more politically active American Studies scholars raised the question whether "myth" was a sufficient framework for understanding American culture. Some turned to political economy to understand the American past and present. Today, innumerable colleges and universities are home to "Studies" departments of all kinds: American Studies, African American Studies, Rural Studies, Native American Studies, Cultural Studies—the list goes on. The word Studies in their titles is a way of announcing their interdisciplinary approach. Slotkin's work anticipated and influenced these developments.

In his final chapters, Slotkin enters the current era. He presents a well-informed analysis of the origins of today's culture war politics, focused on disputes over immigration. The electoral success of Barack Obama, despite the denial of his status as an American citizen by the radical right, helped to propel forward the Myth of the Movement. At the same time, it inspired a resurgence of racialized nationalism. The backlash was exemplified in hostility to the idea, written into the Constitution during Reconstruction, of birthright citizenship, and the spread among conservatives of "replacement theory," which warned of a liberal conspiracy to flood the country with immigrants unfit for participation in democratic politics. Slotkin examines in detail the writings of obscure thinkers who exemplify various strands—cultural, racial, economic—of today's conservatism, including the Koch brothers, determined to repeal the New Deal; anti-immigrant extremists Peter Brimelow and Stephen Miller; climate change deniers; adherents of today's gun culture; and Donald Trump's former attorney general William Barr, who in a recent speech blamed increased toleration of gay men and lesbians for the supposed moral decay of Western civilization (channeling Pat Buchanan, who in a similar speech in 1992 helped to launch the modern culture wars). Given his fixation on a border wall, Trump can be associated with the Myth of the Frontier, although his idea of a frontier seems to begin with Mar-a-Lago. Trump's rise, Slotkin suggests, reflects a merger of the Lost Cause with modern ethnonationalism. How many of Trump's followers read this stuff is difficult to say. But Slotkin insists that these ideas must be taken seriously. Trump's movement, he writes, has become the vehicle for "an authentically American Fascism." "There is always a feedback loop," he warns, "between the dehumanization of foreign enemies and the dehumanization of some classes of fellow citizens."

Where do national myths originate? They do not emerge by happenstance; rather their creation and spread are an exercise of power. Influential historical actors, from antebellum slaveholders to modern-day Hollywood moguls and those Slotkin calls the "political classes," have attempted to develop and disseminate broadly acceptable myths to serve their own self-interest. Then there are historians, seemingly well positioned to invent and develop new national stories. Each side in the culture war, Slotkin writes, appeals to American history. But historians have not taken on the task of devising a coherent national mythology that can bring unity to a fractured republic. Instead, Slotkin notes with dismay, students in red and blue states are being taught radically different versions of the nation's past. All this, he writes, reflects not simply divergent opinions on specific issues, but "disagreements about the fundamental character" of American institutions and "the purpose of the American nation state."

Slotkin credits recent "revisionist historians" for directing attention to the role of racial, class, and gender inequalities in the development of American culture. But one gets the impression that he feels the revisionist wave has gone too far, dwelling obsessively on what is wrong with American society and devoting too little attention to accomplishments such as persistent, and sometimes successful, efforts to combat inequality. These, he suggests, could become the basis for a new liberal national myth that takes as its purpose the enactment of measures that have been on our national agenda for many decades, among them national health insurance, the right to employment, and vigorous public regulation of corporate behemoths, coupled with a tolerant approach to racial and ethnic diversity. In effect, he proposes uniting the politics of the New Deal with the Myth of the Movement. He turns American exceptionalism on its head, pointing out that the same social and political developments that have spawned an authoritarian reaction in the United States have had much the same impact in Europe. In that sense, the United States is not all that different from other countries.

Slotkin acknowledges that his proposed "pluralist national myth" will require ignoring some dark parts of the American experience. But, he believes, a myth focused on the struggles for equality of labor, African Americans, and other groups could inspire a renewed sense of national purpose.

Historians, however, do not seem to be heeding Slotkin's call. Instead, having long since abandoned the quest for an elusive liberal consensus, historians in the past year or so have published important books that trace the rise of reactionary conservatism. These include *Illiberal America* by Steven Hahn, *Democracy Awakening* by Heather Cox Richardson, and Jefferson Cowie's *Freedom's Dominion*. Scholars now, they seem to be saying, should devote themselves to identifying the origins of the current moment, not charting a path to an uncertain future.

What we need to address the current crisis, according to Slotkin, is new national myths. He identifies two possibilities. One, which would turn the clock back to reconstitute the "cultural Lost Cause," would be a disaster. The second, whose elements have not yet coalesced, would unite the country in favor of a tolerant, more equal tomorrow, in effect linking racial justice with greater economic equality. There is something disarming about Slotkin's optimism that a new national myth can help to provide a solution to our current divisions. But readers may wonder if the role of the historian today is not so much to devise new myths as to piece together a candid appraisal, no matter how alarming, of the fraught moment in which we live.

ACKNOWLEDGMENTS

A book of previously published essays like *Our Fragile Freedoms* does not readily lend itself to traditional acknowledgments. But I do wish to thank the authors of the many important works of history with which I engage, as well as the publications where the essays first appeared.

I am very grateful, in addition, to the editorial team at W. W. Norton and Co., beginning with the book's editor, Steve Forman, for shepherding it to publication. Steve and I first worked together in 1990, when he edited a volume that accompanied *A House Divided: America in the Age of Lincoln*, a historical exhibition at the Chicago Historical Society I assembled in conjunction with the talented co-curator Olivia Mahoney. Since then, Steve has cooperated with me on numerous other works of history. Over the years I have benefitted enormously from his careful editing and constructive suggestions as well as his own extensive knowledge of American history. I also wish to thank others at Norton who helped bring this book to fruition: Justin Cahill, Clara Drimmer, Nancy Green, Becky Homiski, and Angela Merela.

Thanks, as well, to my literary agent Sandra Dijkstra, who I have known since we were classmates at Long Beach High School in the suburbs of New York City, and who always offers sage advice to her authors. And I am grateful to her capable staff, especially Andrea Cavallaro, who took on the daunting task of ensuring that all rights required for republication had been obtained.

As always, I owe a debt to my wife, Lynn Garafola, and daughter, Daria Rose Foner, for being willing to listen to my thoughts concerning the issues, historical and political, about which I was writing. An accomplished scholar and writer, Lynn, as always, was my ultracapable first reader. Whatever literary merit this book possesses is due in considerable measure to her meticulous editorial attention. A scholar in her own right, with a doctorate in art history, Daria helped choose the book's vivid cover image.

Our Fragile Freedoms is dedicated to the memory of four superb historians, dedicated teachers, and loyal friends, who sadly passed while I was writing many of the pieces included in this book: Ira Berlin, Alan Brinkley, Fred Siegel, and Judith Stein. Over the years, I enjoyed, and learned from, innumerable conversations with each of them about history and many other subjects. Our political persuasions were not identical, but we shared a passion for history and a wide range of intellectual interests. I benefitted enormously from these ongoing discussions and debates, which contributed greatly to the ideas explored in this book. I will long miss their intellectual and personal companionship.

ESSAY CREDITS

447

New York Review of Books
    Race, Rights, and the Law   190
    Everyday Violence in the Jim Crow South   201
    American Anarchists   321
    Chicago, 1968   342
    Textbook History   376

New York Times Book Review
    Riding for Freedom   251

Montreal Review
    American Exceptionalism, American Freedom   357

Journal of Blacks in Higher Education
    Du Bois   391

Preface to the 1997 edition of Rayford Logan, *The Betrayal of the Negro from Hayes to Wilson;* Da Capo Books   398
Preface to the 1992 edition of Richard Hofstadter, *Social Darwinism in American Thought, 1860–1915;* Beacon Press   416

INDEX